AVA

University of East London

AVA Architecture & Physical Design Yearbook 2022

Publisher
University of East London

Editors
Anastasia Karandinou
Claudia da Palma Romao

Graphic Design
Studio Jon Spencer

July 2022

ISBN 978-1-9989909-5-5 (printed version)
ISBN 978-1-9989909-6-2 (digital version)

University of East London
Department of Architecture and the Visual Arts
Dockland Campus
E16 2RD
T+44 020 8223 2041
F+44 020 8223 2963

www.uel.ac.uk

@uel_art_architecture_design @uel_foundation_arch_design @uel_first_year_architecture @uel_architecture @id_ba_uel @uel_mainteriordesign @uel_landscape @unit8.uel @unit_a__uel

Acknowledgments

We would like to thank the many organisations, companies and individuals who we have had the pleasure of collaborating with, including:

Ablett Architects

ACMI – Thessaloniki

Adrem

Allford Hall Monaghan Morris (AHMM)

APCOR, Portuguese Cork Association

ARB

Barton Willmore Consultancy

Batterea Power Station Development Company

BPTW

British Land Plc

Charles Horne

Chartered Institute of Architectural Technologists (CIAT)

Daria Wong, Daria Wong Architects

Dezeen

Eco Friendly Tiles

Emma Graham, RCKa

Filet Gallery

Frame Magazine

Gareth Morris, What If? Projects

Grimshaw

Hobbs Group

Jayden Ali, JA Projects

Jeff Tidmarsh, Sir Robert McAlpine

Jemma Miller, Tate Hindle

Kalpesh Intwala, Stanton Williams

Karina Williams, British Land

Kazan State Institute of Architecture and Engineering

Lendlease

Liz Waters, Sir Robert McAlpine

London Borough of Waltham Forest

London Legacy Development Corporation

Louise Scannell, Weston Williamson

MAKE Architects

Marija Ambrasaite, Aedas

Mark Lemanski, muf architecture/art

Matter Architecture

Milliken Floors Europe

Morgan Sindall Volker Fitzpatrick

Nakheel Landscapes

Neba Sere

Newham Council

Nia Rodgers, TP Bennett

Nick Evans, Vabel

Nilesh Shah, Russian for Fish

Nimi Attanayake, nimtim architects

Paul Gregory

Pervolarides – Thessaloniki

RCKa

RIBA East London Architects Group (ELAG)

Richard Wentworth

Royal Docks Development Corporation

Royal Institute of British Architects (RIBA)

ScottWhitbyStudio

Shed Life

Sir Robert McAlpine

Skidmore Owens and Merrill (SOM)

Southwark Day Centre for Asylum Seekers

St Helen's Church

Steve Deadman, Pollard Thomas Edwards

Story Garden

Sustainability Research Institute

The Blackhorse Workshop

The Supreme Court

Tom Dollard, Pollard Thomas Edwards

UEL Sustainability Research Institute

Whitby Wood Engineers

Lida Amiri (First Year)

Welcome

Dear Graduates & Colleagues,

I am privileged and delighted to introduce this year's edition of the Architecture and Design Yearbook. We are so pleased to get back to work in the studio on campus after the long Covid outbreak. There was a much-increased engagement with workshops and labs which led to an improvement in 3D work outputs across the School.

It has been an exceptional year with students winning 5 RIBA awards mostly for sustainability at the start of the year. The winners of the RIBA awards are:

RIBA Year 1 Portfolio Prize - Rafael Ribeira Fischer
RIBA UG Skin Thinking Prize - Simone Pamio
RIBA PG Skin Thinking Prize - Paulius Vaizgenis
RIBA UG Sustainability Prize - Viktor Telecky
RIBA PG Sustainability Prize + UEL Sustainability Award - Jun Yap

The School introduced an excellent inter-year project called STEAM to design visionary housing in Docklands. The projects involved level 5 students across the school working in mixed interdisciplinary groups which stimulated their creative thinking and design.

There was a very successful continuation of the Broadgate prize with students working across the architecture cluster on a project with British Land and Sir Robert McAlpine. This provided students with industry experience and the successful students were offered placements.

We had an excellent series of lectures and workshops from Grimshaw Architects who spoke about their work and then met with students to offer technical tutorials on student projects.

We had successful RIBA revalidations of the Architecture courses with three commendations and CIAT revalidation of the ADT course also with three commendations.

Our extraordinary University was ranked amongst the top 20 Universities in the UK for producing most CEOs, as reported by the Business Leader News in June 2021.

This year's book is full of a comprehensive range of very creative and stimulating projects developed by our talented students in partnership with world-class architecture and engineering practices. By closely working with leading practitioners, we strive to offer our students the best experience possible to ensure they are ready for the workplace and capable of providing solutions to complex design challenges. Our highly regarded staff are engaged in high impact applied research areas that shape lives and society.

We are extremely proud to be situated as an anchor institution at the heart of east London and, for the last forty years, have been at the forefront of working in collaboration with a broad range of design practices in order to develop a distinctive portfolio of courses in Architecture and Design.

I am thrilled with the quality and standards of this year's work which presents a comprehensive profile of our students, reflects creative thinking and a holistic approach to design.

My very sincere thanks to my colleagues, practitioners, students and alumni who continue to work together to make architecture and Design the flagship area that it is!

I take this opportunity to wish all graduates a very successful and bright future. We hope you will remain in touch with us as you forge ahead in your careers, remembering that it all began at the University of East London!

Professor Hassan Abdalla PhD PFHEA FRSA
Provost
University of East London

Meditations on the Studio Revisited

The Imagination of Knowledge and Knowledge of the Imagination

The work in this publication celebrates the work and achievements of the Architecture, Art and Design students of the University of East London. All of this work seeks to explore ideas around sustainability and the shared theme for the year was **"Towards Zero Carbon and 100% People"**. This book is by necessity the briefest assembly of many ideas, the briefest glimpse into our unfolding of knowledge and values. It assembles our experimentation that is playful yet underpinned by deeply held values and creative processes.

This has been a particularly successful year for the Department of Architecture and Visual Art (AVA). There are many moments to recall but the overriding sense of relief amongst staff and students followed the return to working in the studio after more than a year of fragmented access. This return brought with it a more social engagement between students and staff. Within the AVA all our creative courses are supported by extensive labs and workshops which serve the creative process and are essential to our learning and teaching. These facilities cover both digital and traditional workshops. Students are encouraged to work in a hybrid approach utilising these diverse technologies and processes. We have the most extensive range of workshop and lab facilities in London located in close proximity to the studios.

As I watched students and staff retuning to the studio I was reminded of my own studio learning experiences both whilst studying and in practice. In the comments below I am indebted to my many tutors including Colin St John Wilson, Peter Blundell Jones, Dalibor Vesely, Peter Carl, Eric Parry and many other colleagues here at UEL and other brilliant staff and students I have worked and studied with over many years of studio life. In this introduction I reflect on this return to studio-based working and take the opportunity of looking at this from a broader perspective including writings I have come across over many years. I will look at exploration of knowledge and imagination made possible in the studio context and situate this is in the broader context of the development of modernist thinking and writing. We will challenge what making really means and suggest it is fundamental to the revelation of knowledge during the design process.

We will explore two themes, abstract knowledge and a more holistic knowledge deriving out of the conditions of reality. We will look at the role imagination plays in the acquisition of knowledge in the creative process and what it means to harness this today. I will also suggest that the relation of the designer to tools and materials has been fundamental to redirecting contemporary Art and Design since the latter half of the 20C.

Thinking about these issues I was interested to read Christian Norberg Shultz's book **Genius Loci** with our first-year students. Norberg Schlutz writes "Our everyday world consists of concrete phenomenon... but it also comprises more intangible phenomena such as feelings...atoms molecules, numbers and all kinds of data are abstractions or tools which are constructed to serve other purposes than those of everyday life. *Today it is common to give more importance to the tools than our life world*". (My italics)[1]

By 1980 Norberg-Schulz was reflecting on the triumphs of reason represented in knowledge revealed through the sciences and the need to balance this with knowledge revealed by "feelings" or our "life world".

The 20C had developed two strongly opposing approaches to the creation process of a work of art, on the one hand abstract art and on the other, art firmly rooted in conditions of reality, of society, material and place.

Fig. 1 Maquette studio Henry Moore (2021) Dane Tree House, Perry Green, Much Hadham.

The argument for the abstract art process is described by Theo Van Doesburg "The work of art must be entirely conceived in the mind before its execution. It must receive nothing from nature's given forms, from sensuality or from sentimentality...Technique must be mechanical, that is exact, anti-impressionistic..."[2]

This Abstract approach to the creative process was challenged by many including Dalibor Vesely. Vesely argued that the abstract approach to the creative process "profoundly influenced the nature of creativity in the twentieth Century .., and, .. translates and reduces reality into an image structured more by our inventiveness and visions than by the given conditions of reality itself."[3]

For Vesely, the creative process needed art to engage with the "given conditions of reality itself" and this offered a very different approach to the creation of a work of art from abstracted process described by Van Doesburg. In the approach described by Vesely the evolution of a work of art needs to engage with the "given conditions of reality itself" because knowledge revealed during the creative process was integral with the artwork. The work of art is not preconceived. Creative and imaginative thought continues through the whole of the creative process. The creative process is a revelation that feeds imagination and vice versa.

During Vesely's studio teaching he stressed this need for the creative process to engage with external conditions, materials and contexts. Vesely felt that through the development of Modernism there had become an estrangement between the artist and the artwork caused by the abstracted means of production of artwork. Vesely sought a new reconciliation between the Modern Artist and the Modern Artwork and he felt this was to be achieved by a re-evaluation of the creative process.

Since the mid 1980s, the creative process at UEL has followed aspects of the creative model outlined by Vesely and is usually referred to at UEL as "learning through making".

The UEL studio has always been the testbed where imagination and knowledge are explored and developed within the creative process. Here at UEL learning through making has been core to our teaching. Within our creative process, students have developed work using their imagination, oscillating back and forth between the studios, labs and workshops. These investigations harnessing material, making and tools in playful experimentation.

In The Origin of the Work of Art, Heidegger reflects on the relation of knowledge and technique. "The word techne denotes rather a mode of knowing. To know means to have seen in the widest sense of seeing... For Greek thought the nature of knowing consists in aletheia, that is the uncovering of beings....Techne, as knowledge experienced in the Greek manner is a bringing forth of beings ....into the unconcealedness of their appearance; techne never signifies the action of making."[4] In this difficult passage Heidegger argues that what we think of as making is actually the revelation of knowledge. We work in the studios, labs and workshops so that art can emerge (be brought forth into the unconcealedness of appearance). Working in the studio is not therefore a problem of manufacture it is the emergence of truthful knowledge in a work of art.

Working in the studio in these terms can be better thought of as gaining different types of knowledge rather than simply making objects. The art emerging through this creative making process is an imaginative rational experiment, but it is an experiment with imagination informed by knowledge revealed in the creative process, it is an art engaged with the "given conditions of reality itself", and with new knowledge embedded in the work at each stage of development.

Reviewing more generally, the year began with very successful upgrades to the main student facing spaces in the AVA building. These spaces are known as the Lightwell, the Atrium and the Gallery. The newly configured spaces have extended our teaching and have been universally popular with students and staff. We have already had some exceptional exhibitions the new Gallery. To give an example, I was delighted by the recent exhibition on new materials called "Wasteless". This exhibition brought together work by staff and students into new and experimental materials mostly grown or made using the by-products of other processes. These experiments add to the work in the research groups and support the growing expertise in sustainability. The year also began with the news of five student RIBA awards in sustainability and I congratulate the staff and students on this outstanding success.

We also had an exceptional input from practitioners including a new series of lectures and workshops from Grimshaw Architects. I would also like to thank the practitioners who contributed to the national lecture series including the Student Society lecture series, the Detour Ahead Art Lecture series and those who visit for crits and reviews. I would also like to thank all our visiting lecturers and especially Professor Patrik Schumacher for his inspiring lecture on the Architecture of the Metaverse. These inputs have considerably enriched the thinking that drives our work.

I would like to thank the students who have assisted with the student societies including the president of the student Architecture and Design Society, Rafael Fischer with Guilherme Bressaneli, Adrienne Mercedes Raleigh, Yoana Miglencheva, Charlie Chinama and team Shreem Khare, Rihab Kharbouchi, Filip Szypula, Khushi Sirvi, Julia Andreea Florian, Jameela Mohamed, Fernando Tagliati, Darnell Carol-Walters and Mahbubur Tahmid.

We are also very grateful to the practitioners who have been mentoring students and offering placements on the RIBA programme and on their own account. In particular we mention Sir Robert McAlpine and British Land for their continued sponsorship of the excellent Broadgate student competition. I thank visiting Professor Charles Horne and Jeff Tidmarsh for their excellent support and expertise in leading the competition.

This year also saw the start of our interdisciplinary project **STEAM** in which year 2 students, representing every undergraduate course, worked together from across the Arts, Computing and Engineering on a specialised housing project in the docklands. The challenge was particularly successful and rewarding giving new insights into the different approaches of the student group as a whole.

At the core of our teaching philosophy is the relationship developed between staff and students and the play of the design process. Students are taught one to one, in small groups, in studios, workshops and lecture halls, and now online. Our project work follows a systematic pattern of setting aims and values, investigation, experiment and innovation. I would like to thank all the staff and students for their excellent work this year and for returning to the studio.

Lastly, I would like to congratulate those students leaving us and wish them every success.

I am reminded that our word University derives from the Latin Universitas meaning whole or community. Please stay in touch with us.

Our knowledge and imagination developed in the studio teaches us that we need to understand the conditions of reality in our Art, Architecture and Design. I hope in your professional life you will be able to learn from your work in the studios, be able to harness your knowledge and imagination in the creative process, understand the "given conditions of realty", and play a part in forming the new work that will enrich our lives. In this way, through your research and innovations, you will fulfil your own potential and the potential of our new century.

Carl Callaghan BA (Hons) Dipl Cantab ARB RIBA
Head of Architecture and Visual Art

Notes

1, Norberg-Schulz, Christian. (1980) "Preface." In: Genius Loci: Towards a Phenomenology of Architecture ." page 6.

2, Van Doesburg, Theo. "Art Concret, no1" (April 1931): 1, trans.in Osborne, Abstraction and Artifice in the Twentieth-Century Art, page 128.

3, Vesely, Dalibor. (2004) "Architecture In The Age Of Divided Representation, The Question of Creativity In The Shadow of Production". MIT Press Cambridge Massachusetts. London England, page 20.

4, Heidegger, Martin. (1935) "The Origin of the Work of Art" trans. In: Hofstadter, Albert. (1975) "Poetry Language Thought" Harper and Row, Page 59.

The Origin of a Work of Art was written between 1935-1937 but made available in English translation in 1971 in Poetry Language Thought. I was reluctant to include this passage initially because it was written during the years when Heidegger was a member of the Nazi party (he remained a member till 1945) and I was concerned about any contextual engagement with the Nazi regime. On further enquiry the section I have used on Aletheia has a longer history in Philosophy. In The History of Philosophy Grayling argues that Heidegger derived his ideas on Aletheia from earlier work by Parmenides (born 515 BCE), Page 479. Interestingly, Grayling also argues that the fact that ours senses mis lead us (Plato's Cave) also derives from Parmenides, Page 35. A fuller account of Heidegger and sculpture can be found in Heidegger Among the Sculptors. See Grayling, A.C. (2019) "The History of Philosophy" Viking, Penguin Random House. Mitchell, Andrew. (2010) "Heidegger Among the Sculptors." Stanford University Press.

Care and Pride

Introduction to the Architecture and Physical Design Cluster

There are many words, and even more fantastic images of work within this book, immortalising a years activity within the Architecture and Physical Design Cluster, which I have had the pleasure of leading for the first time. I will keep my introduction short, and centre it on one of the many shared strands that unite us all across the various disciplines within the cluster, and that is the care and the pride that we all take in what we do here.

At UEL, and in particular within the Architecture and Physical Design Cluster, this notion of care runs through everything we do, inherently impacting all who pass through our doors. From students to faculty, from Torre our ever-present smiling security guard, to Mark Sowden our long standing colleague and master technician, who has for 25 years inspired our students. Our cluster is built on a simple idea that we care. It is infectious, it envelopes us all and it is the foundation for the success of all our graduates.

This book celebrates the incredible work of our current students but will inevitably reach a wider audience through friends, family, colleagues, alumni and future members of our community.

To those of you who are at the beginning of your journey with us, picking up this year book, I hope you are inspired, as I am, by the incredible achievements of our students and excited about what we will achieve together. And if you are asking yourself what it's like to study at the university of East London, I offer you this:

Our staff really care for our students and in return our students really care for their tutors. We are a family, and collectively we care about the future of our professions and their impact on our planet. From the products that our hands will contribute to making, to the spaces our designs will inhabit, to the architecture and cities that we design and contribute to. This is a special place, full of an incredibly diverse group of people, all united in a common goal to make our world better through design.

To our alumni, we are so proud of your achievements, and the stories of your success are an inspiration to us all, from Jayden Ali's co-curatorship of next years British Pavilion at the Venice Biennale, to the many of you who are now in senior positions in world leading architecture and design practices. If you are reading this, and we have not been in touch, please do reach out and reconnect. You are, and always will be a part of our UEL family, and we look forward to welcoming you back to the school in the near future.

To our current students and those who are about to graduate from our cluster. You have not had a normal education and the Covid-19 pandemic has dealt you a really difficult hand. Your resilience has awed and amazed us. In truth it inspired us to do what we do and we could not be prouder of what you have achieved. We hope you will come back, remember your time with us with fondness, and hopefully remember a little of what we have taught you. We look forward to watching you shine bright, rise high and forever change the face of the professions you choose to pursue. Remember your fellow graduates and those you met along your journey, and importantly keep caring for each other, as you have over the past years. You might not know it yet but the class of 2022 will move mountains, especially if you do it together.

To our returning students, your energy is infectious, and we are really excited to see what the next year/s will bring. Rest well over the summer, try something new, see something you haven't seen before and reflect on what you have learnt this year. We look forward to welcoming you back in September brimming with energy, ready to push on and take both you and your studies to new heights.

To our prospective students/potential applicants and your families. This school is a very special place. Now just 15 minutes from the heart of London by Elizabeth Line, we are a school that is consistently moving on an upward trajectory and breaking new ground in creating a careers led education in our subject areas. We care and protect those that step into our 'Factory of Creativity', and will nurture you to be the best that you can possibly be. We are looking for people who care about quality and community, and if you think you are one of those rare, wonderful people then we would love to hear from you.

To the Architecture and Physical Design staff, technicians and ACE School Office Staff, thank you.

Thank you for nurturing our students to be the best that they can be, thank you for caring for each other, and also for putting up with me. This book is a celebration of your commitment to our students and their journeys, and while your hard work and countless briefs occupy the background of this publication, it is very much front and centre of my admiration.

Well done, now onwards and upwards!

Alex Scott-Whitby
Cluster Leader - Architecture & Physical Design

RESEARCH & PEDAGOGY

Image: Dr. Ralph Overill, The Last Cyberman visits Rettendon

Research Group
Culture & Environment

Dr Anastasia Karandinou and Associate Professor Roland Karthaus

With the exceptional support of Dr Julie Wall and numerous colleagues, the new research groups of the School have rapidly developed a clear identity and several initiatives, which promote and support the research culture of the university.

Regarding our group, 'Culture & Environment', social and environmental resilience have been key issues driving the research projects. This research group looks into how political and social phenomena are depicted in visual arts and into how design responds to – and also leads – social, cultural, political change. Creative and transformative analysis and mapping of spaces and phenomena is key to our processes. Mapping and critically transcribing observations and information from one medium to another allows our analyses to be transformative and productive. Architecture, interior and spatial design, photography and visual arts address how we live, and apart from producing spaces and artefacts, they also challenge and propose new paradigms; they constitute a device to think and debate with.

Indicative projects of the group are being presented on our webpage-in-progress - https://uelcultureandenvironment.tumblr.com/ - which also functions as a platform for exchange and an opportunity for conversation amongst the researchers of the group. Short workshops throughout the year supported early career researchers develop links between their teaching and research or practice and research, as well as write a conference abstract, which led to papers being submitted to international conferences. An international conference and network is currently being organised on the theme of 'Repurposing Places'.

Dr Anastasia Karandinou, Literacy Pirates and the MA Interior design students, 'The Storm' community project.

Adam Wiseman, Tlatelolco Disproved, Mexico City

Babylon Blue

Armor Gutierrez Rivas & Rosa Rogina

As part of the academic year 2020-2021, Lecturers Armor Gutierrez Rivas and Rosa Rogina, in collaboration with the Sustainability Research Institute and students from Masters of Architecture Unit 8, engaged in a knowledge exchange collaboration with Babylon Blue, a leading company in Sustainable Water Living Communities. The collaboration included a joint project for the vision, design and execution of a sustainable floating community in the Royal Docks.

The knowledge exchange was developed through a number of workshop sessions where design improvements to the initial vessel design were discussed, including the analysis and potential improvement of the carbon footprint for the vessel. Following these initial sessions Ana Paula Gomes Kouzak, Unit 8 Student, engaged in a paid internship to develop a detailed 3D model of the vessel to be used for quantifying materials and identifying the carbon footprint for each component.

The collaboration included an event as part of the London Festival of Architecture (LFA) on future visions for the Royal Docks, titled 'A Vibrant Civic Waterfront: A collaborative vision for the future of the Royal Docks'. The session was organised as a series of short presentations followed by a round table with Q&A and the audience was able to engage in an open discussion about the future of the Royal Docks waterfront.

The team involved in the project included the following UEL and Babylon Blue staff:

Armor Gutierrez Rivas, UEL Unit 8 Lead Tutor and Senior Lecturer
Rosa Rogina, UEL Unit 8 Lead Tutor, Director of LFA
Daniel Bridge, Royal Docks Programme Director
Darryl Newport, UEL / SRI Environmental Support
Alexander Host, Founder of Babylon Blue
Ana Paula Gomes Kouzak, UEL Unit 8 student
Alexander Host, Founder of Babylon Blue
Maryam Zonouzi, Co-Founder Lemon Leopard

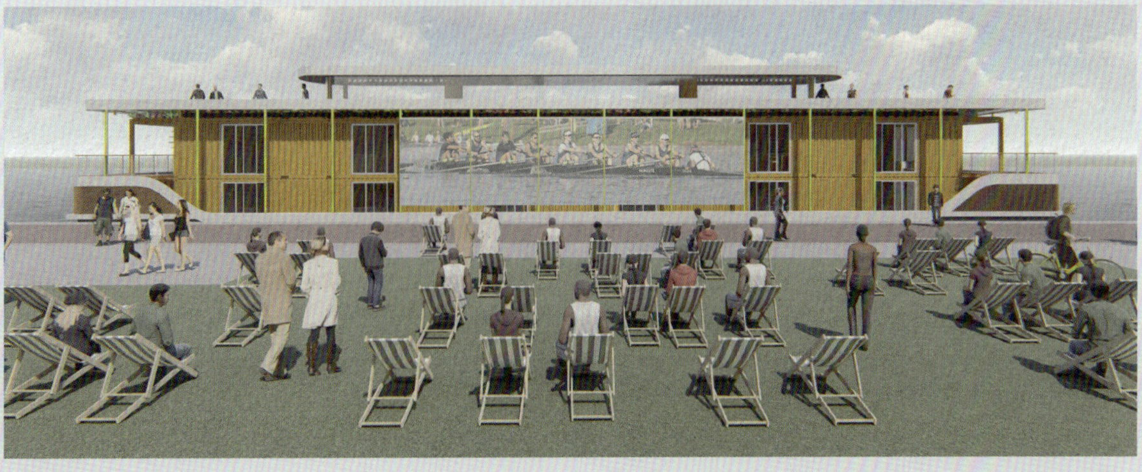

Open Studio Event

This mid-year event allowed invited guests, fellow staff and students to see work in progress and share the diversity of architecture and design at UEL

We held the Open Studio Event with student presentations and guest talks at UEL, over two days in February 2022. The event welcomed invited guests, all students, members of staff and people who were interested in our architectural and design studies.

The Open Studio Event was again a unique opportunity to see work in progress and to share the diversity of studies. The event was organised in such a way that selected students from each Unit or Course presented their ongoing work. As such, it was both, a 'mid-term review' with work in progress and a vital platform for discussion about academic work in architecture.

Special Guests: Baldeep Heer, Philip Christou Baruti, Liam O'Dell.

Thursday 24th February 2022
Following courses presented: Product Design, ADT Architectural Design Technology, Landscape Architecture, MArch Unit 2 (Open Space, Kidbrooke, Greenwich, South-East London), MArch Unit 6 (Sustaining Education or Sustainable Education - UEL Docklands Campus, London), March Unit 8 (Towards a Sustainable De-Industrialisation, Hackney Wick, London), MRes Architecture (Understanding the Neoliberal City), First Year Architecture BSc

Lunch Lecture by Deborah Benrós
Deborah Benrós is an architect and researcher. She holds a doctorate from University College London - The Bartlett School and was a visiting student at MIT. In practice, she worked at several offices including Foster and Partners and Arup. As visiting faculty at Cornell University, she taught design studio and a course focusing on her research field which includes shape grammars and mass customisation of housing.

The lecture explored research work on shape grammars/housing archetypes, past teaching experiences in studio and architectural work which include Foster and Partners' Apple campus, Apple Stores and The Walbrook building in the City of London.

Evening Lecture by Neven Sidor of Grimshaw
Since joining Grimshaw in 1981, Neven Sidor has led design teams on 21 major completed projects. His work spans several sectors, such as transport, higher education, exhibition halls and master planning. He is currently a member of the Stewardship Group, which oversees the values, ethos and standing of the practice.

Grimshaw was founded by Sir Nicholas Grimshaw in 1980. The practice became a Partnership in 2007 and operates worldwide, employing over 650 staff. The company's work is characterised by strong conceptual legibility, innovation and a rigorous approach to detailing, all underpinned by the principles of humane, enduring and sustainable design.

Friday 25th February 2022
Following courses presented: MA Interior Design, BA Interior Design, Degree Unit A (Action Space, Hackney Central, London), Degree Unit B (Rock, Northumberland UK), Degree Unit C (Creat(iv)e Soho, London), Degree Unit E (Brick Lane, London), Degree Unit H (Continuity and Tolerance, Limehouse Cut, London) and MA Architecture + Urbanism

Lunch Lecture by Tony Fretton about Geoffrey Bawa
Tony Fretton is a Visiting Professor at UEL and he is known for his building projects across Europe. He set up his practice in 1982 and his projects include the Lisson Gallery in London and the Fuglsang Museum in Denmark. Tony's architecture is sensitive to local contexts and his approach is centred on people's need, social engagement, perception and proportion.

Tony spoke about the Sri Lankan architect Geoffrey Bawa, who practiced from the late 1950s until the 1990s. Goeffrey Bawa's architecture is often described as 'traditional modernism', combining vernacular and contemporary designs. His architecture relates to an astonishing sense of place and emotional depth. Without falling into common architectural categories, each building understands its location and function, by showing Bawa's architectural intelligence, touch and spatial awareness.

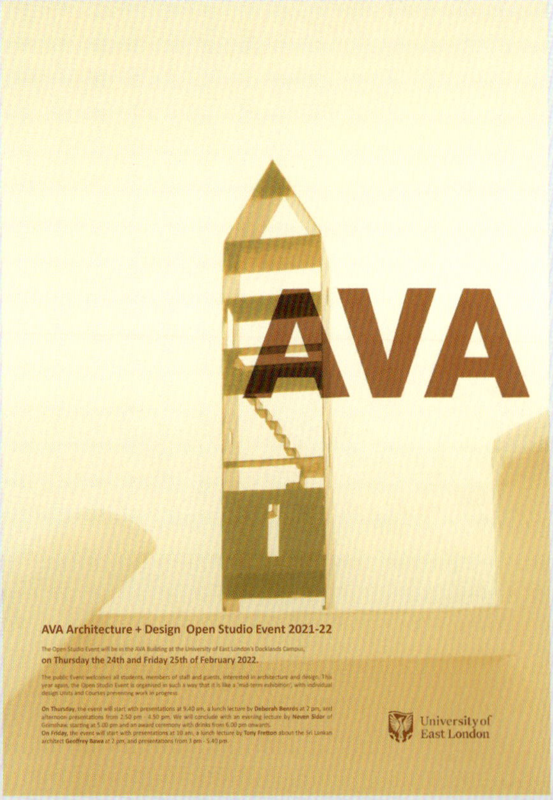
AVA
AVA Architecture + Design Open Studio Event 2021-22
The Open Studio Event will be in the AVA Building at the University of East London's Docklands Campus,
on Thursday the 24th and Friday 25th of February 2022.
The public Event welcomes all students, members of staff and guests, interested in architecture and design. This year again, the Open Studio Event is organised in such a way that it is like a 'mid-term exhibition', with individual design units and Courses presenting work in progress.
On Thursday, the event will start with presentations at 9.40 am, a lunch lecture by Deborah Benros at 2 pm, and afternoon presentations from 2.50 pm - 4.50 pm. We will conclude with an evening lecture by Neven Sidor of Grimshaw, starting at 5.00 pm and an award ceremony with drinks from 6.00 pm onwards.
On Friday, the event will start with presentations at 10 am, a lunch lecture by Tony Fretton about the Sri Lankan architect Geoffrey Bawa at 2 pm, and presentations from 3 pm - 5.40 pm.
University of East London

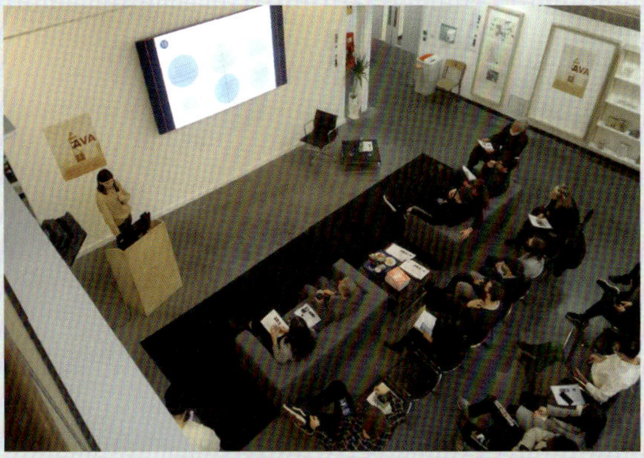

'INTERSECTION'

A degree show at Broadgate, City of London for BA Interior Design

Pol Gallagher & Keith Winter

BA Interiors were tasked with designing and building an exceptional exhibition for the whole of the Architecture and Physical Design cluster as well as UEL Fashion graduates for their final year runway, all housed within the prestigious London centre location of 3 Finsbury Avenue, Broadgate. The developer, British Land, signed off on a 1F floorplate to be used by UEL for this end-of-year show and BA Interior Design Year 02, led by year tutor Pol Gallagher, were given the responsibility of designing it as their main brief for Semester B.

Four groups were created, 1. Walls and Plinths, 2. Entrance Arch, 3. Bar and 4. Reception Desk. Each group was given multiple tasks to assign to each group member and numerous interim crits to check in with tutors and guests along the design journey.

One highlight was the dialogue of Year 02 Interiors and Year 03 Fashion students, collaborating for short snappy video interviews and presentations, that led to the final designs for the exhibition with a custom-designed runway and concept of 'Intersection'. This event has since been listed by London Fashion Week for the first time in UEL's history and is set up to be an incredibly popular weekend for the students, staff and visitors.

The Architecture and Physical Design Cluster then took over the space after LFW and showcased the best work from Architecture, Interior Design, ADT and Product design. With Pol's bright yellow powder-coated scaffold poles and off-set dark blue wall colour, the office space became a transparent labyrinth providing excitable moments around every corner.

BA (hons) Fashion Design
Graduate Show 11-12 June 2022
3 Finsbury Ave, London. EC2M 2PA
INVITATION
INTERSECTION
LONDON FASHION WEEK
11-13 JUNE 2022
PRESENTED BY clearpay
University of East London
11 June 8pm Installations / Presentations
8:30pm Catwalk
9pm-11pm Reception
12 June 12pm-7pm Showcase / Showrooms
RSVP fashion@uel.ac.uk
British Land
BROADGATE
SOLENT UNIVERSITY
HM.

Sir Robert McALPINE

My Own Private Utopia

An exhibition at Velorose Gallery, City of London by Year 02 Interiors
Dr Keith Winter

BA Interiors year 02 had the privilege of showing their Barbican Conservatory projects at Velorose Gallery in the City of London under the watchful eye of gallerist and architect David Rosenberg.

Velorose is an unusual space in that it has a pink carpet on the ceiling and also modular plywood walls that can be adapted to fit different presentations.

Student ambassadors Milena Torres and Aliyah Stewart worked hard to get the 22 x A2 pages printed and meticulously hung for the week of the show 04th-09th April.

The project challenged students to imagine a new bar, mezzanine, staircase and viewing platform in the Barbican Conservatory, to celebrate and delight in the gardens. An in-conversation was had between all students and year tutor Pol Gallagher at the Private View on 08th April. Year 03 Interior students also joined us and were not shy in their critical opinions of the work.

It was a celebration of collage, technical drawing, sketching and 3D softwares that culminated in a rewarding closure to the project and celebration of the possibilities that the Barbican gardens could afford the users.

Private
Utopia
My Own Private Utopia
My Own Private Utopia is a showcase of BA Interior
Design Year 02 work from the University of East London
at Velorose. The project challenged students to imagine
a new bar, mezzanine, staircase and viewing platform in
Barbican Conservatory, to celebrate and delight in the

the problem is, a human is only this big

Virtual + Physical Group Exhibition
April 28th - June 06th 2022

Based on a commissioned text by Gabriel Santamarina + curated by Yeah Totally Ltd

Touchdown at Way Out East Gallery, AVA Building, UEL, London, E16 2RD

Dr Keith Winter ran a book club during lockdown curated by Mexico-City-based writer and psychoanalyst Gabriel Santamarina. In summer 2021 I asked Gabriel to write a short text describing three sacred spaces, which he decided were; a 13th Century Mosque, a 9th Century Buddhist Temple and a cave. Yeah Totally Ltd then translated his text into a set of virtual interior spaces and invited 12 artists to show their works in it.

This was launched both virtually and with a physical touchdown on the April 28th at 5pm. The show ran until the 06th June. On the evening there was an informal artist Q&A in person and online at 7pm for artists from across the world. The virtual exhibition designed by Keith and Nayden was hosted on HUBS Mozilla and allowed anyone, anywhere, will be able to enter from any device and view the exciting work.

Artists: Daryl Brown, Manuela Johanna Covini, Nayden Hadzhiev, Jaimie Henthorn, Khaoula B. Karaweigh, Selecta LDN, Victor Perez-Rul, Parisa Oreizi, Johnston Sheard, Ayesha Singh + misael soto, Daniel Widrig + Keef Winter

yhtotally.com is the experimental design studio of Dr Keith Winter and Nayden Hadzhiev who are both tutors on the BA (hons) Interior Design course at UEL.

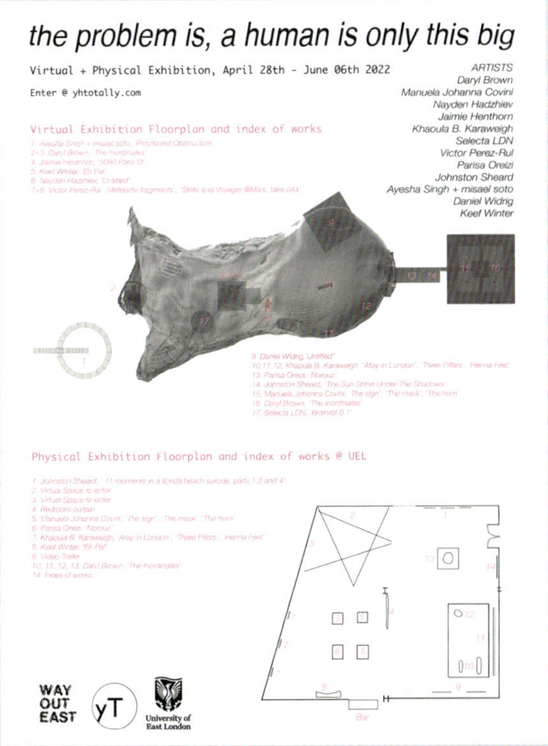

the problem is, a human is only this big
Virtual + Physical Exhibition, April 28th - June 06th 2022
Enter @ yhtotally.com
ARTISTS
Daryl Brown
Manuela Johanna Covini
Nayden Hadzhiev
Jaimie Henthorn
Khaoula B. Karaweigh
Selecta LDN
Victor Perez-Rul
Parisa Oreizi
Johnston Sheard
Ayesha Singh + misael soto
Daniel Widrig
Keef Winter
Virtual Exhibition Floorplan and index of works
1. Ayesha Singh + misael soto, 'Provisional Obstruction'
2+3. Daryl Brown, 'The Inordinates'
5. Keef Winter, 'Eh Pal'
6. Nayden Hadzhiev, 'Untitled'
9. Daniel Widrig, 'Untitled'
10,11,12, Khaoula B. Karaweigh, 'Atay in London', 'Three Pillars', 'Henna Feet'
14. Johnston Sheard, 'The Sun Shine Under The Shadows'
15. Manuela Johanna Covini, 'The sign', 'The mask', 'The horn'
16. Daryl Brown, 'The Inordinates'
17. Selecta LDN, 'Brainrot 0.1'
Physical Exhibition Floorplan and index of works @ UEL
2. Virtual Space to enter
3. Virtual Space to enter
4. Redroom curtain
5. Manuela Johanna Covini, 'The sign', 'The mask', 'The horn'
7. Khaoula B. Karaweigh, 'Atay in London', 'Three Pillars', 'Henna Feet'
8. Keef Winter, 'Eh Pal'
9. Video Trailer
10, 11, 12, 13. Daryl Brown, 'The Inordinates'
14. Index of works
WAY OUT EAST
yT
University of East London

the problem is,
a human is only this big
Virtual + Physical Exhibition, April 28th - June 06th 2022
based on a commissioned text by Gabriel Santamarina (MX) + curated by Yeah Totally Ltd
Touchdown at Way Out East Gallery, University East London, Docklands, London E16 2RD
Private View 5-8pm (UK time) + Artist Q&A 7pm --> All Welcome
Enter @ yhtotally.com
Daryl Brown
Manuela Johanna Covini
Nayden Hadzhiev
Jaimie Henthorn
Khaoula B. Karaweigh
Selecta LDN
Victor Perez-Rul
Parisa Oreizi
Johnston Sheard
Ayesha Singh + misael soto
Daniel Widrig
Keef Winter
WAY OUT EAST
yT
University of East London

Keef Winter

Repurposing Places for social and environmental resilience

Dr Anastasia Karandinou

Whilst the 20th century was mostly about starchitects, the 21st century is about synergies and the relevant complex dynamics that these allow to grow. This shift happens in parallel to others; reusing, retrofitting, and giving a new life to the existing places, buildings and neighbourhoods, in an environmentally and socially resilient manner, developing ways for the existing communities to grow in a symbiotic relationship with new ones, designing processes of circular economy and upcycling that allow people to collaborate and find viable solutions. Participation in architecture is a notion that continuously evolves, even more so in recent years. Knowledge and innovation that contributes to social justice and responsible design emerges from complex networks and agile cross-disciplinary collaborations.

In this context, the conference we are organising for 2023, aims to discuss the link between social and environmental resilience, by looking into designed projects, cross-disciplinary research, participatory and collaborative design methods. It welcomes architects, designers, artists, planners, academics, educators, who have addressed the above themes through their work. Projects on adaptation and retrofitting of places in an environmentally and socially responsible way will be discussed, as well as ongoing collaborative and cross-disciplinary projects with open-ended questions, and which drive the relevant conversations forward.

Image created by MA Interior Design student Rushil Gaba.

Topic 1: Retrofitting places with focus on the cultural and social context. Design proposals, built precedents and critical analyses of case-studies.

Topic 2: Cross-disciplinary collaborations on innovative approaches to retrofitting places.

Topic 3: Innovative approaches to mapping, analysing, understanding a place and its inhabitants; new approaches to participation. Projects and critical analyses of this theme, in the context of architecture, art and urbanism.

Topic 4: Repurposing places and relevant investigations through educational briefs and student projects. Driving the conversation forward through linking teaching and research.

Conference organisers: Dr Anastasia Karandinou (UEL), Florence Lam (Arup)

Advisory Committee: Prof Hassan Abdalla, Carl Callaghan, Alan Chandler, Prof Gail Findlay, Prof David Tann, Dr Julie Wall.

Scientific committee is being developing and will be communicated through the UEL website.

The conference is supported by Arup.
Venue: Arup, London
Dates: 23-24 March 2023

In parallel to this conference, an international research network is being formed, which is addressing this subject through developing links between teaching and research.

For further information on this conference, please visit: www.counterarchitecture.com/repurposing-places-conference

Rosina Rogina appointed as Director of the London Festival of Architecture

UEL Lecturer and Unit 8 Lead Tutor Rosa Rogina has been appointed as director of the London Festival of Architecture (LFA). The LFA is the world's largest annual architecture festival and is exploring the theme of 'act' through a hybrid programme in 2022. The LFA is part of New London Architecture (NLA), and has a mission is to support London's architectural and design talent, enthuse and engage with the public, and find new ways to look at familiar places. In 2021 the LFA explored the theme of care, and celebrated innovation and design through a hybrid events programme last June. A year-round programme of design competitions, design charrettes, campaigns and other activities also champions London as the best place in the world to practice and enjoy architecture.

Rosa Rogina has been programme director of the London Festival of Architecture since 2016. She was part of an international team representing Montenegro at the 2018 Venice Biennale and was curator-in-residence at Vienna Design Week 2020.

Rosa holds a MA degree in Architecture from the Royal College of Art and an MA in Research Architecture from Goldsmiths, University of London. She has worked for some of the world's leading architecture practices including MVRDV, Grimshaw and Farshid Moussavi Architecture. Her writing has been published widely and she is a regular speaker and moderator on contemporary architecture and design.

Rosa Rogina said:
"I am thrilled to become the new director of the London Festival of Architecture. I cannot wait to work with my festival colleagues and the New London Architecture team, as well as our wonderful network of supporters to shape the future of the festival. Ever since joining the festival team in 2016 I have been struck by the LFA's ability to impact everyday experiences of the city: something that's going to be needed more than ever as London emerges from the Covid-19 pandemic, and as we focus more keenly on the climate emergency. I'm proud to be part of a team that does so much to promote the value of London's built environment, and I'm excited for the festival's future."

Peter Murray, curator-in-chief at New London Architecture and founder of the London Festival of Architecture said:
"I'm very pleased that Rosa has agreed to take on the role of director of LFA. She is well known to all those who have been involved with and supported the festival in recent years and brings a welcome continuity to the role which is enhanced by her work in practice, academic teaching and international curatorial projects."

www.londonfestivalofarchitecture.org
Twitter: @LFArchitecture
Instagram: @LondonFestivalofArchitecture

ZEMCH 2021

International Design Workshop UAEU

The ZEMCH International Design Workshop 2021 was held from 20th to 24th October 2021 (9am - 5pm) at the United Arab Emirates University (UAEU) in Dubai in partnership with ALDAR. The workshop was held online with 95 undergraduate and postgraduate students and 19 tutors taking part from Australia, Belgium, Cyprus, India, UAE and the UK. In partnership with ALDAR, a range of plots in Abu Dhabi was provided to the students aiming to deliver and explore innovative concept solutions for the vertical sustainable houses for Emiratis that safeguarded the contextual socio-cultural norms and preferences.

The students had to develop a mixed-community apartment/residential unit that have a max of 3-4 floor of low-rise for 10 units considering a diverse range of families. The proposed designs were supposed to meet the general project goals by creating good design, indoor air quality, adequate thermal comfort, stimulating daylight, acoustic environments, and energy efficiency according to the relevant national standards. We are pleased to announce that two groups involving our Architectural Design Technology students were selected as the 1st and 2nd winners. Their achievements were announced and showcased at the ZEMCH 2021 International Conference in the UAE. The judges provided highly praised the quality of our students' works.

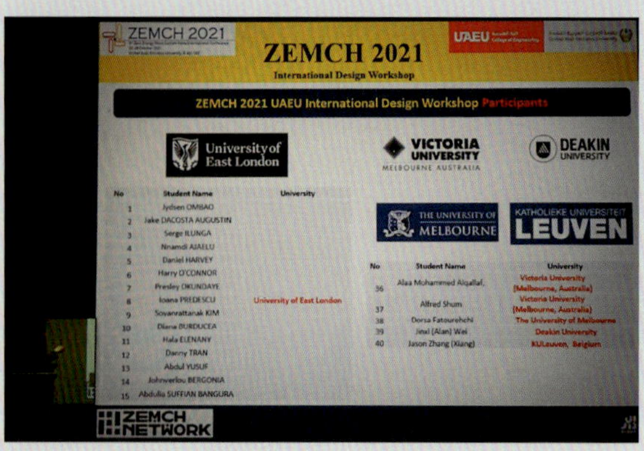

Sustainability Decathlon 2023

Dr Arman Hashemi (Principal Investigator, UEL)

We have been successful in securing $100K to design and build an Affordable Prefabricated Carbon Neutral House in California, Orange County (OCSD 23) as a collaboration between The University of East London and Tongji University at the Sustainability Decathlon.

"OCSD23 is a new competition that challenges teams to design, build, and market innovative model homes that demonstrate a range of solutions to some of California's most urgent problems."

Eighteen teams have been selected and each will receive $100,000 to help fund the project. Dr Arman Hashemi will be leading the project on behalf of UEL at the Sustainability Decathlon which aims to bring bold and inventive ideas to be designed, built and marketed that are carbon neutral, resilient, water- and energy efficient and affordable. The homes will be displayed in October 2023 in a Solar Village which will be open to the public.

Sustainability Decathlon
ORANGE COUNTY

Modular Design in the UK and China - Towards Zero-Carbon Mass Customised Housing

Dr Arman Hashemi (PI)

This UEL funded project is a collaboration between UEL and Tongji University that will identify strategies for designing and manufacturing zero carbon modular homes, followed by virtual, physical and environmental performance assessments of designed prototypes. Conclusions will be drawn, followed by publications on the impacts of offsite modular construction on achieving zero carbon homes in the UK and China. The project facilitates the following:

- Encourage collaboration and knowledge exchange between the academics and industry partners in the UK and China on subjects relevant to Modular Offsite Construction and Zero Carbon Building.
- Both UEL and Tongji universities closely work with the industry and local governments on delivering sustainable affordable housing.
- We will extend our international collaboration with the Zero Energy Mass Custom Home (ZEMCH) network that has over 800 members worldwide and over 10 years of experience on subjects relevant to zero energy and modular construction around the world.

The partnership aims to integrate this project within some of our modules to facilitate student participation in Architecture, Architectural Design Technology, Interior Design and Engineering.

Buildings in Russia – adaptation and mitigation for climate change

Dr Arman Hashemi (PI)

Architectural Design Technology (ADT) students successfully completed a £30K British Council funded research/teaching project, entitled "Green Buildings in Russia – adaptation and mitigation of existing buildings to a changing climate", in collaboration with the Institute of Architecture & Civil Engineering MITU – MASI, led by the Dr Arman Hashemi as the Principal Investigator.

The project involved Russian and ADT students at UEL, who assessed energy consumption and thermal comfort using Dynamic Thermal Simulation and Physical Measurements in three case study buildings including a multi-storey office and residential block and a school. Energy and comfort were assessed against the benchmarks and solutions were suggested to improve conditions.

Both UEL and MASI students participated and presented the results of the project in an international conference "Green Buildings- optimisation through research" held in February 2022, at the Moscow Institute of Architecture & Civil Engineering MITU – MASI in Russia.

UK-RUSSIA YEAR OF KNOWLEDGE 2022/2023

BRITISH COUNCIL

UEL Staff longlisted in Dezeen Awards 2022

Alice D'Andrea and Alex Scott-Whitby

The Dezeen awards are a global search for the worlds top architecture projects and this year attracted over 5400 entries from 90 countries. The 5400 entries were long listed down to less than 300 entries spread out over 12 categories.

UEL Staff have been successfully involved in 2 of these entries.

Alex Scott-Whitby
The Jubilee Pool in Penzance has been longlisted in the Rebirth Category. This was designed by Alex's practice, ScottWhitbyStudio.

https://www.dezeen.com/awards/2022/longlists/architecture/rebirth-project/

The pool has also been shortlisted for the AJ Architecture awards.

Alice D'Andrea (BSc Architecture - Unit C)
Alice was project architect for The Gathering Place, longlisted in the Landscape Category, with her practice KHBT.

https://www.dezeen.com/awards/2022/longlists/architecture/landscape-project/

Top: Jubilee Pool (photograph by Jim Stephenson)
Above: The Gathering Place (photograph by Robert Omerod)

Conservation projects in Chile

Alan Chandler

Alan Chandler collaborated with the architect Cecilia Puga on a competition winning scheme for the reinvention of a derelict urban palace in Valparaiso, Chile. He was involved in developing the conservation strategy and looking at how the new building is inserted within the existing external façade. The project was awarded in March 2022 by the Chilean Government to create a regional archive.

This year also saw the opening of the another conservation project and collaboration between Alan and Cecillia – the Palacio Pereira in Santiago de Chile. The historic Palacio Pereira in Santiago has been transformed onto Chile's Ministry of Culture. Again Alan was supporting the conservation aspect of the project.

From top: Archivo Regional de Valparaiso, Palacio Pereira (photograph by Cristobal Palma)

House of Lords Built Environment Select Committee Inquiry into Housing Demand

Dr Anna Minton

Following on from Big Capital: Who is London for? (Penguin 2017), Anna Minton has continued to write about the housing crisis for academic and mainstream publications, including the Guardian and the Financial Times.

She was invited to give oral evidence to the House of Lords Built Environment Select Committee Inquiry into Housing Demand, which published its report in January 2022.

In June she gave a keynote at the 13th International Space Syntax Symposium in Norway.

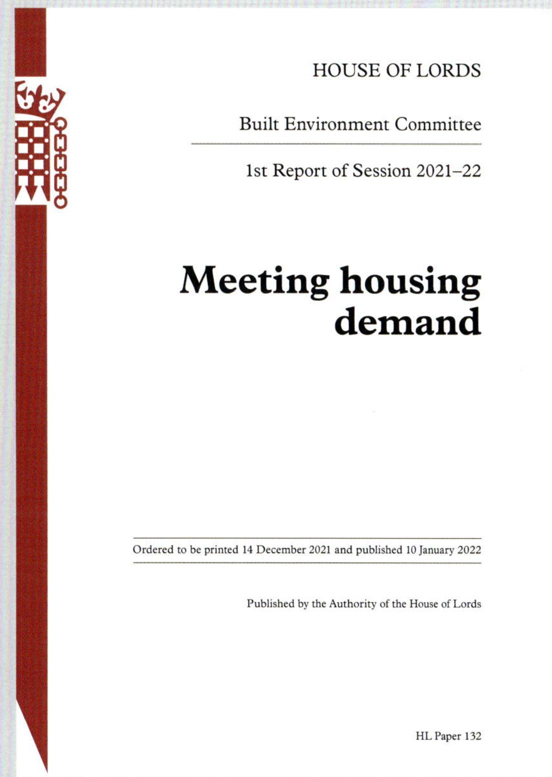

HOUSE OF LORDS

Built Environment Committee

1st Report of Session 2021–22

Meeting housing demand

Ordered to be printed 14 December 2021 and published 10 January 2022

Published by the Authority of the House of Lords

HL Paper 132

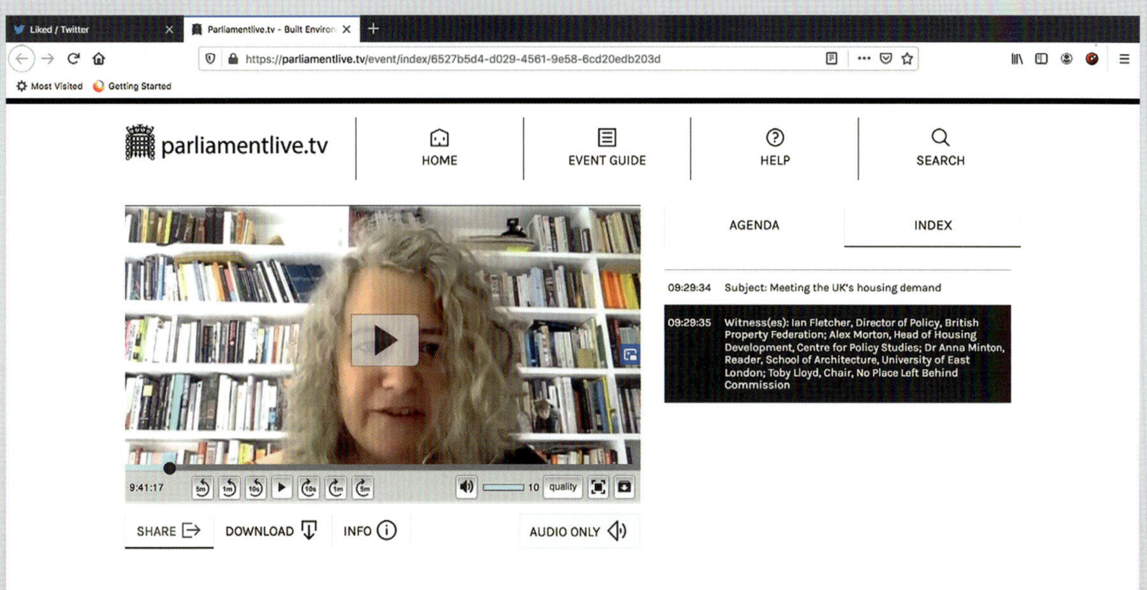

An Archaeological Model for St. Mary's Field Museum

Collaboration between UEL Unit A and L - P : Archaeology working for Fusion-JV on behalf of HS2

In June 2021, six UEL architecture students engaged in a work experience programme on an active construction project, they designed and digitally manufactured physical archaeological representation models to help communicate the findings from the excavation project of St. Mary's Church in Stoke Mandeville (Buckinghamshire). The archaeological site was being excavated as part of the construction of HS2.

The UEL students visited the excavation, were briefed by the archaeology team and museum curator and worked to a detailed brief for the design and development of the models. During the design phase, the students produced numerous drawings and prototypes and attended design reviews with the archaeologists and the museum team. Because this was a live project which happened alongside the excavation itself, the challenge was to represent the spatial conditions and changes of the site and landscape in relation to space and time, translating this relational understanding into tactile and interactive models that, despite being physical, had to still remain open to interpretation and to possible changes in order to incorporate the new findings as they were uncovered.

The final models were designed in acrylic, using layers, colours and transparency to overlay the different phases and features of the site. The models were also designed to be played with, and to be arranged in multiple constellations. This multi-dimensional approach helped to communicate how the spaces of interest had changed over time, as well as enable the team of archaeologists to creatively explore the site and its surrounding landscape, supporting the process of interpretation and understanding of the site during the excavation, an unexpected but highly appreciated aspect of the students' model.

The project for the St. Mary's Field Museum's models resulted from a collaboration with L - P : Archaeology, as part of their delivery of SEE (Skills, Employment and Education) and Public Engagement programmes for HS2. It provided a real life project experience for the UEL students who had to respond and deliver the project using the tools offered by their architecture training, architectural language and critical design thinking, while learning: how to work in a construction environment; archaeological practice; historical phases and building typologies; and most importantly, learning how to engage in a collaborative process of trans-disciplinary knowledge exchange.

The models were presented to the team of 65 archaeologists and construction professionals by the students and exhibited to the public at the St. Mary's Field Museum, a pop-up museum on site, between July and September 2021. During the exhibition, the representation models became key elements of the exhibit and proved to be highly popular with public audiences of all ages. It was seen by more than 1700 visitors. Some parts of the models featured in the BBC's 'Digging for Britain' programme on BBC1 and BBC i-player (Series 9- Episode 2).

Awards:
- Archaeology Achievement Award 2021 (highly commended)
- Public & Community Engagement Award 2022 (winner in partnerships category)

Project Lead: Carsten Jungfer and Fernanda Palmieri (Unit A degree unit)

Degree Student Participants: Aya Nasr, Busthana Nusren Odayapurath, Claudiu Theodor Cazan, Haleema Ahmed, Michael Ngam, Muhammad Tawfik

Special Thanks to UEL staff Paul Nichols, Rob Pyecroft, Daryl Brown, David Morgan and Mark Sowden.

Also, special thanks to Guy Hunt (L-P), Rachel Wood (Fusion-JV), Lily Hawker-Yates (L-P) and Susan Greaney (English Heritage) for making this collaboration project a reality.

Plato for Architects
Thinkers for Architects series

Renée Tobe

Plato for Architects in the Thinkers for Architects series will be published by Taylor and Francis in 2023.

The aim of this book is to examine the nature of thinking itself, which is the basis for design and architectural decision making. Plato asks what it means to know, and how we can ever communicate what we know to others. Introductions to Plato situate his thinking in his own era, and dissect his thoughts one from the other in the different dialogues. The dialogues are structured to be interpreted and translated in our own eras, so that they are always contemporary. This book carefully extracts the points relevant to architects and urbanists, weaving them together so that we can learn from them while maintaining continuity with the discussion from which they derive.

Excavation through layers of Western thinking identifies two distinctly divergent directions for architects and urbanists both of which trace their origins back to Plato. In the first, lie centrally planned ideal cities; Utopias, urban typologies in the structured language of the new order of the French Republic and the architecture of 20th century fascist regimes. The canonical texts of urban design by Jan Gehl, Kevin Lynch, Gordon Cullinan, among others that describe forms of communicative and community life or Christopher Alexander's *The Pattern Language* combinations of urban elements to enhance our existence follow the second line of thought. Many of our current structures whether in government, urban design or education find their descriptions in the Platonic dialogues. This book helps decode terms and provides the points relevant to architects. The objectives are to deliver them in a manner that informs other thinking about architecture, and how we practice it.

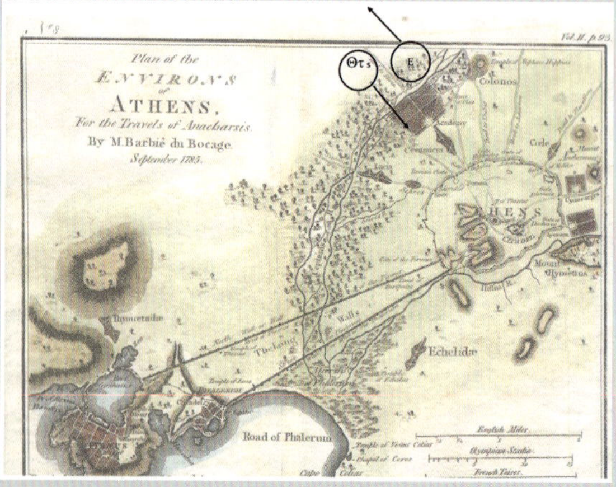

Location map of the *Theatatus*, showing position of characters.

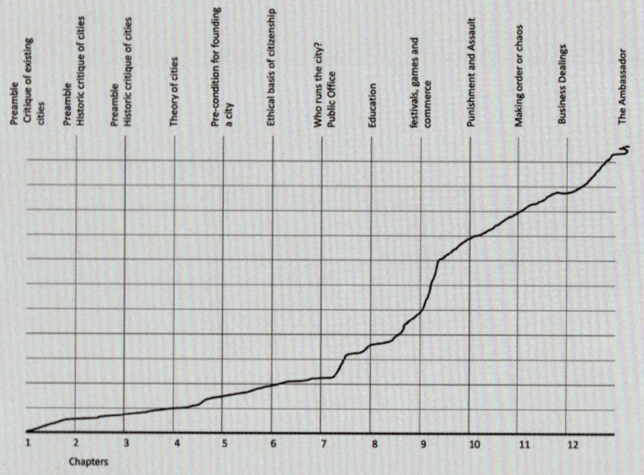

Spatialisation of The Laws

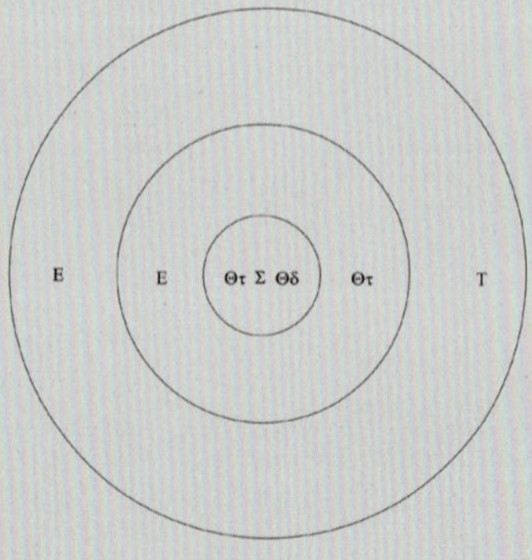

Diagram of the characters and structure of the *Phaedrus*

Professional Practice
BSc(Hons) Architecture (ARB/RIBA)

Stephanie Schultze-Westrum

RIBA collaboration
RIBA Mentoring - Part 1 Year 3
Special thanks to Jessica Davies and Dian Small from the RIBA for organising the RIBA mentoring scheme for our Part 1 Year 3 students.

We are extremely grateful to the following mentors for giving the students insight into the professional world of an architecture practice and for their support with portfolios and job application preparations:

Anne-Sophie Doneche - ADAD Architecture
Esther Jimenez Herraiz
Gordon Shrigley - Gordon Shrigley Architecture
James Nutt - Foster + Partners
Max Fraser - Atomik Architecture
Morgan Wild - HTA Design
Rupert Bucklad - Stiff + Trevillion
Steven King
RIBA Future Architects - We further would like to thank Victoria Adegoke for her valuable insight into RIBA Future Architects geared at Part 1 and Part 2 students looking for guidance and inspirations around employment.
RIBA ELAg - Thank you to Mike Jamieson from Tate Hindle for the introduction to the RIBA East London Architects Group (ELAg) and his invitation to students to get involved in planning and organisation of events, whilst meeting professionals and East London stakeholders.

Professional Practice - Job Applications
CV workshops and mock interviews, Part 1 Year 3
We are very grateful to Romy Berlin from Allies and Morrison for her insightful talk about graphic layout of CVs, cover letters and portfolios. Discussing fonts, font sizes, margins, tonality, but also inviting the students to see text based documents like a design project, to give the white space in between text blocks/images similar attention given to spaces in between buildings.

Following the workshop, the students were assigned an architectural practice for a mock interview. A big thank you to the interviewers. It was a fantastic experience, and the subsequent written feedback was gratefully received by the students.

Romy Berlin – Allies and Morrison
C.F. Møller
Emily Farmer - Grimshaw
Naomi Danos - Grimshaw
Sun Yen Yee - Grimshaw
Beata Szkotak - Grimshaw
Annelie Kvick Thompson - Grimshaw
Ben Clark - Grimshaw
Lee Herrick - Grimshaw
Frederick Fasola - Maccreanor Lavington
Jonathan McDowell - Matter Architecture
Paul Dunphy - Perkins & Wills
Rafael Marks - Penoyre & Prasad (Perkins & Will)
Kalpesh Intwala - Stanton Williams
Jemma Miller - Tate Hindle
Fiona Young - Tate Hindle
Alfonso Padro - HKS
Teddy Laurence - Urbanauts
Jerry van Veldhuizen - Haworth Tompkins
Gareth Morris - what if: projects
CV and job application talk and workshop - adrem recruitment agency

A big thank you to Carl Nevil from adrem for industry insights into recruitment and what practices are looking for in 2021/22.

Mental Wealth Professional Practice - London Walks: Kings Cross
Part 1 Year 1 and Year 2 could experience in depth tours of the Kings Cross Redevelopment. We are very grateful to Antje Saunders - Allies and Morrison and Julia Finlayson - Argent, for the two different perspectives of the project from conception to realisation.

UEL Students Redesign Disused Office for 2022 Showcase

Students from the University of East London transformed a disused office space at Broadgate into an architectural and design showcase.'Show 22' featured the work of students across all levels from the School of Architecture, Computing and Engineering (ACE).

It proudly revealed the work of a cohort of students with diversity at its core, as the University boasts a minority majority with a focus on a local east London intake. Some 72 per cent of students are from minority backgrounds and 68 per cent are the first generation in their family to go to university.

The disused office space, which is owned by British Land, was donated to the University and staff and second year students used recycled scaffolding gifted from Westfield Shopping Centre and Zap Architecture to create a maze displaying work including models, design sketches, paintings and visual pieces. The office furniture including tables, cabinets and drawers were repurposed into seating and plinths which presented the best work from the architecture and design cohort.

Many of the exhibiting students chose to focus on creative reuse projects, as well as explorations into new materials that could be developed from waste products. This includes a community pavilion set within a ruined landscape in the village of Rock, Northumberland (Korell Llaudes); clothes formed out of orange peel (Maria Castro Paredes); and a concept for a new restaurant that sits atop a mushroom farm, with pods made out of crushed eggshells (Joana Miglencheva).

There is a strong community focus too - the AJ Student Prize-nominated Hamda Jama has developed a Youth Parliament in Hackney that spreads into the market next door, becoming a completely public building.

The exhibition space enables visitors to immerse themselves in all aspects of exciting and creative architectural and design courses as well as viewing work which incorporates practices from both engineering and computing. The building itself will be pulled down at the end of July to make way for new construction. Earlier in June, students from the School of Arts and Creative Industries (ACI) held a London Fashion Week event at the space.

The show, which is sponsored by British Land and Moet & Chandon, was embedded into architectural and design courses as second-year students will earn credits for their work displayed in the exhibition. British Land has employed around 50 students from the University, inviting them onto summer programmes and to take part in the Broadgate Prize, a collaboration including leading construction company Sir Robert McAlpine.

Alex Scott-Whitby, leader of the architecture and physical design cluster, said, "This show represents an enormous investment into UEL from British Land, so we are incredibly grateful to them for giving us this opportunity. Our students have designed and built this incredible exhibition space which complements their work. This exhibition is focused on employability and engagement as our students can display their work to professional architects and the whole of London. Our students are the people who will change the face of architecture and design and this exhibition is an opportunity for us to showcase our students' talents to the public and the professional world."

Bianca Radoanca, BA Interior Design, who was part of the curation team, said, "As part of this project we were required to completely redesign the office space for the UEL fashion show as well as architecture and design exhibition. Our focus in creating the show was to make sure we reuse and repurpose as much materials as we can. By reusing the office furniture, we have breathed new life into everyday materials and designed the perfect stage for our work. The yellow scaffolding, which we have prevented from going to waste, contrasts against the blue walls in the space to create a maze effect which guides visitors through the work that hangs off the beams. We also used the scaffolding as table spaces so visitors can have a closer look at the designs and models. The exhibition has been five months in the making and we're incredibly proud of the space we have created and our work which is being displayed."

Photographs: Simon Williams

University alumnus Jayden Ali, founder of J.A_P and course tutor at the University of the Arts London (UAL), spoke about his journey and the important role that architecture plays in developing and strengthening communities.

He said, "UEL was critical in developing how I practice as an architect and allowed me to build lasting networks that I still use today. At UEL I learnt how I can project who I am in my work and how my life experience adds value to what I do. Now in my practice, I have been able to explore issues that are important to me. Whether that be highlighting the importance of decarbonisation and decolonisation or producing cities that are much more representative of the people that they serve, architecture has an important role to play in improving and developing opportunities for us all."

Professor David Tann, dean of ACE, said, "This show represents an opportunity for us to showcase the dedication and hard work of our students and staff. We're extremely pleased to welcome many of our alumni back to the UEL community. We are grateful to British Land for the continuous support throughout the years, and for generously providing us the use of this great venue especially dedicated for this STEAM show.

In this exhibition you will see work from our students - the future artists, architects, designers, engineers, construction managers and IT professionals, who have demonstrated the knowledge, skills, and intelligences required to contribute to building a better and sustainable world."

Jayden Ali speaking at Showcase 22, photograph: Simon Williams

UEL rated first in London for student satisfaction in architecture

NSS 2022 shows positive results for UEL's architecture and design courses

Architecture at UEL was ranked the highest in London for overall student satisfaction, teaching on my course, academic support, learning community and students' union, National Student Survey (NSS) 2022 reveals. The rankings also placed architecture in second place nationally with an overall satisfaction rate of 95 per cent.

For the second time in two years, BA interior design at UEL also received 100 per cent student satisfaction in the rankings. Design studies at UEL ranked fourth out of 12 higher education institutions nationally.

The NSS invites students to share their experiences of studying at universities and ranks them according to overall satisfaction. Topics measured include, course organisation and management, assessment and feedback, academic support, quality of teaching, development opportunities, student unions and more.

This survey was one of the largest on record – with around 325,000 responses from students across the UK.

UEL possesses international renown architecture and design courses, where students have access to our brand new state-of-the-art facilities including wood, metal and plaster workshops, digital fabrication areas, high spec computer labs and more.

Our courses focus on employability and our architecture and design students receive excellent career opportunities with our industry partners including The Royal Institute of British Architects (RIBA) and British Land.

The positive results come after UEL students transformed a disused office in London showcasing Show 22 – UEL's end-of-year architecture and design exhibition.

Mr Carl Callaghan, head of the department of architecture and visual arts, said: "This is an impressive achievement, and our staff can be very proud of their hard working in creating such a positive and impactful learning environment for our students. Our architecture and design courses have been tailored by our partners in industry and uses cutting edge equipment to challenges and prepares students for the jobs of the future."

Professor David Tann, dean of ACE, said: "I am extremely proud to see that our architecture and design courses achieved such great student satisfaction results in the recent NSS survey. Student feedback is incredibly important to us, and we have listened diligently to what our students have said, so we're very proud that this has been reflected in our results.

Our staff work incredibly hard to ensure that our students have the best possible experience when studying at UEL. We will use these fantastic results to continue our work in enhancing student experience and provide them with opportunities to grow and develop as they prepare for their future careers."

Some of this year's field trips and workshops

Open Lectures

Our ongoing lecture series during 2021-2022

ONE SCHOOL - ACE AVA PRESENTS
CAN
University of East London
Mat Barnes is the director of architecture studio CAN. He is a former member of the teaching and arts collective STORE and has delivered lectures on his work across Europe. He consolidated his various creative practices to form CAN in 2016 which has built a reputation for creating striking and idiosyncratic projects, underwritten by cultural and historical research, that reflect the unique personalities and needs of their clients.
13:00-14:00, Tuesday 16th Nov, IN PERSON - UEL AVA LIGHTWELL &
ONLINE - ONE SCHOOL on TEAMS, all welcome

Architecture & Design Society Presents - The Future is Now!
Studio Ben Allen
University of East London
Studio Ben Allen is a multidisciplinary design practice. they undertake a wide range of projects at the intersection of architecture, design and art. Each of our projects has at its core an open collaborative dialogue between participants and disciplines, from concept to production, in order to create unique and engaging spatial sequences.
13:00, Tuesday 29th March, IN PERSON - UEL AVA LIGHTWELL &
ONLINE - ONE SCHOOL on TEAMS, all welcome

Architecture & Design Society Presents - The Future is Now!
Bureau de Change
University of East London
Their architectural strategy can be described as a desire to bring a sense of theatre, playfulness and innovation to the design of spaces, products and environments. The result is a studio where rigorous thinking and analysis are brought to life through prototyping, testing and making. BDC is an award-winning studio and is considered to be a prominent young practice in the UK with a strong attention to detail, resulting in very powerful projects.
13:00, Tuesday 22rd March, IN PERSON - UEL AVA LIGHTWELL &
ONLINE - ONE SCHOOL on TEAMS, all welcome

ONE SCHOOL - ADSOC PRESENTS
Alison Cooke
University of East London
Alison Cooke works with clay dug from interventions such as mining, engineering or scientific research and looks for where histories of a location relate to and impact on our lives today. She is a member of the Royal Society of Sculptors, co-founder of ceramics collective the Associated Clay Workers Union, and recipient of grants and awards from Henry Rothschild and Arts Council England.
13:00-14:00, Tuesday 26th April, IN PERSON - UEL AVA LIGHTWELL &

Architecture & Design Society Presents - The Future is Now
Nick Newman
University of East London
The first invitee of the student-led lectures is Nick Newman, the director of Studio Bark and one of the writers of the book "Everything Needs to Change". This year, ADSOC focused on discussing our generation's main issues and how the guest lecturers see the future of architecture. Climate emergency being the most worrisome, no one better to start this series than Nick! Hope to see you there.
13:00, Thursday 3rd February, IN PERSON - UEL AVA LIGHTWELL &
ONLINE - ONE SCHOOL on TEAMS, all welcome
EVERY-THING NEEDS TO CHANGE

Architecture & Design Society Presents - The Future is Now
Robert Jamison
University of East London
Robert Jamison is an award-winning architect from Northern Ireland. Bold, innovative and boundary-pushing with his designs, he certainly knows how to make a statement with his architecture. His travels around the Indian sub-continent have greatly influenced his practice and ethos as an architect. Robert Jamison is also well known from BBC's series "Your Home Made Perfect" where he shows his innovative designs, with bench seating and adaptable multi-function rooms among his signature style.
13:00, Thursday 17th of March, IN PERSON - UEL AVA LIGHTWELL &
ONLINE - ONE SCHOOL on TEAMS, all welcome

Architecture & Design Society Presents - The Future is Now!
StudioMK
University of East London
Studio MK27, from São Paulo, was founded in the late 70's by architect Marcio Kogan and today is comprised of 30 architects and various collaborators worldwide. The architects of the team, great admirers of the Brazilian modernism generation, seek to fulfill the task of rethinking and giving continuity to this iconic architectural movement. The projects of Studio MK27 place value on formal simplicity and are elaborated with extreme care and attention to details and finishings.
13:00, Thursday 24th March, IN PERSON - UEL AVA LIGHTWELL &
ONLINE - ONE SCHOOL on TEAMS, all welcome

A+DC PRESENTS
Tony Tremlett
University of East London
Tony Tremlett is a curator based in London. His curatorial work focuses on art practices that engage with the spiritual, emotional and political command of place and material. He currently operates a new public arts platform named CIRCA which takes over the advertisements on the Piccadilly Lights screen in London with contemporary art. He also co-directs Betts Project, a commercial art gallery focusing on the intersection of art and architecture. He graduated from Goldsmiths College with an MFA in Curatorial Studies. Recent exhibitions include: Keeping Time, Ceretto, Alba (2020); Out of eye, Laure Genillard Gallery, London (2019); RÊVE SONORE, Espace Le Carré, Lille, France (2019); Günter Günschel: Freigeregelte, Betts Project, London (2018); Waves and Sirens, with Nicolas Jaar, Torre Bonomo, Spoleto, IT (2018)
12:30-14:00, Tuesday 19th Oct, ONLINE - ONE SCHOOL > TEAMS, all welcome

CASE Team + One School AVA presents
career zone
Simon Hamilton
University of East London
Design & Diversity: The changing face of the workplace
Simon Hamilton is a designer, careers mentor, diversity & inclusion consultant and a presenter (recently featured as design expert on 'Virtually Home' BBC1's latest Interior Design daytime show. Attend this webinar to be inspired by his career journey and learn how being different can be of benefit in the world of interior design. He will also be sharing his golden nuggets about the value of collaborative work and networking (yes- there was a reason for all that group work you are assigned to do!) and how this can help you building your career.
14:00-15:15, Thursday 27th Jan,
ONLINE - ONE SCHOOL on TEAMS, all welcome

HISTORY AND THEORY

Image as Argumentative Tool - Aby Warburg Workshop by Dr Renee Tobe

History and Theory

An Introduction

Year 1: The Vernacular International
Module Leader: Cláudia da Palma Romao
Contributors: Andrew Wright, Carl Callaghan, Mark Sustr, Susan Ginsburgh

As we know, the ongoing destruction of our environment by anthropogenic pollution is pushing us toward catastrophic circumstances. This situation promises to only worsen as we advance toward a series of climate-change tipping points. Amounting to the most momentous experimentation with the earth's living systems in human history, this environmental alteration, put in place by industrial modernity (with roots in the formation of capitalism centuries before), threatens increased temperatures, plummeting agricultural yields, wide-ranging droughts and consequent raging wildfires, massive flooding, extreme weather events, the collapse of fisheries, and public health breakdowns with spreading of epidemics. (Demos, 2016)

Employing a comprehensive perspective which includes the primitive, vernacular, regionalism, and pluralism, this module aims to critically reflect and inquire about the classical history of architecture and design. And it further examines the relationship between humans and the natural environment.

From technological developments, industrial and scientific revolutions, imperialism and war, this module demonstrates how cultural, political and ecological issues have been represented globally in architecture and design.

Weekly lectures and course readings will provide an orientation in fundamental ideas, while written assignments emphasise the development of debate and criticism within responsible design development.

Essays explain concepts of dwelling and domesticity through "The House as an instrument for Living" by revisiting an (eclectic) collection of international Houses of Modernity. Through seminars and tutorials, students analyse how each case study encapsulates a particular architecture and design intention and how it translates through continuity or discontinuity to the central topic of the Vernacular International and architectural past – from the Hut to the Machine. Quoting Latour: have we always been modern? (1993) and how shall we go from here?

Demos T.J. (2016) *Decolonizing Nature, Contemporary Art and the Politics of Ecology.* Sternberg Press (page 8,9)
Latour, Bruno. (1993) *We have never been modern.* Harvard University Press

Year 2: Cities
The Building as a City: London as a case study
Module Leader: Cláudia da Palma Romao
Contributors: Aleks Catina, Miho Nakagawa, Dr Renee Tobe

In the second year, H&T examines the topic of Cities, presenting students with historical and theoretical analysis that intersect the contemporary city with its past. Building on an understanding of the political, economic, social, and cultural landscapes, we explore how concepts, positions, and propositions of certain "typological" constructs serve as exercises to be analysed, questioned and transformed in a world dominated by uncertainty, speculation and ultra-technological change. Historical and contemporary projects and writings are studied in context and part of the theoretical discourse of the (non)urban architecture and design.

The Unique City (Steen, 1937) provides a starting point for investigating how a building could represent a city. Through various architectural buildings and typologies, which are part of a global-oriented history, we will primarily inquire how can we understand a building as a fragment of the city? How does the building reflect and relate to the city and its memories? How does the building reflect the technologies of a particular time? Are these typological constructs (models) serving the contemporary city and its peoples? Which new models are necessary for the present and (near) future?

Rasmussen, Steen. (1937) London: The Unique City. MIT Press

Year 3
Tutors: Miho Nakagawa and Renee Tobe

In the final year of the BSc, seminars encourage students to speak with their own voice and develop individual thought. Students engage with textual and linguistic means of expression of space and place using non-discriminatory language and references. Engaging with the inherent ambiguity of how we experience the world around us many questioned how to improve our planet, tackle the climate change emergency, and challenge received opinions. Space is never neutral and writing emphasised reflection about the subjectivity of each perspective and criticality of its position. The three essays presented here demonstrate the search for the ideal, the exploration of the public realm, and postcolonial expression in West Africa.

Robert Venning
What Happens When Any Architect Can Create Their Own Perfect World; How the Technological Shift from Representation to Simulation has Distorted the Architect's Ability to Envision Utopia

The switch from representation to simulation in architectural image making does not negate the architect's ability to propose utopias that promote social goods. However as the medium allows every architect to envision their own perfect world in a simulated environment that is in and of itself with no external reality the desires of individuals necessarily supersede the aims of the collective. The innovations that allow for this switch from representation to simulation run in parallel with the rise of neoliberal politics and economics becoming the popular system through which the world orders itself. In the work of Archigram we can see early signs of consumerist imagery dictating the vision of speculative architecture but it's context of the benevolent British Post War state and modernist architecture kept the group's vision focused on improving forms of public life. Though architects such as Peter Eisenman used hybrid methods of simulation and representation to envision projects that aimed to promote scientific discovery and innovation, simulation has overtaken representation and with that the celebration of the individual is promoted.

With the emerging metaverse offering the potential for economic opportunities to migrate into virtual worlds more architects may move to designing buildings in the digital environment. But as has been displayed the architects behind these utopias so far seem content with creating designs that promote a form of digital capitalism that prioritises the display of wealth and technological progress and any cost.

Cristina Roscolute
Public Realms of Soho

'The dismal quarter of Soho seen under these hanging glimpses, with its muddy ways, and slatternly passengers, and its lamps which had never been extinguished or had been kindled afresh to combat the mournful re-invasion of darkness, seemed in lawyers' eyes. Like the district of some city in a nightmare.'

– The Strange Case of Dr Jekyll and Mr Hyde, Robert Louis Stevenson, 1886

Aristotle, In the Politics, 'ten people would not make a city, and with a hundred thousand it is a city no longer.' When it comes to Soho, this quote states how a community should be big enough to be 'self-sufficient for living the good life after the manner of a political community.' (Kevin Lynch, 1981, p.239). While people need a community to function, enjoy themselves and have a healthy mind, overpopulation can also be damaging. Like in everything, there needs to be a balance for people and societies to flourishes. Currently, there are 3,054 people residents in Soho, which is double the number since 2001 (1,412 residents). Throughout time, Soho has been through major population changes. The outbreak of cholera in 1854 was a devastating event for the Soho residents. Broad Street, now known as Broadwick Street and the neighbourhood street, has lost around 700 of its residents. (Publica, 2014, p.142). The epidemic was caused by a water pump outside No. 41 Broad Street. It took seven years to figure out what was causing the epidemic. Dr John Snow's measures aided in halting the spread to the rest of the homes along Broad Street. The pump was designed with pink granite curbstone and is still an important artefact on Broadwick Street today. The residential district began to grow in tandem with the expansion in business usage. Bad residential neighbourhoods like Brewer Street and Ingestre Place were planned to be demolished to make way for new 'model housing'. These neighbourhoods can still be seen today and had a significant effect on the sort of space, streets, and courts that comprised Soho's public realm. The buildings within the neighbourhood were being used on a smaller scale in relation to the streets. Their usage became influenced by the streets' narrowness and the area's enclosure, and later on, repurposing them. These public realms have stayed within the two neighbourhoods till our days and have been used since then. Soho works as a public space not merely because it possesses all of the necessary instruments to be recognised as one, but because of the district's unique traits. According to Google Maps, the park's separation in terms of public spaces could be improved and additional vegetation could be added to the space. In reality, according to Léon Krier, the ideal ratio for public space inside a city, or in my case, a district, is somewhere between 25 and 35% of the facility's capacity.

Balla Ngam
Investigating Architecture in Senegal

This essay examines the architecture of two cities in Senegal through historical research into Senegal in colonial and postcolonial times as well as personal narrative from those who experienced life at that time. The essay will focus on the similarities and differences between colonial and post-colonial approaches to building and dwelling, from an African point of view. It begins with a discussion about the story of colonial French Africa in general then focus a little about Senegal, on the role of religion in Senegalese culture, and primarily on the Mouride tariqa. The Mouride tariqa is a spiritual brotherhood founded in 1883 in Senegal by Amadou Bamba. Mouride comprise almost half the population of the country and have strong influence on everyday life in Senegal. Their headquarters are in Touba (Villalon, 2004). Senegal is in West Africa, subdivided by The Gambia and with a capital city, Dakar, on a promontory on the coast and second city Touba, inland to the East. It was colonised by the French and achieved independence in 1960. To contextualise all the points in this essay an understanding of 'sacred' and profane' as defined by Mircea Eliade sheds light on how the city is experienced and understood. Senegal is defined by religion; the mosques are always at the centre of the city, and they regulate the activities during the day (through prayers). Personal narratives from different generations, both those who grew up in colonial times and those who experienced independence help to evaluate the differences and changes during those times and put them in comparison to today's life. I will talk about how waste management, that is, the actual cleanliness of the streets themselves, also affects the country and how it relates to society and religion.

Personal Narratives
"It was very difficult in our time, we used to go to the fields to harvest the crops (bodj in Wolof, a word I had to ask my mother the meaning), then we would come back home to manually prepare them with our equipment, then transform the product to millet to eat or sell. After that, us women would go to the well to collect water in our barrels (every family must fill up their own) then go again to the fields to help and after noon come back to prepare lunch, usually 'thiére' (a Senegalese dish prepare from millet, still very popular to this day, it can be mixed with a sauce with either chicken, fish, or meat) for the men to come and eat together . After lunch again go back to help in the fields to help until 'takkussan' (prayer time around 5pm) and come back to prepare the millet that is going to be used for the next day. We used to work all day". (Ngom, 2022). When I asked the question

'how was life during your times in Senegal?' to my aunt (Faty Ngom) her first reaction was of laughter maybe it was a bitter smile remember her childhood and early adult life because she started by stating how tough those times were in rural areas in Senegal in the 1950s. Also, this helped me realise how crucial the role of women is in Senegalese culture, granted they don't or didn't have a strong or equal voice (in fact they didn't have a voice in political matters, now they are getting more empowered), their hard work supporting their husbands, children and themselves made Senegal what it is today in a positive while politician do what is best for themselves and not the society.

I started the essay by talking about the personal experiences because I wanted to give the reader a first insight of how the life was through three different perspectives (poor adult woman in rural areas, young man looking for a better life and rich young woman), this would help me later highlight these differences and give a chronological order to the events. I talked about the history of Senegal but in relation to the religion and the governing bodies (colonial administration and post-colonial state) because religion is at the centre of the Senegalese lifestyle. I talked about the provision of land, how there is no service that surveys it and the challenge it is to develop the country if the land in which a person lives is not registered to his name and how the State makes it very difficult to have these regulations. I talked about the African urban model, with the mosque in the centre as a reference, a fixed point in the chaos that is the world, the house of the Chief near it, a public square where the elderly discusses under a tree (called 'penc' in Senegal) the matters of the city, big wide streets converging on it. After my research I have done in this argument the thing that jumped to my eye is the relentlessness of Senegal society. They did not wait for the government in colonial times and post-colonial times to today. They are a very inclusive culture, getting in small groups of families or neighbours and organising themselves appointing 'Chef de quartier' and 'Chef de village' to regulate their own problems what they have. This fact of not waiting for the State derives from religion, the fact that the believer must work for the forgiveness of God and thank him for everything that happens in life. With this mentality they built these cities and mosques. Being a country so religious, where cleanliness of the soul is sought after, is why it is surprising that they still have major problem with trash because it represents the profane, something that contradicts what the general population believes in.

Foundation

Architecture + Design

Keita Tajima, Course Leader

The course aims to provide a broad range of experiences in the culture of spatial design. "Thinking through making" is at the core of this course, which is a tradition of architecture and design at UEL. We aspire to make the foundation studio into a creative laboratory where students will explore, discuss and cultivate individual creativity and critical thinking through studentship. Our aim is to stimulate students to find joy and enthusiasm in making and designing through the framework supported by experienced and enthusiastic tutors.

Keita Tajima

Foundation

Keita Tajima (Programme Leader),
Irina Maria Georgescu, Catalina Pollak,
Andrew Wright

Foundation in Architecture and Design is a gateway to the culture of design. The course aims to provide a broad range of experiences in the culture of spatial design. "Thinking through making" is at the core of this course, which is a tradition of the architecture school at UEL. We aspire to make the foundation studio into a creative laboratory where students will explore, discuss and cultivate individual creativity and critical thinking through studentship. Our aim is to stimulate students to find joy and enthusiasm in making and designing through the framework supported by experienced and enthusiastic tutors. Each module in the foundation program is set to provide briefs to enable students to discover their talents, and develop them further to be ready for their challenge as a first year student in a specific field of design.

2021-22

We started the year by building up a series of skills and experiences through drawing and making from a scale of a pencil to a body, and exploring the relationship between a body and space at the end of first semester. The online workshop with a choreographer stimulated the fresh discovery of the movement of a body, and provided students with further insight into the spatial relationship between a body, movement and space. The workshop allowed students to document and experiment in full scale drawing and collaborative digital collage.

Design Project

The final design project allows students to go through a series of design processes from observation, interpretation, and experiments to develop an imaginative design propositions. This year, the site for the project was set in Wapping, along the Thames foreshore, a hidden pocket of spaces which reveals layers of history, as well as spaces under the water through the tidal change. The students were asked to develop a room as device to register the unique setting and environment, and it also provides a space for refuge. Students have observed the area by various ways of recording, and explored a series of spatial narratives and possible scenarios

Students:
Bryce Clarke James Douglas Aisha Drysdale Eraee Jargaui Niyaz Hussain Jhan Carlos Lobaton Alay Carolina Machado Yogesh Mall Karleen Christiane Menes Mrugaya Nagdeve Prince Raymond Partee Melissa Sarango Rivas Ammar Ali Abubakar Abdirahman Sharif Sameer Zahid Adijat Abass Ivana Plamenova Panayotova Cianka Powell Farhan Rehman Michelle Richards Alfred Storer Azra Tahtali Alanna Terpilowski Imad Hussain Salima Rahman Emmanuel Torson Maria Badea Naivasha Francis Shahida Hassan Moses Jenga Diana Mihaela Stoica

Special thanks to:
Ektoras Arkomanis Adam Nathaniel Furman , Akil Scafe-Smith (Resolve Collective) Ivana Sehic, Carsten Jungfer, Ioana Marinescu, Keith Winter. Mark Sowden, Gaynor Zealy, Paul Nichols, Craig Madden, Daryl Brown, David Morgan

1

Previous page **1** Spatial installation by all students + Ivana Sehic **2** Michelle Richards, fragment sketches **3** Michelle Richards, dissected pomegranate **4** Alfred Storer, orange section drawings **5** Alanna Terpilowski, pepper measured drawings **6** Michelle Richards, dissected pomegranate (photo) **7** Alanna Terpilowski, casting process **8** Ivana Plamenova Panayotova, model **9** Salima Rahman, sketch models **10** Carolina Machado, slotting joints model **11** Mrugaya Nagdeve, axonometric of fragments casts **12** Karleen Christiane Menes, model **13** Karleen Christiane Menes, axonometric collage **14** Mrugaya Nagdeve, fragment plaster casts **15** Ivana Plamenova Panayotova

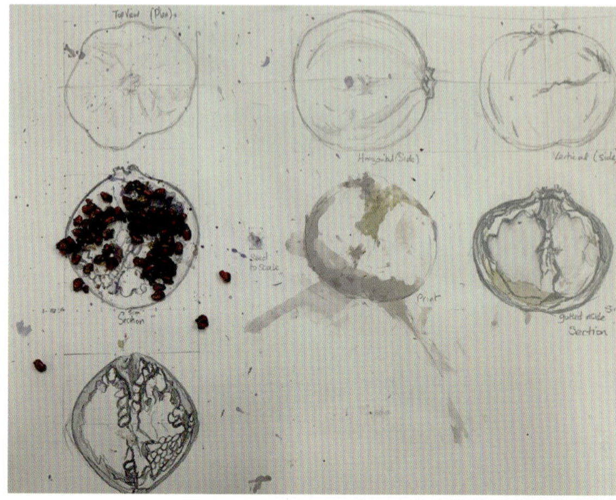

3

2

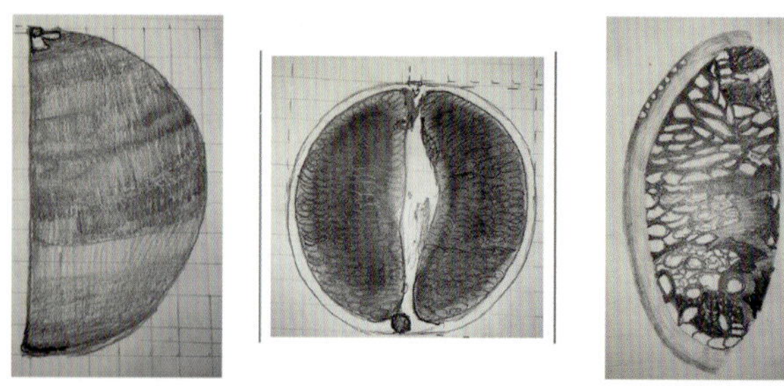

4

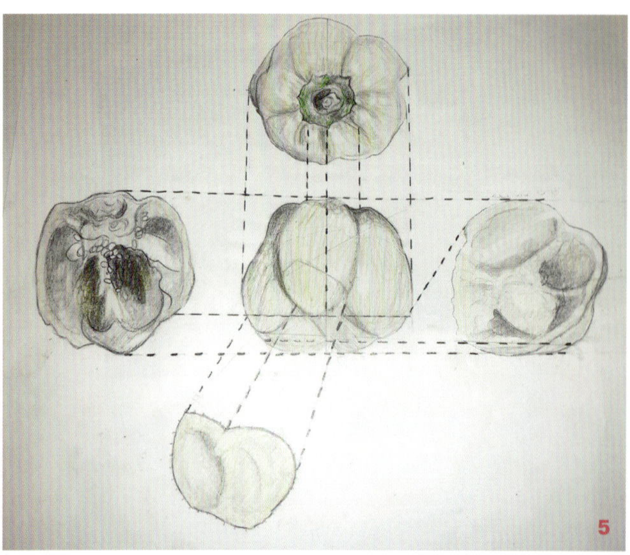

5

6

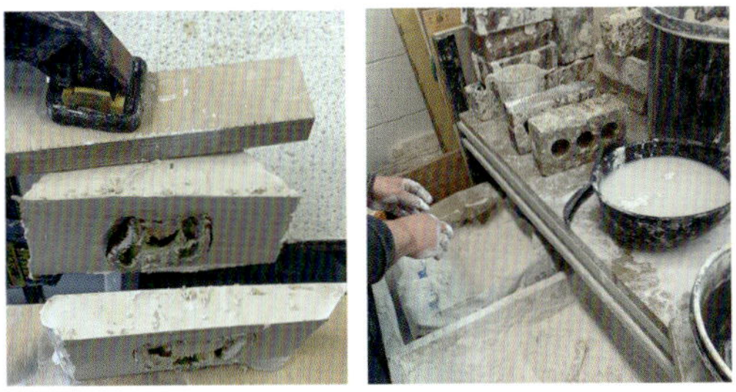

7

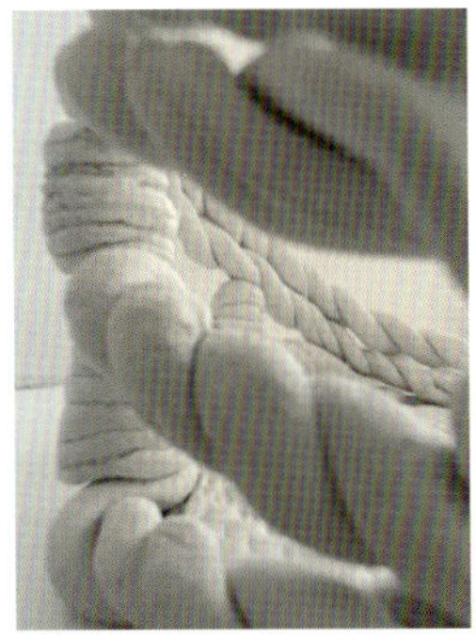

8

10

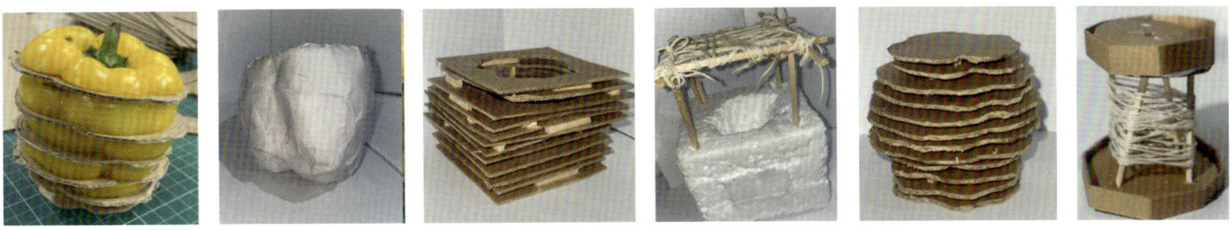

9

11

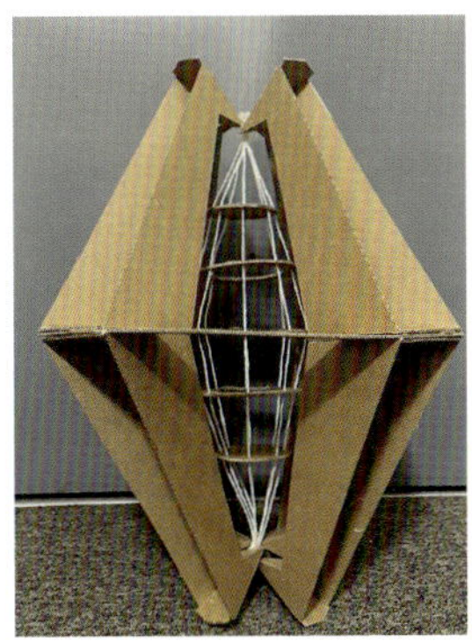

12

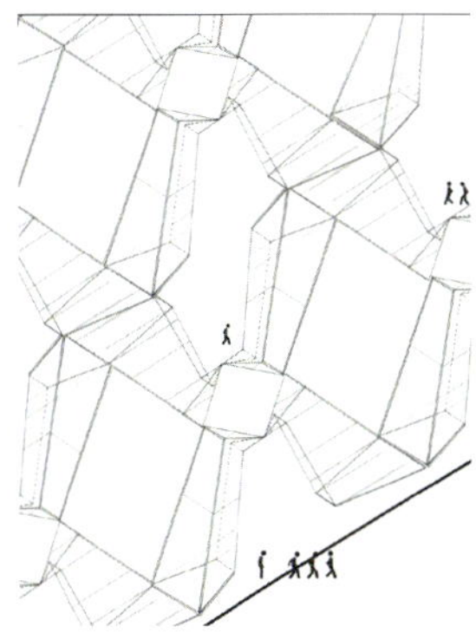

13

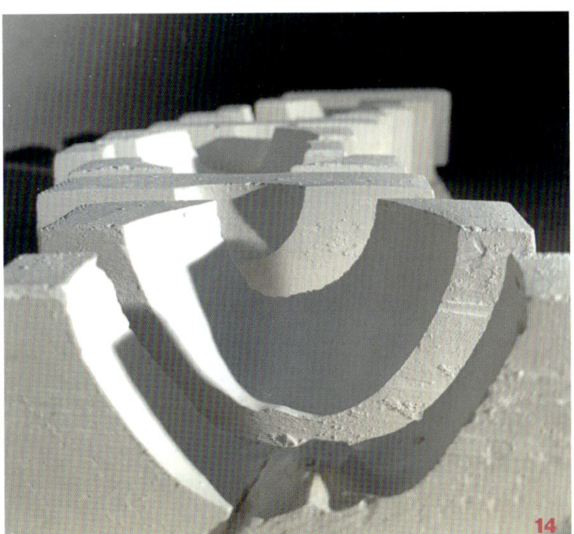

14

15

16 Eraee Jargaui, photographic exploration of plaster cast **17** James Douglas, inhabitation study **18** Salima Rahman, paper collage **19** Karleen Menes, speculative collage of elements from Wapping foreshore site **20** Karleen Menes, acrylic laser engraving and resulting intaglio and relief prints **21** Alanna Terpilowski, monotype study of materials **22** Yogesh Mall, intaglio silvercard drypoint print **23** James Douglas, digital spatial collage **24** Alfred Storer, embossing print **25** James Douglas, spatial collage of National Theatre perspective **26** Eraee Jargaui, 3d paper collage **27** Bryce Clarke, photoshop movement sequence

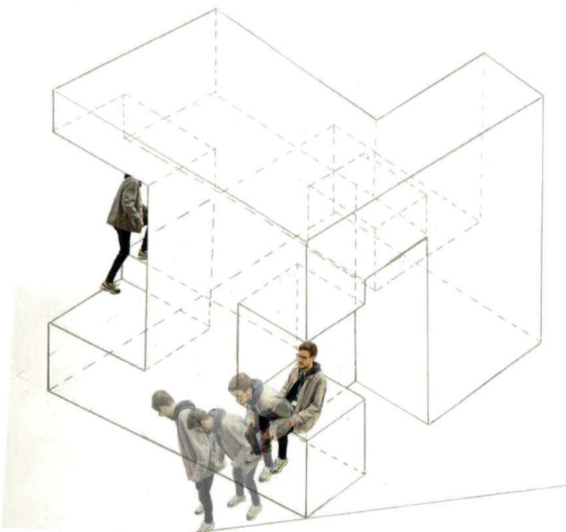

17

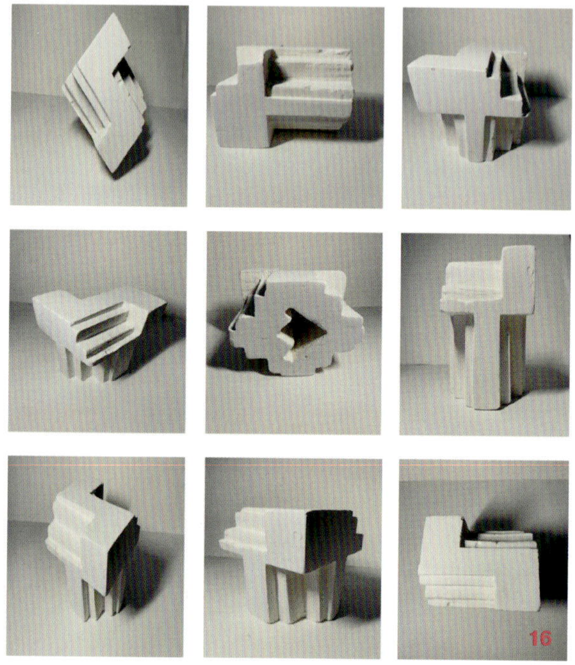

16

18

19

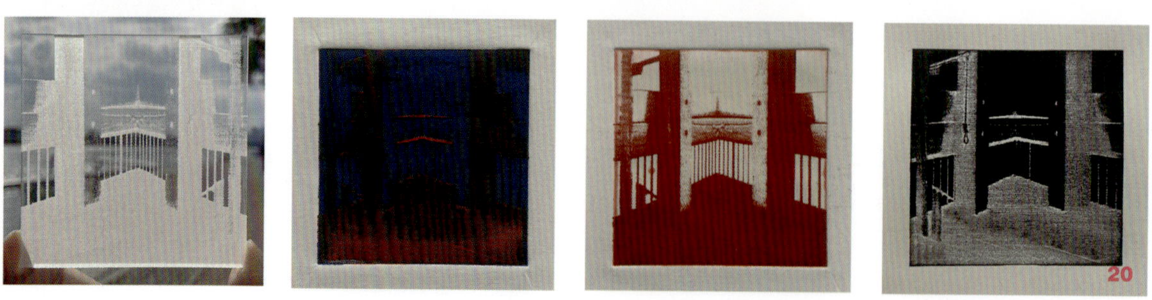

20

21

22

23

24

25

26

27

28 Thames boat trip and drawing session **29,35** V&A visit and sketching sessions **30** RESOLVE Collective lecture by Akil **31** Architecture visit in North Greenwich **32** Exhibition visit at The Building Centre **33** Serpentine Pavilion visit and drawing sessions **34,36** Mark making workshop at the Barbican centre

28

29

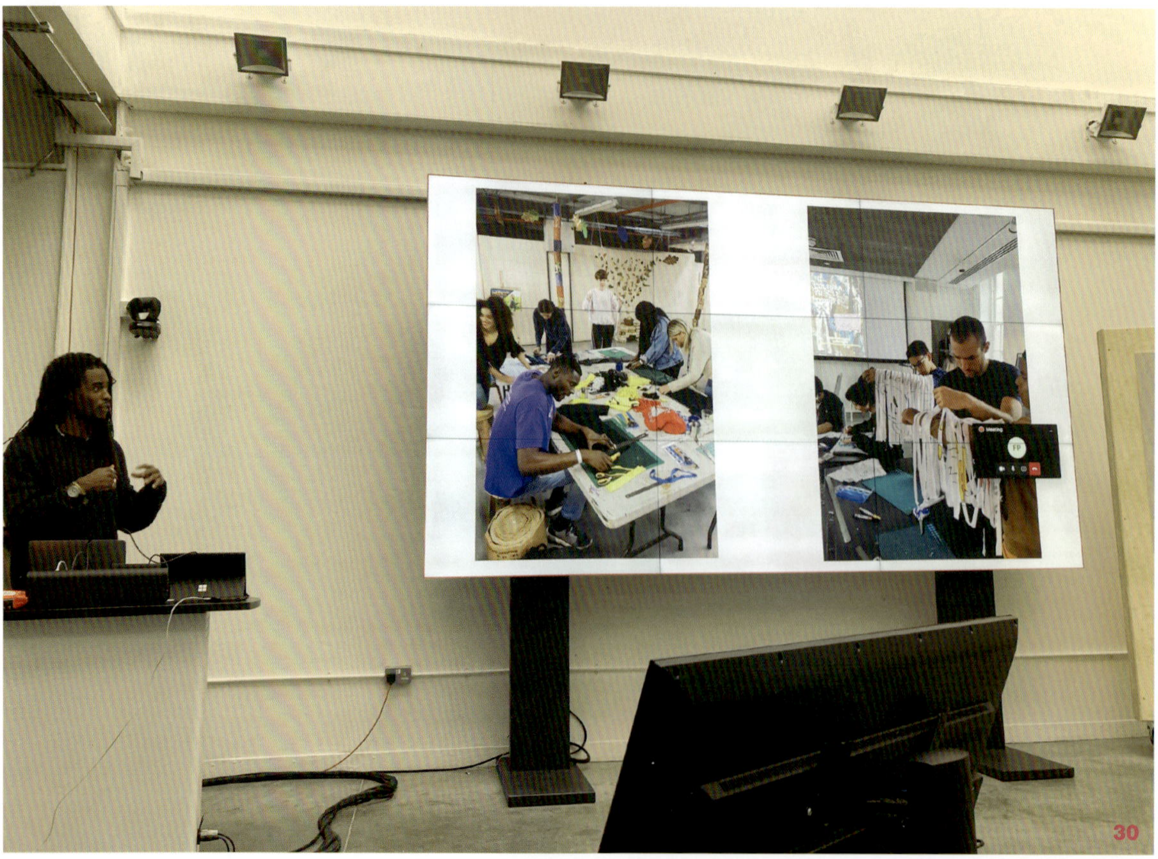

30

31

32

33

34

35

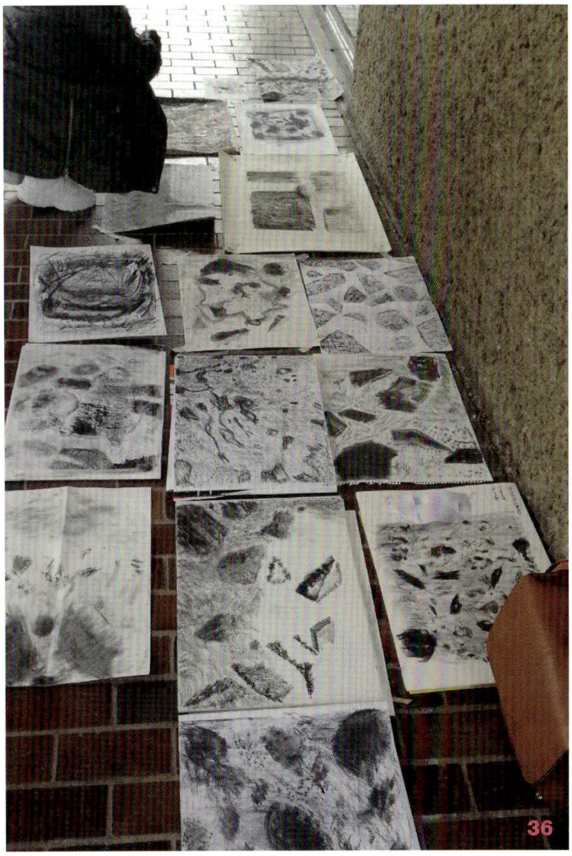
36

34 Karleen Christiane Menes, activity photo-montage **35** Yogesh Mall **36** Karleen Christiane Menes, activity mapping **37** Yogesh Mall, axonometric **38** Karleen Christiane Menes, test models **39** James Douglas, detail from the site **40** Farhan Rehman, model **41** Yogesh Mall **42** Jhan Carlos Lobaton Alay, sketch **43** Klaudia Depczynska, model **44** Farhan Rehman, model

37

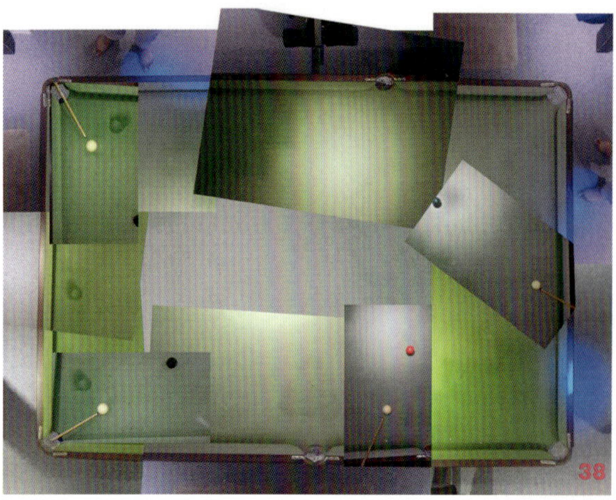

38

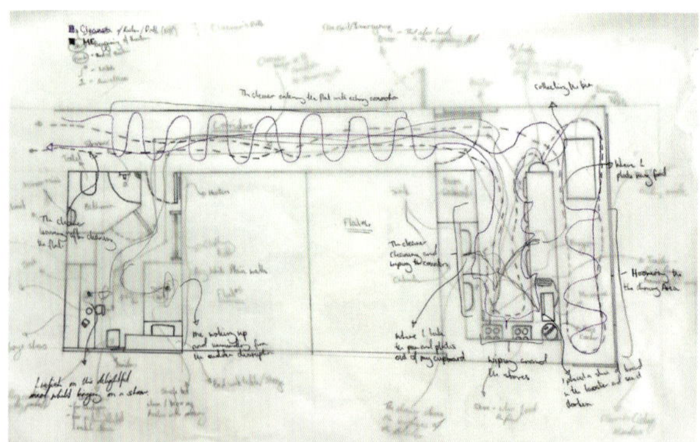

39

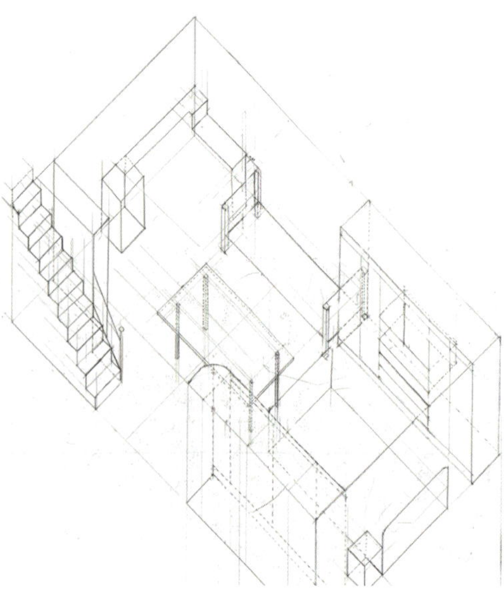

40

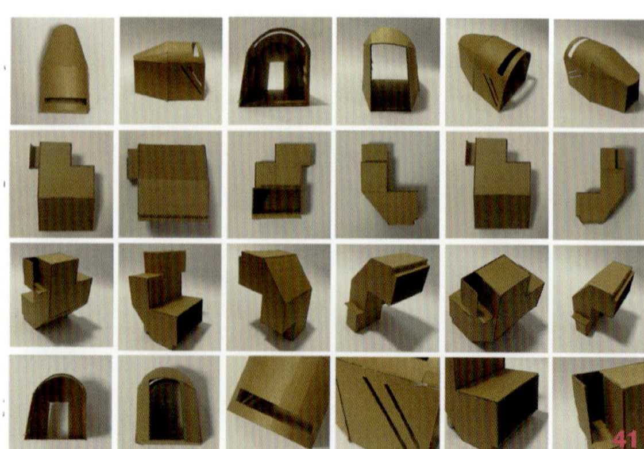

41

42

43

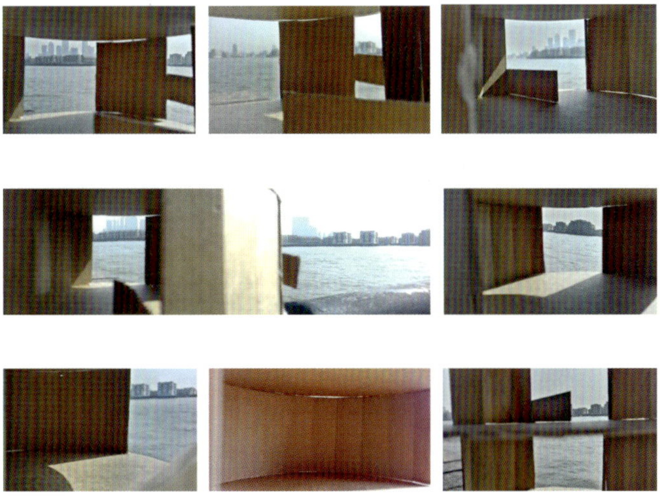

44

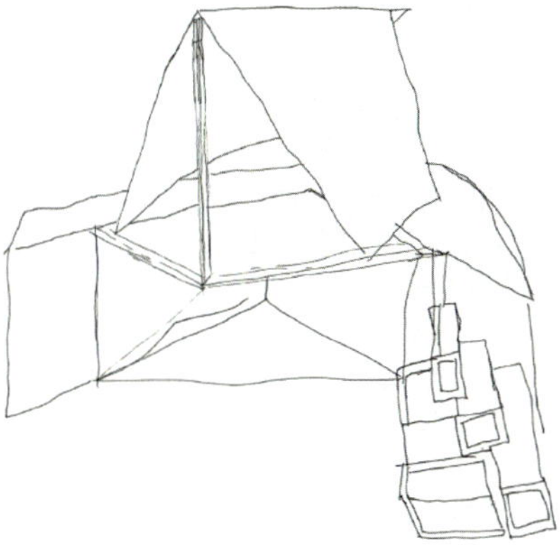

45

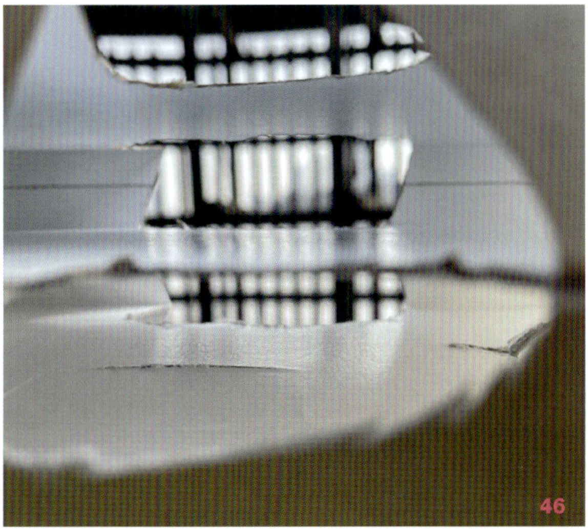

46

47

45 Karleen Christiane Menes **46** James Douglas, model **47** Farhan Rehman, model **48** James Douglas, model **49** Jhan Carlos Lobaton Alay, model **50** Karleen Christiane Menes, collage **51** Eraee Jargau, proposal model

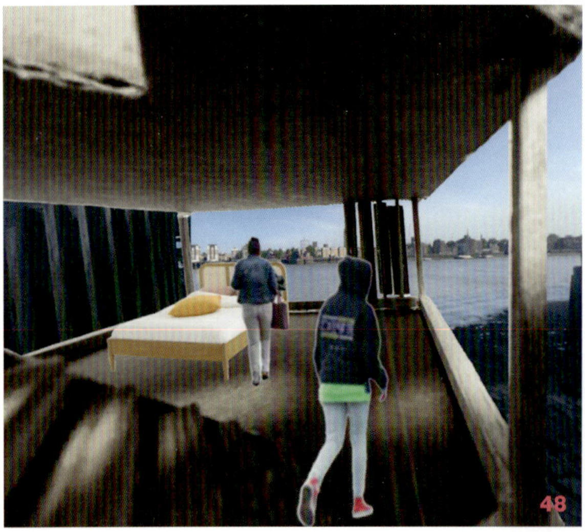
48

49

50

51

52

53

54

Architecture

BSc (Hons) Architecture
ARB/RIBA Part 1

Alex Scott-Whitby, Course Leader

Architectural Design Staff:
1st Year Team - Christian Groothuizen (Lead), Charlotte Harris, Toshiya Kogawa, Phillipa Longson, Dianna Cochrane, Isaac Cobo Displas, Armor Gutierrez, Jeff Tidmarsh.

Unit A - Carsten Jungfer, Fernanda Palmieri
Unit B - Alex Scott-Whitby, Stephen Baty
Unit C - Alice D'Andrea, Robert Whitlock
Unit E - Michele Roelofsma, Nasios Varnavas
Unit H - Keita Tajima, Charlotte Harris

History & Theory teaching staff:
Renee Tobe, Claudia Palma, Miho Nakagawa, Susan Ginsberg, Aleks Catina, Andrew Wright.

Technical & Environmental Studies teaching staff:
Armor Gutierrez, Teresa Serrano, Jeff Tidmarsh, Deborah Do-Rosario-Benros, Andy Downey.

Professional Studies teaching staff:
Stephanie Schulz-Westrum, Teresa Serrano, Deborah Do-Rosario-Benros.

Technicians & Demonstrators:
Daryl Brown, Luiz Bueno, Garry Doherty, Paul Nichols, Mark Sowden, Phillipe Murphy.

External Examiners:
Teoman Ayas, Julian Cross, Raymond Quek, Jessica Reynolds, David Short, Michael Trousdel.

Through the professionally accredited RIBA/ARB Part 1 programme, our students develop a rigorous and strategic understanding of context encompassing social and environmental, physical and non-physical concerns, enabling them to make engaged and critical architectural proposals.

Our teaching is centred on the interface of social and spatial structures, on people and place. Our location in East London gives unique opportunities to understand, critique and reimagine how regeneration and redevelopment impact upon existing places and communities, bringing case studies from across Europe and beyond back into a critical reflection on London and its future. At the core of this education are our design units in Years 2 & 3, each of which provides students with a particular thematic and methodological approach to design, and as a whole contain a diversity that stimulates critical awareness. The design units operate as autonomous research teams and consist of two tutors and between 16 to 20 students. Supporting the design units is a framework of teaching in essential technical, theoretical, regulatory and practical knowledge that enables a fully integrated design process. Students must construct with both materials and ideas, and in final year BSc are expected to develop their design proposals as a personal thesis.

In Year 1 the teaching is centred on a sequence of design projects that work through from the scale of the body to the scale of the city. The year aims to provide a broad platform for exploring creativity and introduces a set of skills and standards that range from surveying and technical drawing, to sketching and model making. Embedded within the schedule of projects are lectures, seminars and practical workshops that provide an introduction to the social concerns of architecture, knowledge of historical context, and understanding material properties and capabilities. The year is structured to guide every student along these first steps on the path to becoming an architect, building confidence and developing a strong sense of purpose and direction.

In Years 2 & 3 the design units lead an iterative design process that is driven by creativity, imagination and critical self-reflection. The course is designed to educate students to think seriously about the world around them, to consider occupiers and users, buildings and spaces with an approach that is both critical and poetic. The supporting strands of History and Theory, Technical and Professional Studies, Computing and Representation, inform and enrich an integrated design approach. Students test and apply learned knowledge, practical skills and critical enquiry to a personal architectural proposition; this forms the basis of the architectural education. The technical teaching instils an appreciation of site and context, the art of construction, economy of structure and the nature and complexity of materials, using knowledge- based lectures and analysis of precedent as a route to integrate this understanding in the unit-based design proposals. Our hands-on approach to a poetic materiality is characterised by exploratory model making across multiple scales.

Preparation for professional practice integrates essential technical, philosophical, regulatory and practical knowledge as baseline skills that enable the final thesis at BSc and MArch to critically extend beyond the RIBA/ARB requirements. Decision making and technical innovation develop from and relate to wider socio-political contexts, grounding the design work and the critical task of detailing to make tangible connections to wider architectural ideas. The professional Architecture programmes at UEL produce directed, responsible and socially aware graduates that understand architecture as a beautiful, radical tool to make 'place' and engage with the complexities of social and environmental interaction, and to equip our diverse talented graduates with the skills needed to face, and make positive change to the challenges and opportunities the 21st century will bring.

First Year
Repair / Reuse / Recycle

Diana Cochrane, Isaac Cobo Displas, Christian Groothuizen, Armor Gutierrez, Charlotte Harris, Toshiya Kogawa, Phillipa Longson, Claudia Palma, Jeff Tidmarsh, Nasios Varnavas.

Seeing From Memory

The year started with the exploration of a personal ritual from an important memory or moment hidden in everyday life. Through drawing, text and photography we revealed the narrative of the ritual and the ways it changes the space in which it is enacted. Taking the ritual as a starting point, students adapted their personal spaces to propose a 'Space for Performance' through a new ritual space, piece of furniture or object.

By far the greatest challenge facing us in 2020 is the climate emergency. In the UK, 49% of annual carbon emissions are attributable to buildings. Over the next 40 years, the world is expected to build 230 billion square metres of new buildings, the equivalent of building a city the size of Paris every single week. To meet UK Climate Change targets, the London Energy Transformation Initiative, the World Building Council and Architecture 2030 insist that all new buildings must be net zero carbon by 2025.

Learning from segal

Often compared to traditional domestic Japanese structures, and based on timber frame building techniques, The Walter Segal Self Build method eliminates the need for high carbon building methods such as bricklaying and plastering. The resulting light-weight structures can be built with minimal experience and are ecologically sustainable. Another advantage of the Segal method is that it incorporates standard sized materials to avoid waste. In term two we explored how to incorporate environmental design into our design proposals reducing their carbon footprint.

Our client is a modern day mudlarker — a treasure hunter and curator of London's social history, who scours the river edge searching for objects from the city's past. The site is Trinity Buoy Wharf, near Canning Town. The proposal brief consisted of an artist's studio/workshop and a small public museum or archive.

Connecting Space / Threshold Space

Underpinning the intricate moments between public and private points within these mudlarkers' spaces, students used a range of techniques, from surveying and drawing to printmaking and casting, to make studies of threshold spaces within larger architectures. These could be connecting spaces, inserted spaces, or a space that sits between other, adjacent spaces. They denote transitions between conditions, qualities or use, and are highly relatable to the human body and all its senses.

DEPTFORD CREEK, LONDON
LOGNE, WUPPERTAL, GERMANY

Students:
Saidumarkhon Abdimajitov, Khateeja Afreena,Taha Ahmed, Asfia Alam, Lida Amiri, Tarannum Anam, Safiya Baaz, Edmund Balasca, Valeria Beregoi, Sara Bonito, Azriel Buckley, Teodora-Marilena Busnosu, Alejandro Castro, Charlie Chinama, Md Chowdhury, Kai Davis, Klaudia Depczynska, Daniel Ferrari, Baris Freed, Blazej Goralczyk, Yunus Gureli, Zahid Hafesji, Billy Hale, Brendan Hampton, Ines Isidro Ramos, Ozgur Karadag, Nehal Khan, Mohammed Khan, Divine Lembe Dodiya, Jamilah Mahdi, Kledjan Mangaj, Silvia Marin Giraldo, Roderick Montero, Krishnan Nagarajan, Mae Allen Nerona, Agata Nyckowska, Temitope Ogunbiyi, Helly Pandya, Jamie Parmenter, Maharshikumar Patel, Yaisa Pulido Gil, Zuhaida Salum, Rosalia Sanchez Rojas, Mariam Tarek Khalil, Marwan Tawfik, Tatianna Teca Nsamba, DariaTecza, Maryam Uddin, Rudson Valacio, Nabiha Warsame, Toshiyuki Yasue

Critis and Collaborators:
Halima Ali, Sena Bektasoglu, Jana Dockalova, Alfred Hatch, Michele Roelofsma, Nima Sadar, Alex Scott-Whitby, Keita Tajima

Special thanks to:
Mark Sowden

@uel_first_year_architecture [Instagram]

01

01 Agata Nykowska, final proposal section **02** Kai Davis, collage of ritual space **03** Klaudia Depczynska, cast model reconfigured **04** Agata Nykowska, National Theatre as a threshold between the city and the river **05** Yaisa Pulido Gill, room for a chess game **06** Saidumarkhon Abdimajitov, timber frame model **07** Rosalia Sanchez Rojas, National Theatre sketch **08** Yaisa Pulido Gill, ritual space collage **09** Rudson Valacio, South London Gallery threshold study **10** Silvia Marin Giraldo, experimental frames on site **11** Rosalia Sanchez Rojas, inhabited timber frame model

02

03

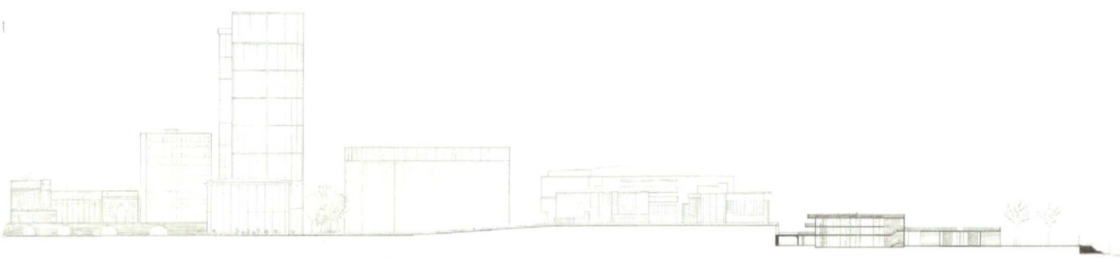

04

05

06

07

08

09

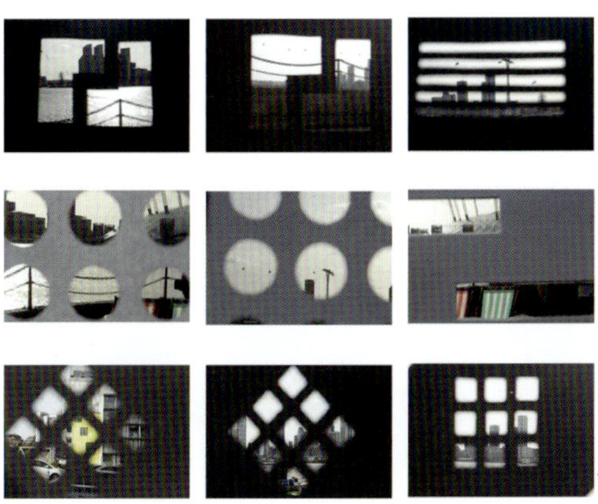

10

11

12 Rosalia Sanchez Rojas, intaglio print threshold analysis **13** Lida Amiri, phototransfer prints of threshold analysis **14** Nabiha Warsame, axonometric and printmaking sequence studying Sir John Soane's Museum entrance **15** Agata Nykowska, cast photos exploring levels, material continuity, multiple thresholds, and absence plus slippages **16** Brendan Hampton, threshold section cast **17** Ozgur Karadag, spatial study model **18** Temitope Ogunbiyi, Whitechapel Gallery stair section **19** Agata Nykowska, National Theatre study sequence looking at layering, overlaping, insertion and 'floating' layers **20** Nabiha Warsame, Tate Modern Turbine Hall section with light study **21** Group site model at 1:200, Alejandro Castro, Yaisa Pulido Gill, Silvia Marin Giraldo and Rosalia Sanchez Rojas **22** Roderick Montero, threshold section cast **23** Rosalia Sanchez Rojas, threshold cast study **24** Temitope Ogunbiyi, threshold cast study **2l** Charlie Chinama, final proposal section model at 1:20 scale

12

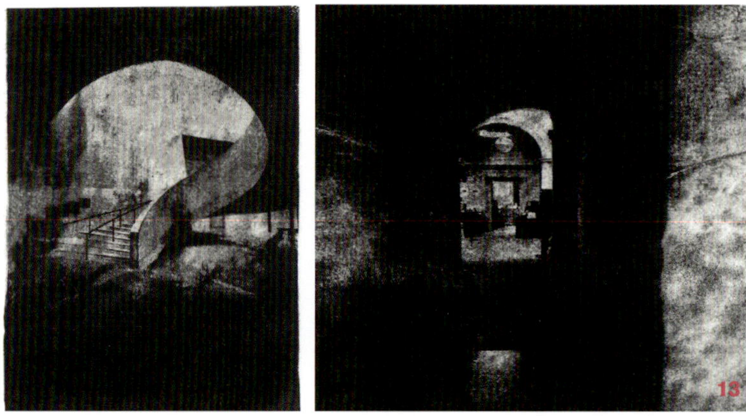
13

14

15

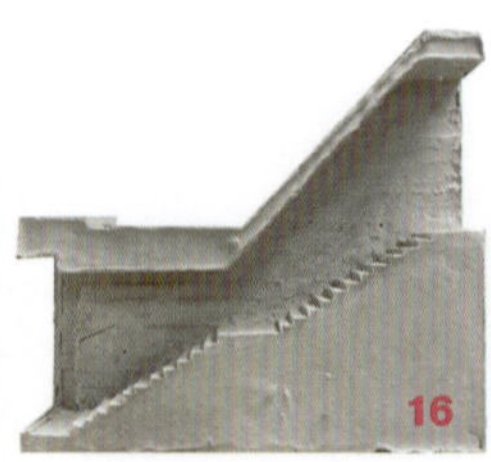
16

17

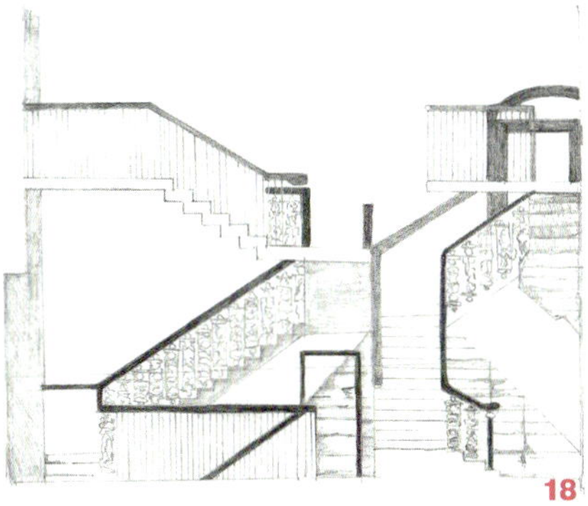

18

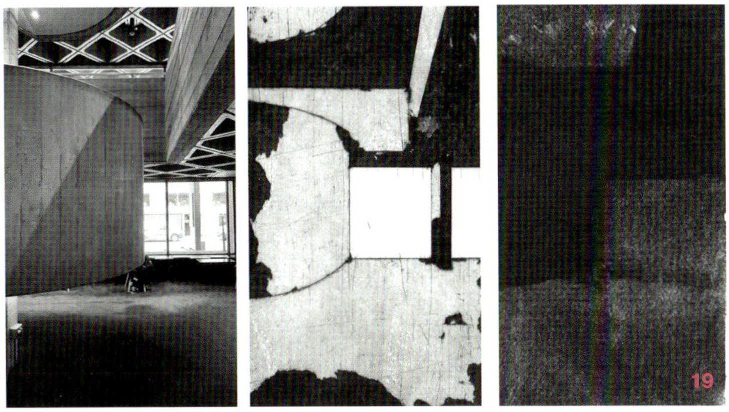

19

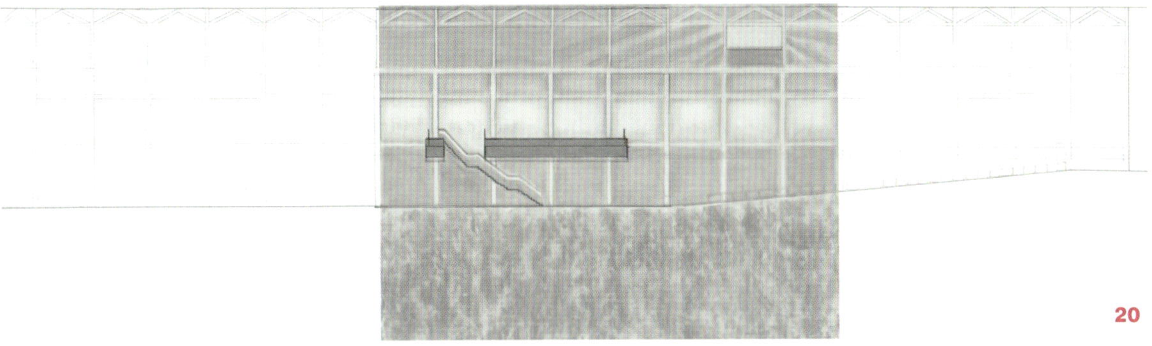

20

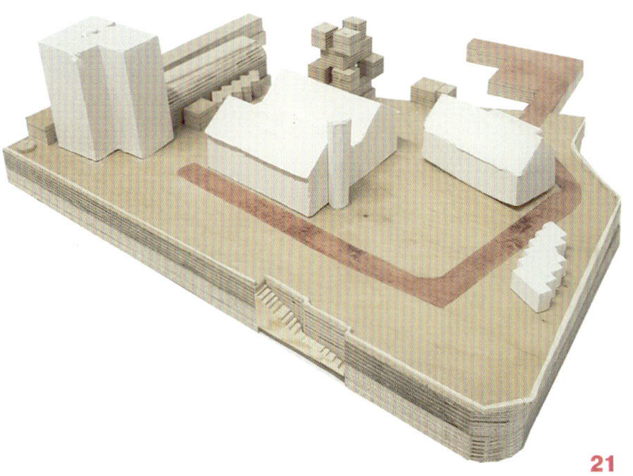

21

25

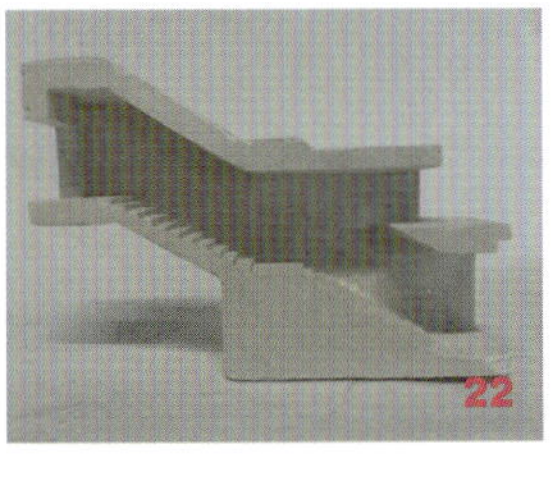

22

23

24

26 Temitope Ogunbiyi, threshold analysis exploring the city in the building **27** Silvia Marin Giraldo, experimental collages with cast fragments to create unexpected spaces **28** Charlie Chinama, light and inhabitation tests through model-making **29** Rudson Valacio, model investigating light qualities **30** Silvia Marin Giraldo, elevations to understand how the pier and bridge work together during tidal movement **31** Brendan Hampton, re-imagining thresholds through cast and collage **32** Nabiha Warsame, casting historic maps of the site as tiles for final proposal **33** Agata Nykowska, final proposal plan **34** Brendan Hampton, cast model testing excavated spaces **35** Mariam Elkashory, site model testing proposal **36** Brendan Hampton, spatial qualities through modelling **37** Alejandro Castro, testing proposal on site model

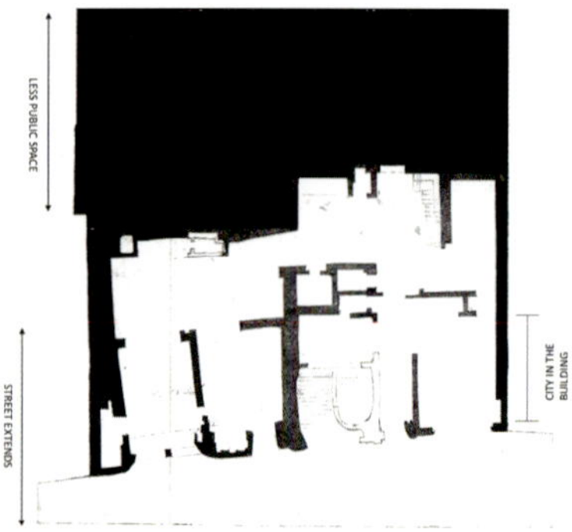

26

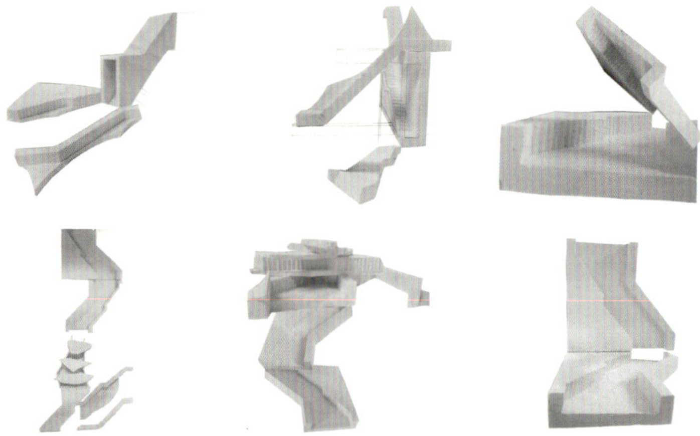

27

28

29

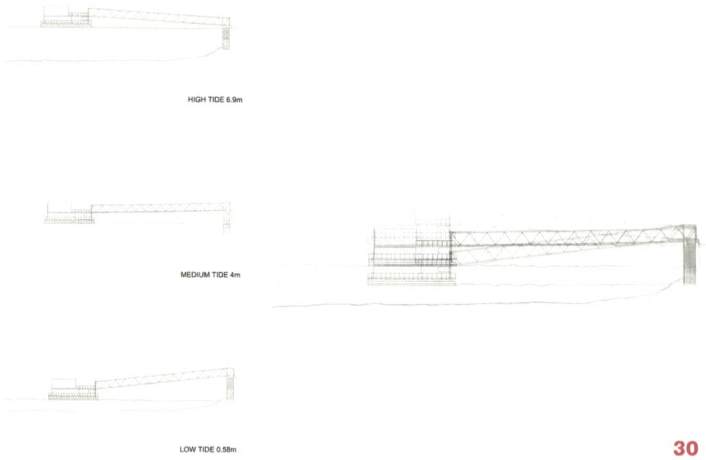

30

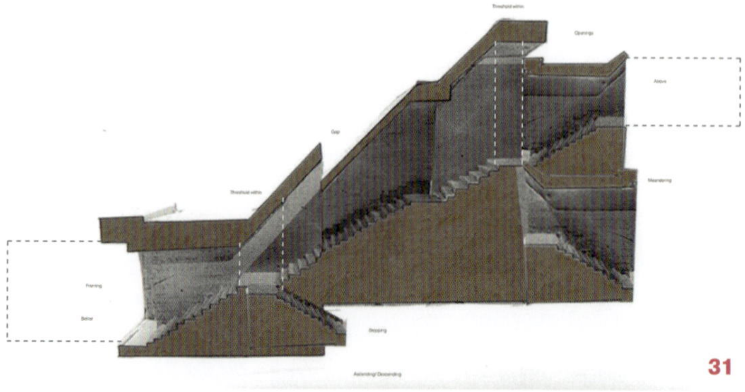

31

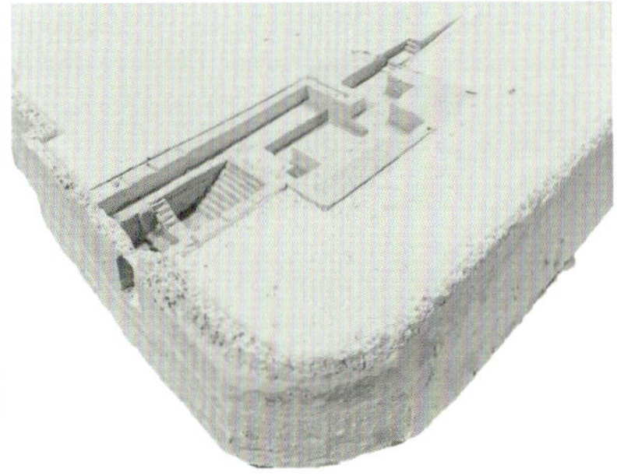

34

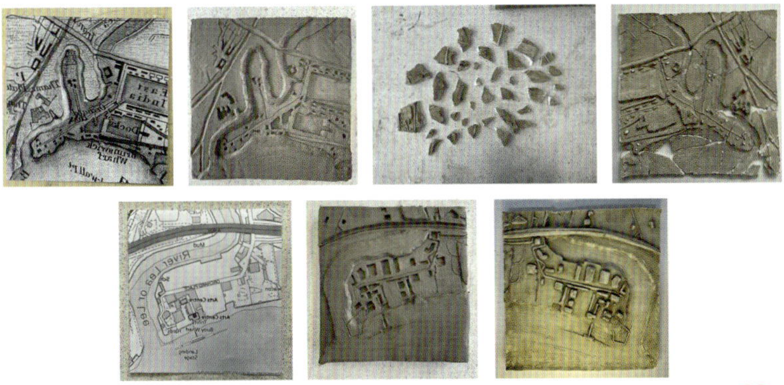

32

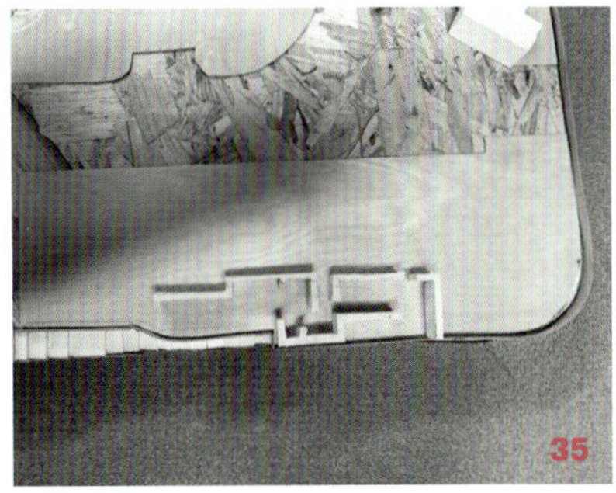

35

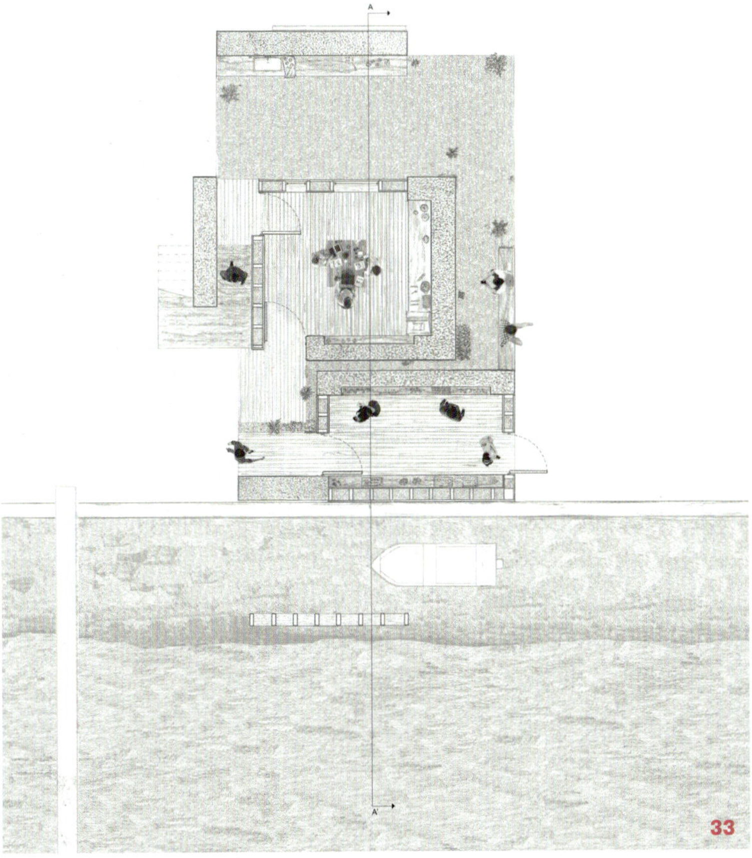

33

36

37

38 Mariam Elkashory, proposal collage **39** Brendan Hampton, intaglio concept print **40** Nabiha Warsame, process of making 1:20 Roman tiles **41** Agata Nyckowska, journey from East India Basin to Trinity Buoy Wharf along the 'green promenade' **42** Mariam Elkashory, cast analysis **43** Rosalia Sanchez Rojas, timber frame model **44** Silvia Marin Giraldo, testing propsal iterations **45** Edmund Balasca, perspective section of final proposal **46** Rudson Valacio, 1:200 massing tested on site model **47** Alejandro Castro, proposal sketch **48** Sara Bonito, concept model

38

39

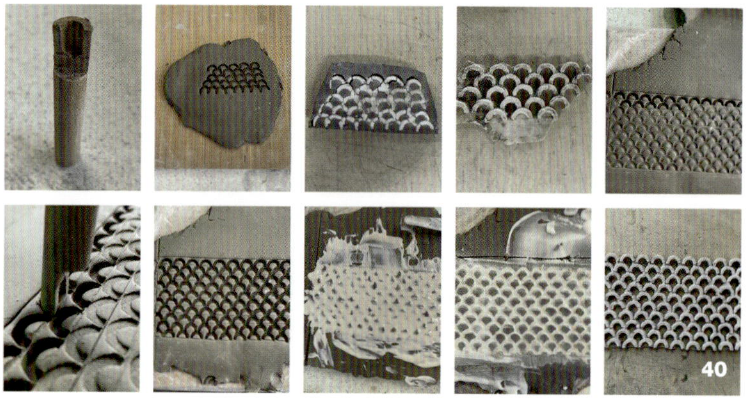

40

41

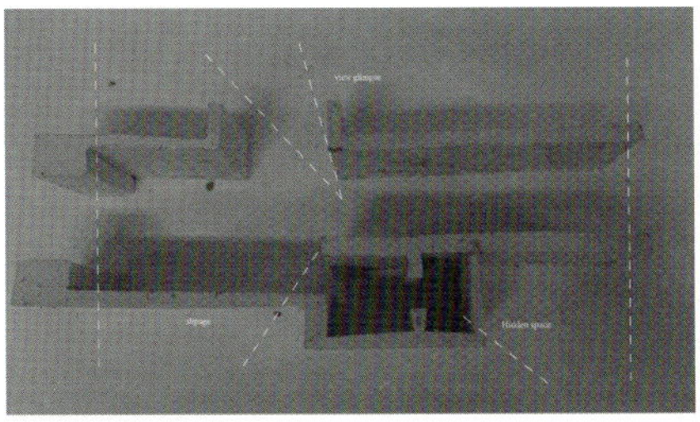

42

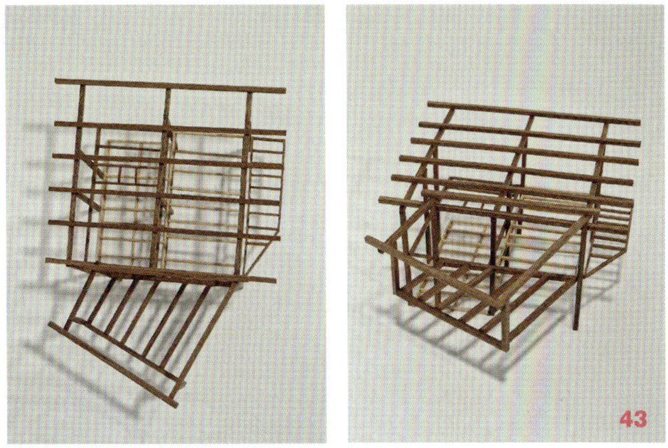

43

44

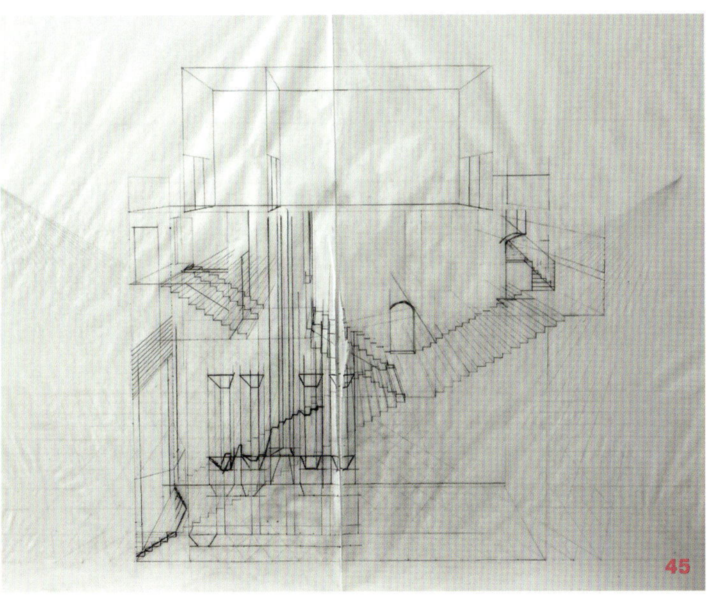

45

46

47

48

49 Agata Nyckowska, tectonic section of final proposal **50** Agata Nyckowska, dismantling and erosion changes the proposal over time **51** Sara Bonito, possible inhabitations **52** Brendan Hampton, proposal model **53** Brendan Hampton, final proposal plan **54** Marwan Tawfik, sketched key view of the final proposal threshold **55** Alejandro Castro, interior sketch **56** Alejandro Castro, section exploring materiality **57** Brendan Hampton, proposal model **58** Edmund Balasca, perspective section drawing of key spaces **59** Nabiha Warsame, model testing spatial qualities of the entrance **60** Rudson Valacio, final proposal section **61** Edmund Balasca, final proposal section **62** Jamie Parmenter, section and model collage **63** Jamie Parmenter, collage envisioning proposal at Trinity Buoy Wharf

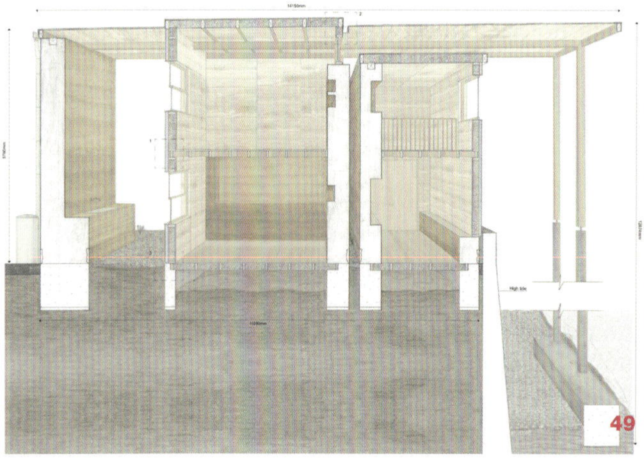

49

50

52

51

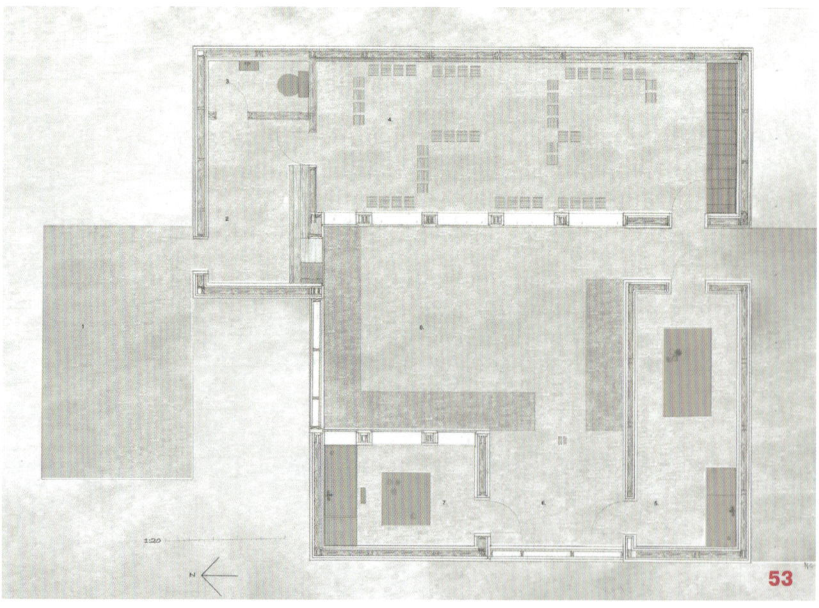

53

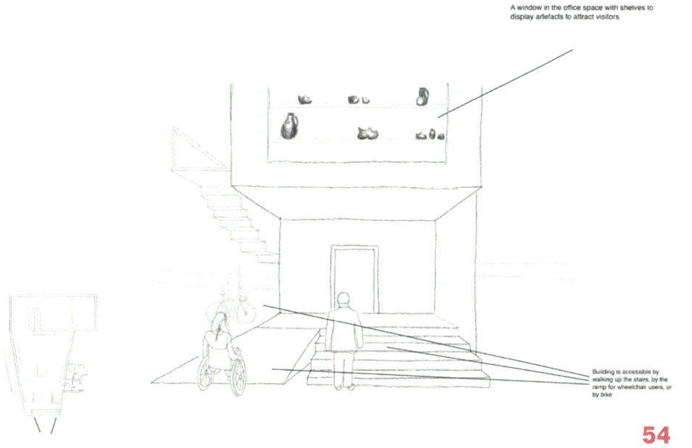

54

55

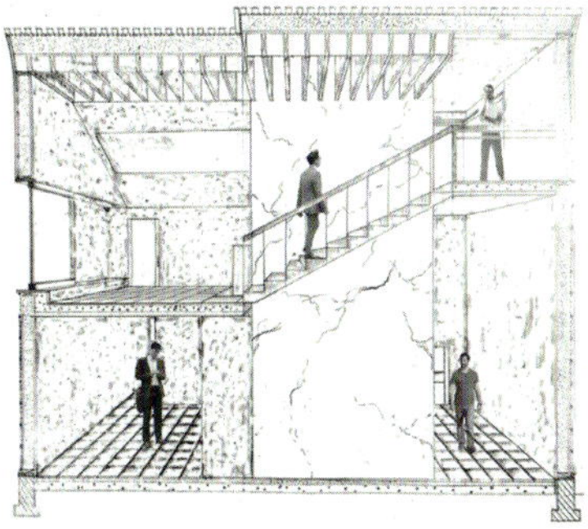

56

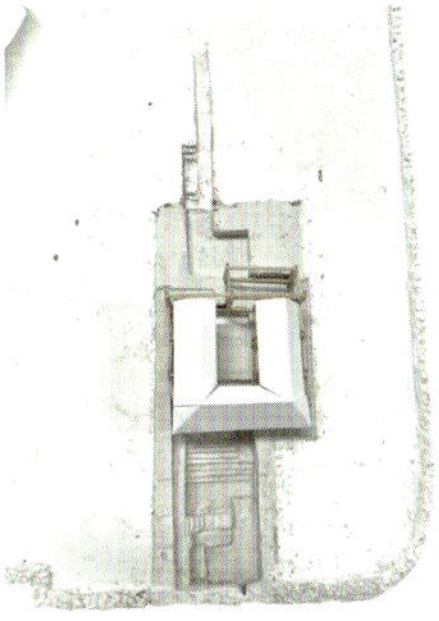

57

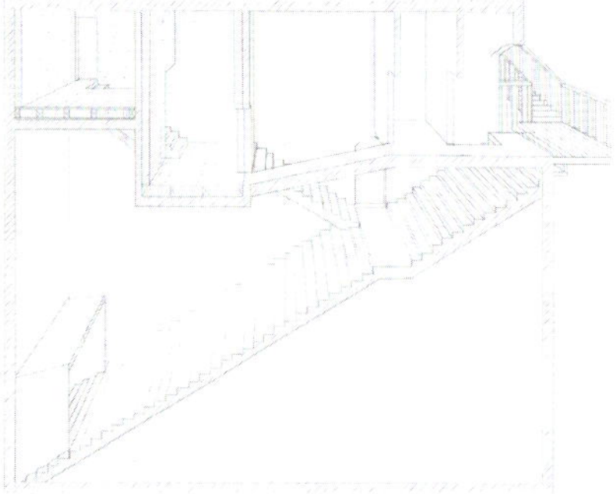

58

59

61

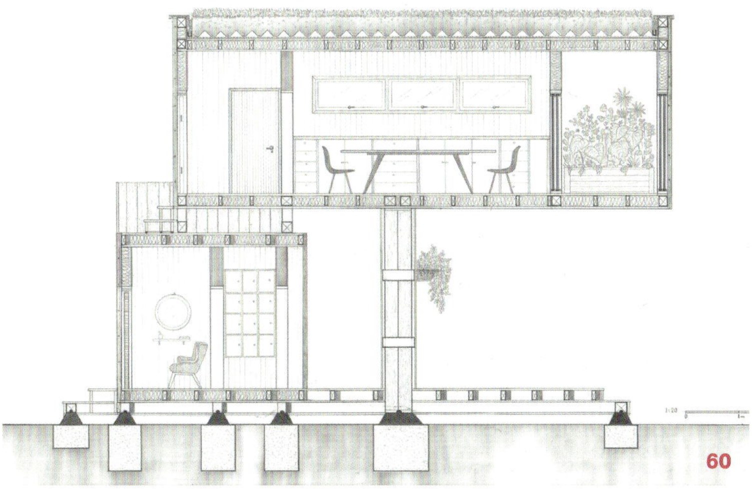

60

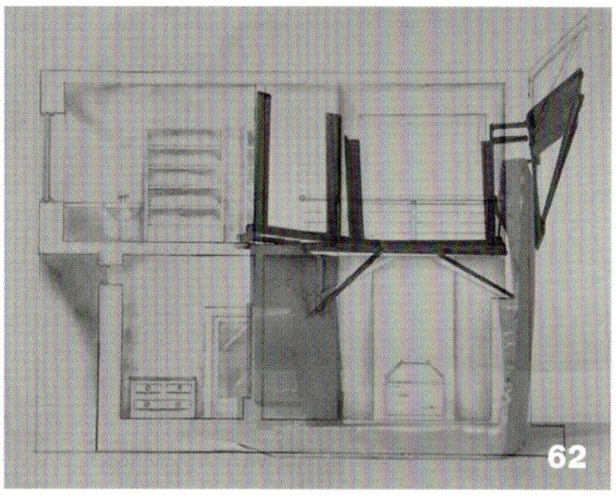

62

63

Unit A
Action Space

Carsten Jungfer, Fernanda Palmieri

Re-thinking space for activism, education and play in context of the climate emergency: A new building for Hackney's Youth Parliament.

Johan Huizinga, a Dutch historian and linguist famous for his work about the play element in culture (1949), argues that the free realm of ludic activity, or the act of playing, is the lone field of true life, and that play precedes culture as well as it is the source of cultural production itself. If play is life and culture, then the need for play in the city is not, or should not be, restricted to formal situations or to children and young people only, but should be made possible for everybody, everywhere.

This year, Unit A investigated existing social-spatial situations with opportunities for play and cultural production. The students critically reflected on the idea of common and shared spaces in contested urban contexts, not as spaces for profit, but as spaces for people, play, participation and freedom of expression. We continued to work with complex social and urban conditions across different areas of Hackney, which has been a focus of study over the past 5 years. The work of the unit, has lead to research projects commissioned by the London Borough of Hackney and live-project collaborations between community stakeholders and UEL students.

Collectively, we revisited the urgent and latent question asked by the Mayor of London's planning guidelines 'Making London Child-friendly' (2020), on how to achieve healthier and safer urban environments for children and young people, because a city that works for children will work for everyone.

Hackney has a rich history of democratic political activism, however it has seen a significant increase in spatial and social inequalities across the Borough in the past decades. Hackney Youth Parliament, an elected representation of young Hackney residents aged 11-19, was established in 2011, just after the London riots, and works with its youth electorate on issues related to inequality, inclusion, learning and climate change. Hackney Young Parliament intends to make space in the political realm to better represent the large population group that, despite being the most affected by social stress and climate change, have no saying or agency over how their own environment is managed.

Hackney Youth parliament, which currently doesn't have a home of its own, became the focus for the design project this year. The students explored different approaches of spatial production, sourcing recycled materials and speculated on accessible, open and informal building typologies that can respond to change better and are able to anchor a multiplicity of activities to build new relationships across all ages groups of the local community. Students explored questions relating to urban context and designed spaces that promote interaction and also informal spaces that support the formal spatial requirements of a chamber conducting the operations of the youth parliament.

Students:
Y3: Hamda Jama, Hanan Al-hilli, Mohammed Hamza Ahmad, Robert Venning, Seyed Mohammad Rezvani, Shuhada Binti Sabri, Silvia-Mihaela Gramada, Stephanie Stocks, Vatsal Javiya
Y2: Adriana Bostan, Carl Reyes, Charles Mendoza, Darnell Carol-Walters, Federica Guarini, Francesco Narcis Stefan, Hamid Ebdali, Hannah Beernaerts, Horacio Araujo, Josephine Nyanteh, Lewis Curtis, Melisa Mjekra, Naafiah Miah

uel23ua.blogspot.com
@unit_a__uel (Instagram)

Special thanks to:
Visiting Critics: Alan Beverdige (RCKa), Amor Guiterrez, Dickon Hayward (Material Works), Kiesse Andre, Mark Sustr, Norbert Kling (zectorarchitects), Renato Pimenta, Teresa Serrano

Contributors: Denize Bisset (Montpelier Community Nursery), Kelly Bradley (Sands End Arts & Community Centre), Lucy McMeneny (LBH), Cllr Michael Desmond (Speaker of Hackney), Muhammad Rahmani (TNG Youth & Community Centre), Paul Nichols, Peter Algacs (LBH), Tom Gibson (Eleanor Palmer Primary School), Yeoryia Manolopoulou & Anthony Boulanger (AY Architects)

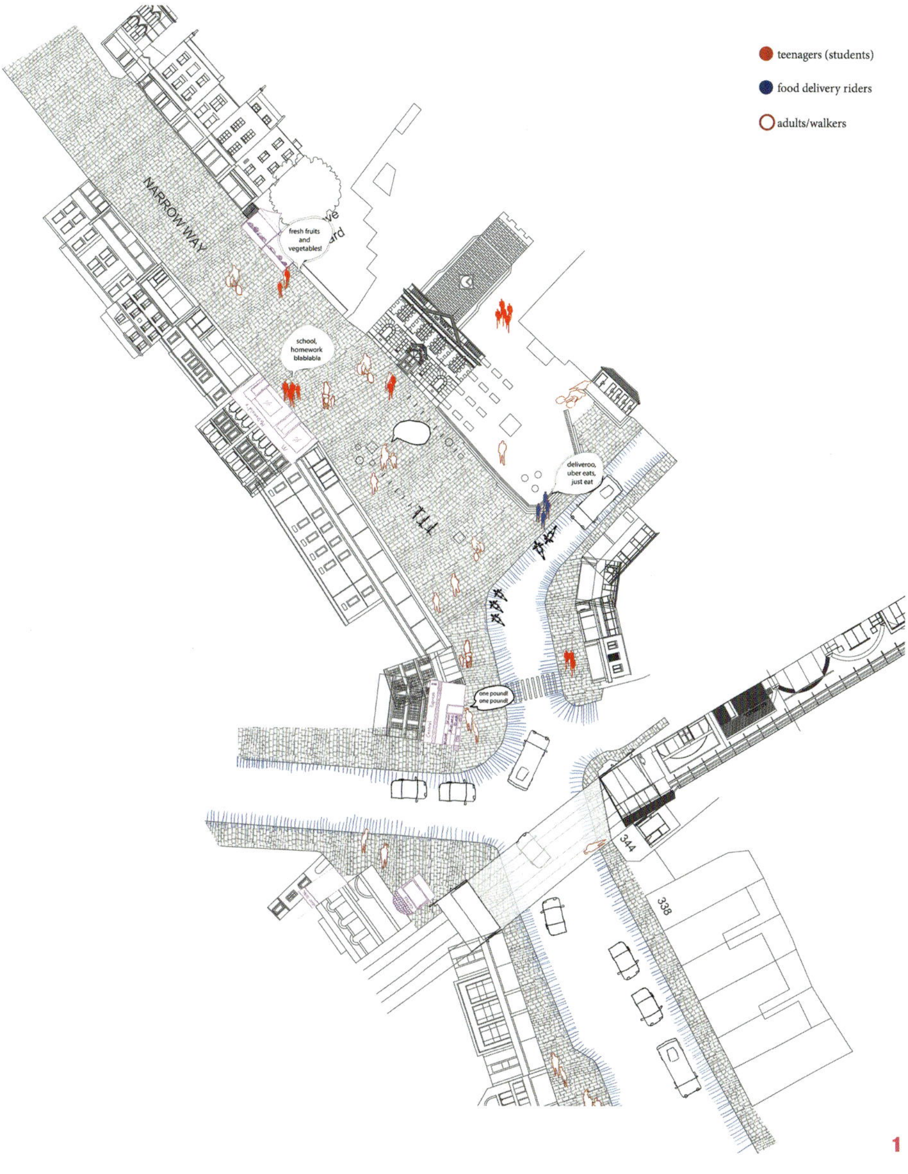

1

1 Socio-spatial analysis drawing investigating relationships between activities and spatial conditions along Narrow way's public realm by Shuhada Binti Sabri. **2** Location plan with Hackney Central project site. **3** The open circulation is designed as an in-between space to promote casual and informal use. **4** Sketch model interpreting Federica's personal experience of spaces at the Montpelier Nursery in Camden, one of the buildings visited by the unit. **5** Model exploring permeable and tectonic qualities of a folded roof and facade design **6** Proposal for temporary meeting space applying a circular economy design approach by using waste material from nearby refurbishments. **7** Long section through sequence of circulation and informal meeting spaces in context . **8** Urban axonometric exploring relationships of proposal with key stakeholder and its wider impact onto Hackney Central's socio-spatial context.

Project and drawings by Federica Guarini.

2

3

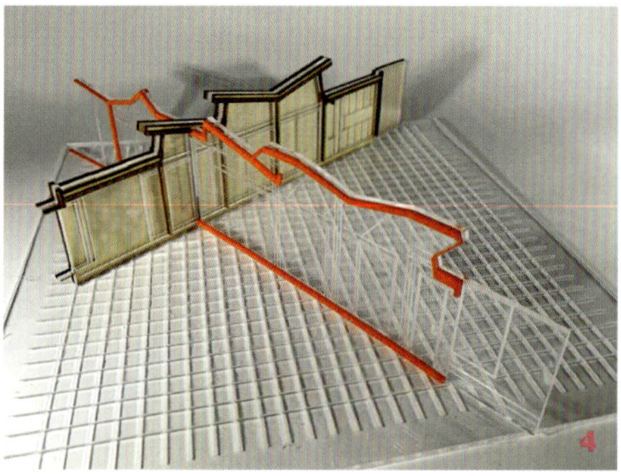

4

5

6

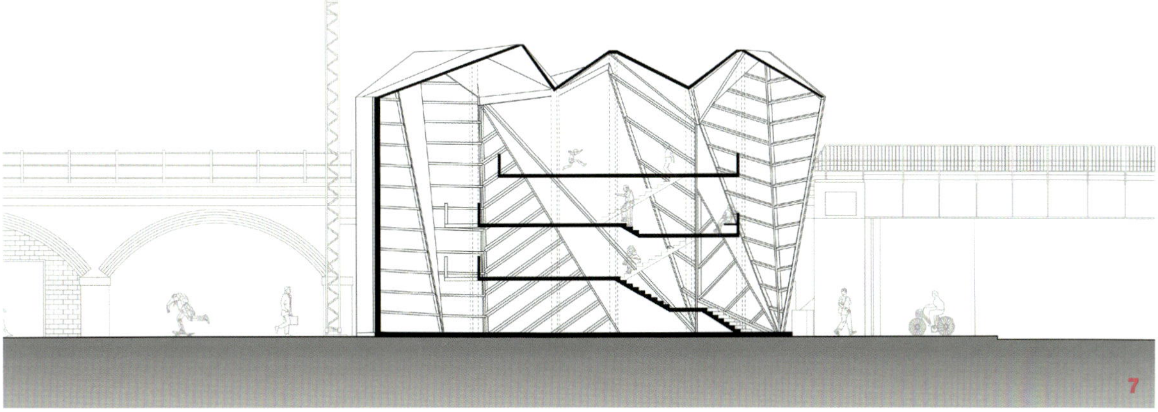

7

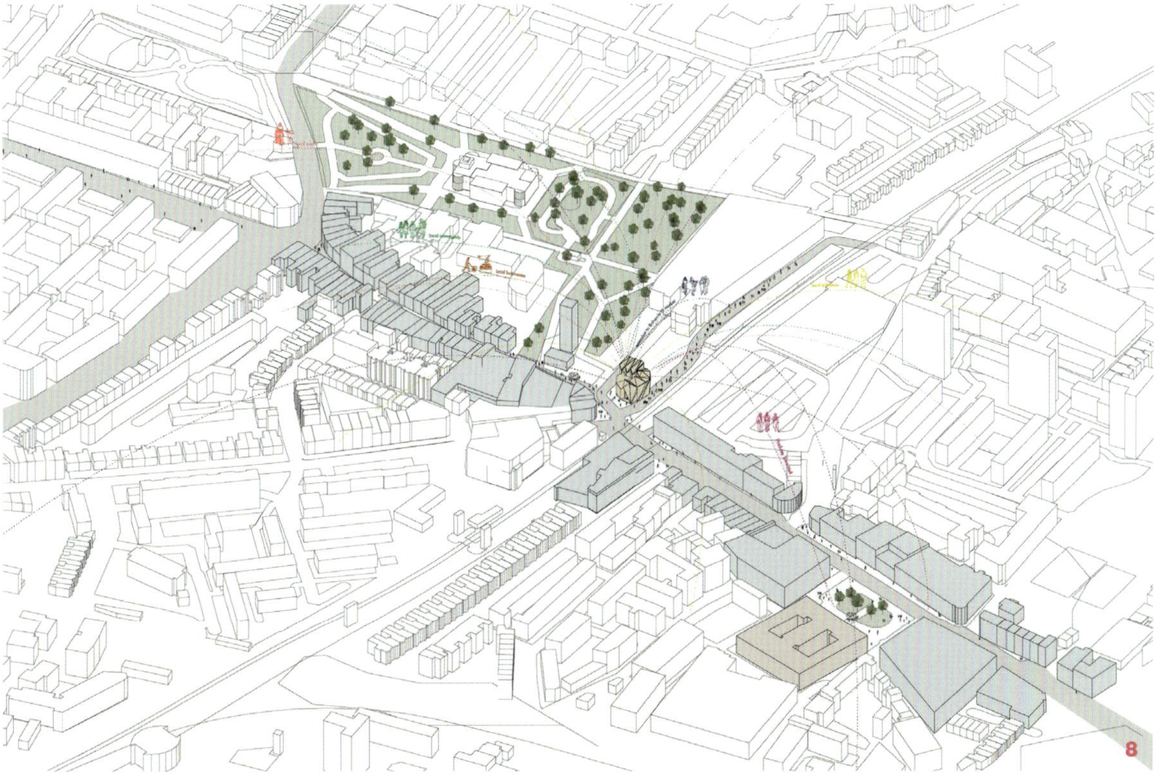

8

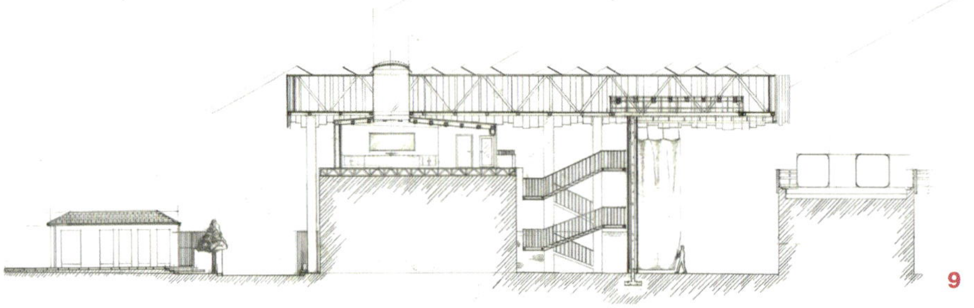

9

10

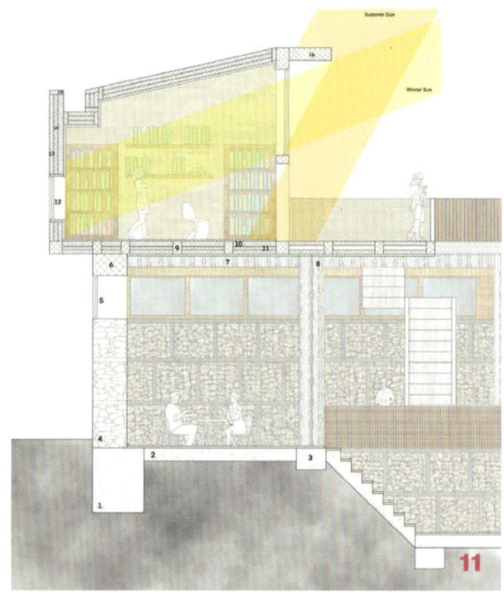

11

12

13

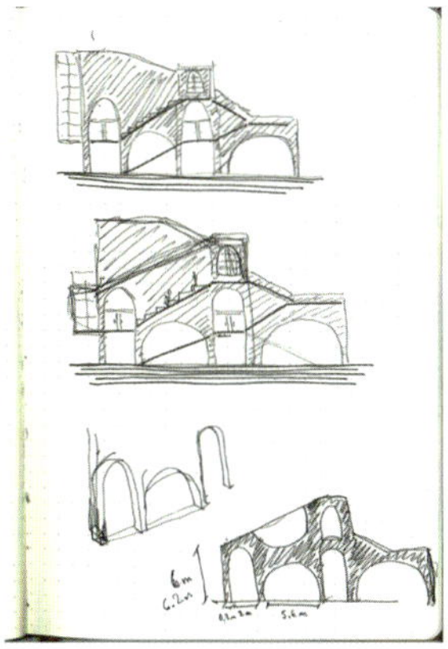

9 Cross section through proposal of superstructure providing meeting spaces above existing 'Paper Dress Vintage', accessibility upgrades and a new event space for Bohemia Place, by Darnell Carol-Walters. **10** 'People's Kitchen' is an intergenerational hub for food, learning and well-being, by Robert Venning. **11** Gabion-walls lock-in carbon by re-cycling construction waste from demolition on site to create new a place of exchange, by Mohammed Hamza Ahmad. **12** 'Theatrical Pavilion' is a temporary multi-use and performance space for Narrow way, constructed solely from up-cycled construction waste sourced form nearby facade-renovation at Dalston Square, by Carl Reyes. **13** Exploration of spatial sequences through sketching and digital model-making, reflecting on Adam Kahn's Plot 10 precedent, by Charles Mendoza. **14** 'Edificio-Piazza' is extending the public realm of Hackney Central's square into a civic hub with the youth parliament at its centre, by Silvia-Mihaela Gramada. **15** 'Protest Pavilion' is a space-frame, constructed entirely from building waste that aims to make political space for placard-making and display, designed by Naafiah Miah and inspired by her experience of school children's climate protest at Hackney's town hall.

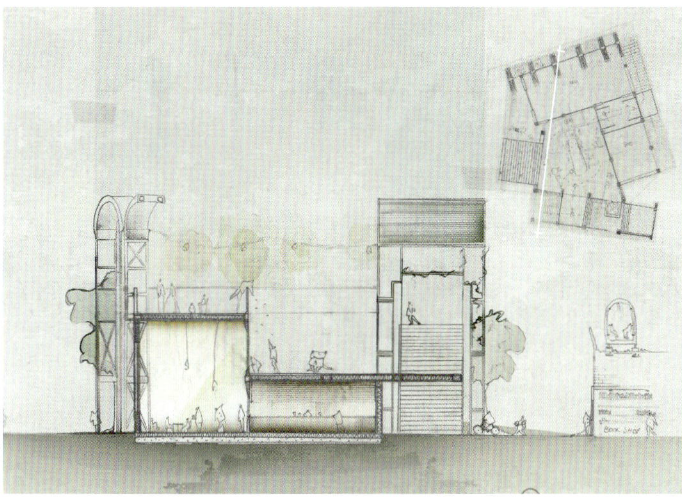

14

15

16 Digitally produced model reflecting on Shuhada's personal experience of spatial sequences from visiting the C1 Building by Architecture 00. **17** Collage exploring relationship between sketch proposal, existing building and urban context. **18** Detail of socio-spatial analysis investigating relationships between activities and spatial situations in the study area. **19** Cross section of proposal in dialogue with re-programmed existing building, using recycled steel structure and a cladding made from locally sourced and up-cycled materials. **20** Sectional development model testing relationships with surrounding spaces and context. **21** Internal visualisation of formal meeting spaces for the Hackney Youth Parliament. **22** Physical model exploring spatial and material relationships between proposed and existing, with intent to promote accessible and inclusive spaces to engage Hackneys youth and local stakeholders to collaborate, exchange, learn and address local challenges in context of the climate emergency. Project and drawings by Shuhada Binti Sabri.

16

17

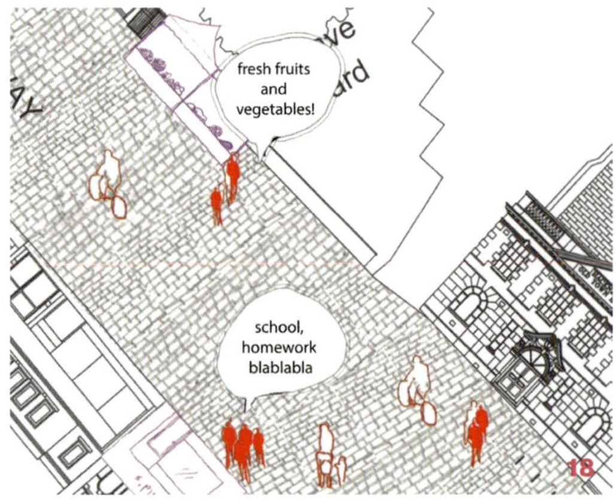

18

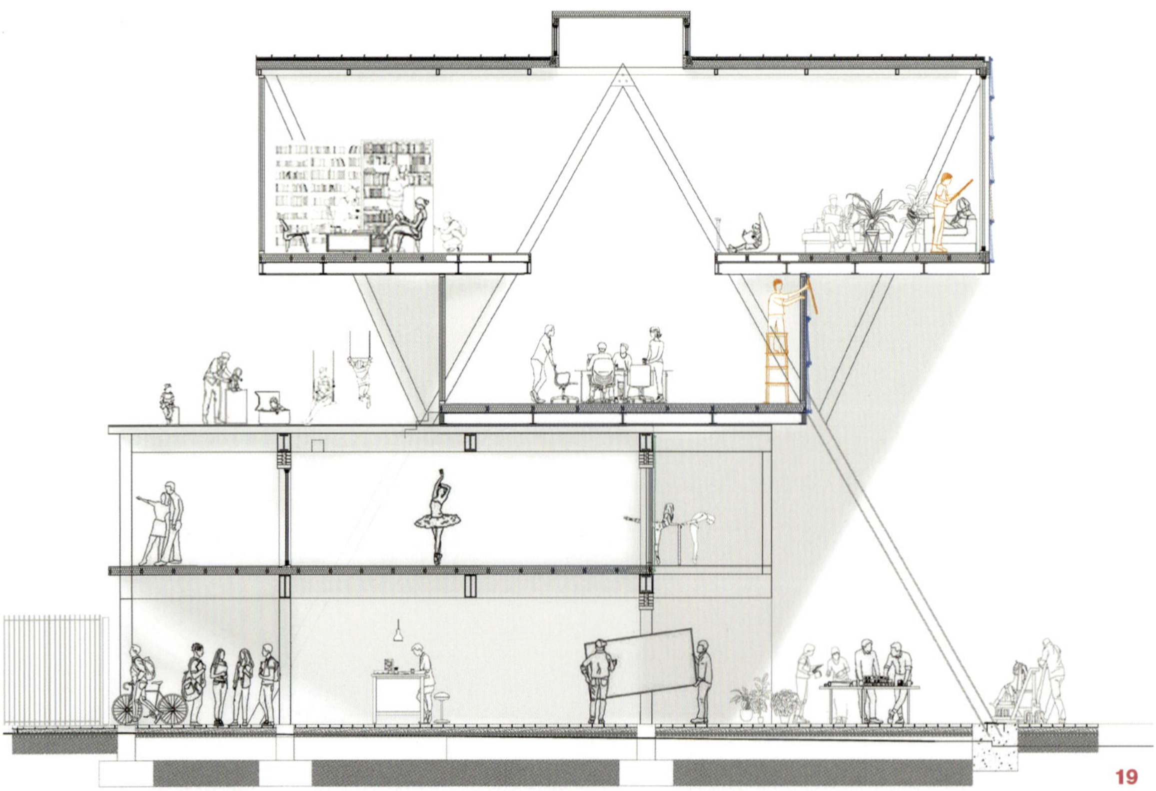
19

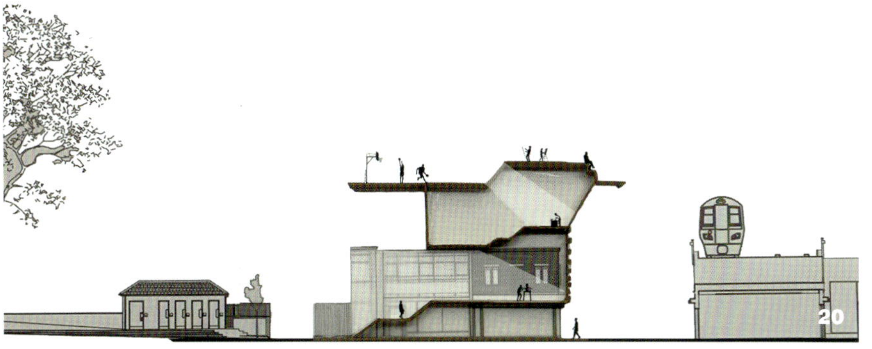

20

21

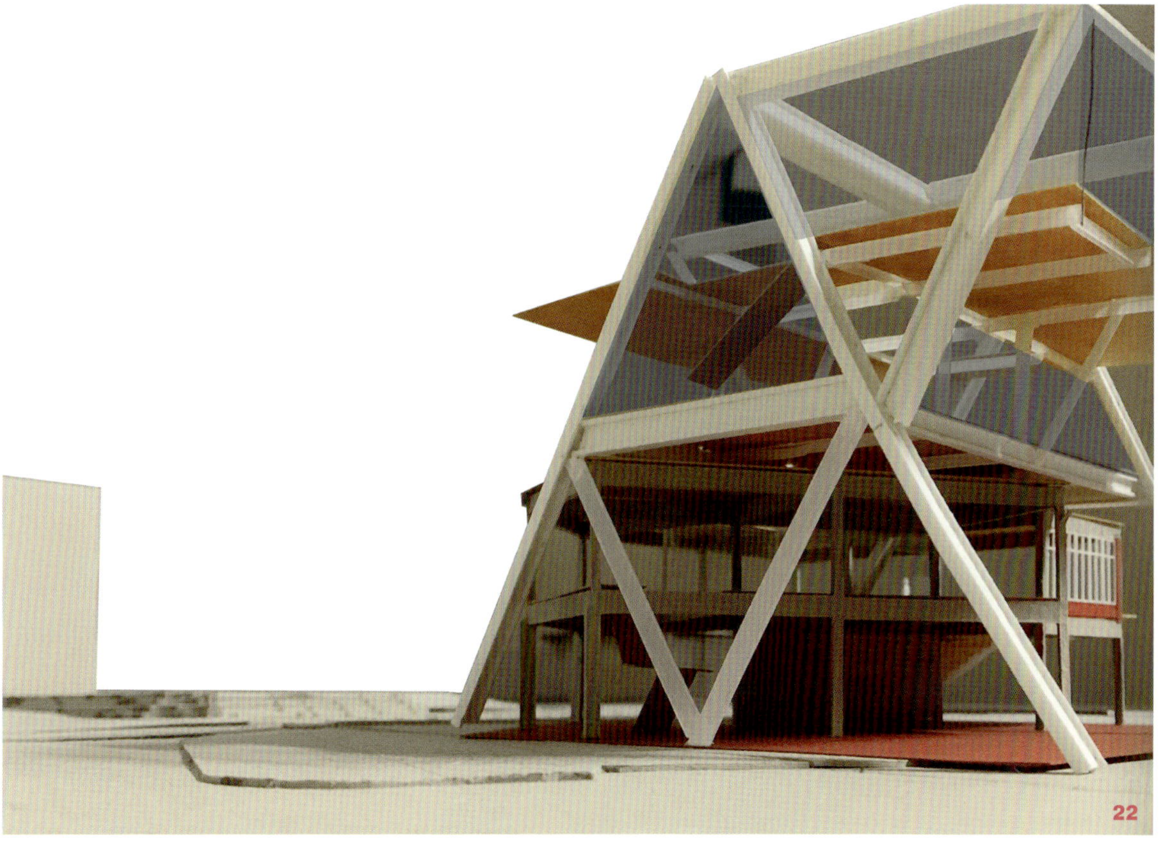

22

23 Model exploring internal spatial relationships, circulation and structure. **24** Cross section of Hackney Youth Parliament proposal in context, for a new type of public building that acts as extension to the public realm and is fully accessible. **25** Digitally produced model interpreting Hamda's personal reading of spatial sequences experienced at Kingston University Town House by Grafton Architects. **26** Axonometric precedent study. **27** Digitally produced sectional model exploring informal qualities of space **28** The fluid qualities of the proposed spaces and the open circulation aim to invite a broad range of activities and interaction, not only between members of the youth parliament, but between all members of the local community. **29** Floor plans starting with ground floor from left; atrium facing Narrow way's civic square with open auditorium and workshop, 1st and 2nd intermediate floors containing formal meeting spaces of varying sizes and informal reading areas; 3rd floor sports-hall and roof-garden. Project and drawings by Hamda Jama.

23

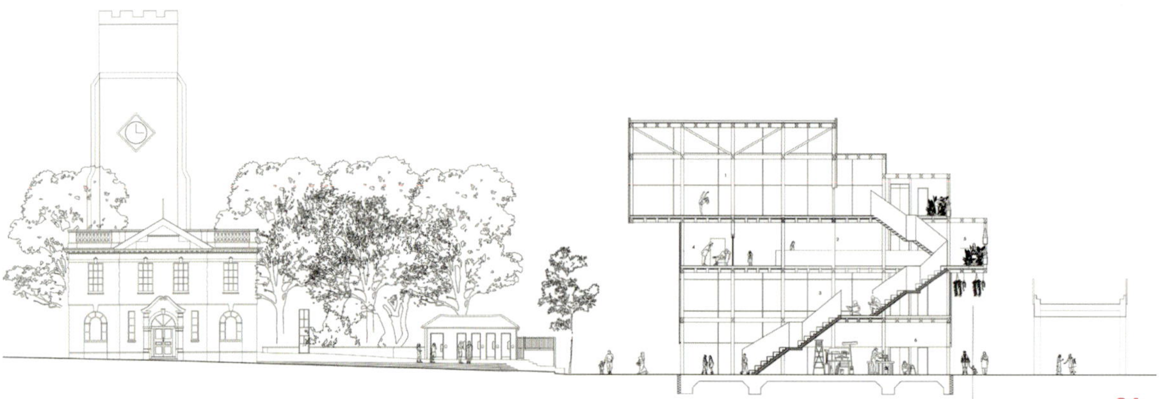
24

25

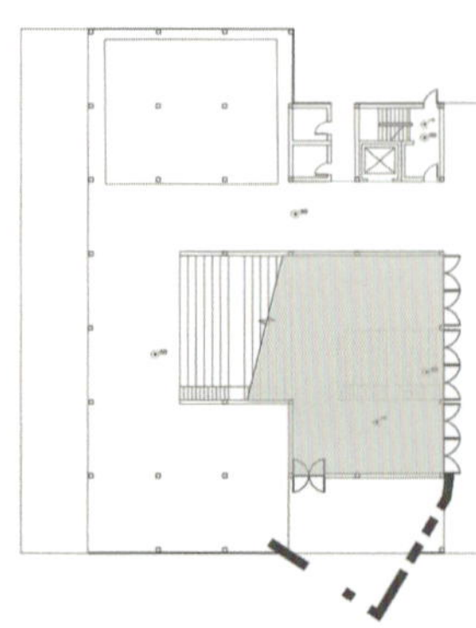

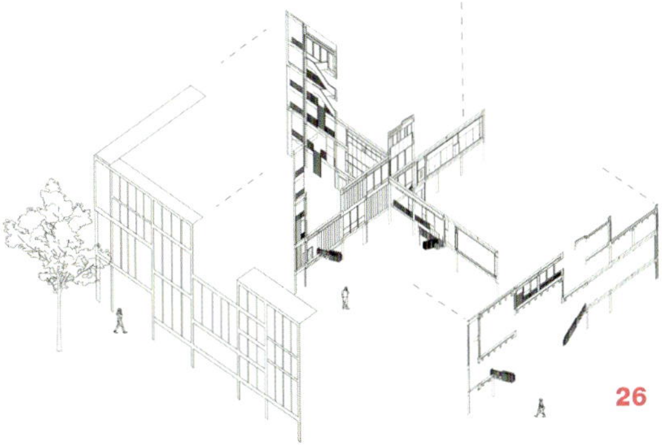

26

27

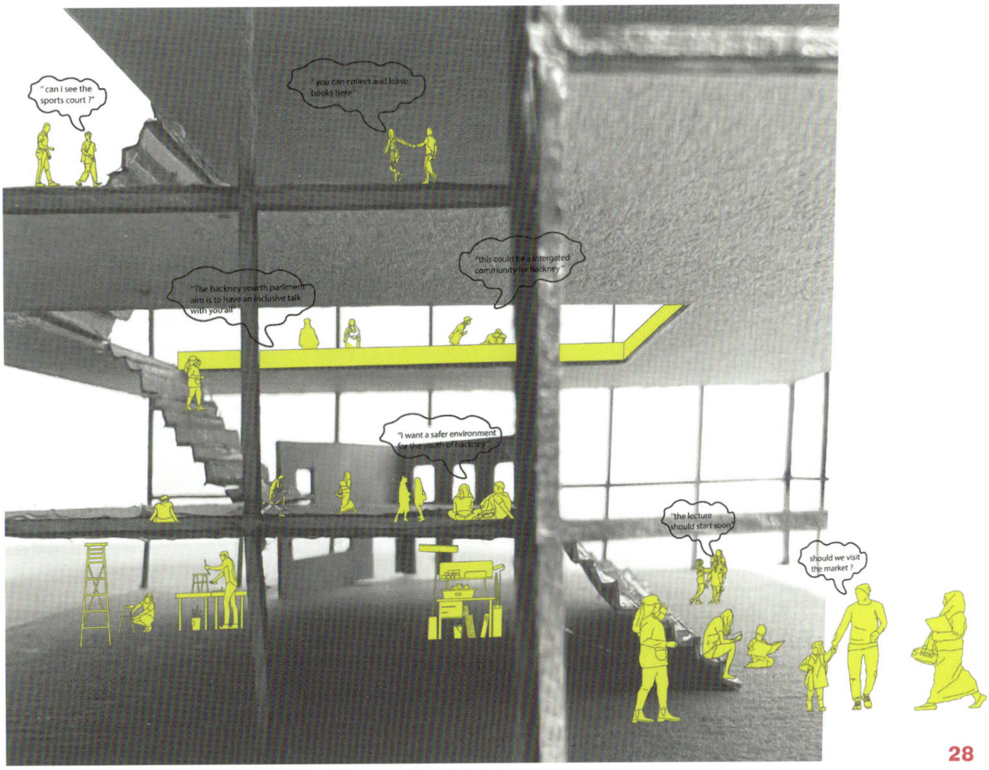

" can i see the sports court ?"
" you can collect and leave books here"
"this could be a intergated community for hackney"
"The hackney yourth parliment aim is to have an inclusive talk with you all"
"i want a safer environment for the youth of hackney"
"the lecture should start soon"
should we visit the market ?

28

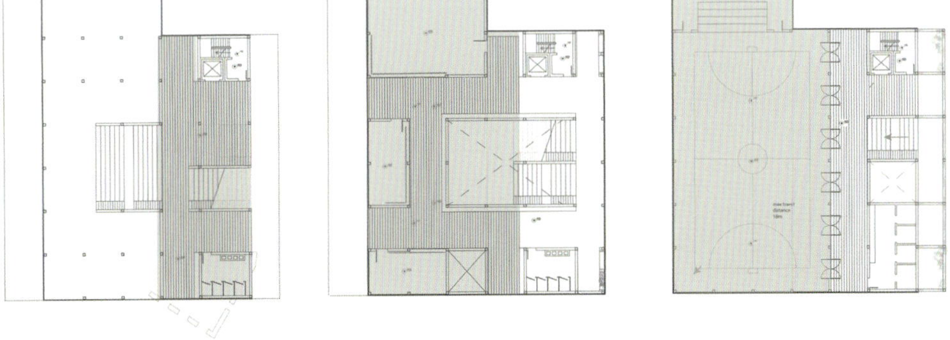

29

Unit B
Rock Hall

Alex Scott-Whitby, Stephen Baty

'No industry today is interested in repairing things'[Dieter Rams], instead the phenomena is better to buy new than repair and buy more than you need. Growth, expansion, renewal drive our economies. Old buildings considered outdated are demolished to make way for new development. Resources taken from the ground are processed to make the things we use, however the more we process, the more complex it is too reuse. What if we were to waste less as we once did in ancient times? How could we use materials to maximise longevity and re-use? What strategies could we develop to give new life to the things that already exist. Should shaping our environment to work more efficiently be the most important thing we do? Is this the moment to reconsider what architecture should be? This year the studio continued its investigation into the idea of re-use and retrofit and looked at the rural settlement as a model for future development. Associated with agriculture, we used this typology to explore building with local natural resources and how to minimise energy use.

Our Site was the historic estate village of Rock on the Northumberland coastal plain. A designated conservation area, Rock is surrounded by fields, woodlands and farmsteads belonging to the Rock estate. The village is connected to the old A1 road by a private avenue, an early nineteenth century landscape feature created to provide a grand approach to the Grade II* Listed Building. The client is keen to improve the village by building on its heritage. Part of this vision includes, the improvement of an existing community facility current a dilapidated Cricket Pavilion and the re-creation of a new village hall within the ruins of their

existing hall. The studio was lucky enough to spend 7 days in the Northumberland and Scotland on their first unit trip since Lockdown. In one day the unit travelled from the sea (Lindesfarne Castle) to the Sky (James Turrell's Skyroom) via forests and roman ruins. The trip ended with a dinner in Edinburgh hosted by some of Scotland's leading architects.

Students:
Y3: Ahmad Feroz Bahar Bozyigit Haider Kahn Jennifer Glowacka Korell Llaudes Le'quan Bailey Nazia Begum Rova Taha Tobi Yeoman
Y2: Aagaman Limbu Alina Obreja Bisera Ruseva Jameela Mohamed Jordan Perry Kostadin Topalov Linda Jennifer Martinez Ubilluz Mariana Marian Rafael Ribeiro Sami Begum Tanjina Hossain

Special thanks to:
The Bosanquet Family, The Rock Estate, A1 Taxi's, Alnwick Gin Distillery, Mark Whitby, Andy Downey,
Tom Joy, Osman Marfo-Gyasi, Graeme Massie, Ronnie Murning, Charlie Sutherland, David McKenna,
Rebecca Madden, Conor Poland, Jemima Elliott, Deborah Benross

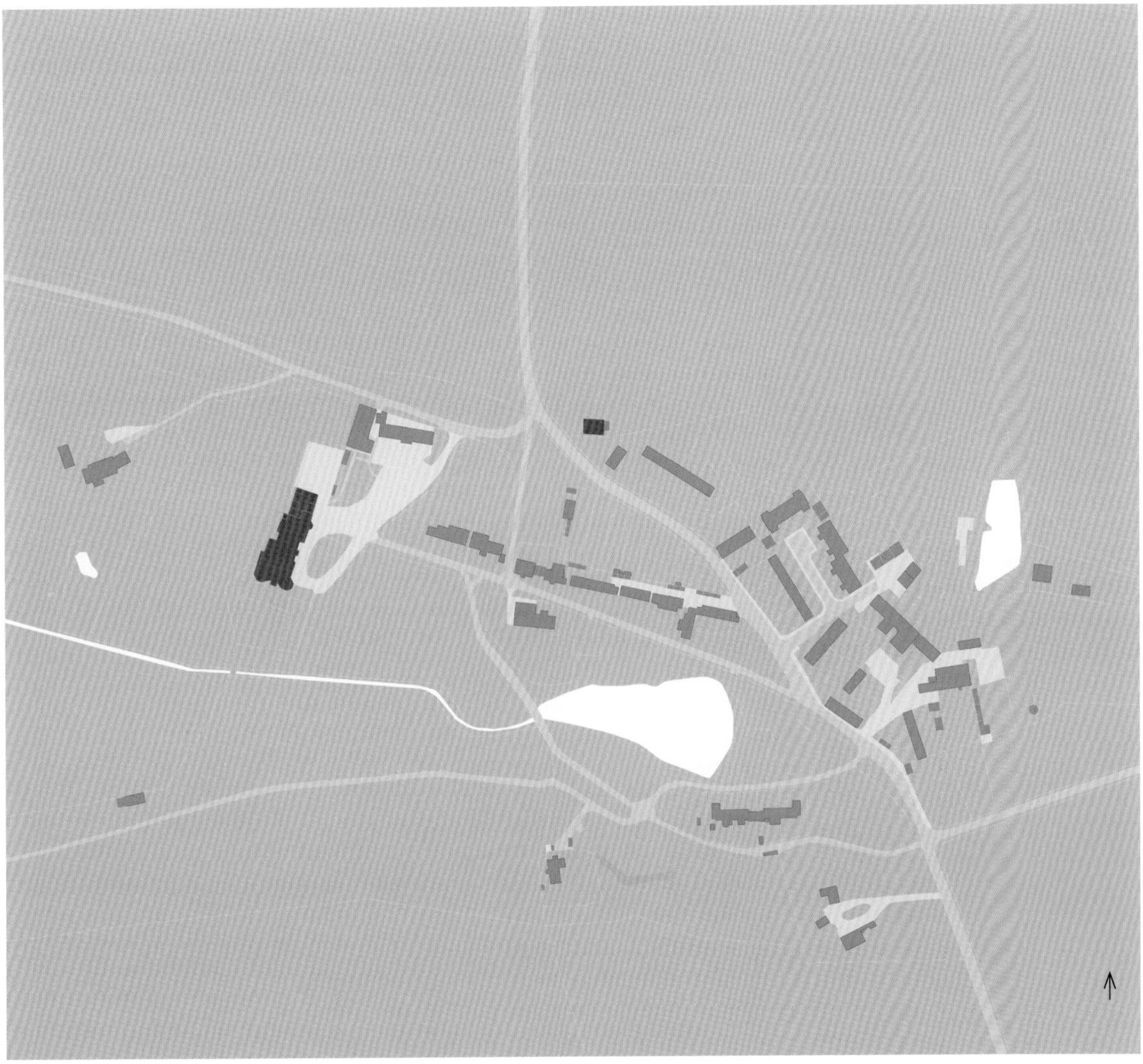

1 Sketch over 3rd model iteration of the Rock Pavilion project by Korell Llaudes **2** Hand drawn section of the Rock Pavilion, showing texture and lighting conditions by Ahmad Feroz **3** On site hand drawing/sketch of Lindersfarm Castle by Bahar Bozyigit **4** On site hand drawing/sketch of an old ship converted into a small hut by Bahar Bozyigit **5** Hand drawing/sketch of the existing Rock cricket club house by Aagaman Limbu **6** Proposal image of Rock Pavilion using final model and post-poduction, photoshop, to include context and atmosphere by Linda Jennifer Martinez Ubilluz **7** Internal view of the tea area and covered terrace of a Rock Pavilian proposal by Linda Jennifer Martinez Ubilluz **8** Internal view of foyer/waiting area for a Rock Pavilion proposal by Jordan Perry **9** Internal view of structural proposal model for Rock Pavilion by Alina Obreja **10** Side elevation of Rock Hall proposal model (1:50 scale) by Rafael Ribeiro

1

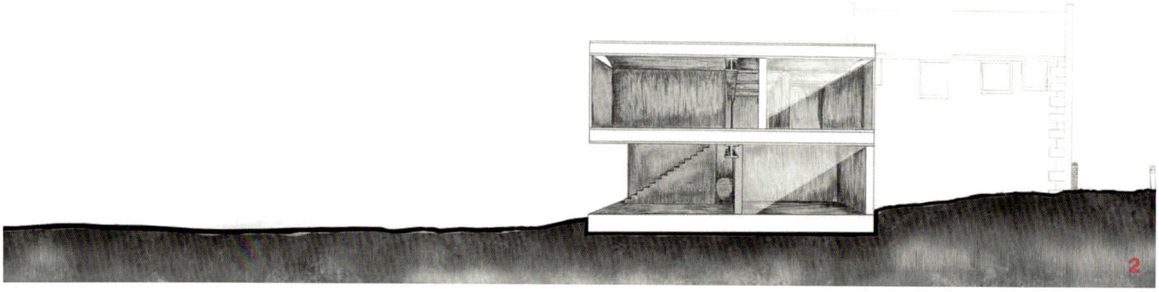

2

3

4

5

6

7

8

9

10

11 .Structural proposal model of Rock Pavilion by Linda Jennifer Martinez Ubilluz **12** Proposal model (1:50 scale) in context of existing site model by Korell Llaudes **13** Internal view of proposed Rock Hall model by Rafael Ribeiro **14** Proposed structural model photoshoped into context by Rafael Ribeiro **15** External view of Rock Hall proposal model (1:50 scale) by Tobi Yeoman **16** Internal view of proposal model for Rock Pavilion model showing 'light at the end of the passage' by Jameela Mohamed **17** Internal view of proposal for Rock Pavillion, inhabited by Tobi Yeoman **18** Detailed connection of Rock Pavilion structure by Tobi Yeoman **19** Thematic model, which was the starting process that progressed the concept and form of Rock Pavilion by Bahar Bozyigit **20** Internal view of proposal structural model for Rock Pavilion by Alina Obreja **21** Structural proposal model for Rock Pavilion by Bisera Ruseva **22** Proposed Rock Pavilion site model (1:500 scale) by Linda Jennifer Martinez Ubilluz

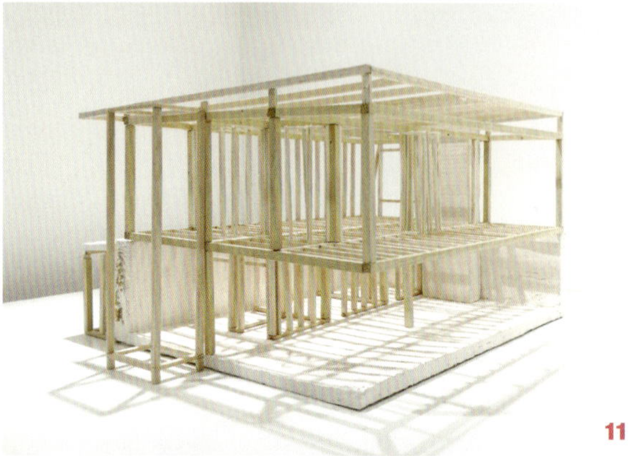

11

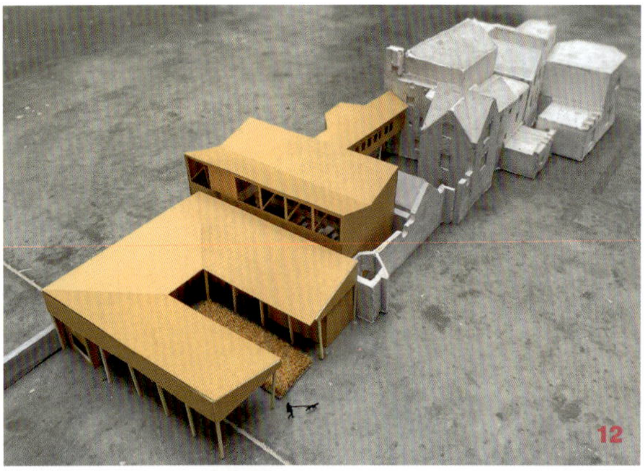

12

13

14

15

16

17

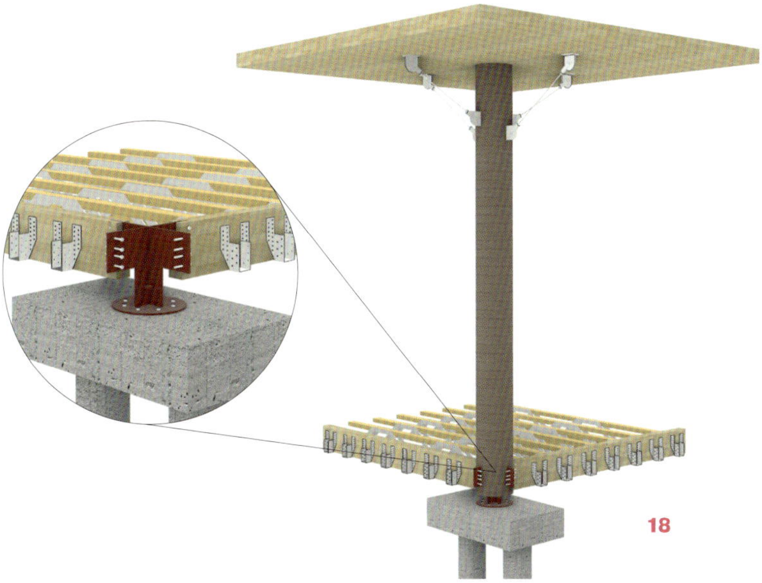

18

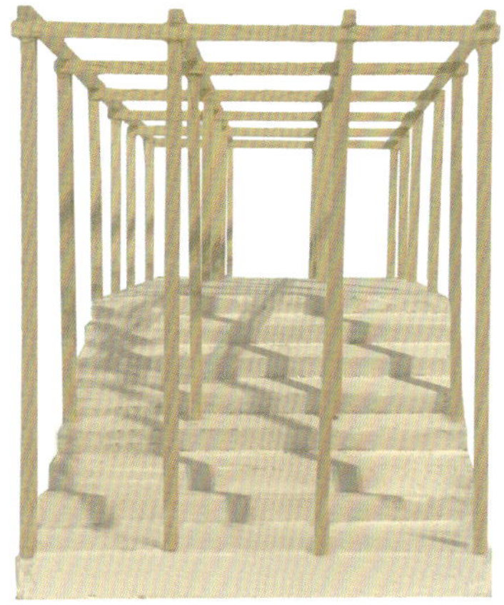

19

20

21

22

23 Internal view of proposed Rock Hall model by Rafael Ribeiro **24** Internal view of Rock Pavilion proposal with photoshopped inhabitation and post production by Korell Llaudes **25** Internal view of proposal structural model for Rock Pavilion by Alina Obreja **26** Internal view of proposal final model for Rock Hall venue space and inhabitation models by Korell Llaudes **27** David Chipperfield inspired section (1:200 scale at A3) by Korell Llaudes **28** Detailed section for Rock Pavilion by Jordan Perry **29-30** Internal views of proposal model by Jordan Perry **31** Final mass model to explore the form, highlighting the different views by Tanjina Hossain **32-33** Selection of work final proposal models by Jordan Perry, Tobi Yoeman, Tanjina Hossain, Rafael Ribeiro and Ahmad Feroz,

23

24

25

26

27

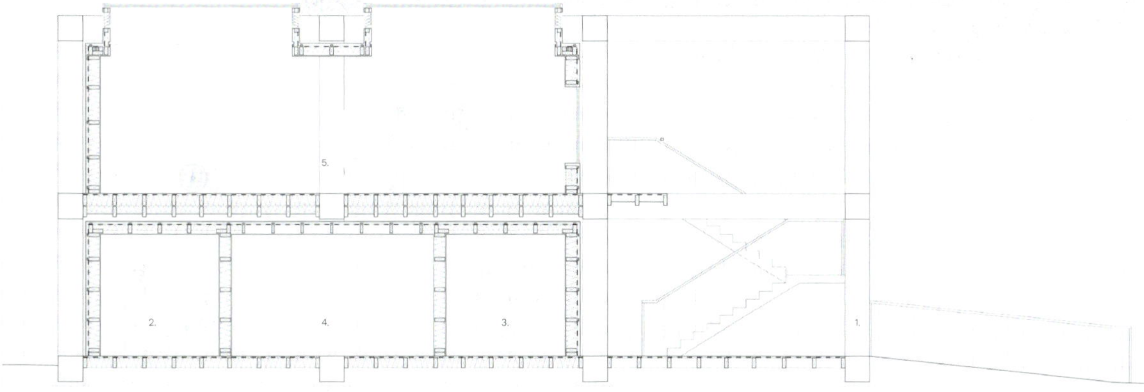

28

29

30

31

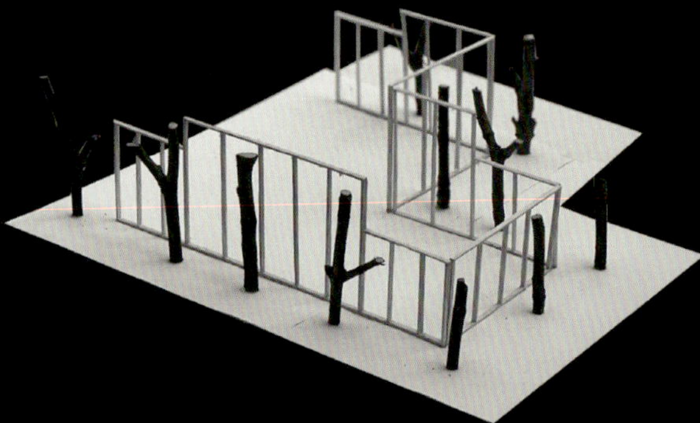

Unit C
Creat(iv)e Soho

Alice D'Andrea, Rob Whitlock

United Kingdom Government figures show that the creative industries contributed £111.7 billion to the national economy in 2018. The London Borough of Westminster contains 7% of those creative industries and it has been estimated that Soho contains one of the highest concentrations of creative businesses in the UK.

In Unit C the students were required to develop a space for creative industries in Soho and to infill an urban void (existing or created), exploring the potential of the site and the opportunities that are created by its setting.

The presence of creative industries within Soho and their value to the local economy is highly valued by Westminster Council, which recognises that they are under threat and facing numerous challenges. Westminster's Planning Policy specifically prioritises and encourages the provision of workspaces for small and medium creative enterprises in Soho.

It has often been said that Soho has something of the atmosphere of a village within the city. Unlike the surrounding areas of Mayfair, Fitzrovia and Bloomsbury most of the area was not controlled by a single aristocratic landowner developing to a more formal urban plan of streets and squares. This made the area less attractive to wealthier residents, and from the early eighteenth century Soho was transformed into an area for artists, merchants', craft and manufacturing. Ever since the area has been constantly remade by the variety of communities that have made Soho home. This history is evident in Soho's surviving architecture today, a rich collage of architectural layers accrued over time.

Careful consideration is given to how architecture can be made within such settings. The students were encouraged to undertake a thorough site analysis and research on the physical, social, cultural and historical qualities of the chosen site.

Year 2 students had a choice of two sites. One is an urban gap site in Frith Street, the other a gap site on Duck Lane, which is part of a building that has its principal frontage onto Berwick Street market.

Year 3 students had a choice of two sites. The Frith Street site, and an urban void which is used as parking lot, sitting between Ingestre Place and Hopkins Street.

The category of 'Creative' could be broad covering advertising, design, fashion, film, photography, galleries and more. The UK's creative industries are a diverse and interconnected sector that is far greater than the sum of its parts, and the majority of creative enterprises are small, employing fewer than 10 people. Students will research into a specific creative industry to understand its condition and needs.

The proposed space should be different from the neutral space the market tends to offer. How can this be achieved? How can we create a different or new type of (communal) creative studio that works with its immediate and future challenges including environmental issues and a potential crisis as we have just experienced with COVID 19?

The proposals range from single studios to medium density studio space that explore opportunities of a new collective art studios model, up to exhibition spaces, workshops and so on.

Students:
Y3: Ionut Stefan Apostol, Claudiu Theodor Cazan, Patryk Filuk, James Hancock, Zoe Kalou, Maddassar Khan, Paula Mema, Musfica Rahman, Cristina Maria Rosculete, Kiana Shokrani Chaharsoghi, Taylor Stephens
Y2: Anoeda Chikungwa, Holly Franks, Malachi Henry, Ritesh Ajay Karelia, Ahmed Khan, Doua Khila, Samuel Littlewood, Karen Moussaid, Afshan Anjum Parvez Shaik, Ruby Mae Walsleben, Jake Whiley

Special thanks to:
David Connor (David Connor Design), Kate Darby (Kate Darby Architects), Deborah Do-Rosario-Benros, Andy Downey (elliottwood), Marco Fedrigo (astudio), Armor Gutierrez, Teresa Serrano, Marco Strizzolo (Citizens Design Bureau), Jeff Tidmarsh, Martin Williams (Williams Griffiths Architects)

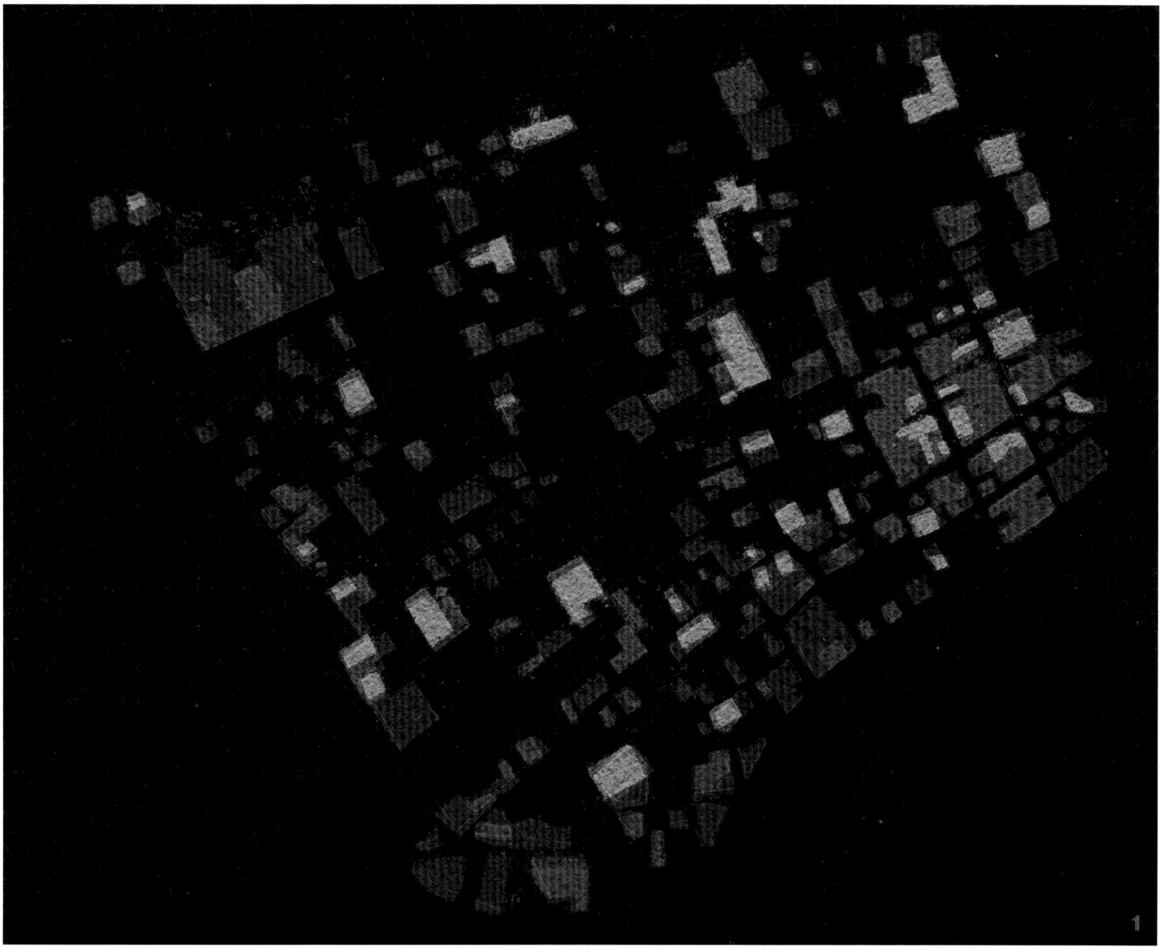
1

1 Map of the night activities in Soho by Patryk Filuk, representing the opening hours of all premises with a license to sell alcohol from Thursday to Saturday **2** Observations of the site area between Ingestre Place and Hopkins Street, canopy of the neighbouring tower being the main element of focus, by Kiana Shokrani Chaharsoghi **3** The three unfolded sections of elevations of Duck Lane, by Jake Whiley. The rear of the dry cleaning shop at 7 Duck Lane is shown in the centre with the infill site above **4** Frith Street and surroundings site model **5** Connection between 13 and 14 Frith Street and wall between 14 and 15 Frith Street by Samuel Littlewood **6** Sketch from the rear open space of the 14 Frith Street existing building 'Garlic and Shots' showing the cluttered garden by Holly Franks

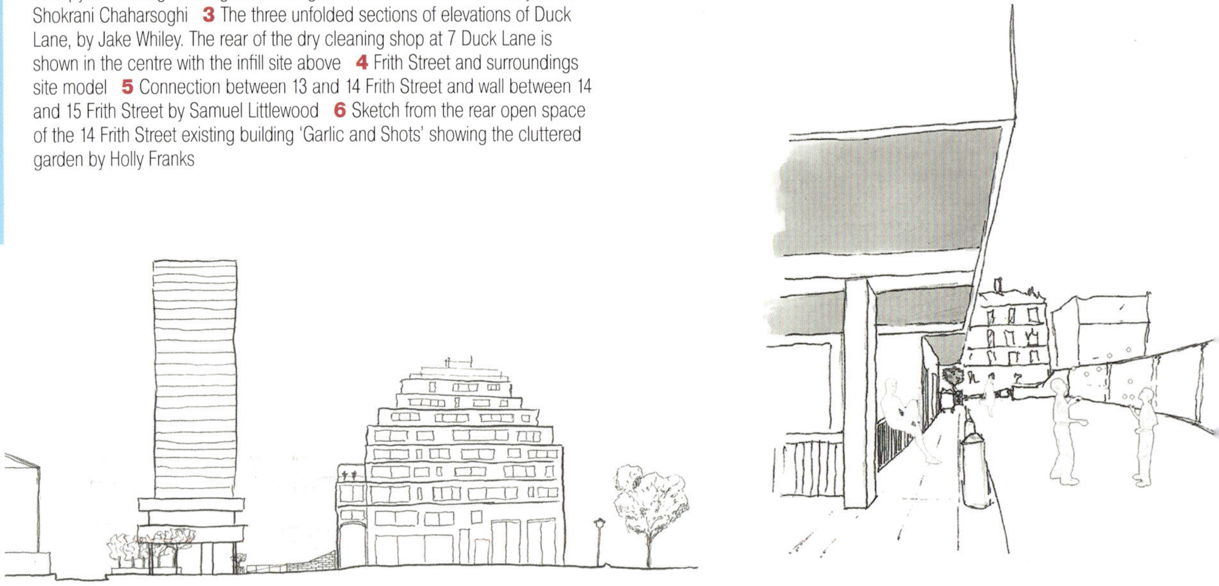

2

3

4

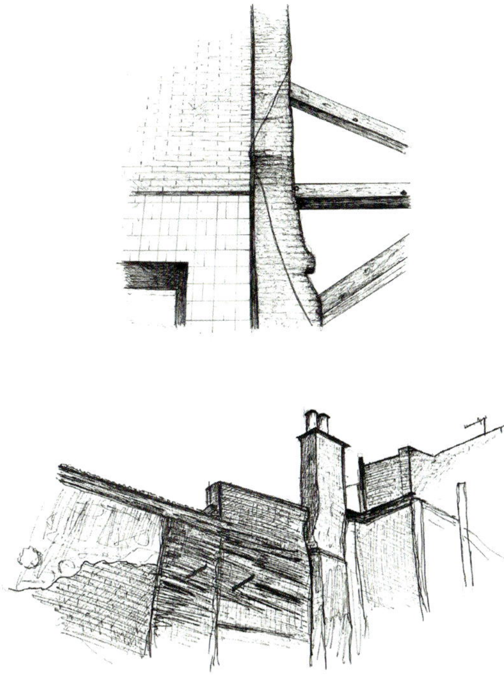

5

6

7 A pencil drawing showing the 2nd floor sculpture terrace that spans from the front to the rear of Holly Franks's proposal 'An Oasis for the Creative Industries'. The core that runs through the vertical of the building just like a bone is also shown **8** Front view and rear view from the second floor communal terrace at '14 Frith Street' by Samuel Littlewood. The proposal serves as a gallery space welcoming the people of Soho and all visitors to experience exhibitions hosted by the creatives based in the building itself along with those from the wider area. The studios will provide a space for creatives to gain footing in Soho and to set up in the area. Communal spaces within the building will create an informal space for the creatives to share knowledge, pushing ideas and growing talent. **9** A cardboard model of the 1st floor at 'Number 14 Frith Street' by Ritesh Karelia testing different volumes and shapes created by the nets between the three existing wooden structures. The installation is meant to create a relaxing space within the gallery space **10** Infill experimentation at Portland Mews by Ruby Mae Walsleben. The concept is inspired by abrupt scene changes in film: discontinuity editing. The proposal was to create a brick facade replicating the others in Portland Mews that encases a plaster space with a circular skylight in the middle of the ceiling. Utilizing natural light during the day and artificial light at night, filling up the plaster cave to achieve the 'cut' feeling I was pursuing. The scene change from reality to a distant place, all in the span of a few meters. **11** Located between Berwick Street and Duck Lane, 'Untitled Gallery' by Jake Whiley explores and promotes the merging of the exhibition and creation of artworks, offering a unique experience for both visitor and artist. A large studio space made from translucent and transparent glass sits suspended above and between the public spaces and levels of the gallery, allowing a limited yet beguiling connection between private and public.

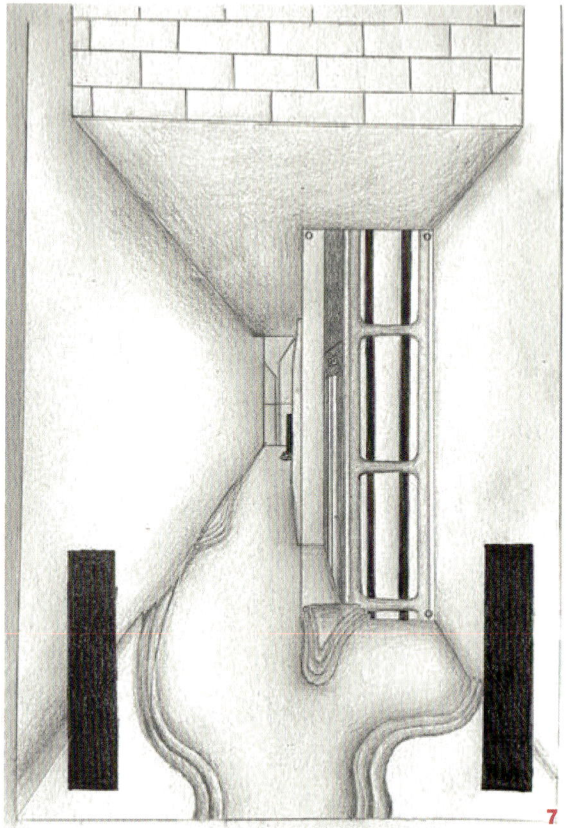

7

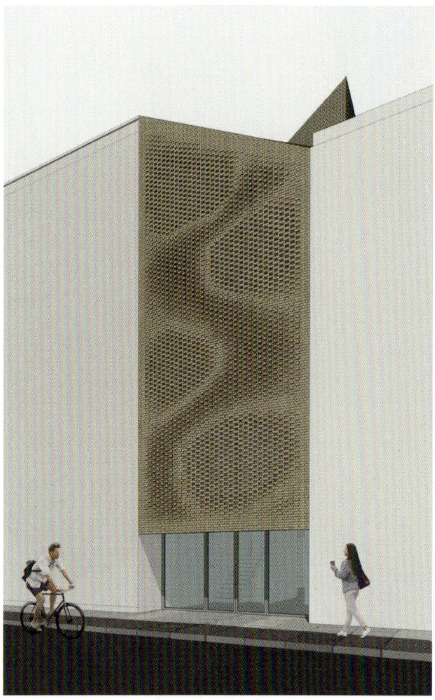

8

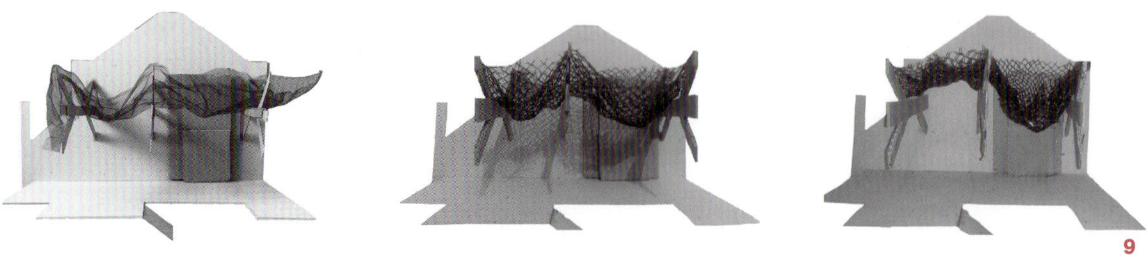

9

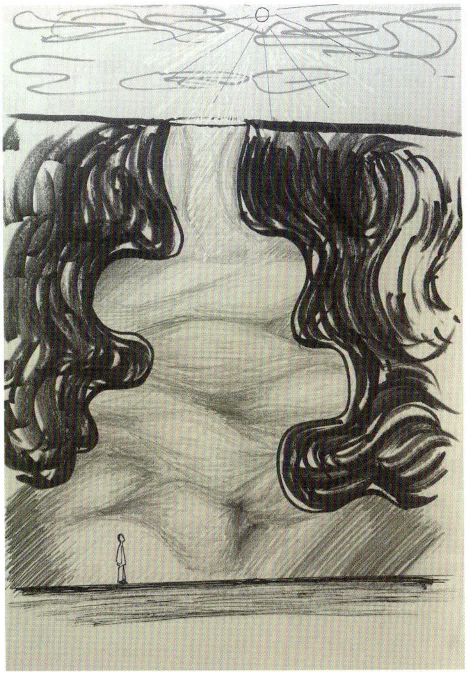

10

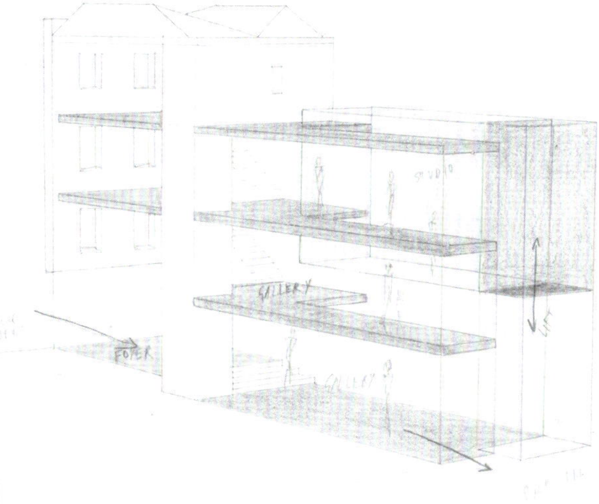

11

12 With the project 'Viga Voladiza', Taylor Stephens creates a space for Part 1 and 2 graduates as well as young practitioners to start their carrier paths. Open studio spaces and private studios offer different working environments. Outdoor terraces and the café at ground floor level aim to bring people together and create networking opportunities **13** Development of the proposed volumes forming the roof of 'Leaning Lights', a proposal by Maddassar Khan. The design concept consists of pyramidal forms reaching for the natural light within the narrow space created by the void between the existing buildings at 14 Frith Street. The form leans on the walls of the buildings on either side to further resemble reaching out towards the light **14** 'Soho Creative Gardens' by Patryk Filuk aims to build a strong community of local artists and people who will collaborate, acquire new skills, and support one another. To maintain the history of this place, this project proposes a green courtyard with elements of the original building from 1733 as a respect to the past. The preservation of the Garlic & Shot will keep the atmosphere of the entertaining culture of Soho. The new building will house the Gallery space on the ground floor and affordable open-plan studios for artists on the upper floors.

13

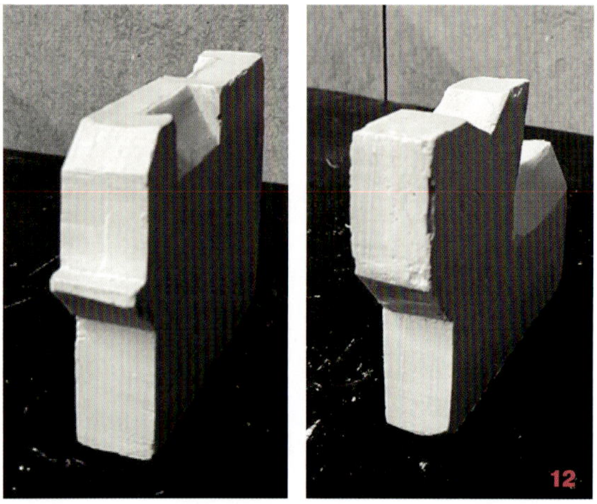

12

8

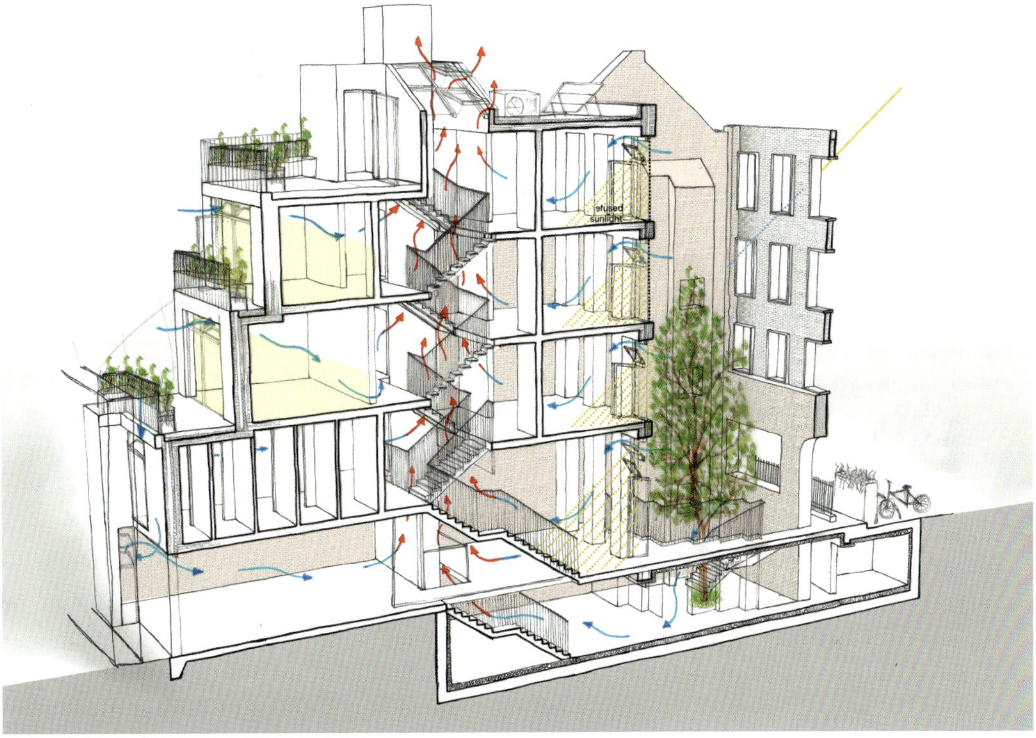

15 'Labyrinth of Passageways - Soho' by Kiana Shokrani Chaharsoghi aims to create a social public space for the neighbourhood of Soho. Celebrating the fabric of the city with attention to materiality and boundaries, the proposal focuses on the creation of a flexible performance space, a multi-purpose space to accommodate meetings, lectures, workshops, rehearsal practices, and a public space/public passageway widely accessible by everyone, incorporated into existing fabric of the urban block **16** The new Soho's Fashion centre, 'Kusokan', by Cristina Maria Rosculete, is intended to be a safe place where young new artist have the opportunity of presenting and creating their new work. The centre will accommodate exhibition spaces and workshops. Experimenting with materials is paramount. Sustainable aspects are considered in order to incorporate natural features into the design **17** 'Project Galaxia' by Musfica Rahman, aims to accommodate modern artists that are inspired by cosmology concepts and want to inhabitate a space in order to make their video/sound art a reality. **18** 'Going Underground' by Ionut Stefan Apostol is a recording studio and music venue that gives young musicians a place to perform and record their music. The proposal explores the idea of retaining the connection between Ingestre Pl and Hopkins St, creating a public space which serves also as occasional open air performance space, whilst the venue and studios are underground to not interfere with the residencies around the site

15

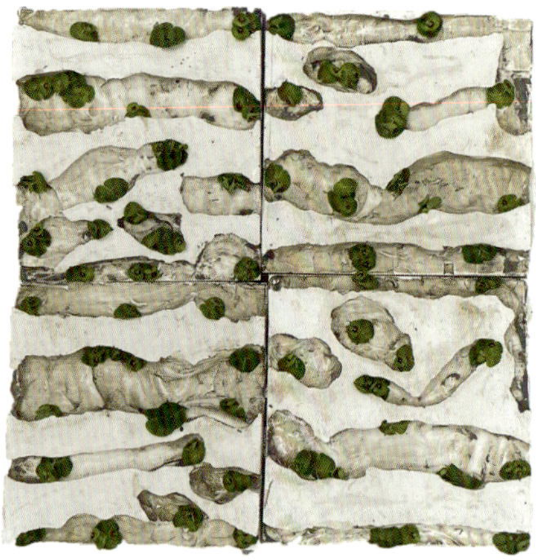

16

17

18

Unit E
"A room for Brick Lane"

Michele Roelofsma, Nasios Varnavas

1.1

Over the years, Unit E and Diploma 7 have been working in complex urban settings. Whether it was Fez's medina, with an incredible cultural and environmental challenge, or the desire of Madrid and Seville for urban inner-city regeneration, or on a much smaller scale Thessaloniki's mercado and last year's site The Lower Marsh in London.

The driving factor for our architectural discussion on these sites is the discussion of current social, economic, and political themes already embedded in these sites and the effect of possible architectural and urban "imposed" proposals.

The recently approved planning permission for development of the Truman Brewery site in Woodseer Street, East London, is a good example of the disconnected manner in which neighbourhood, council and developers are operating. Tower Hamlets Council approved the planning application although there was great objection from locals. The Group "Save Brick Lane" developed a number of points and comments on the approved proposal, which was used as the platform of discussion for the some of the units' proposals.

The second main development of discussion is on the north side of Brick Lane, the Goods Yard. Where The Goods Yard reaches Brick Lane is where the introduction project was set. It is visible how fragments are cut away and the "cut" became part of the Architectural design discussion. Students were asked to complement the east entrance of Goods Yard with the 18 century Oriel on the west celebrating the entrance to the arches, the walk to Brick Lane and creating a Brick Lane-Goods Yard threshold.

1.2

The brief asked for a design of two rooms, one facing the west and the proposed park referred to as future fields (as mentioned in the Master Plan) + proposed high-rise developments, and the second room facing Brick Lane and the East. The challenge was how the the "Cut" proposal could connect the Goods Yard with Brick Lane be part or use elements of the Master Plan. Exiting master plans became a platform for discussion and proposition. Especially in the case of Brick Lane it affects a large community. The students tried to accommodate the needs and desires of the Neighbourhood, given its complexity as a playground of Social, Political, Environmental landscape. Students were forced to take a position in this highly charged environment.

On just 1km of length, Brick Lane contains over 100 food related businesses, some of them permanent, some of them temporary. During the weekend, market stalls enter the lane and quite literally change its occupation. The density is strengthened, becoming almost overwhelming. The Asian style of street food is introduced to Western Europe. As a result, food acts as strong social glue for Brick Lane.

Brick Lane sits on the edge between the deprived borough of Tower Hamlets and the prosperous City of London borough. This schizophrenic condition is pushed to the extreme with the approval of the new Goods Yard development. The economic power of the development has a potential of seriously overrunning the current state of Brick Lane. Consequently, the development introduces an unprecedented "bigness" into the human-scale lane. In the visuals, the meeting point with Brick Lane is depicted as a square, introducing a condition that might result in breaking the flow, dispersing people in all directions. The harsh contact between the big and the small must be rendered much softer.

> "The street is a room by agreement.
>
> Louis Khan

Students:
Y3: Delrick Adikar ,Gabriel Rebec-Permo, Sumaiya Binte Ismail, Simone Pamio, Viktor Telecky, Yucel Seckin Karatas, Maria Zegheru, Joseline Daniela , Czerrina Salayog, Balla Ngom, Abir Hussain
Y2: Cristian-Luca Serbu, Aurorinia Roman, Elonas Butrimas, Cristian Severin, Daniela Herteg

Special thanks to:
Visiting Critics: Craig Bamford (Sasa Works), David Bass, Daniel Meier, Will Lindley Stephania Solomos
Contributors: Amor Guiterrez, Teresa Serrano, Andy Downey (ElliotWood), Louis Schulz (Assemble), Laura Mark (Walmer Yard)

1.1 "Save Brick Lane" protest by locals. **1.2** Goodsyard oriel. **1.3** Flow of people in "the cut" during market da. **1.4** Old entrance of the old bishopsgate station. **1.5** Site context analysis, by Viktor Telecky. **1.6** New development proposal against locals newspaper, by Simone Pamio.

1.3

1.4

1.6

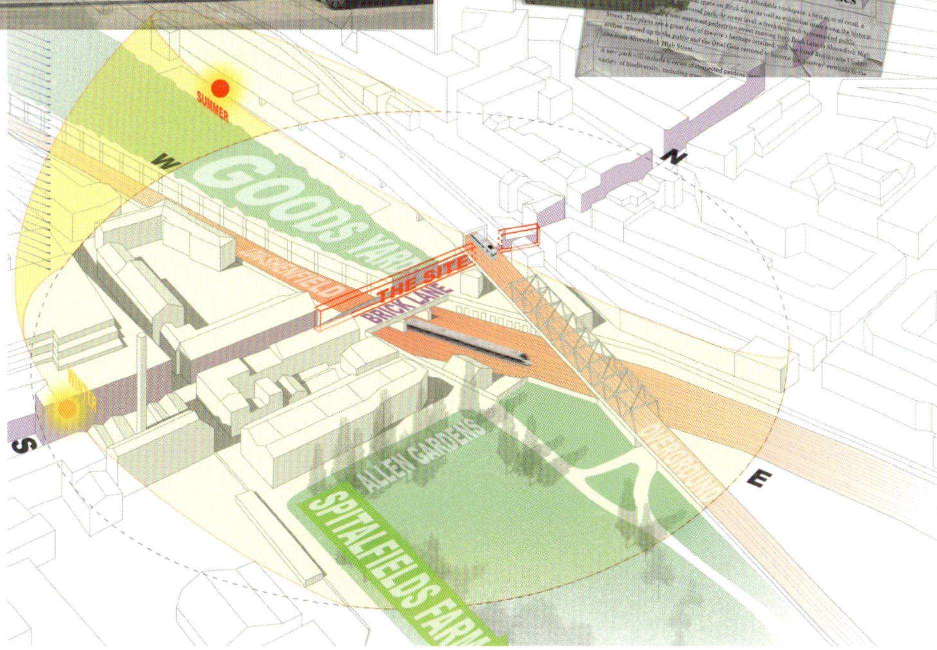

1.5

3.1 Site remnant of the old Bishopsgate station, by Simone Pamio. **3.2** Sketches of the design process of the walkway, by Simone Pamio. **3.3** Fragment of the new walkway following the same materiality of the site, by Simone Pamio. **3.4** Light experience under the walkway, caustic reflections on the existing wall and the new arches, by Simone Pamio. **4.5** Exploded isometric of the overall intervention for the goodsyard, by Simone Pamio. **4.6** Spatial experiences in the landscape as a room to get lost, by Simone Pamio **4.7** Architectural movement gesture and breakdown of planning, by Simone Pamio. **4.8** 1:20 Section illustrating the tension between Brick Lane and the new intervention overhanging on top of it, by Simone Pamio.

3.1

3.2

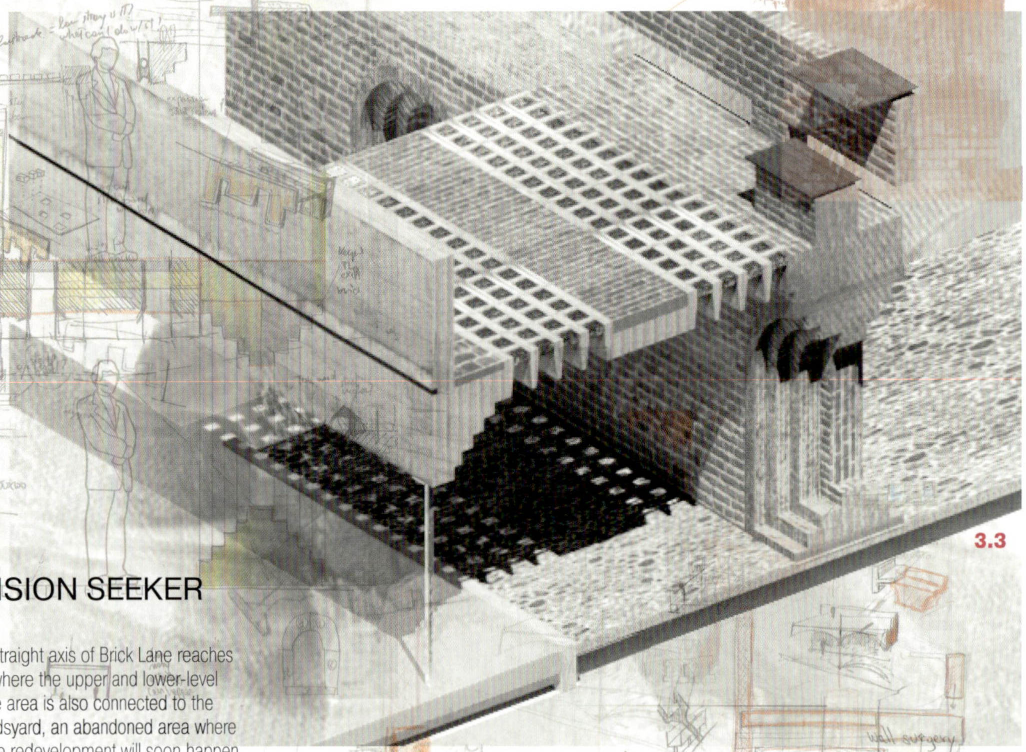

3.3

A-(T)TENSION SEEKER

The continuous straight axis of Brick Lane reaches a breaking point where the upper and lower-level railways meet. The area is also connected to the Bishopsgate Goodsyard, an abandoned area where an approved future redevelopment will soon happen.

The first phase of the project will focus on the redevelopment of the Cut, which is now being used as a circulation space for both people and vehicles. Part of the development will happen alongside the new masterplan, focusing on the access between the street and the Goodsyard and in the way people access and interact with the top part of the Goodsyard. The abandoned Goodsyard presented a lot of interesting remnants of the old Bishopsgate station that people seemed to overlook while experiencing and moving in the Lane. The first part of the project thus seeks to create a new walkway.

The second part of the project will focus on the re-establishment of the top part of the Goodsyard, now an abandoned roof with ubiquitous wild flora. The project will make use of the large soil excavation of the masterplan housing to create a brand-new natural landscaping on top of the Goodsyard old structure. Moreover, an Urban Garden Centre, designed to sit on top of the new landscape, will provide a vertical farming fo the community.

The landscape of the top floor is designed as to be "a room to get lost". The journey plays a crucial role on this matter, as the space-time experience of the journey is the means necessary to explore the area by entering new realms but be constantly reminded of the context people are in.

3.4

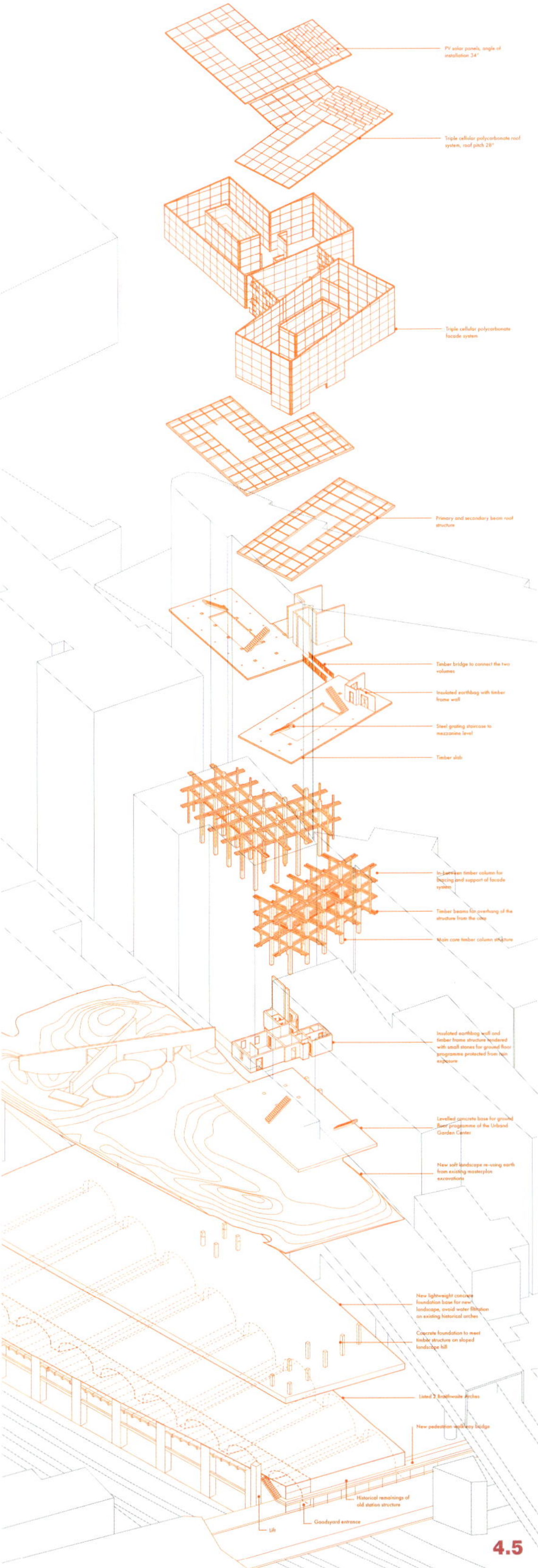
PV solar panels, angle of installation 34°
Triple cellular polycarbonate roof system, roof pitch 28°
Triple cellular polycarbonate facade system
Primary and secondary beam roof structure
Timber bridge to connect the two volumes
Insulated earthbag with timber frame wall
Steel grating staircase to mezzanine level
Timber slab
In-between timber column for bracing and support of facade system
Timber beams for overhang of the structure from the core
Main core timber column structure
Insulated earthbag wall and timber frame structure rendered with small stones for ground floor programme protected from rain exposure
Levelled concrete base for ground floor programme of the Urband Garden Center
New soft landscape re-using earth from existing masterplan excavations
New lightweight concrete foundation base for new landscape, avoid water filtration on existing historical arches
Concrete foundation to meet timber structure on sloped landscape hill
Listed 2 Braithwaite Arches
New pedestrian walkway bridge
Historical remainings of old station structure
Goodsyard entrance
Lift

4.5

4.6

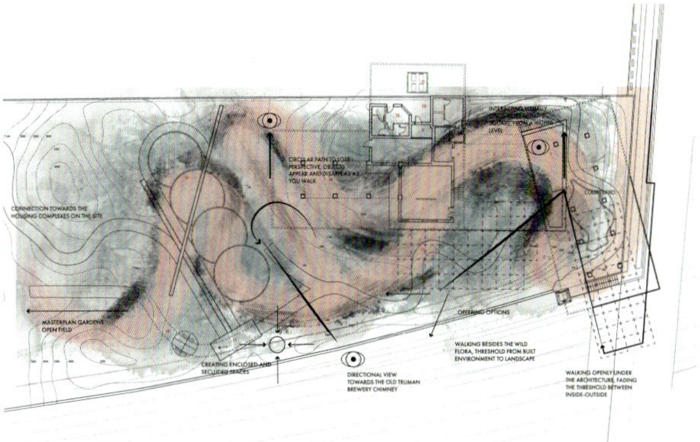
CIRCULAR PATH TO LOSE PERSPECTIVE, OBJECTS APPEAR AND DISAPPEAR AS YOU WALK
CONNECTION TOWARDS THE HOUSING COMPLEXES ON THE SITE
COURTYARD
OFFERING OPTIONS
MASTERPLAN GARDENS OPEN FIELD
WALKING BESIDES THE WILD FLORA, THRESHOLD FROM BUILT ENVIRONMENT TO LANDSCAPE
CREATING ENCLOSED AND SECLUDED SPACES
DIRECTIONAL VIEW TOWARDS THE OLD TRUMAN BREWERY CHIMNEY
WALKING OPENLY UNDER THE ARCHITECTURE, FADING THE THRESHOLD BETWEEN INSIDE-OUTSIDE

4.7

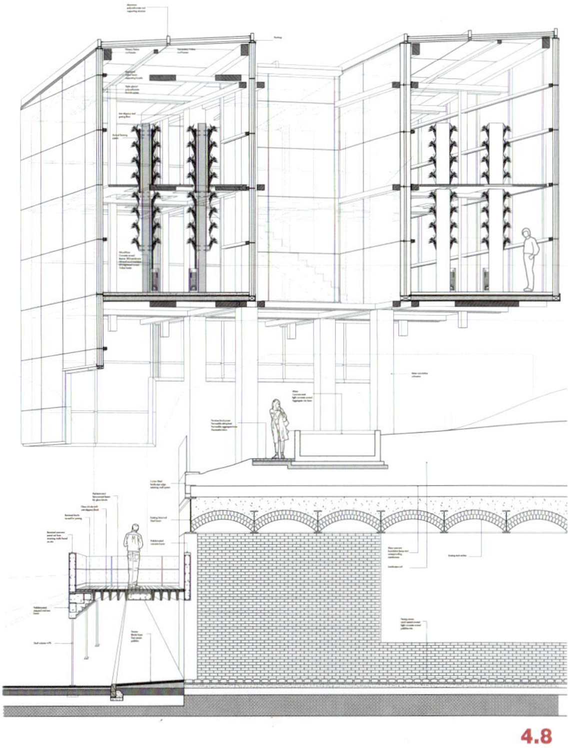

4.8

5.1 Life happens near ground. **5.2** Pushing and pulling. **5.3** Food education centre. **5.4** Food banks + (s)eating space. **5.5** Food museum. **6.6** Welding. **6.7** 1:200 massing model. **6.8** Food education centre. **6.9** Framing the street. **6.10** How it all comes together. **6.11** Food museum. **6.12** Long section. **6.13** Light study. (Project done by Viktor Telecky).

5.1

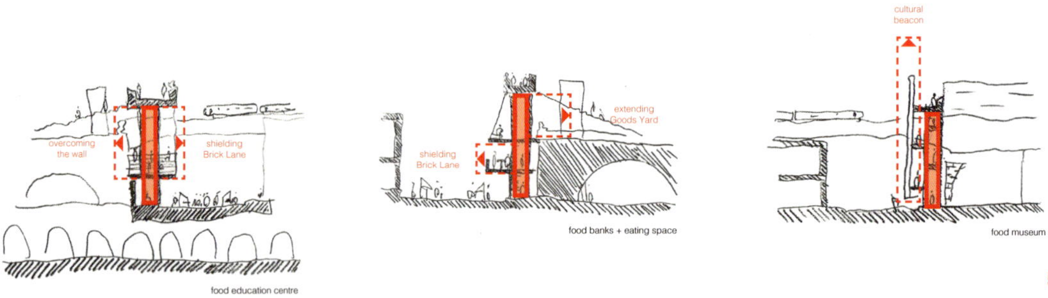

5.2

5.3

5.4

5.5

6.6

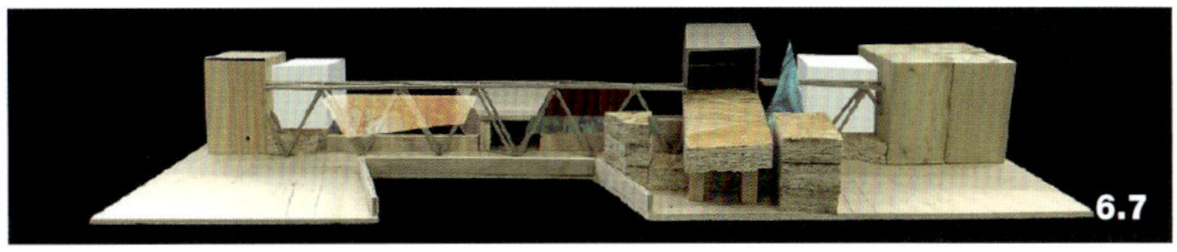
6.7

6.8

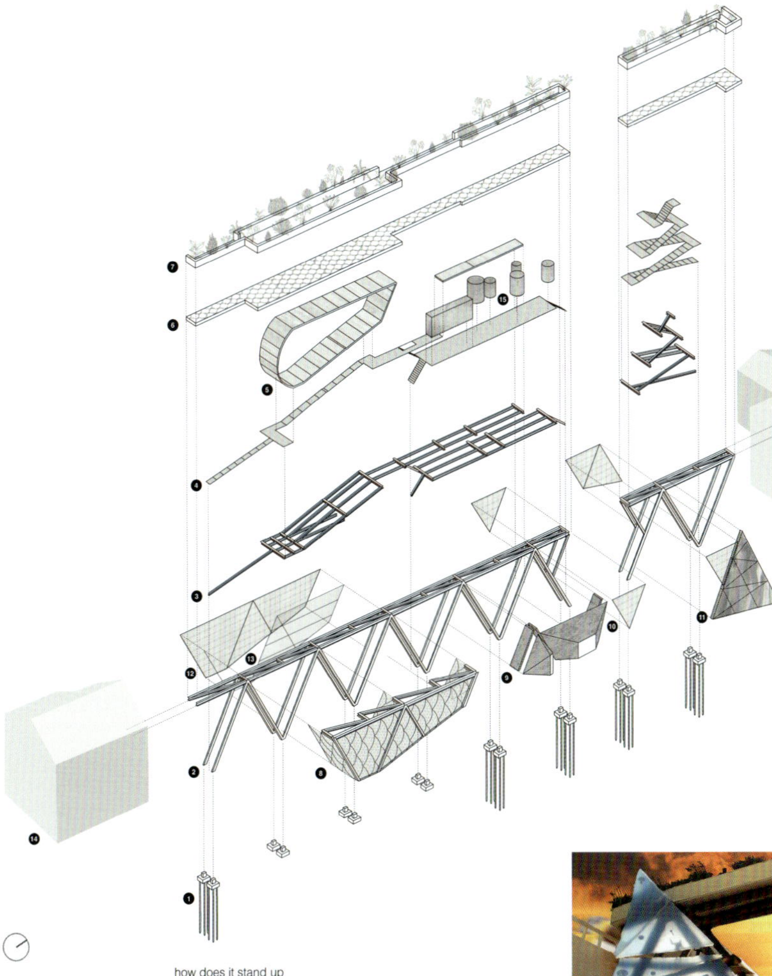

6.10

6.9

6.12

6.11

6.13

Proposal for cricket practice room in Pedley Street. Partly occupying the former Brick Lane rail station. Embankment condition on the north and Pedly Alley way (street) on the south **7.1** Wall Brick lane **7.2** Room and threshold proposal for Bricklane and Goodsyard **7.3** Bricklane Station North facade **7.4** Proposed Lower Basement Plan **7.5** Proposed Upper Basement Plan **7.6** Proposed Ground Floor Plan **7.7** .Study model north facade **7.8** West facade facing Allen Gardens **7.9** structural diagram **7.10** Brick lane meeting Pedley street **7.11** Proposed long section (Project done by Delrick Adikari)

7.1

7.2

7.3

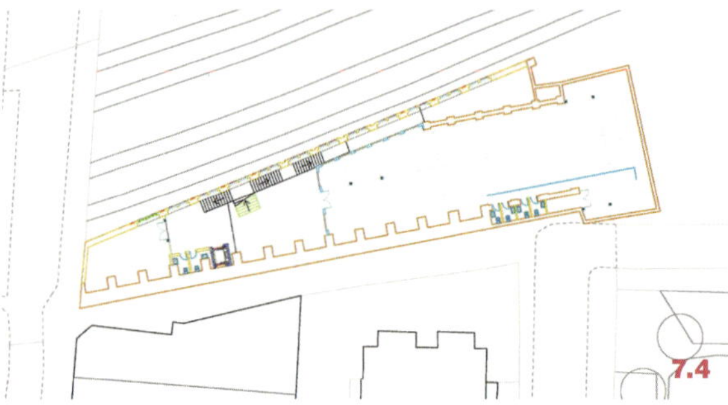

7.4

7.7

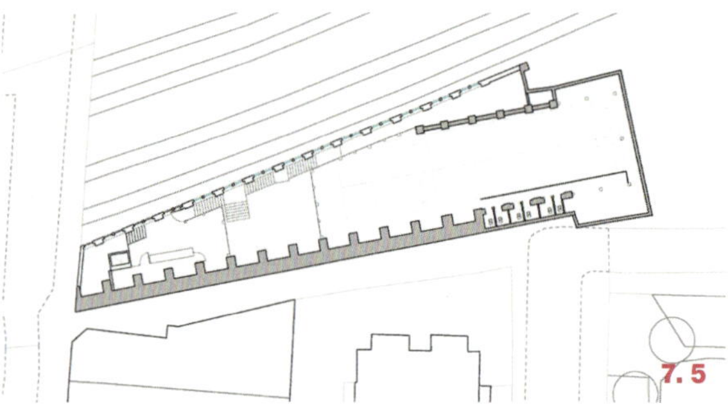

7.5

7.8

7.9

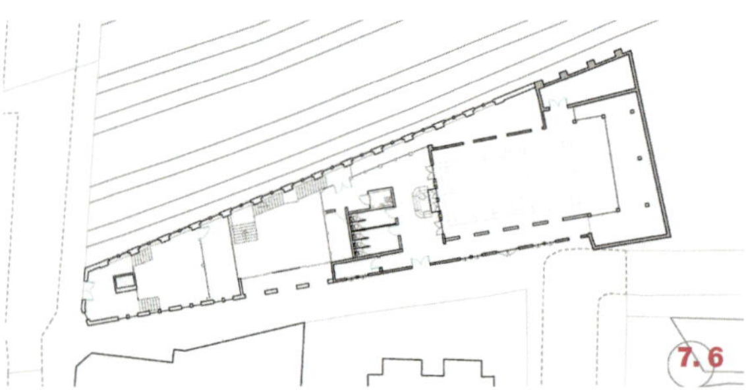

7.6

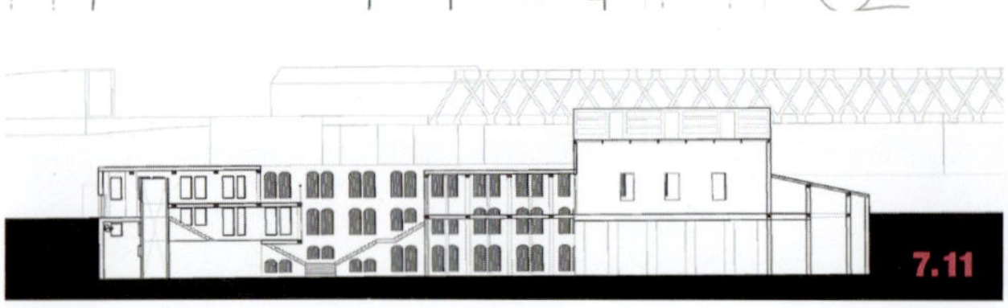

7.11

7.10

8.1 Model of the proposal development **8.2** Ground floor of the new residential buildings **8.3** Section of the new proposal and the existing Truman brewery **8.4** New courtyard in conversation with the historical site. **8.5** Nature and light experience in the courtyard **8.6** View of the courtyard from the new housing complex.

The Project looked into the social, political and spatial complexities of Brick Lane in relation to the city of London. The Project responds to the proposed large scale redevelopment master plan for the Goodsyard and Truman Brewery, shaping an architecture of the in between- A public room for London. The architectural idea of the project is the journey through a series of courtyards experiencing threshold between public and private spaces. The co housing project for Truman Brewery site is designed for the local Bangladeshi community by involving the existing building with the new built to form a courtyard in between- a place to gather. (Project done by Sumaiyabinte Ismail)

8.4

8.1

8.5

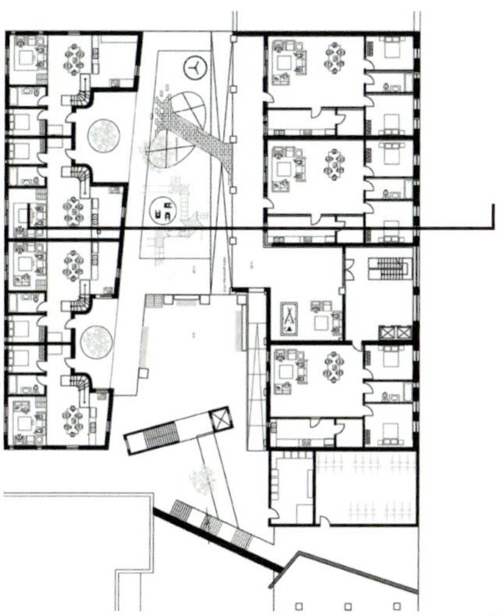

8.2

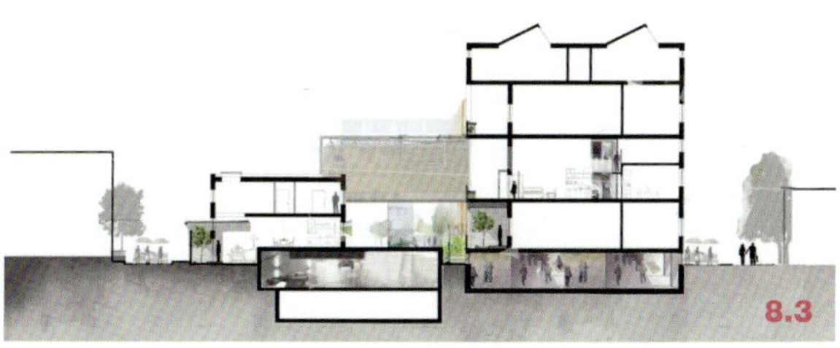

8.3

8.6

10 'Gabriel Rebec Permo:The focus was the abrupt ending of west part of the lanes building fabric. The buildings on the south are concluded Pedley Street the building row with a designed façade facing the north. Reference Smithson's Summer Pavilion and Assemble where discussions point in the design process. Social Club "Art Academy" "The Belt Shop "where integrated in "The neighbourhood workshop for brick lane" the celebration of the North Façade of the urban block. The replacement of the connection of the West with East with a room Bridge connecting the workshops with the proposed Brick Lane Gallery in the former station.

10.1 Located Site and Wall of interest **10.2** Day & Night Render of Proposal **10.3** Sketch model workshop space **10.4** Diagraming new ending to bricklane **10.5** 1-25 Section in Context **10.6** First Floor Proposal Plan **10.7** Second Floor Proposal Plan **10.8** 1-100 Section through Proposal

10.1

10.2

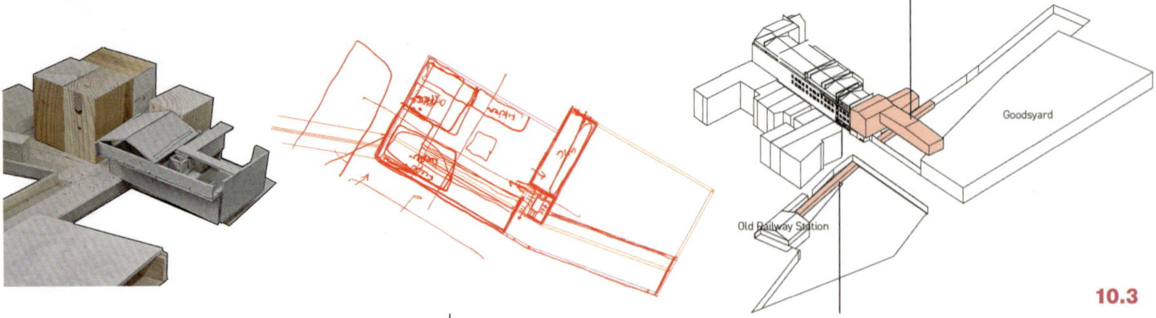

10.3

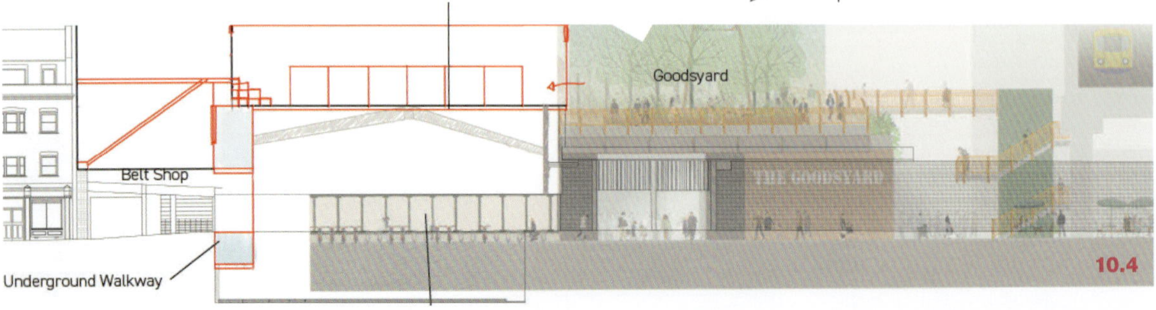

10.4

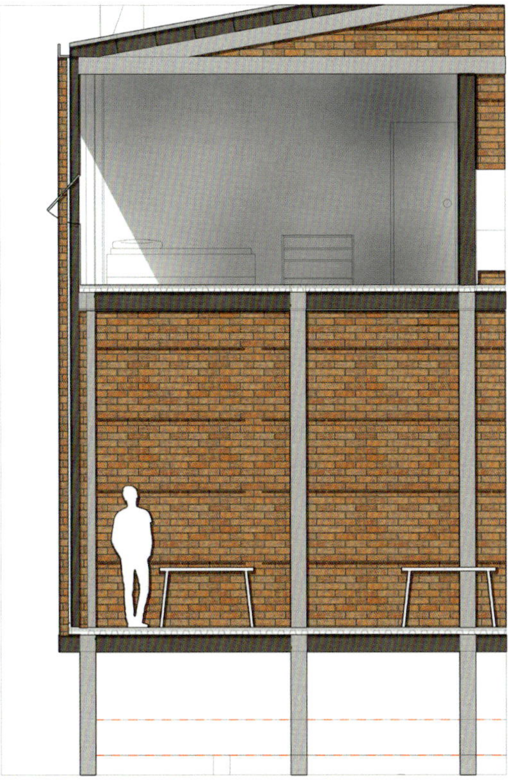

10.5

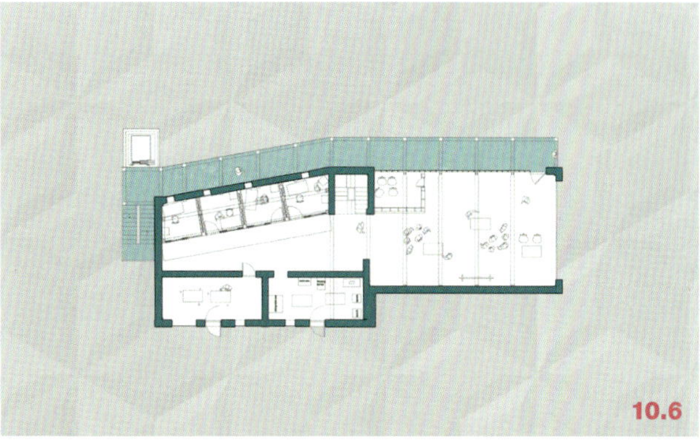

10.6

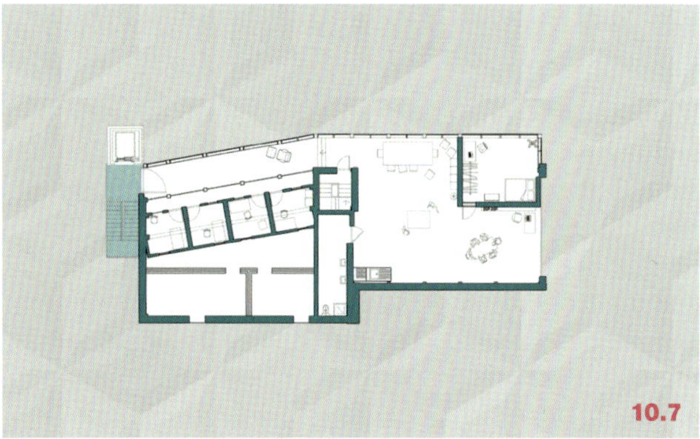

10.7

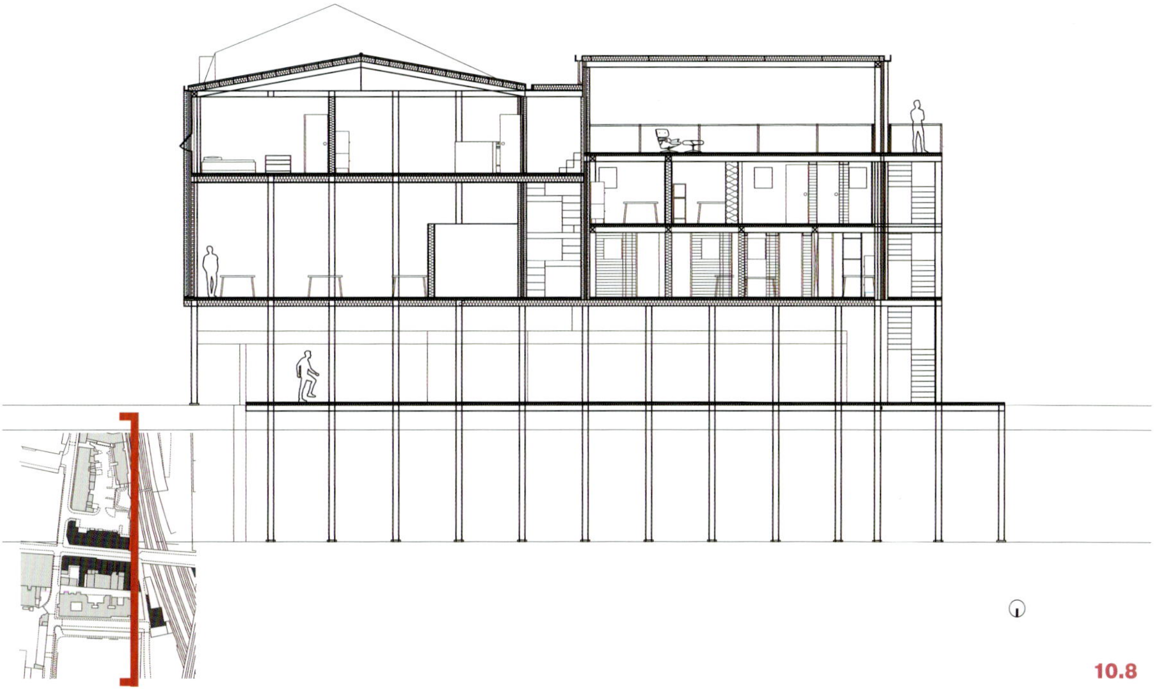

10.8

Unit H
City Land Process III
Continuity and Tolerance

Keita Tajima, Charlotte Harris

This year Unit H focused on the notion of "Continuity and Tolerance" in architecture.

The unit is interested in how materials of the land and city can be re-thought and formed to express a specific spatial sensibility and experience, enriching our architectural approach to the city and design of spaces whilst revealing the intricacies of place-memory. By considering a decarbonization of the city as one of the urgent global issues, we will investigate the city and its building stocks from very micro scale by evaluating their material performance and construction, spatial quality and architectural merit, and unravel their further potentials by re-composing with new architectural elements. We will make an archive of experimental materials and speculative architectural fragments from that can be tested and developed in relation to the specific site context and available resources.

SITE: Limehouse

We based our site study along the Limehouse Cut, the first navigable canal in London, opened in 1770 in order to connect the River Thames and the Lee navigation for boat traffic, transporting raw materials to a place of manufacture or finished goods to consumers. Since the second half of 20th century, the use of canal as trading route has declined, subsequently the buildings along the canal have lost their relationship to the water, a half of its stretch has been replaced by new residential blocks with little to no interaction with the canal and minimal public accesses. Students have formulated their architectural potential and questions based on the value and the obsolescence of this ex-industrial urban landscape, and to develop an urban strategy to create local network of publicly accessible shared resources or "urban commons".

LIMEHOUSE, LONDON

Students:
Y3: Kacper Jajuga , Christos Karamanos, Ainsley Moffat, Ali Mohammed, Mohammed Abdul Mubin, Kathlyn Pagador, Mahbubur Rahman Tahmid, John Paul Nasayao, Simran Maria Pires, Filip Szypula, Roland Vata,

Y2: Ashia David, Mohamed Lamine Dif , Guilherme Bressaneli, Adrian Grant , Kiranjit Kaur , Milesa Khan , Adrienne Mercedes Raleigh , Maria Isabel Salazar, Tobias Scriven, Sonia Elena Stefanescu, Arlinda Zenelaj

Special thanks to:
Visiting Critics: Pierre D'Avoine, Alfred Hatch, Amor Guiterrez, Adam Cheltsov, Andrew Houlton (, Ingrid Petit (Feiden Fowles), Nikolay Shapazov , Colin O'Sullivan, Hanna Tweg, Christopher Thorn, Mo Woonyn Wong (MOCT Studio)

Contributors:
Vincent Cullane (Hone Studio), Jim Matthews (H.G Matthews) Studio 2 London Metropolitan University, UEL workshop: David Morgan, Daryl Brown, Mark Sowdon,

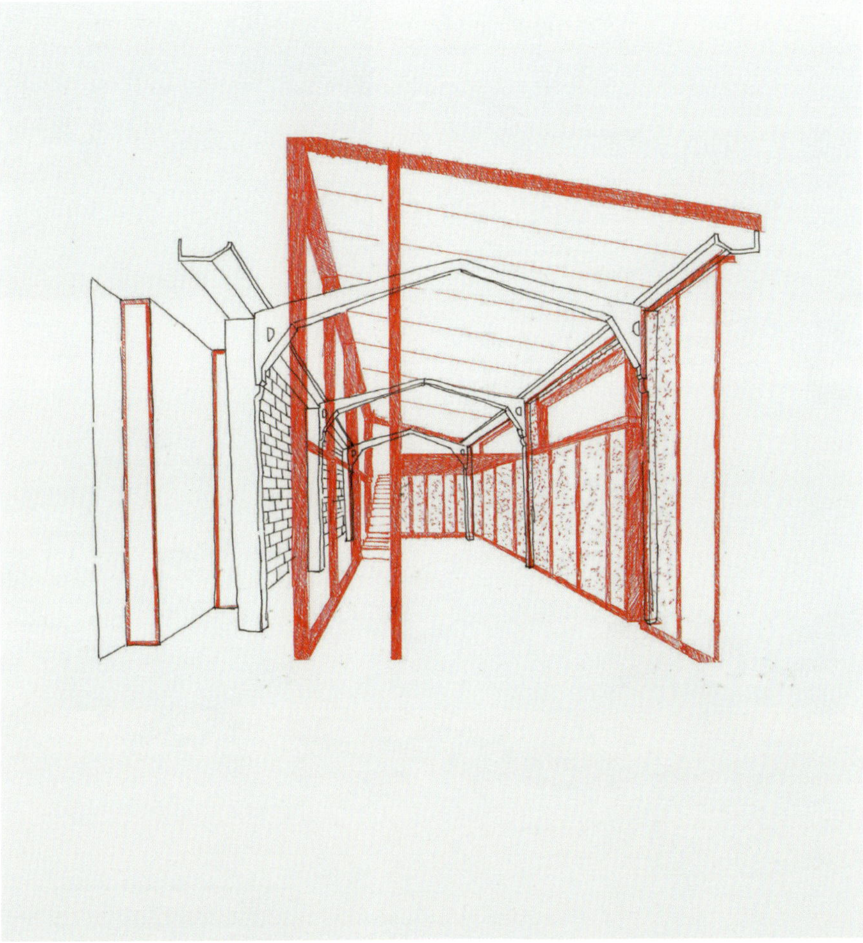

1

1 Loose-ness and tight-ness, spatial exploration through perspective sketch by Adrienne Mercedes Raleigh **2** Location map in relation to available public space around Limehouse cut by Adrienne Mercedes Raleigh **3** View of Limehouse Cut from the towpath, Kathlyn Pagador, **4** Hone Studio courtyard photographed by Adrienne Mercedes Raleigh **5** Spatial sequence through Limehouse Cut, Kathlyn Pagador. **6** Hone studio spatial mapping by Arlinda Zenelaj **7** Detail sketch of existing brick wall to explore the history and textural quality around the site by Arlinda Zenelaj **8** Physical model exploring spatial intervention and material (hempcrete) application to Hone Studio by Arlinda Zenelaj.

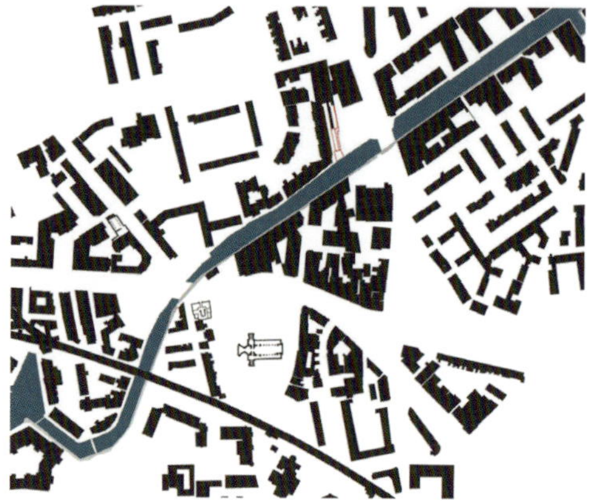

2

3

4

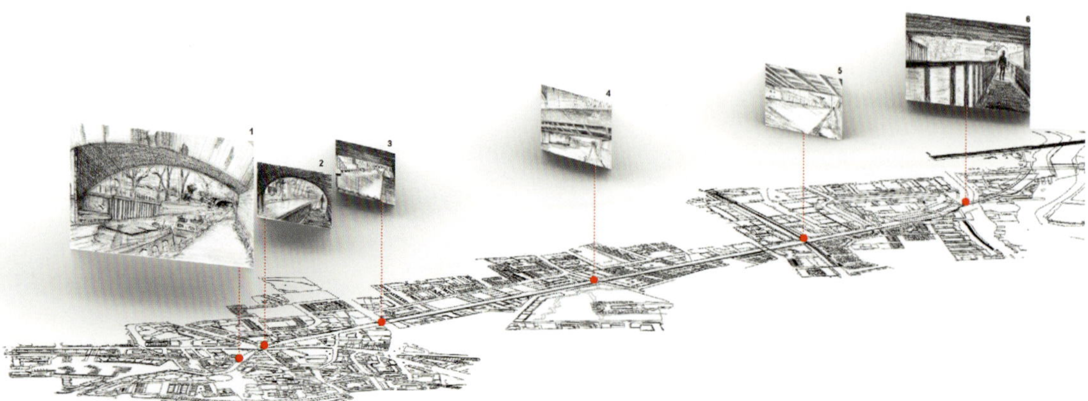

Bridges frames a view. It has multiple architectural qualities and functions.
The quality over the years from bricks , concrete to steel can generate a sense of feel of its strength. It carries people, vehicles and trains.
Bridges can act as a form of shelter too when it rains.
Bridges connect one place to another, thus connecting people to get to and from places.
Overall bridges are places of transition too, like a threshold or the place in between- to identify a sense of place.

5

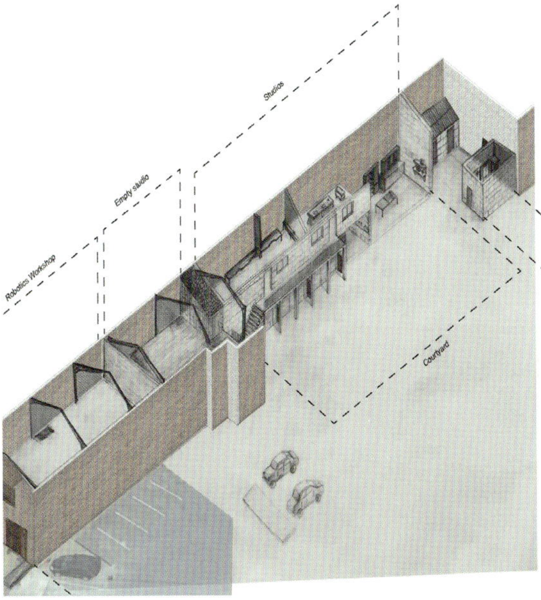
Robotics Workshop
Empty studio
Studios
Kitchen
Courtyard

6

7

8

9 Field trip to H/G Matthews **10** Material experimentation workshop. Group work, photographed by Kathlyn Pagador **11** Experimenting with charred timber by Kathlyn Pagador **12** Internal view of gathering space extension to Hone Studio by Roland Vata **13** Walled garden extension to Hone studio by Simran Maria Pires **14** Exploring the application of sacrificial mould with earth filling by Ainsley Moffat **15,16** Exploring idea of connection-disconnection by Christos Karamanos **17** Sketch model exploring a removal strategy and additional structure to Hone Studio by Adrienne Mercedes Raleigh **18** Extraction and new insertion into existing wall of Hone revealing the historical layer found in existing wall by Guilherme Bressaneli **19** Exploring idea of flat-pack structure by Filip Szypula **20** Initial sketch exploring proposal for walled garden and natural dye workshop by Simran Maria Pires

9

10

11

12

13

14

15

16

17

18

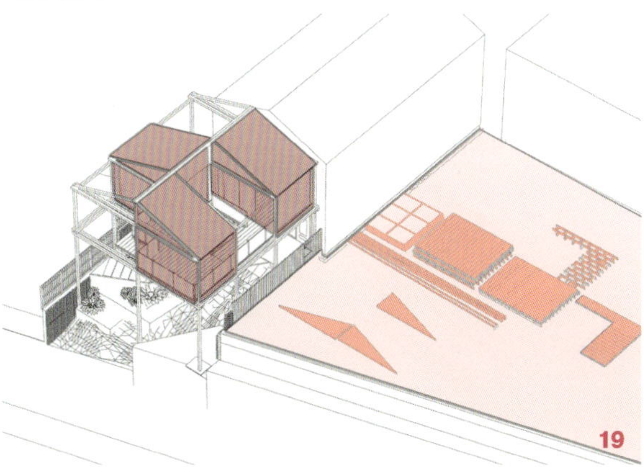

19

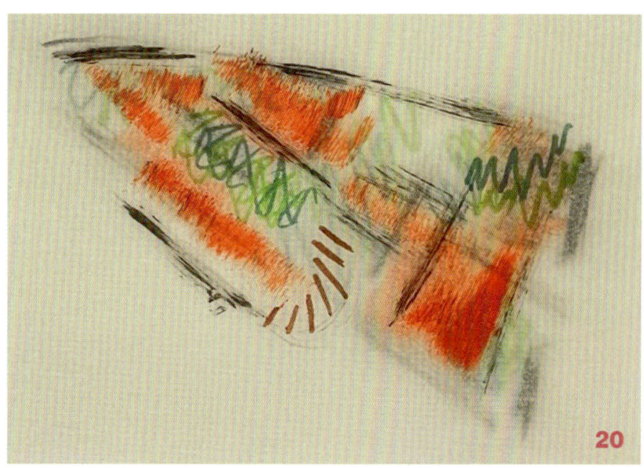

20

21 Physical model exploring the structural relationship between existing concrete portal frame and new timber frame structure to Hone Studio by Adrienne Mercedes Raleigh **22** Sketch model to explore the spatial quality after removal of existing floor and wall at Hone Studio by Guilherme Bressaneli **23** Detail section showing the relationship between new structure and existing portal frame to Hone Studio by Guilherme Bressaneli **24** Exploded axonometric demonstrating the proposed permanent arch space by using Catalan vault structure and lightweight adaptable timber frame structure by Kathlyn Pagador **25** The model of public hall as a part of adaptable shed structures by John Paul Nasayao **26,27** The photomontage and the physical model shows the proposed yard space between proposed jewellery maker workshop, gallery and by Mohammed Abdul Mubin **28** Proposed ground floor plan for the urban plaza with three proposed buildings on the site to improve the public access to the canal while proving affordable studio space for makers and artists.by Mahbubur Rahman Tahmid **29** Longitudinal section through the proposed adaptable shed structures that provide shared workspace, public hall and live/work spaces by John Paul Nasayao

30 Section cutting through the towpath, proposed studios for makers and shared courtyard by Kathlyn Pagador **31** View to proposed urban plaza which mediates space between two proposed studio/workshop spaces as well as topography. Print by Mahbubur Rahman Tahmid **32** Proposed elevation in relation to existing urban landscape by Ainsley Moffat **33** View to the proposed walled garden and natural dye workshop by Simran Maria Pires **34** Internal view of proposed long room by Guilherme Bressaneli **35** View from the proposed arch space for wood workshop into new shared courtyard for makers.

21

22

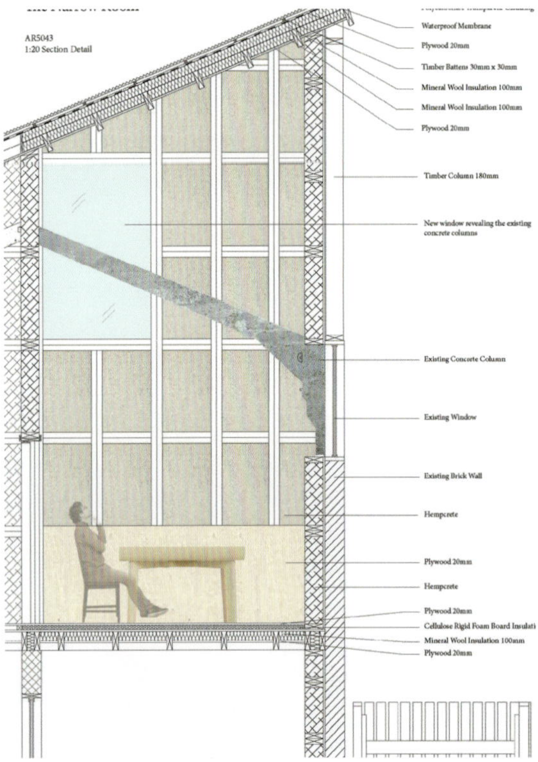

23

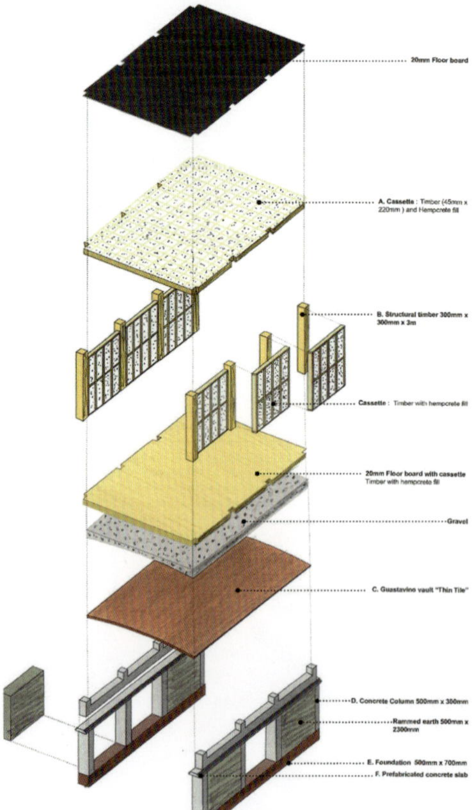

24

25

26

27

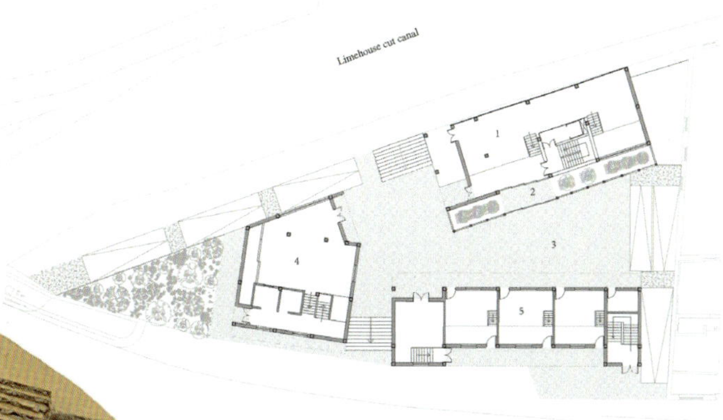

28

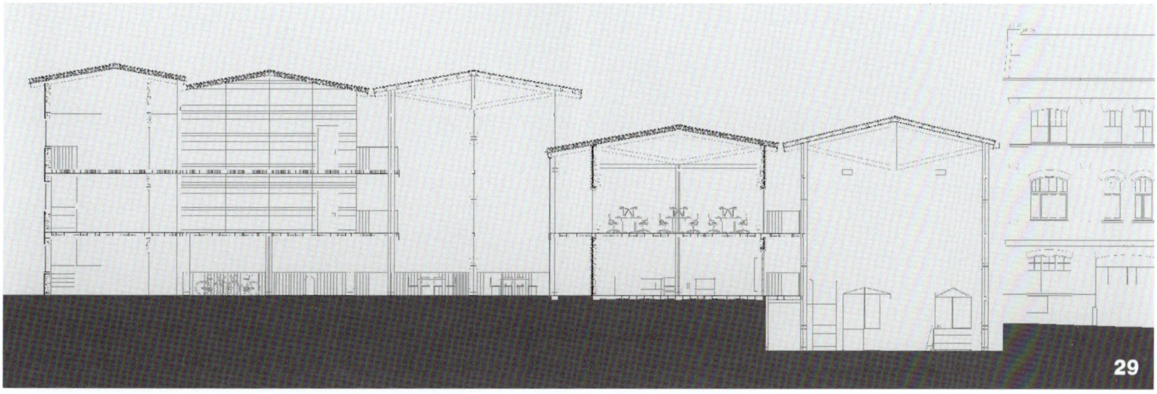

29

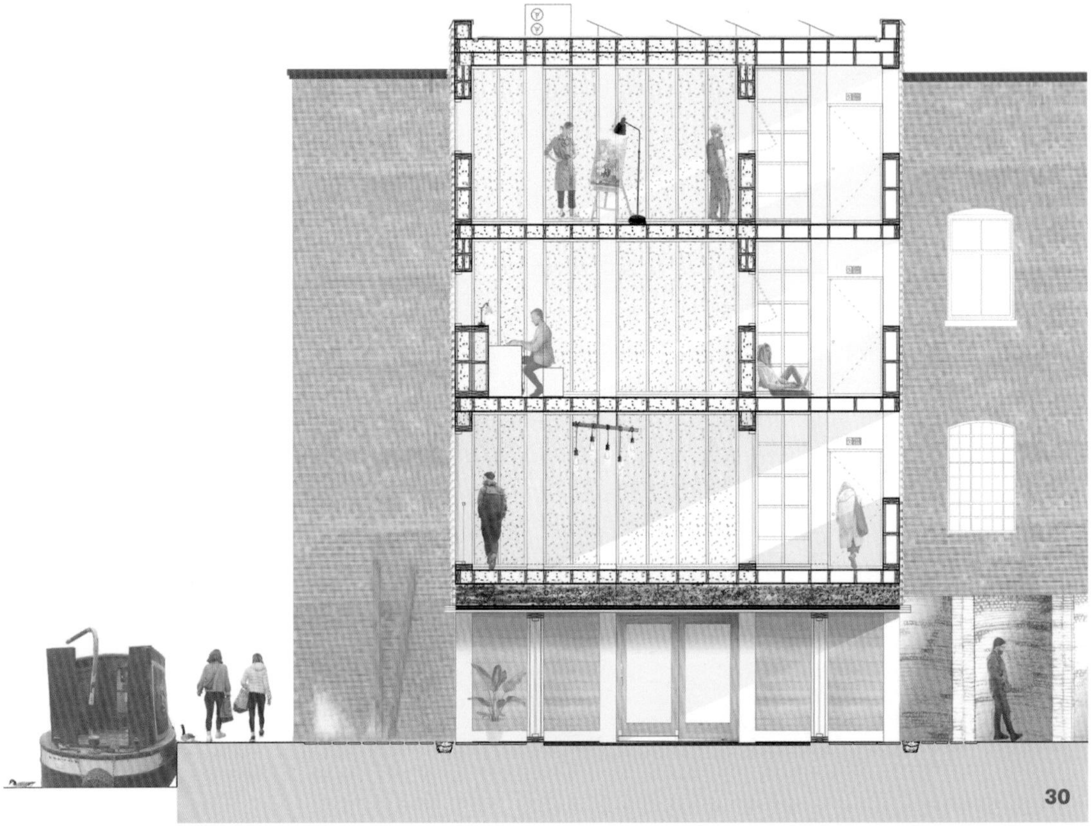

30

31

32

33

34

35

Architectural Design Technology

BSc (Hons)

Dr Arman Hashemi, Course Leader

The BSc (Hons) Architectural Design Technology (ADT) programme has received full accreditation by the Chartered Institute of Architectural Technology (CIAT) for the next five years. The CIAT panel provided very good feedback and commended on the staff passion and dedication, university facilities, integration of research and knowledge exchange activities within the course, digital fabrication activities, great approaches on technical studies, strong industry links, integration of sustainability and mental wealth modules within the course.

Similar to the previous years we have been very keen on developing the subject specific knowledge and employability skills to support our students who aspire for a rewarding career in this field. The introduction of Digital Fabrication and Assembly in SolidWorks proved to be very successful with many students producing outstanding digital and physical 3D printed models.

This year, our ADT year 3 students took part in the ZEMCH International Design Workshop 2021 that was held from 20th-24th October 2021 in the UAE, with 95 undergraduate and postgraduate students and 19 tutors taking part from across the world. Two groups involving our ADT students were selected as the 1st and 2nd winners. The judges highly praised the quality of our students' works and their achievements were announced and showcased at the ZEMCH 2021 International Conference in the UAE.

Our students also took part in a £30K British Council funded research/teaching project, entitled "Green Buildings in Russia – adaptation and mitigation of existing buildings to a changing climate", in collaboration with MASI university. Energy consumption and thermal comfort were assessed in three case study buildings, using Dynamic Thermal Simulation and Physical Measurements, and the results were presented in an international conference held in February 2022 in Russia.

Next year, our ADT students will be joining the Sustainability Decathlon 2023 as a collaboration between The University of East London and Tongji University to design and build an Affordable Prefabricated Carbon Neutral House in a Solar Village in California, Orange County.

We are indeed very proud of our students' achievements and will keep working closely with the CIAT and the industry to improve the quality of our course and provide employment opportunities to our students.

Dr Arman Hashemi (BSc, MSc, PhD, FHEA, MCMI, ACIAT)

BSc (Hons) Architectural Design Technology

Arman Hashemi, Alfonso Senatore, Michele Roelofsma, Niall Healy, Raquel Castro, Shahrokh Zandi

The Design modules are delivered in close relation to the Technical and Professional Studies modules. In the design modules, students develop their design and drawing skills while in technical modules they do comprehensive studies aimed at exploring technical aspects of the proposed designs, including the production of detailed construction drawings.

In Year 1, we designed a sustainable two storey house, on a site at UEL campus overlooking the Royal Docks. The project aimed at developing our design and technical understanding of small residential structures, building materials, construction processes, sustainability and technical details.

Year 2 and 3 ADT, had the opportunity to engage and develop a comprehensive design proposal located within The Regeneration Carpenter Estate Housing Project, in the London Borough of Newham. Some of the strategic questions included:

-What are the limitations and potentials of the site and context?

-How can the design proposal meet the RIBA 2030 Climate Challenge Targets for operational energy use, climate resilience, embodied carbon, and water conservation?

-What could be the most effective building form and fabric for the chosen site?

-How can buildability, adaptability, disassembly, low-maintenance, use of low carbon materials and occupants' health and wellbeing be incorporated in your design?

In Year 3 we designed a multi-storey office building while in Year 2 we designed a new housing development. In Term 1, we carried out a site visit and worked in teams of 3-4 people to assess the site on various aspects including the history, weather/climate, geology, architecture & materials, planning, traffic, site usage, mass, green areas etc. We also built a virtual model and a 1:500 scale physical model of the site for all students to use and test their ideas while developing their concepts.

This was followed by some case studies, feasibility studies, concept and architectural design, construction drawings and 3D visualisation of the final design. In Term 2, we developed the initial concepts into a set of architectural and construction drawings, and virtual 3D models. In addition to planning and design requirements, we focused on various building regulations including Part A, E, M, L, K with a specific attention to the Part B (Fire Safety).

During the last year, we enjoyed learning Revit, Lumion, SketchUp, InDesign and AutoCAD as well as some state-of-the-art energy and building performance simulation software packages including EnergyPlus and IES(VE). In the research module we had the opportunity to work on various subject including Passive Design, Thermal Comfort, Indoor Air Quality, and History and Theory of Architectural Technology. The design, technical and research modules are linked in a way to help students become more competent in the analysis and interpretation of the site, feasibility studies, concept design, architectural and detailed drawings as well as in developing project-specific research methodologies.

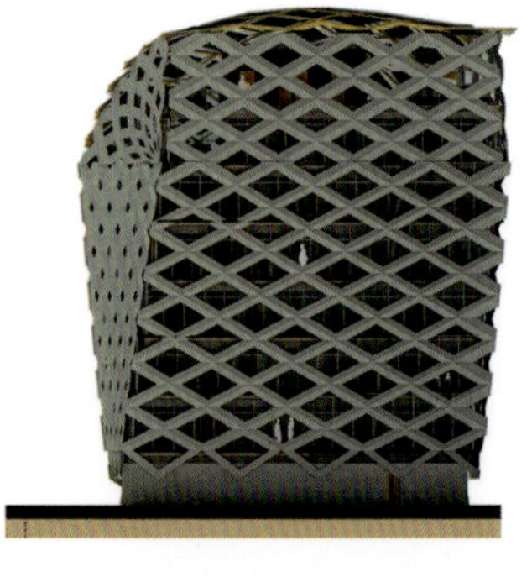

Students
Year 3; Nnamdi Ajaelu; Johnverlou Bergonia; Diana Andreea Burducea; Hala Elenany; Serge Ilunga; Sovanrattanak Rattanak Kim; Harry O'Connor; Presley Osa Okundaye; Jydsen Zchrlyn Ombao; Ioana - Madalina Predescu; Abdulia Suffian Bangura; Danny Tran; Abdul Yusuf; Jake Dacosta Augustin; Sosan Khalid; Joel Shroader

Year 2; Jason Bailey; Jordan Moore; Maryam Nasar; Sophie Naylor; Jeremiah Olabode; Muhammad Saqib; Thomas Wheeler; Attila Borca; Mathulan Paramanadan; James Landen

Year 1; Abu Jalloh; Jeremiah Olabode; Abir Choudhury; Daniel Bonney-Andrews; Nathaniel Akinlolu; Udeme Asanga; Jason Bailey; Promise Fayose; Omid Rahat; Arda Arslan; Aliyah Hoque; James Heath; Hamdi Sufi.

Special thanks to
Professor Sean Smith; Dr Masoud Sajjadian

www.uel.ac.uk/undergraduate/courses/bsc-hons-architectural-design-technology

@ADT_UEL (Twitter)

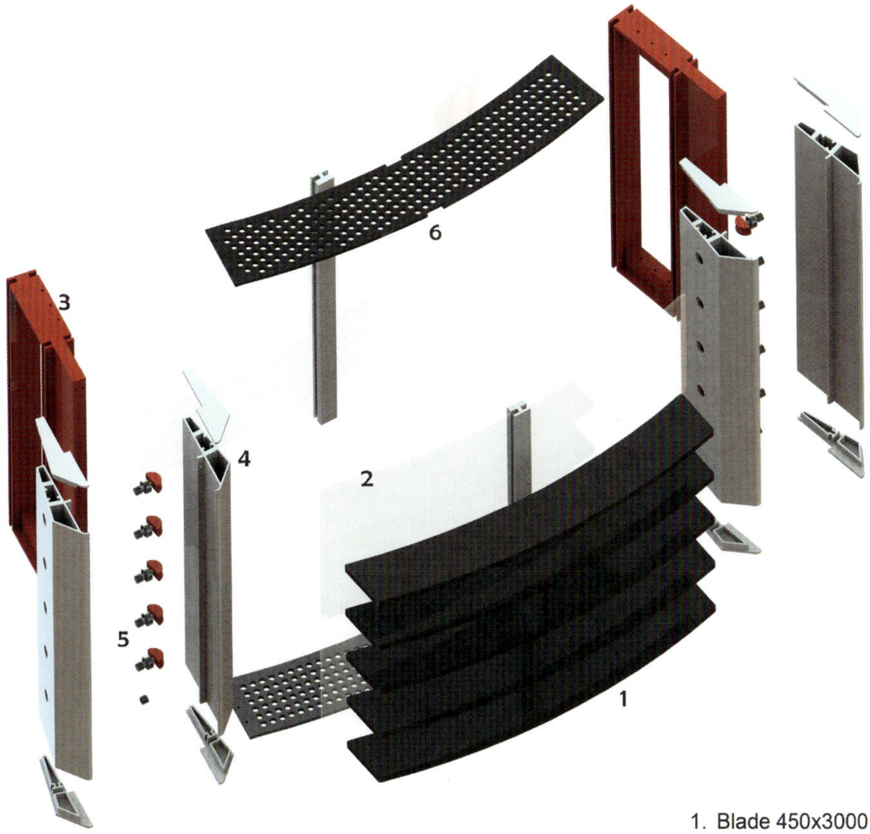

1. Blade 450x3000
2. Single glazed
3. Mullion
4. Cassette structure
5. Bearings
6. Perforated decking

01 Year 3; by Danny Tran **02 & 04** Year 3; by Ioana Predescu **03** Year 1; by Aliyah Hoque **05 & 06** Year 3; by Serge Ilunga

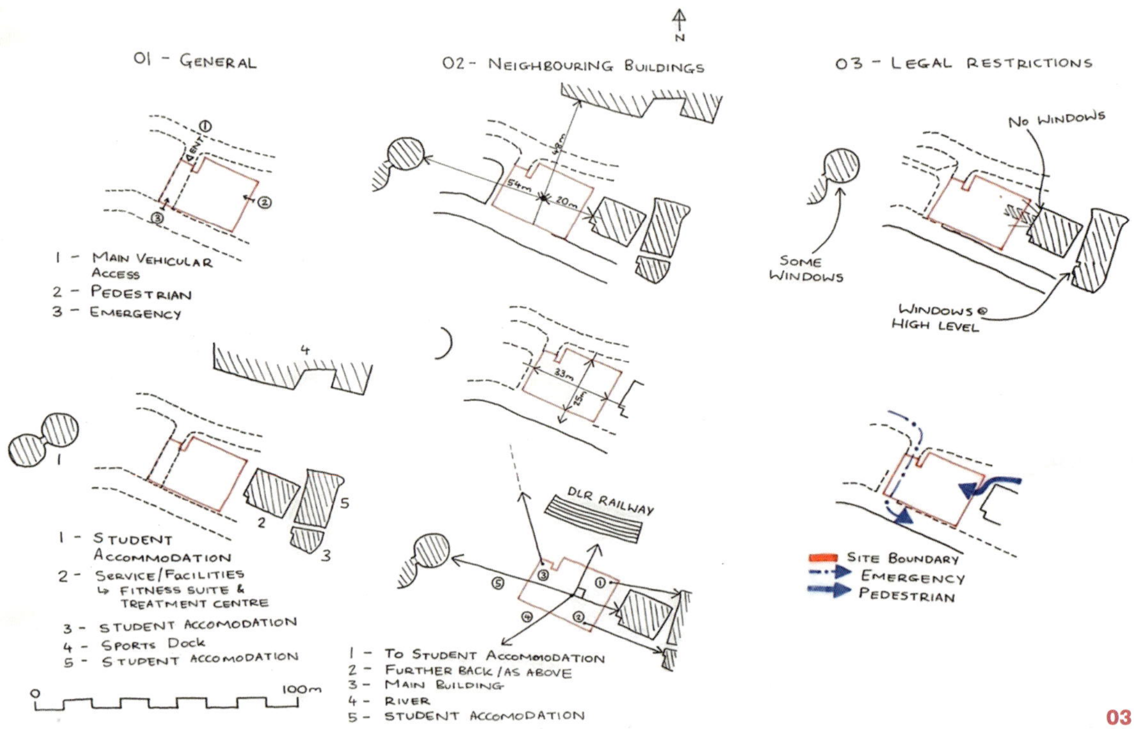

03

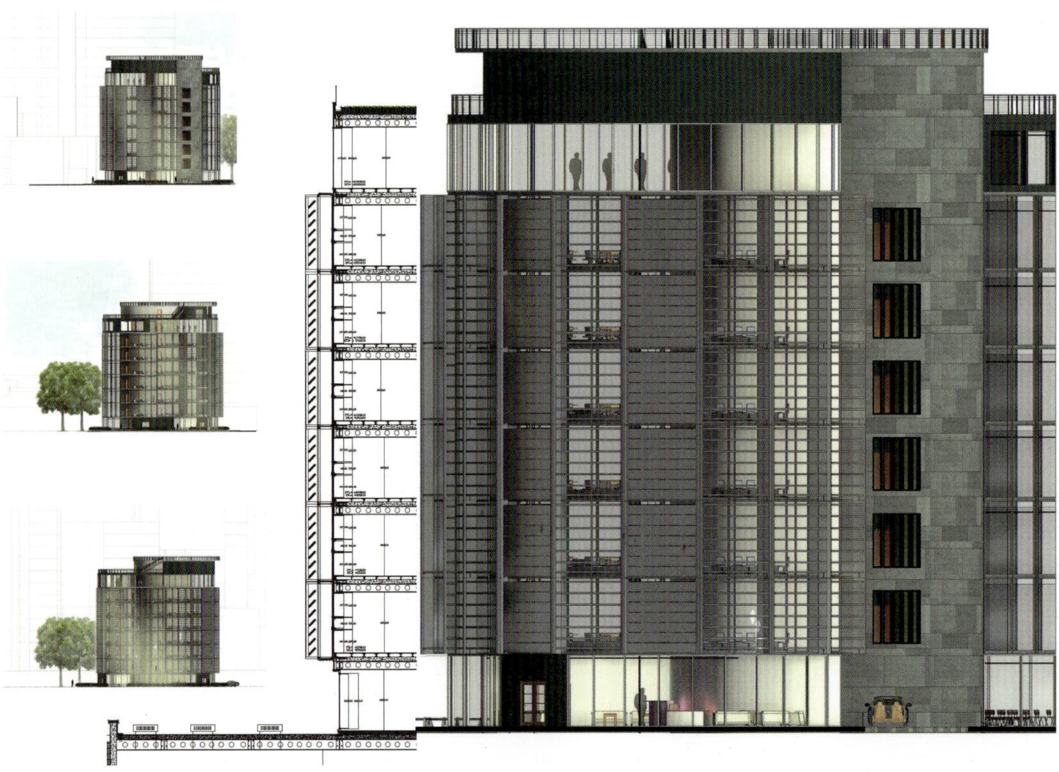

04

G
F
RoofTop
30000
Level 6
23700
Level 4
16300
Level 3
12600
Level 2
8900
Level 1
5200
office ground level
6300
1200
3800
1300
3700
900
2700
100
4200
2464
1802
2163
6849
3647
815
2580
2277
3000
1122
3000

05

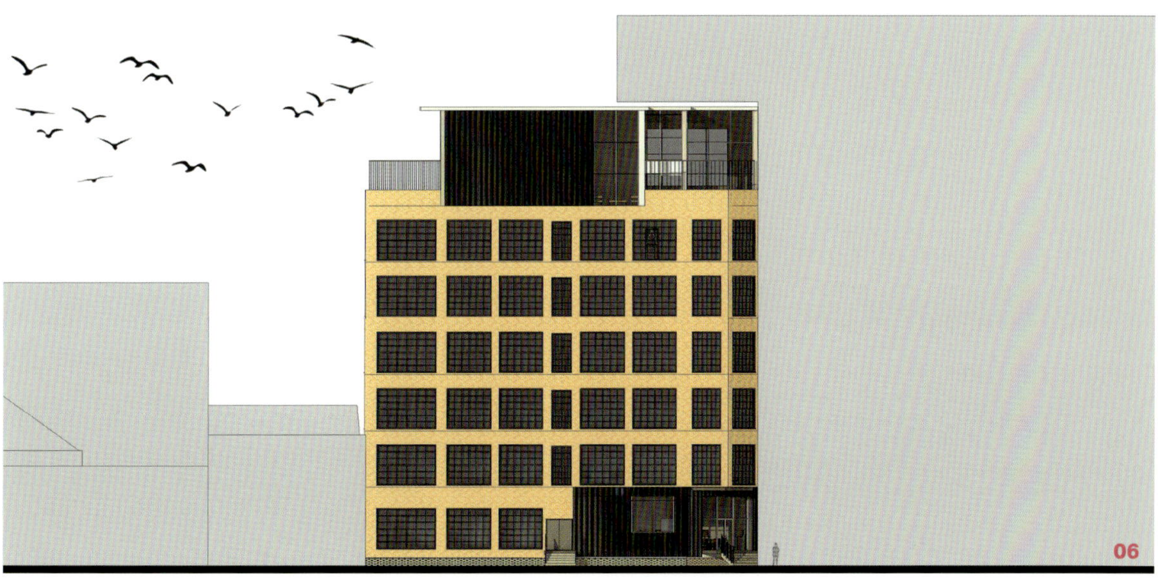

06

07 & 08 Year 1; by Daniel Bonney-Andrews **09** Year 3; by Johnverlou Bergonia **10** Year 3; by Ioana Predescu

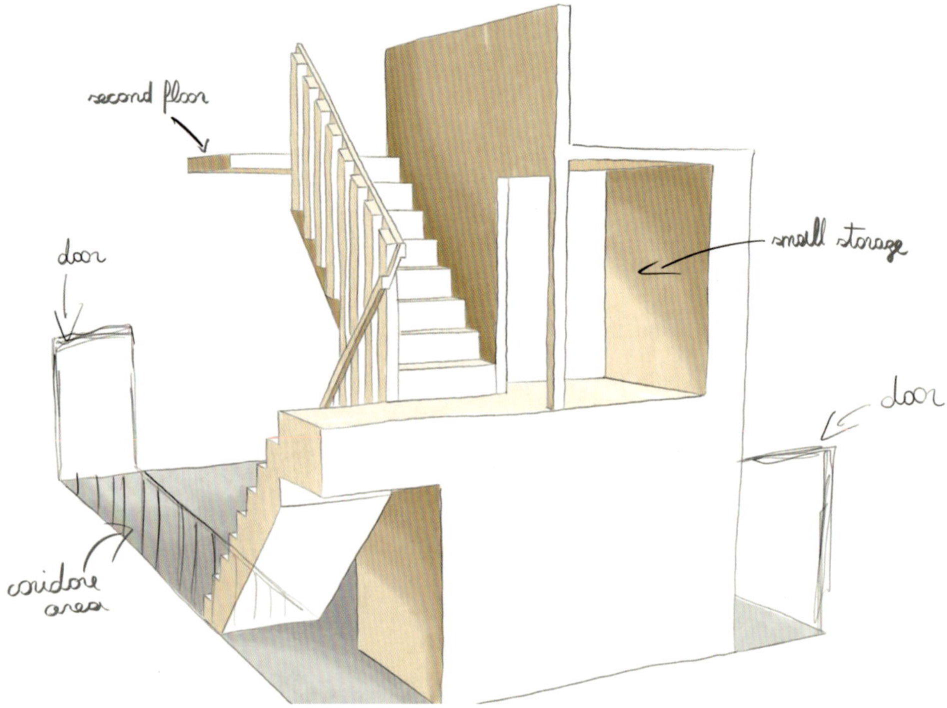

07

08

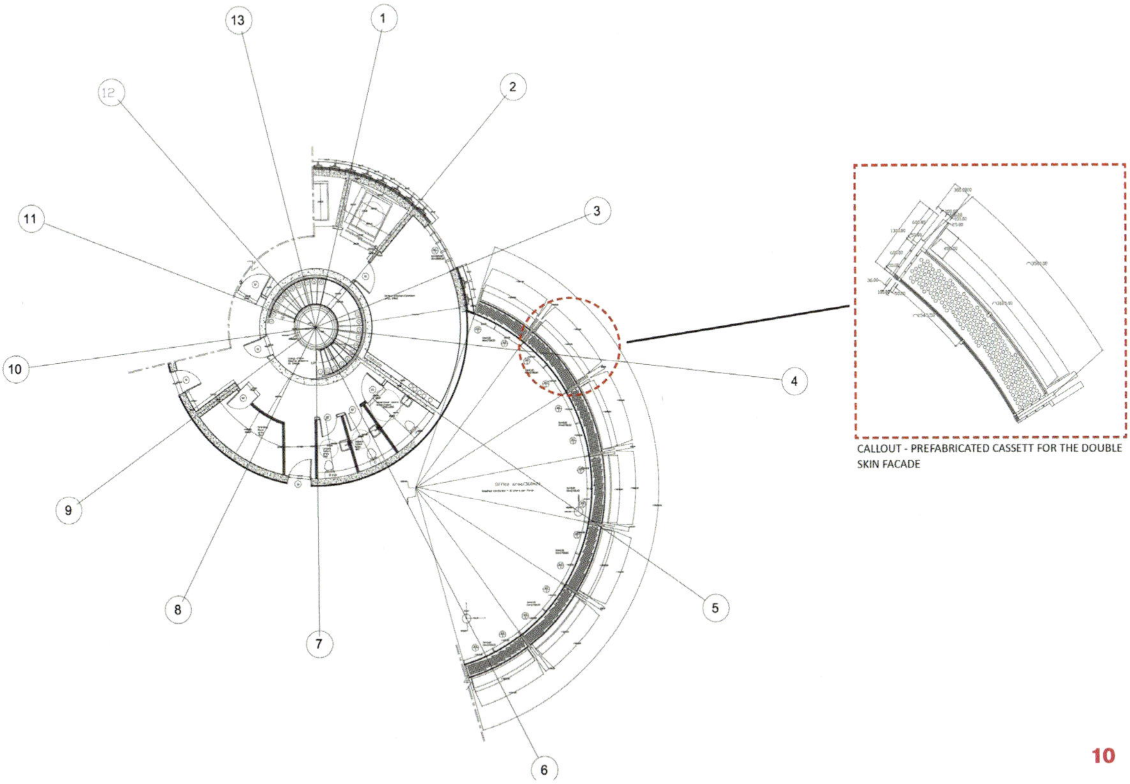

CALLOUT - PREFABRICATED CASSETT FOR THE DOUBLE SKIN FACADE

11-15 Year 1; ADT Students

11

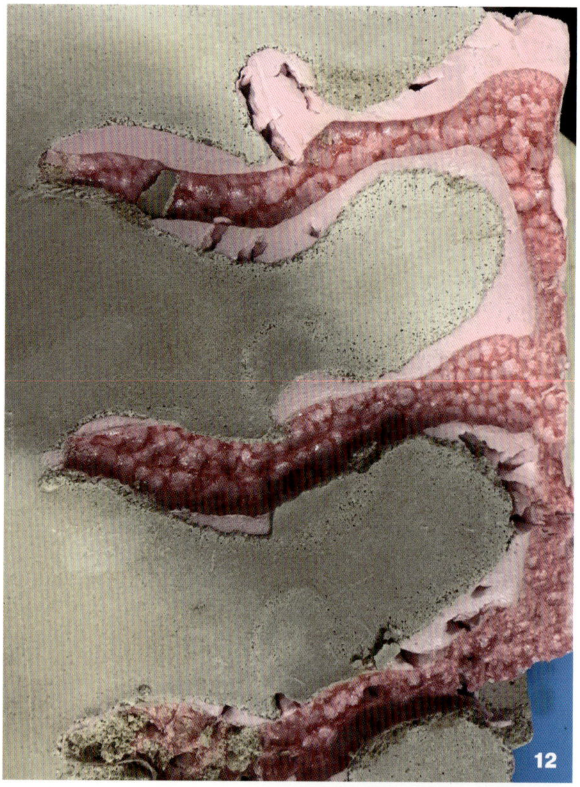
12

13

14

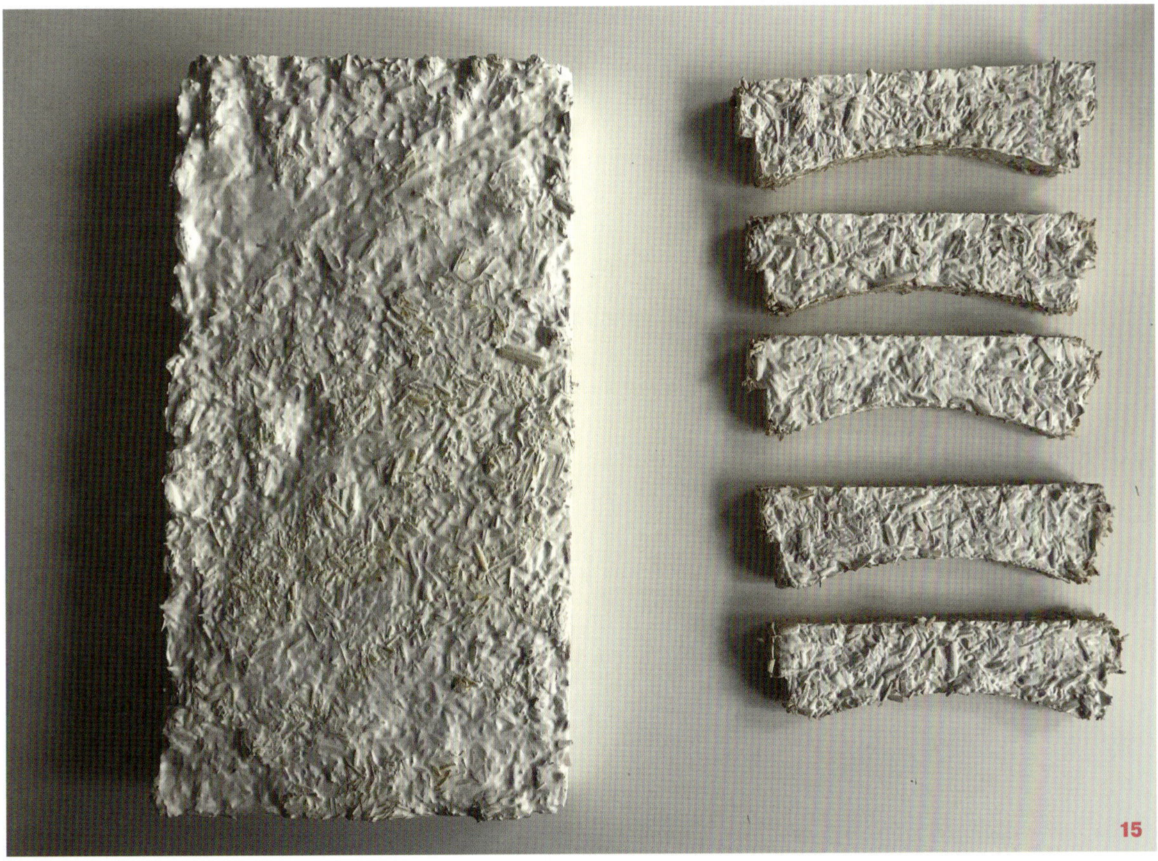

15

16-17&19 Year 3; by Danny Tran **18** Year 2; by Attila Borca

16

Tag	No.	Handed	Location
D1			
	01	RHR	External
D2			
	01	RHR	External
	02	LH	Internal
	03	RHR	Internal
D3			
	01	LH	Internal
	02	RHR	Internal
FD			
	01	RH	Internal
	02	LHR	Internal
	03	LH	Internal
	04	RHR	Internal
	05	RHR	Internal
	06	LH	Internal

17

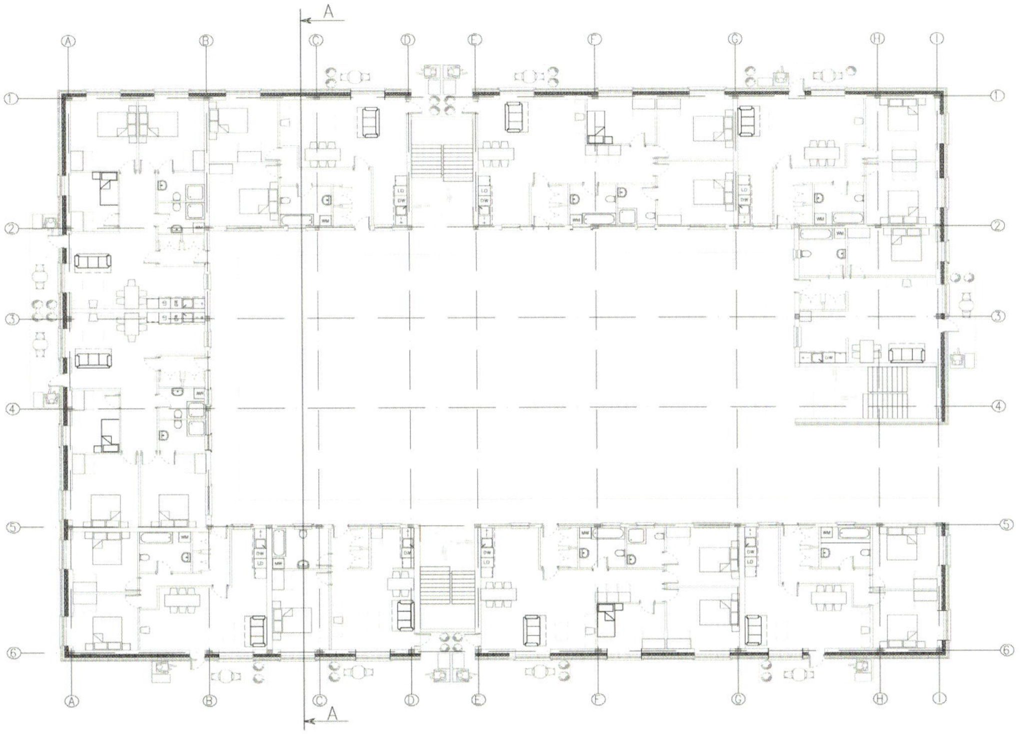

18

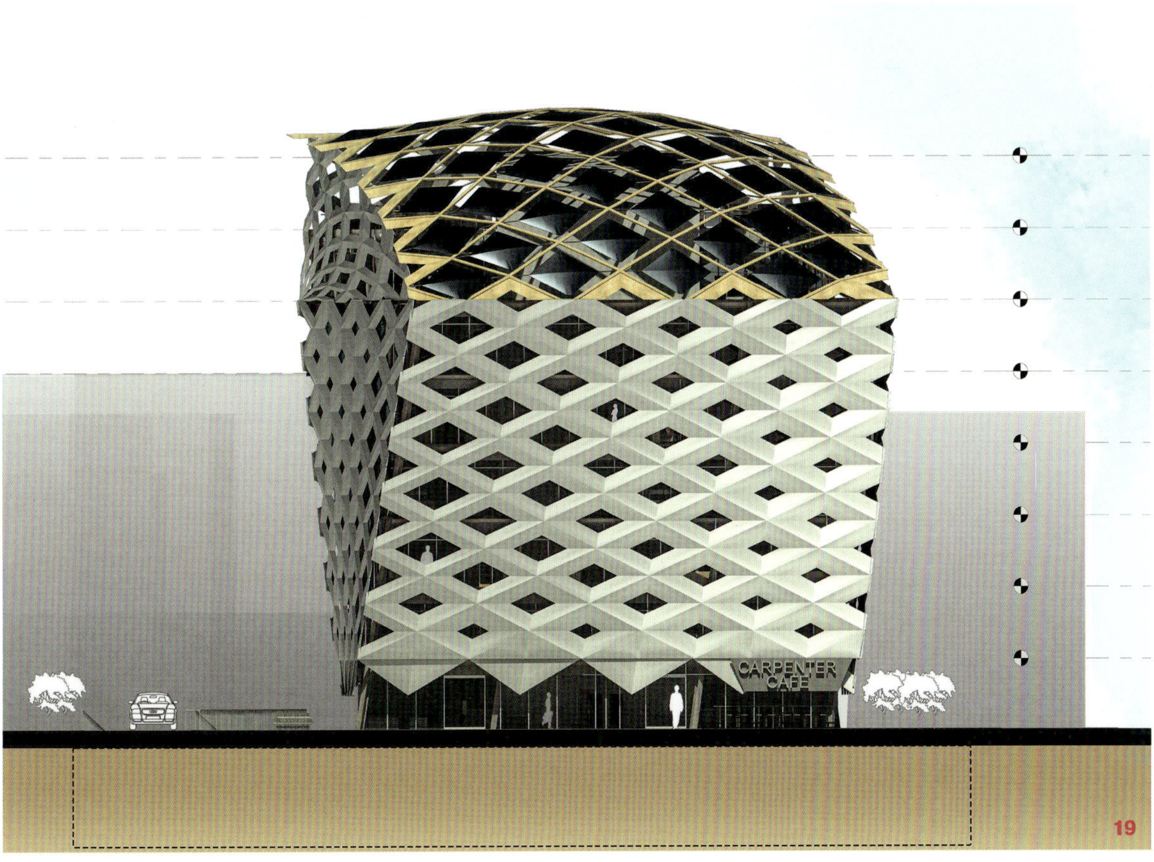

19

20-22 Year 3; by Danny Tran **23** Year 3; by Ioana Predescu .

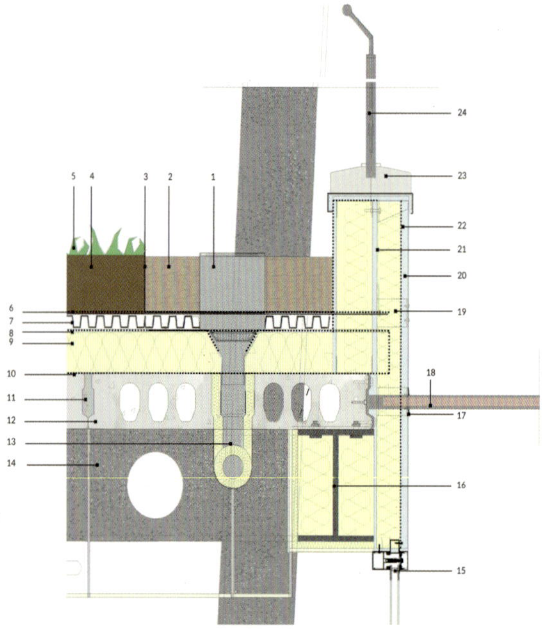

1: Chamber to Rainwater Pipe Drainage
2: 300mm Gravel edge channel
3: Retention Trim
4: Plant Growing medium
5: Plant and vegetation
6: Filter fleece preventing substrate entering drainage mat
7: Drainage Mat
8: Waterproof Roof barrier
9: 150 Rigid Insulation
10: Vapour control membrane under insulation
11: Grout between precast slabs
12: 200mm Precast Concrete Slab
13: Insulated 70mm Pipe - Rockwool T90/450 Insulation to pipelines
14: 400x400mm Steel Beam with Intumescent Coating (M61/120)
15: 70x150mm Transom unit
16: 400x 00mm Steel Beam with Intumescent Coating (M61/120)
17: Rubber Gasket
18: Facade Skin Anchor, with Thermal Break
19: Support Bracket
20: Aluminium Cladding
21: Steel Wall with Insulation and weather resistant membrane
22: Cladding Rail
23: Parapet Cap for Handrail Mount
24: ASF L30/55 Proprietary balustrades 1200mm handrail in case of tolerance mistakes.

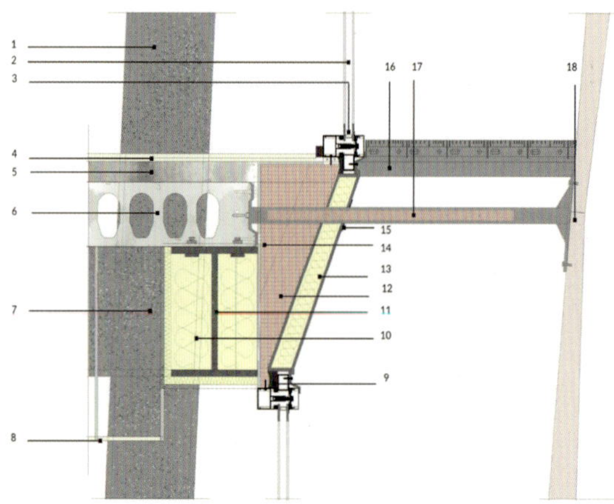

1: 320x400mm Steel Column with Intumescent Coating (M61/120)
2: Double Glazed panes with argon
3: EW50 (Aluminco) Transom unit
4: Floor Finish
5: Cemfloor CT C25F5 M10/160 Proprietary self smoothing levelling screeds 100mm
6: 200mm Precast Concrete Slab
7: 400x400mm Steel Beam with Intumescent Coating (M61/120)
8: Norwood Metal Pan modular suspended ceilings K40/10 Unit/ with 600x600mm tiles
9: Rubber Gasket
10: 150mm insulation protecting perimeter beams
11: 400x400mm Steel Beam with Intumescent Coating (M61/120)
12: Fire Stop between Levels
13: Insulated Spandrel Panel
14: Transom to Structure Bracket
15: Rubber Gasket
16: Elefant Mesh Q10/312 Footway grating
17: Facade Skin Anchor, with Thermal Break
18. Aluminium Facade

20

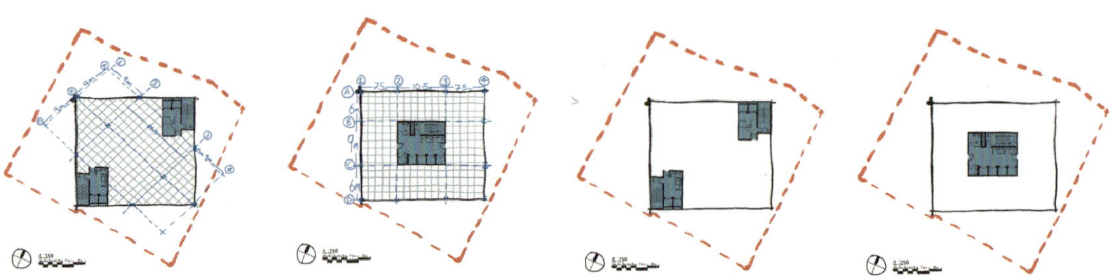

22

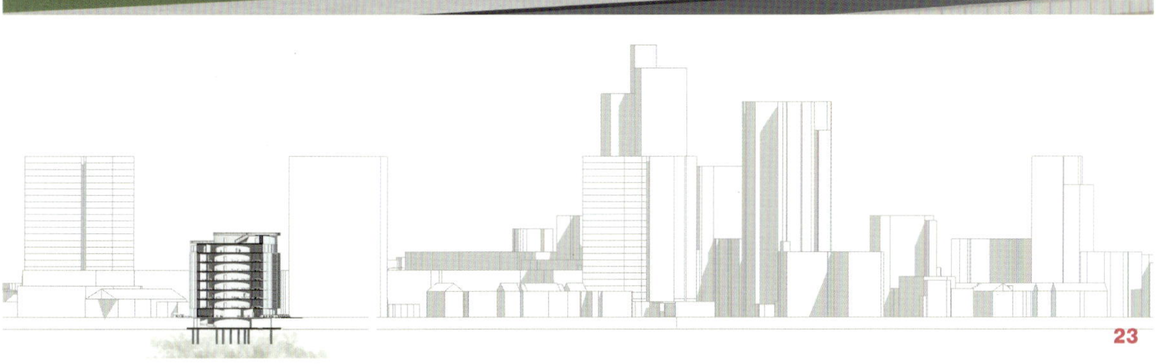

23

24 Year 2; by Jordan Moore **25** Year 3; by Ioana Predescu
26 & 27 Year 3; by Danny Tran

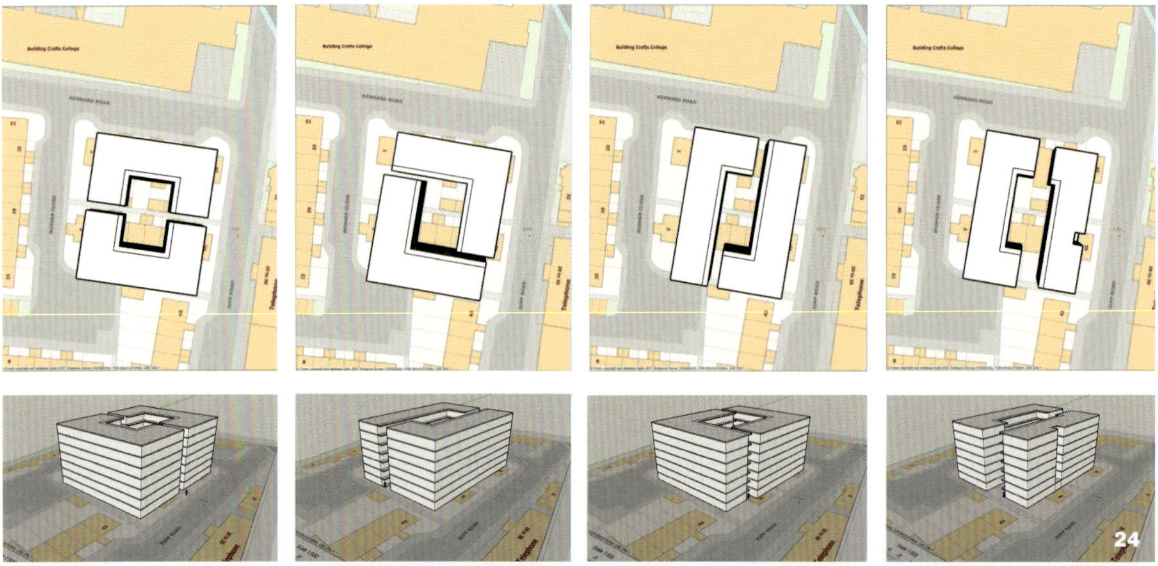

24

25

26

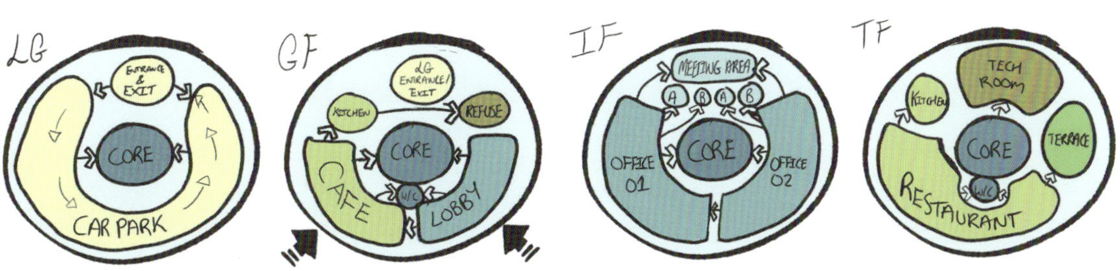
LG
ENTRANCE & EXIT
CORE
CAR PARK
GF
LG ENTRANCE/EXIT
KITCHEN
REFUSE
CORE
CAFE
W/C
LOBBY
1F
MEETING AREA
A
B
A
B
OFFICE 01
CORE
OFFICE 02
TF
TECH ROOM
KITCHEN
CORE
TERRACE
W/C
RESTAURANT

27

28 Year 3; by Ioana Predescu **29-31** Year 2; by Thomas Wheeler
32 Year 2; by Attila Borca .

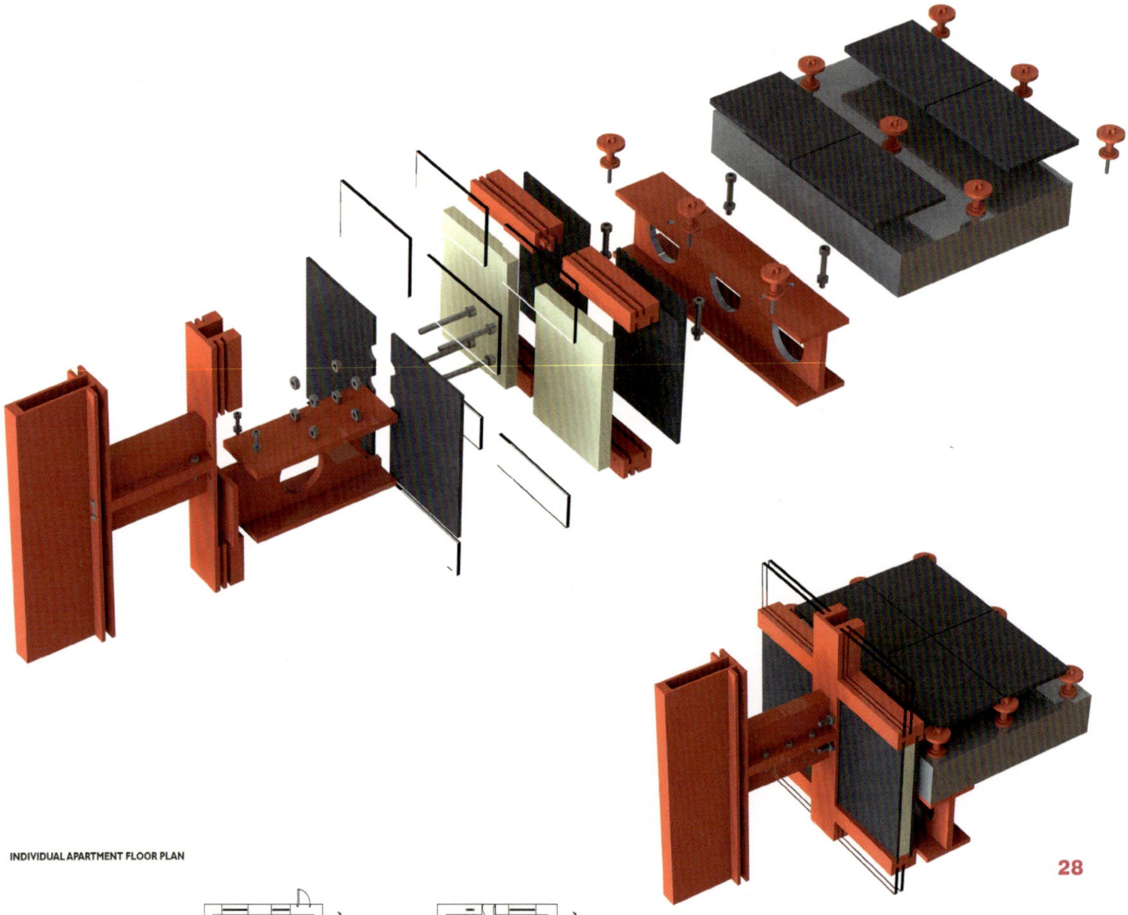

28

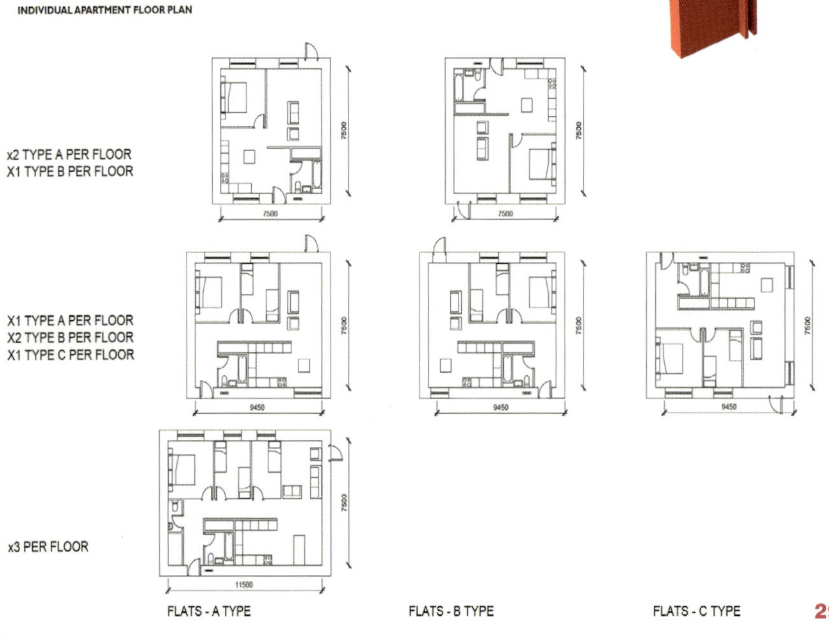

29

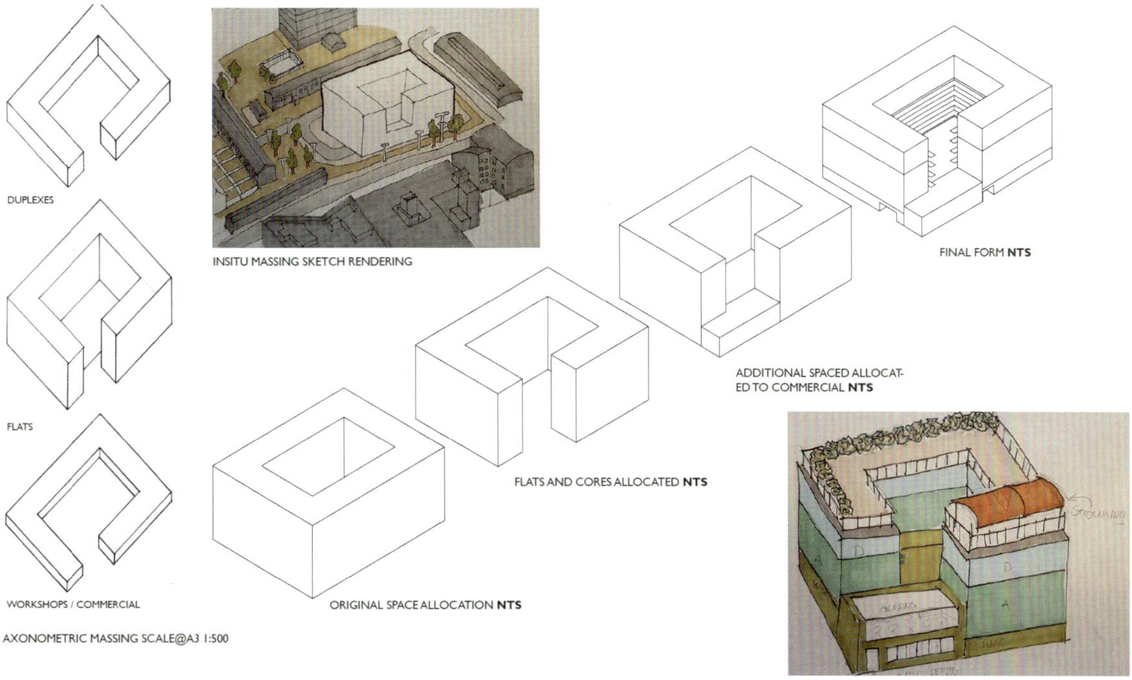
DUPLEXES
FLATS
WORKSHOPS / COMMERCIAL
AXONOMETRIC MASSING SCALE@A3 1:500
INSITU MASSING SKETCH RENDERING
ORIGINAL SPACE ALLOCATION NTS
FLATS AND CORES ALLOCATED NTS
ADDITIONAL SPACED ALLOCATED TO COMMERCIAL NTS
FINAL FORM NTS

30

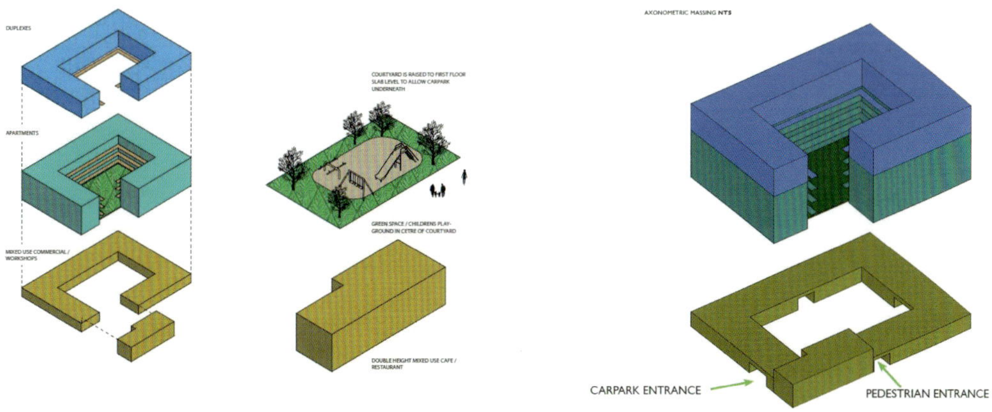
DUPLEXES
APARTMENTS
MIXED USE COMMERCIAL / WORKSHOPS
COURTYARD IS RAISED TO FIRST FLOOR SLAB LEVEL TO ALLOW CARPARK UNDERNEATH
GREEN SPACE / CHILDRENS PLAYGROUND IN CETRE OF COURTYARD
DOUBLE HEIGHT MIXED USE CAFE / RESTAURANT
AXONOMETRIC MASSING NTS
CARPARK ENTRANCE
PEDESTRIAN ENTRANCE

31

N

32

33 & 34 Year 3; by Johnverlou Bergonia **35 & 37** Year 3; by Danny Tran
36 Year 1; by Aliyah Hoque

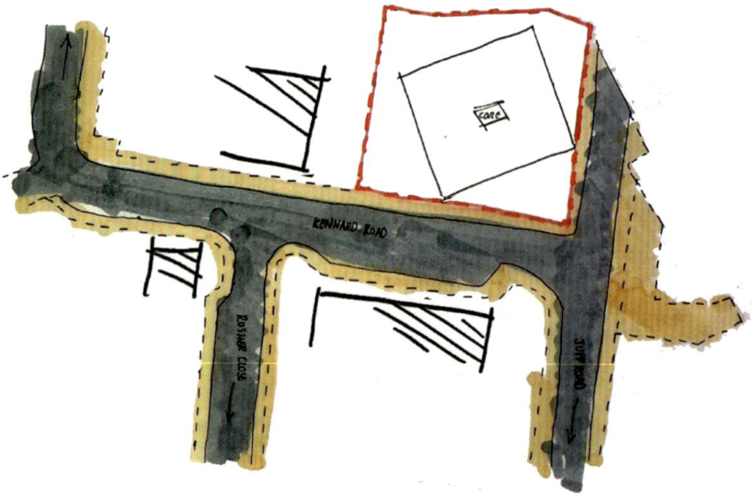

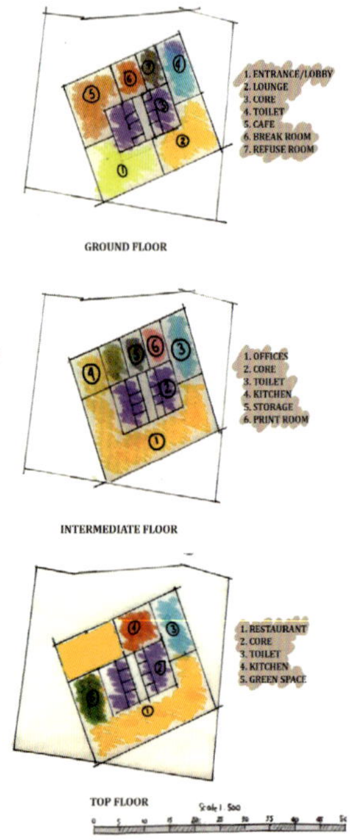

33 **34**

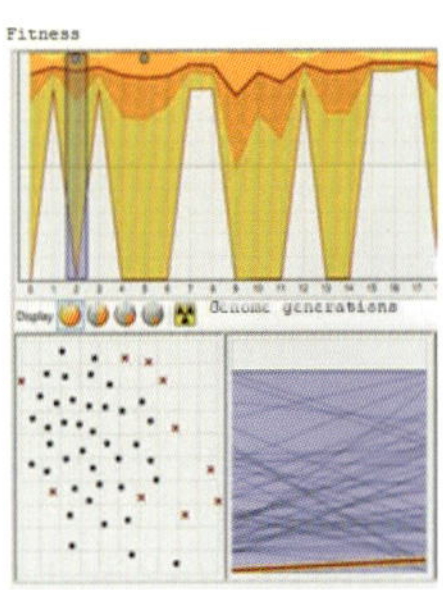

Figure 95: Galapagos Results - Best from Genome 2

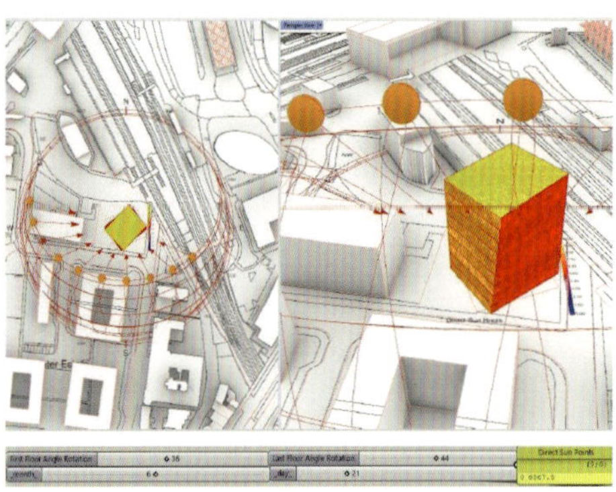

Figure 96: Genome 2 Summer Solstice Analysis (Direct Sun Score: Lower the better)

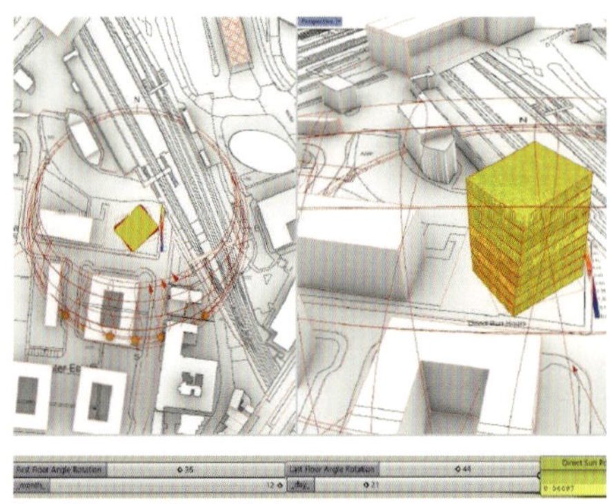

Figure 97: Genome 2 Winter Solstice Analysis (Direct Sun Score: Higher the better)

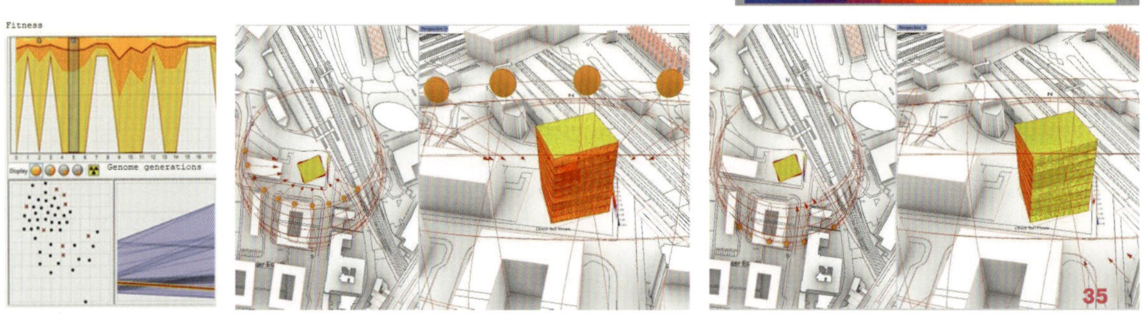

35

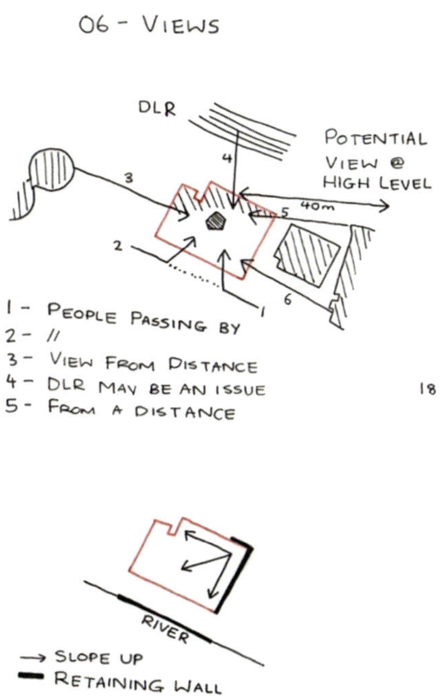
06 - VIEWS
DLR
POTENTIAL
VIEW @
HIGH LEVEL
40m
1 - PEOPLE PASSING BY
2 - //
3 - VIEW FROM DISTANCE
4 - DLR MAY BE AN ISSUE
5 - FROM A DISTANCE
RIVER
→ SLOPE UP
▬ RETAINING WALL

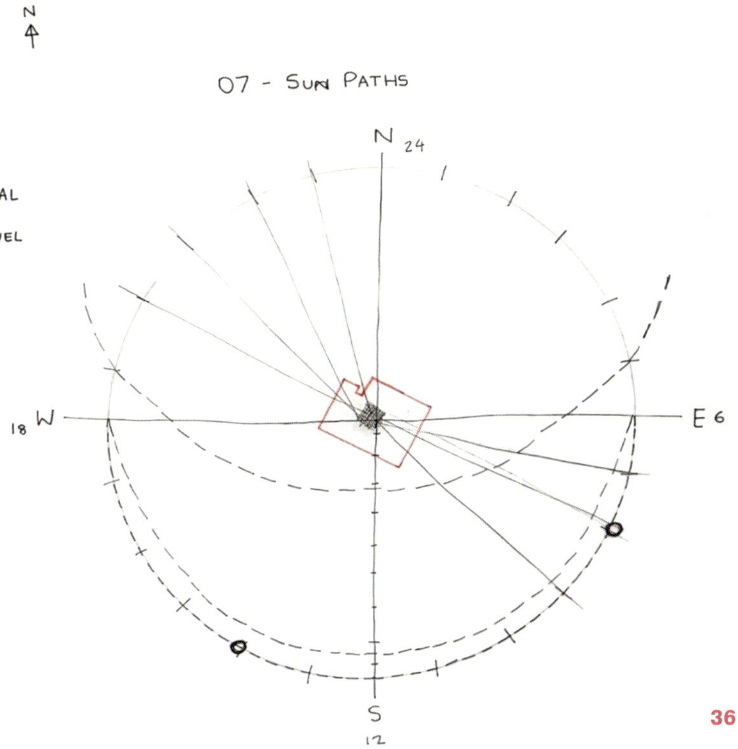
N
07 - SUN PATHS
N 24
18 W
E 6
S
12

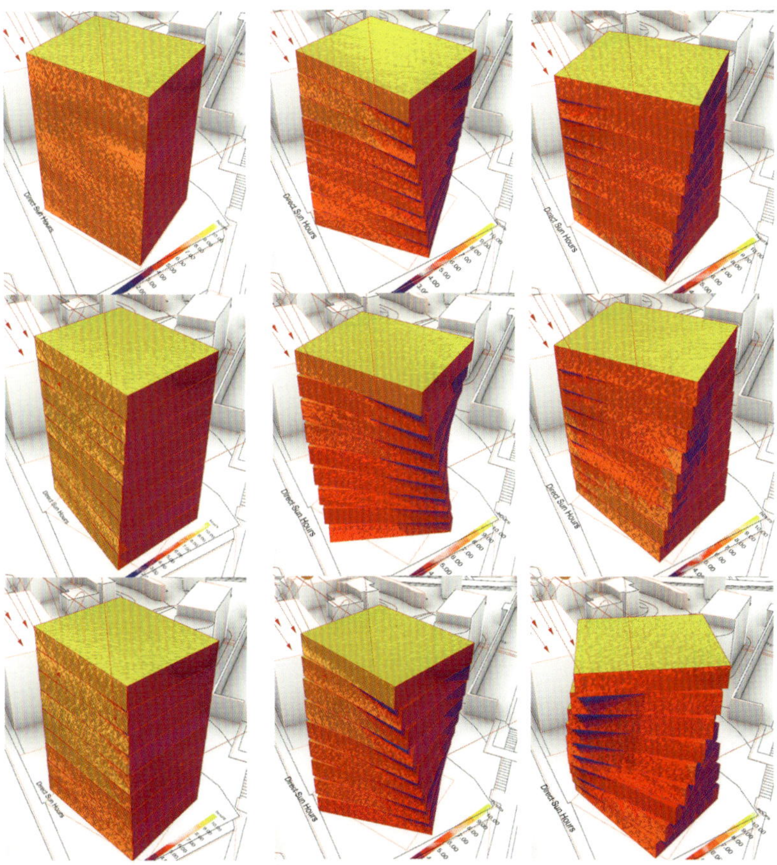

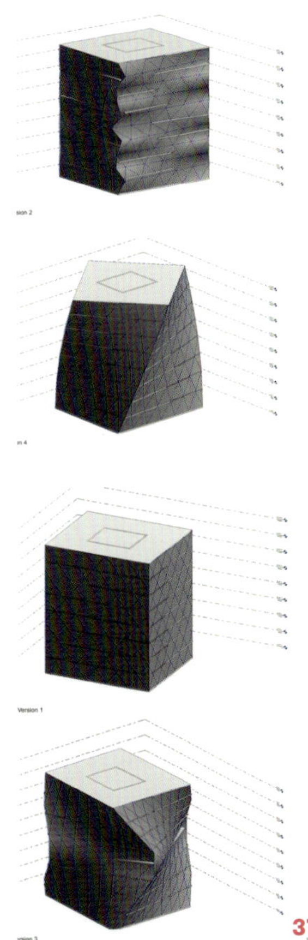
Version 1

38 Year 3; byJydsen Zchrlyn Ombao **39 & 40** Year 3; by Ioana Predescu
41 Year 3; by Serge Ilunga **42** Year 2; by Thomas Wheeler .

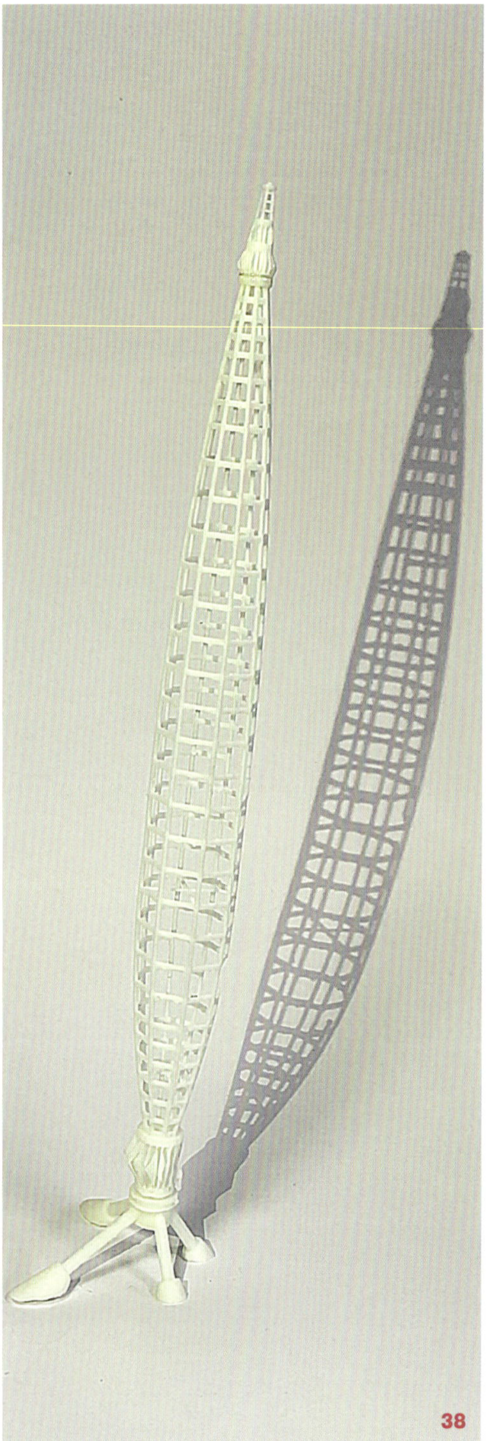

38

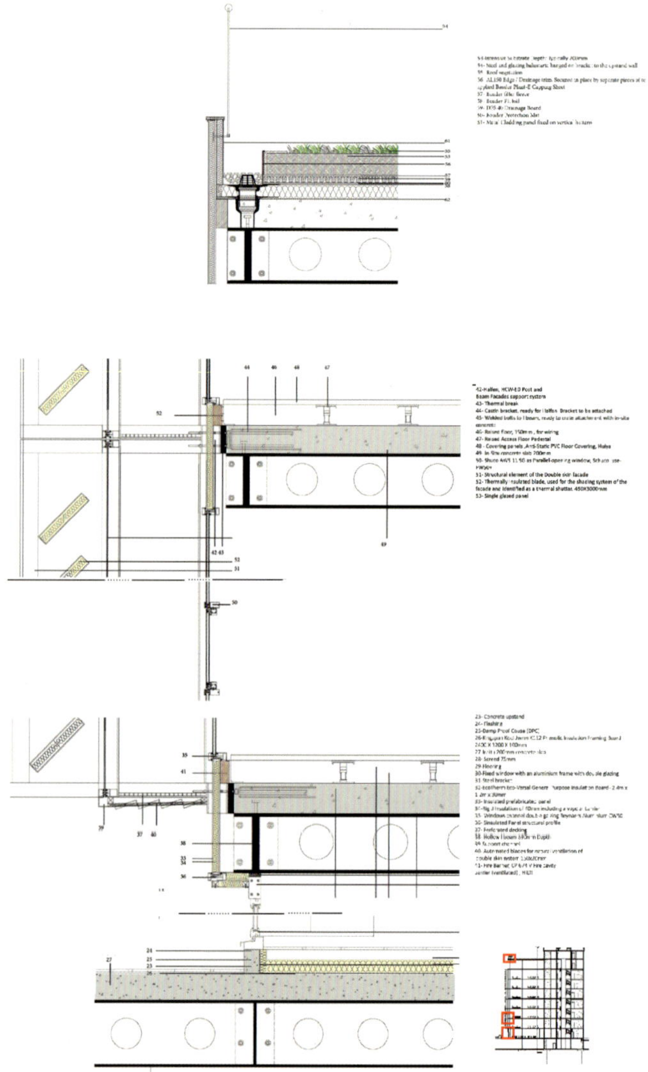

39

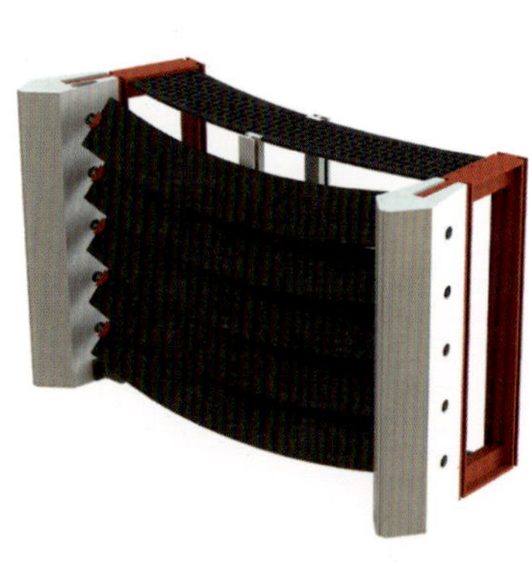

40

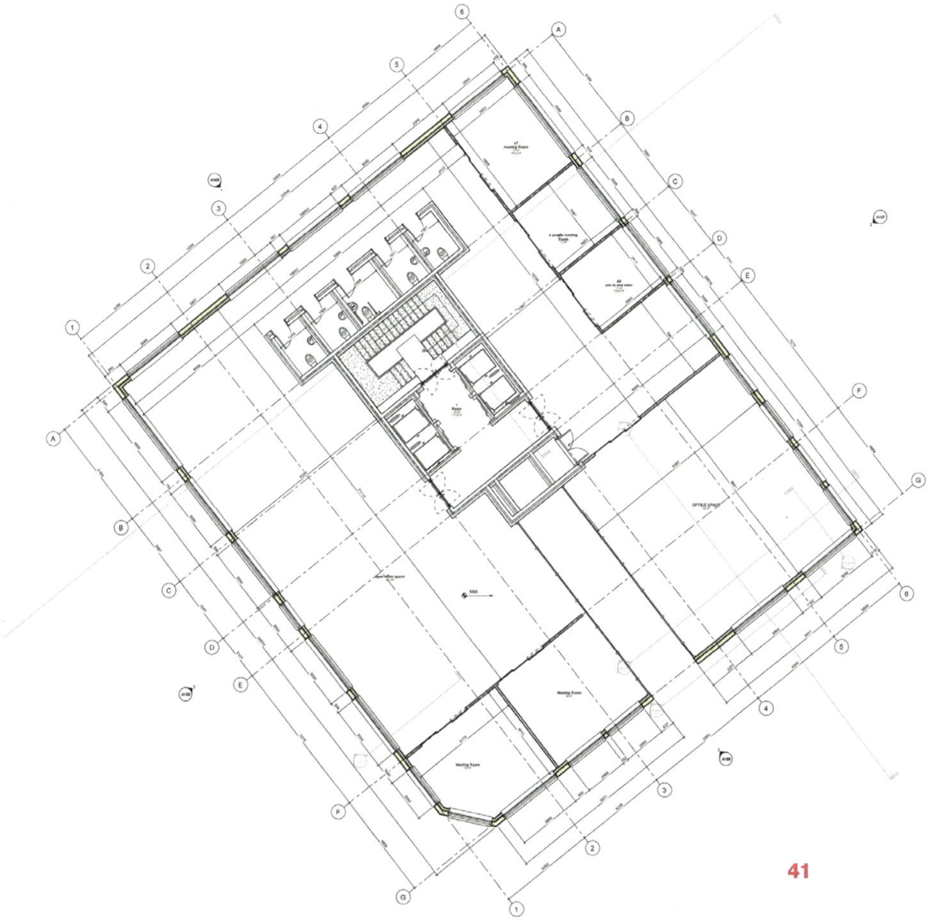

41

42

43 & 44 Year 1; by Udeme Asanga **45-47** Year 1; by Daniel Bonney-Andrews **48 & 49** Year 2; by Maryam Nasar **50** Year 3; by Ioana Predescu.

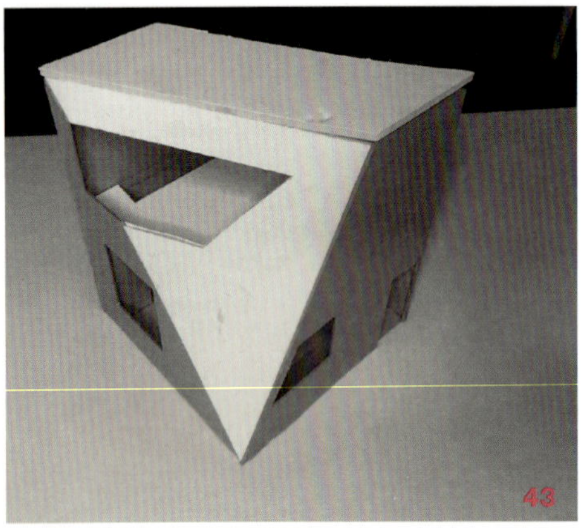

43

45

44

46

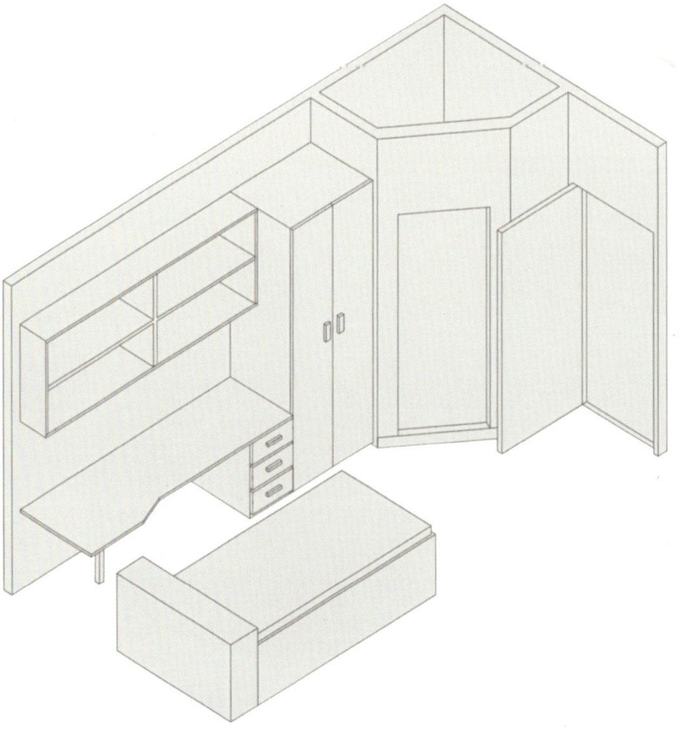

47

TOWERS

48

PRESPECTIVE

49

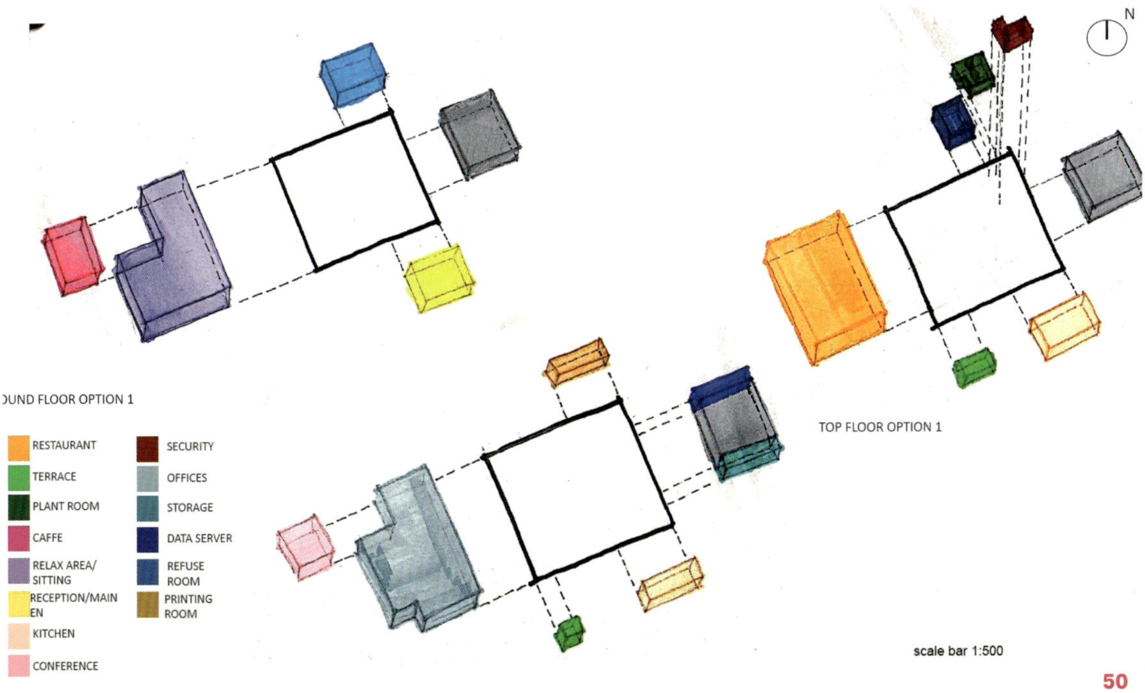
N
OUND FLOOR OPTION 1
TOP FLOOR OPTION 1
RESTAURANT
TERRACE
PLANT ROOM
CAFFE
RELAX AREA/ SITTING
RECEPTION/MAIN EN
KITCHEN
CONFERENCE
SECURITY
OFFICES
STORAGE
DATA SERVER
REFUSE ROOM
PRINTING ROOM
scale bar 1:500

50

51-53 Year 1; by Omid Rahat **54** Year 2; by Jordan Moore **55** Year 2; by Thomas Wheeler **56** Year 2; by Attila Borca.

51

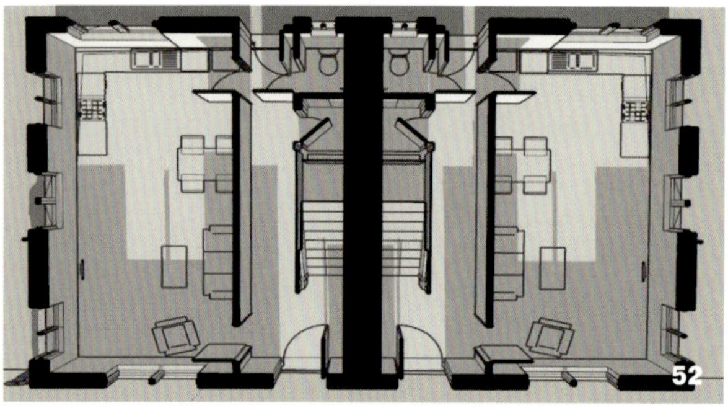

52

53

54

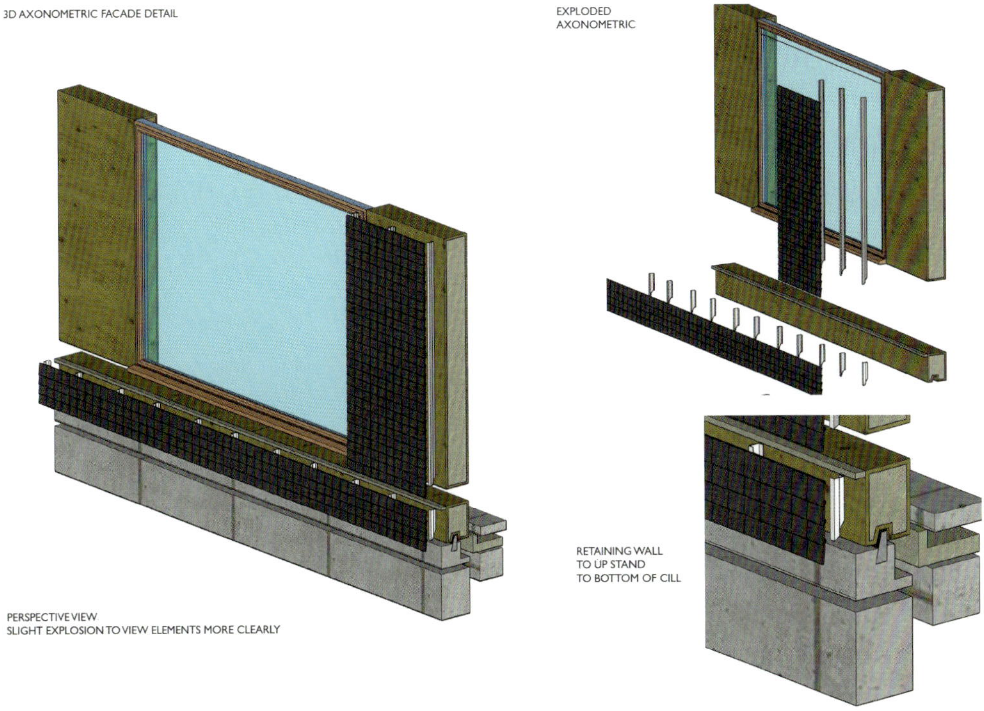
3D AXONOMETRIC FACADE DETAIL
PERSPECTIVE VIEW
SLIGHT EXPLOSION TO VIEW ELEMENTS MORE CLEARLY
EXPLODED
AXONOMETRIC
RETAINING WALL
TO UP STAND
TO BOTTOM OF CILL

55

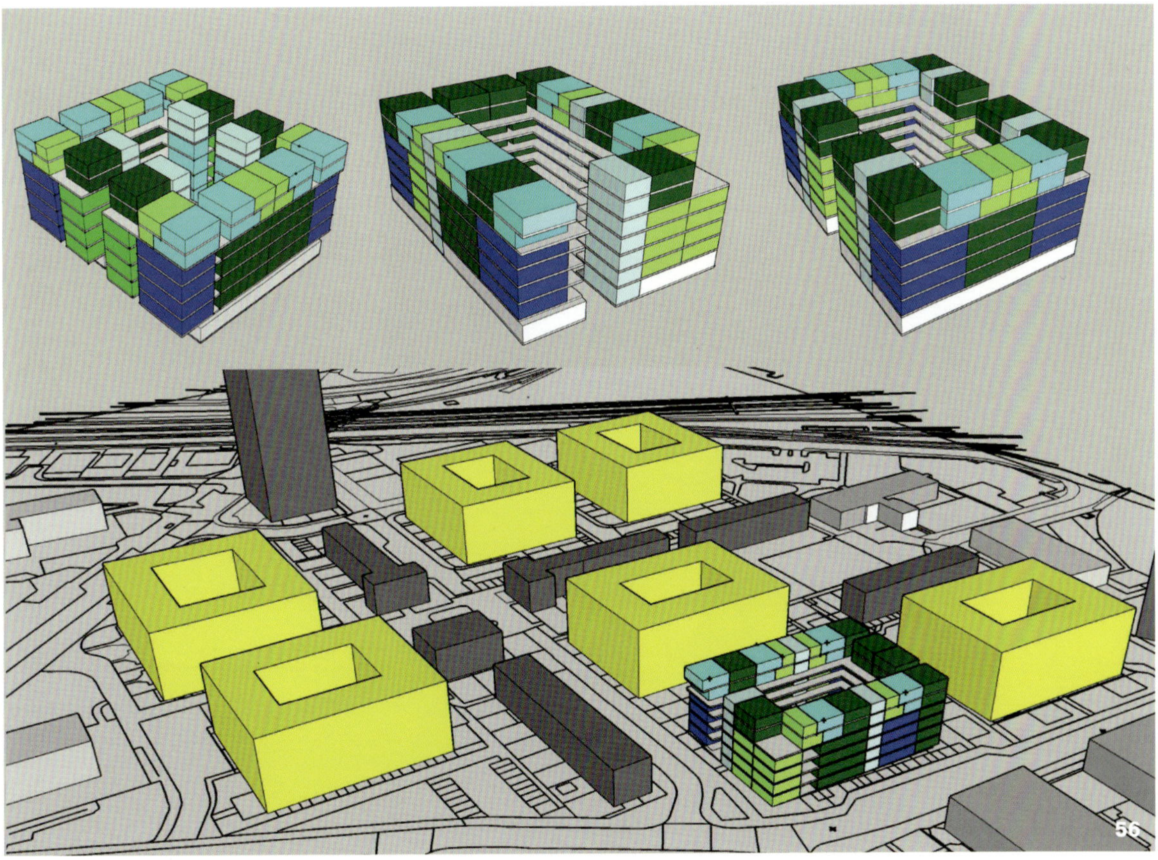

56

57 Year 2; by Thomas Wheeler **58-60** Year 3; by Danny Tran **61** Year 1; by Nnamdi Ajaelu **62** Year 3; by ADT Students **63** Year 3; by Ioana Predescu .

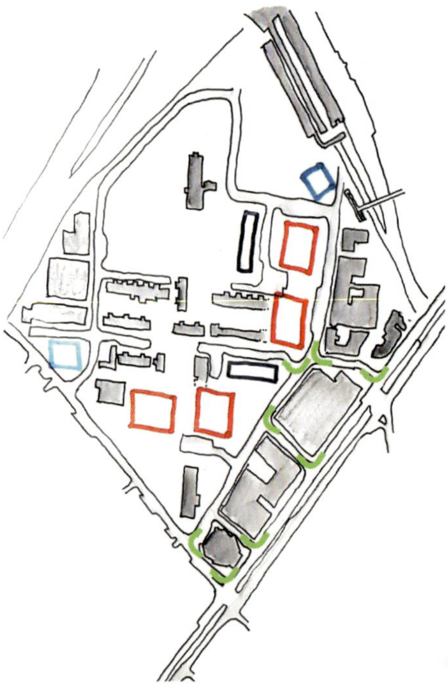

57

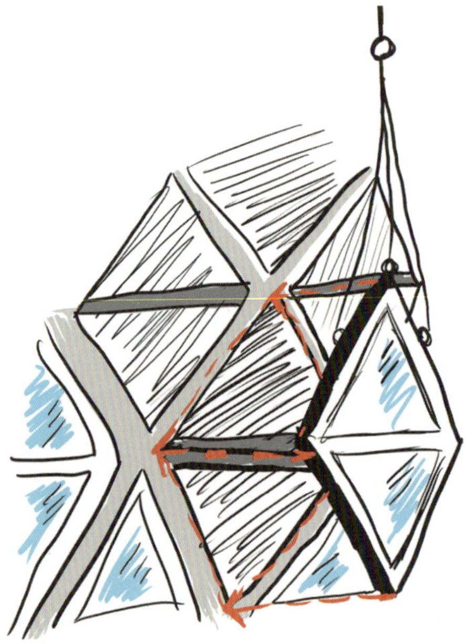

58

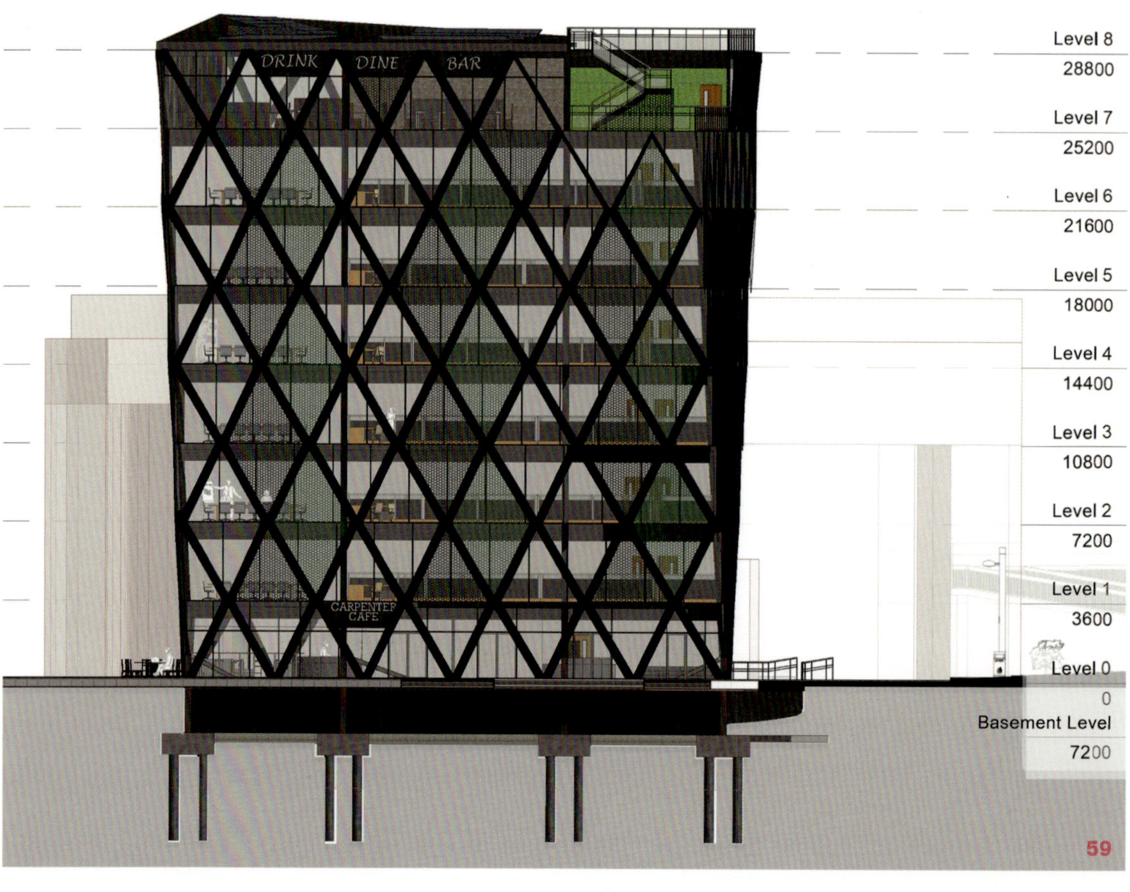

59

62

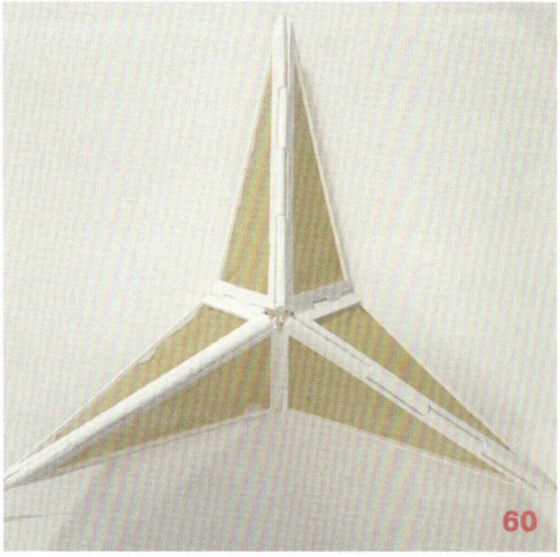
60

61

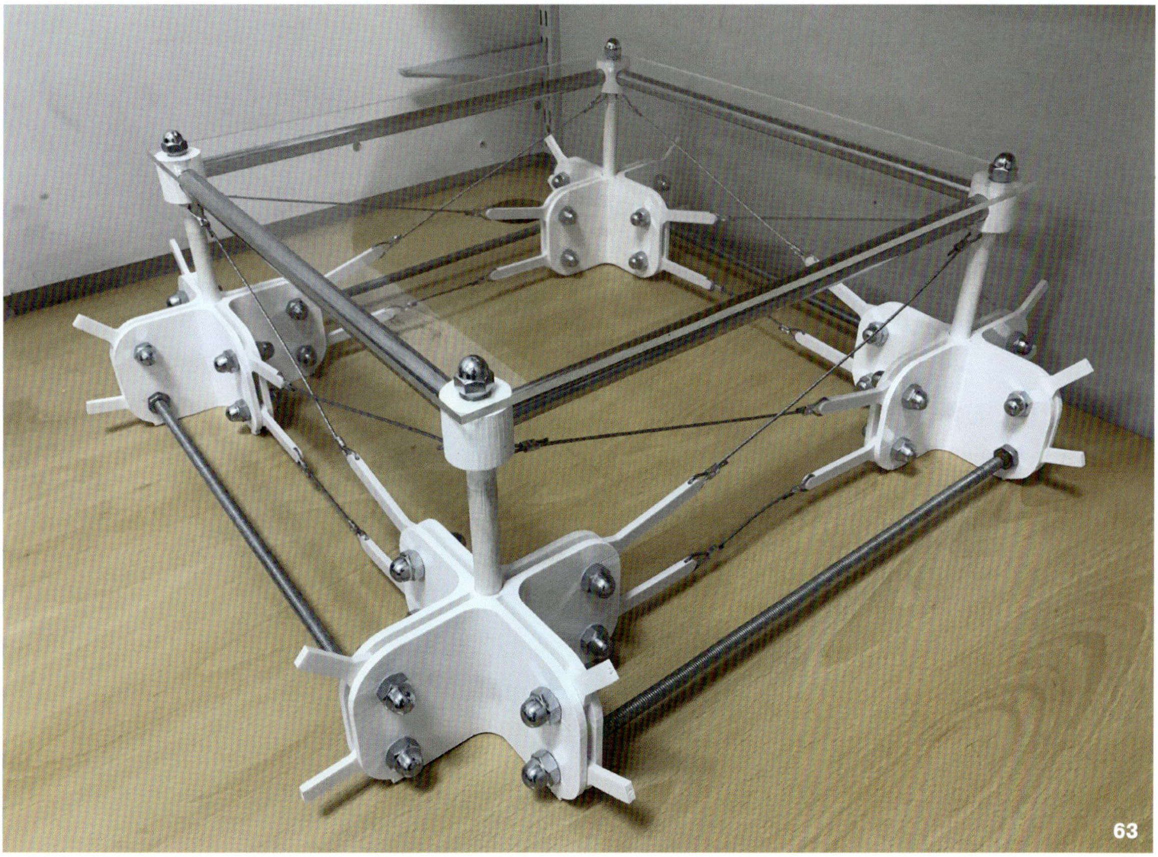
63

64 & 67 Year 3; by Ioana Predescu **65 & 68** Year 3; by Johnverlou Bergonia **66** Year 3; by Nnamdi Ajaelu

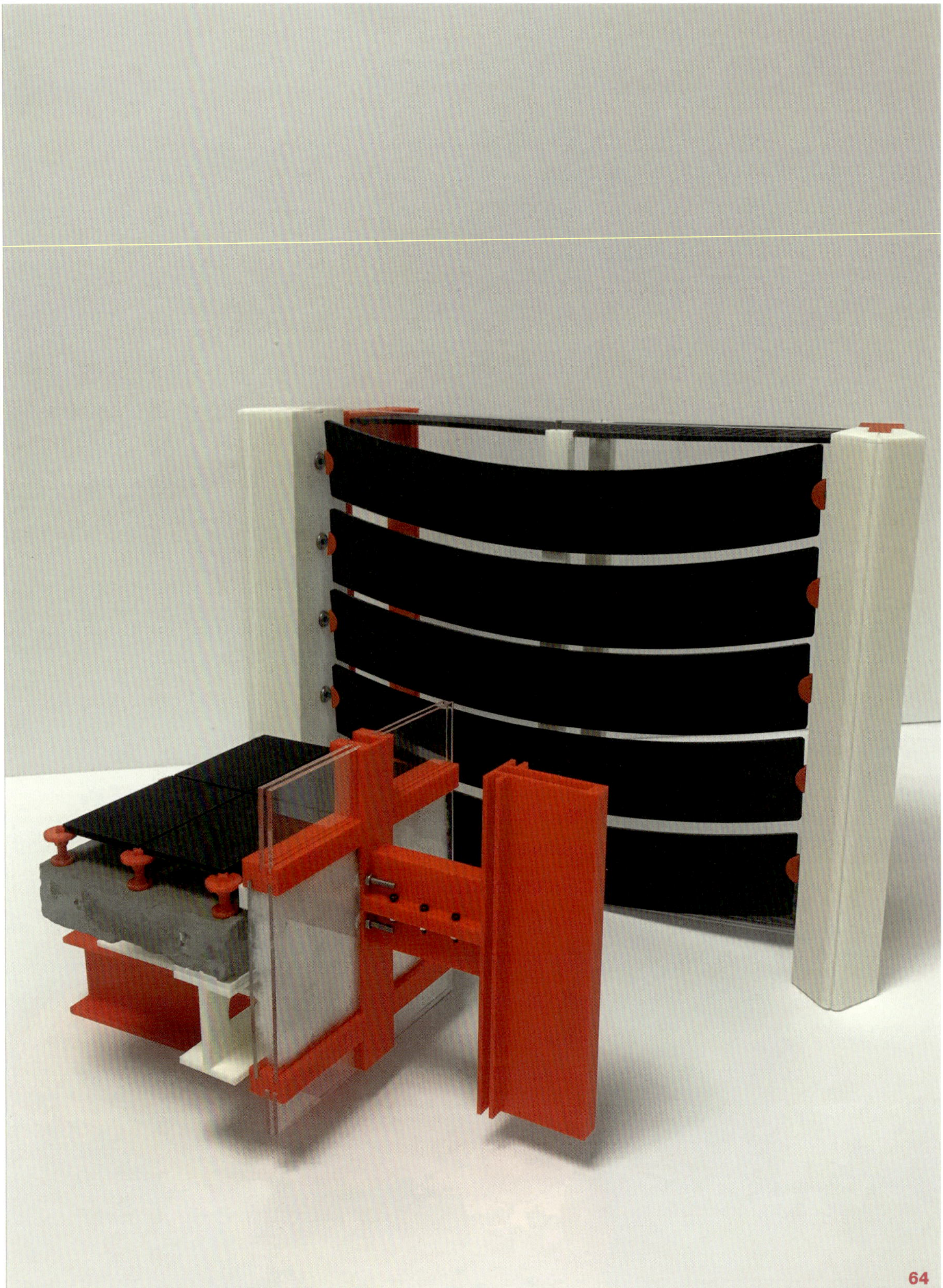

64

65

66

67

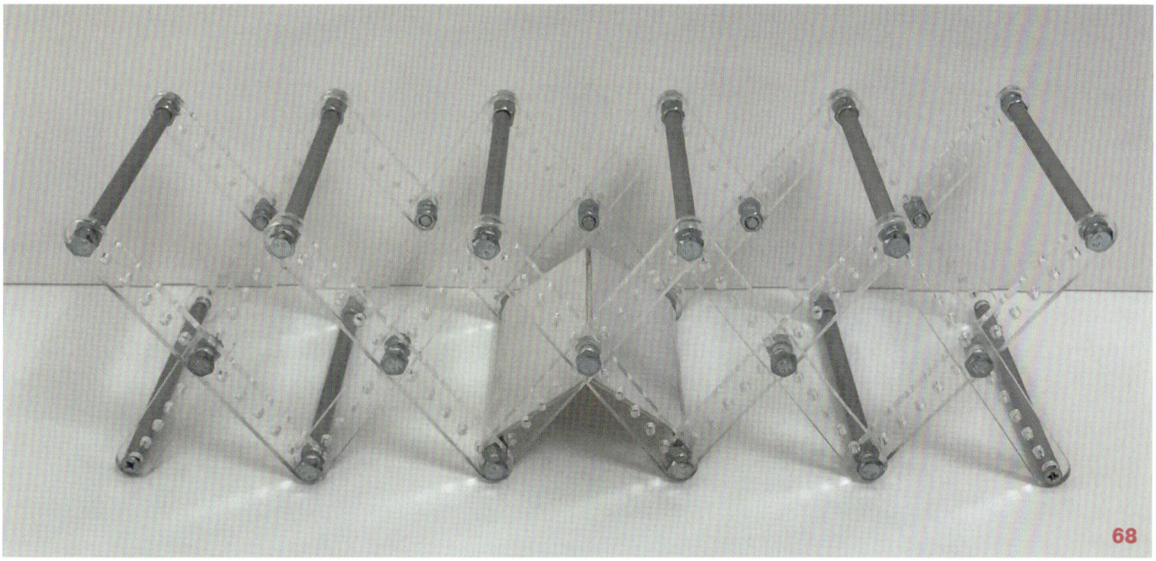

68

Interior Design

BA (Hons)

Dr Keith Winter, Course Leader

2021/22 was a year to get in and get busy as the doors opened up again and sterile computer screens became messy upcycled pots, Microsoft Teams became handmade collages and paintbrushes and PDF's became bespoke publications. We had a large cohort of 87 students this year across Level 4-6. With a 100% score in NSS in 2021 we had a lot to live up to. 'Mental Wealth 3' was a new Year 03 module launched this year as part of a new framework. I ran this alongside Claudia Palma and built in a professional skills program based on industry and readiness that included Stages of Work, CV's, selected work portfolios, cover letters, mock interviews, professional headshots (kindly taken by Adam Wiseman and his Level 4 students from photography!) and finally a week-long 'Job-Shadowing' in 17 different practices and studios across London. The submission for this module required a 1000-word reflective report by the student, illustrating what they had learned by critically evaluating their experience. A highlight was one of our top students Laylaa Osman gaining work experience at Adjaye + Associates. The list of practices can be seen in the following pages.

BA Interior Design saw a new Year 02 lead tutor Pol Gallagher being appointed permanently to the teaching team. Year 02's in SEMA carried out a feature staircase and viewing platform project in the Barbican that culminated in an exhibition in the adjacent Velorose Gallery, housing the work of the 22 students neatly compiled onto A2 competition boards and carefully hung under the guidance of gallerist David Rosenberg. In SEMB Year 02 Interior Design students were tasked to design the mighty Broadgate Exhibition in 3 Finsbury Avenue, opening 11.06.22 for UEL Fashion graduates and Architecture and Fine Art on 22.06.22. The students worked in groups to create designs for an Entrance Arch, bar, reception desk and walls and plinths as well as a fashion runway. A major feature being the first-time listing of UEL within London Fashion Week's official schedule.

An online article in Dezeen will be launched in July 2022 to highlight the success of the Broadgate exhibition and the hard work of our Year 02 students. Our other physical exhibition this year 'Does that make sense?' presented all of our students' prototypes and drawings and models as a complete Interior BA show in Way Out East Gallery in AVA, where we had several crits amongst the works and an opening to celebrate the Mid Year despite a freakish hurricane blowing through London.

Interior Educators takes place in a much larger format this year where we are sided up against the other Interior Design courses within the UK such as Kingston, GSA, ECA, Manchester MET and more in the OXO Barge building where we will carry through a version of our Broadgate structure and show our best work.

Broadgate Competition was a massive success where three of our year 02 and 03 students were finalists and moved through to the last 6 teams of 50.
When the opportunity was present we used workshops and studios on campus making prototype receptions desks in Year 01 using Laser-cutting and 3d printing. In Year 03 recycled and upcycled plant pot 1:1's as well as large 1:20 scaled models of a new Mahler + Lewitt residency centre project in De Beauvoir made sure interiors were once again the dominant course using our excellent UEL workshops (big thanks to all the techs for their help!).

Our Semester 01 guest lecture series was packed this year in collaboration with Architecture and ADSOC, held on a Tuesday Lunchtime for which we designed the poster series. These included Patrik Schumacher, Keef Winter, Alison Cooke, CAN, Guy Robertson, Tony Tremlett, Nicholas Szczepaniak, Simon Hamilton, Grimshaw, Amy Frearson, DEZEEN, Maliha Haque, Robert Jamison, Niall McLaughlin, Richard Wilson Resolve Collective Atsushi Iwata All of these guests brought an important piece of current relevant information to the table, giving our cohort an elegant array of confident creatives to bolster their own belief in themselves.

Dr Keith Winter
PhD MArch DipArch BSc Arch (hons) ARB

BA (Hons) Interior Design

Keith Winter, Susan Ginsburgh, Pol Gallagher, Nayden Hadzhiev, Karen Byford, Claudia Palma

1

LONDON

Students:
Year 01: Cristina Ben Ammar, Florin Matei- Sascau, Nicoleta Matei-Sascau Andreaa Cheptea, Dalal Bandar, Fatima Noor, Hafiza Sultana, Ishya Thompson, Jessica Olseen, Joseph Pearce, Joy Raj, Kidst Belete, Kinga Sobolewska, Kizrene Kenton, Lana Russo, Loubna Zein Eddin, Migle Gjocaj, Millie Lawrence, Miurjina Miah, Nadine Haven, Prince Garcia, Simona Dilyte, Tonisha Lee-Harvey, Maneesha Wijekoon Mudiyanselage

Year 2: Immanuel Kisakye, Gizem Atici, Cintia Szabo, Karysse Jno-Baptiste, Aleksandra Pieron, Isobel White, Stoimen Dzhukanov, Mahfooz Abdalla, Keeji Hondi-Medi, Milena Torres Toscano, Aliyah Stewart, Yogesh Bipinbhai Chhayani, Bianca Radoanca, Adrienne Mcken, Tahsin Mahita, Fernando Da Silva Tagliati, Emiliana Lance, Hussain

Year 3: Axelle Assi, Jasmine Assi, Stephanie Balde, Sara Barod, Yasmin Benrakad Imlahi, Rushaun Buchanan, Nelly Dibaud, Jazmine Fagbayi, Julia Florian, Lorenza Haddow, Humayra Haque, Zainab Jimoh, Sevgi Karaagachla, Emmanuel Muhangi, Rihab Kharbouchi, Sidra Khouli, Laura Lukacova, Michelle Ly, Yoana Miglencheva, Tasneem Mohammed, Solveiga Murauskaite, Anastasia Mustapha, Osama Medhat Mahmoud Nehad, Mettwaly Sead, Laylaa Osman, Jordan Grant, Joanne Kannikaklang, Nauma Patel, Nicusor Pocitar, Taiwo Popoola, Leanne Rosemary Taylor, Ridwan Salman, Khushi Sirvi Nitesh, Matea Soljak Palwahs Chugthai, Yusur Derzi

Special thanks to:
VELOROSE, Patrik Schumacher, Keef Winter, Alison Cooke, CAN, Guy Robertson, Tony Tremlett, Nicholas Szczepaniak, Simon Hamilton, Grimshaw, Amy Frearson, DEZEEN, Maliha Haque, Robert Jamison, Niall McLaughlin, Richard Wilson Resolve Collective Atsushi Iwata

2

1 Feeding the 5000 sustainable restaurant and Food Centre by Laylaa Osman **2** Mahler + Lewitt Residency 1:20 model by Yoana Miglencheva **3** CV + Selected Portfolio covers by Yr03 **4** Residency rear view by Laylaa Osman **5** List of practices and students for Yr03 Job Shadowing **6, 7** Design Development sketches by Rihab Kharbouchi **8** Mock Interviews with Yr03 **9-16** Jordan, Khushi, Jazmine, Tasneem, Matea, Ridwan, Julia, Rihab professional Headshots of Yr03 students by Yr01 BA Photography and Adam Wiseman **17** Upcycled Plant Pots by Yr03 including Nic, Laylaa, Anastasia, Tasneem, Rihab, Ridwan, Joanne and Yoana **18** Feeding the 5000 sustainable restaurant designs by Ridwan Salman **19** Mahler + Lewitt Residency by Julia Florian **20** Mahler + Lewitt Residency floorpans by Jazmine Fagbayi **21, 25** Mahler + Lewitt Residency by Yoana Miglencheva **22** Feeding the 5000 sustainable restaurant and Food Centre by Tasneem Mohamed **23** Mahler + Lewitt Residency analysis and material palette by Laylaa Osman **24, 27** Restaurant and FC by Laura Lukacova **26** Restaurant Sketches by Ridwan Salman **28** M+L Residency Site Analysis by Tasneem Mohamed **29** Barbican Terrace visual by Bianca Radoanca **30** Barbican Utopia plant shop by Mahfooz Abdalla **31** Barbican Terrace by Sharon Gomes **32, 33** Bar Group design by Yr02 for 'SHOW' **34, 37** Walls + Plinths Group design by Yr02 for 'SHOW' **35, 36** Entrance Group design by Yr02 for 'SHOW' **38** Reception Desk Group design by Yr02 for 'SHOW' **39** Reception desk prototype by Tonisha Lee-Harvey **40** 'Dream Bedroom' interior view of model + plan by Joe Pearce **41** Reception desk model by Loubna Zein Eddin **42, 43** Reception desk prototype by Miurjina Miah **44** Express Yourself Analysis and design by Hafiza Sultana **45** Express Yourself sketch models by Tonisha Lee **46** Express Yourself plan by Jessica Olseen **47** Sketch model and drawing for reception desk by Prince Garcia **48** Collage by Prince Garcia **49** Dream Bedroom Axonometric by Joe Pearce **50** 'Express Yourself' interior visual by Millie Lawrence **51** Reception Desk designs by Ishya Thompson **52** Dream Bedroom 1:20 physical model and Axonometric by Maneesha Wijekoon

3

4

Company	Online/ONSITE	No placements offered	Emailed	Form Sent	Agreement Signed	STUDENT NAME
Fred Rigby Studio		1	YES By TT	YES	YES	Julia
ALEX SCOTT WHITBY		2	YES BY KW	YES	YES	Yoana, Rushaun
Studio M London	OnLine	1	YES BY TT	YES	YES	Sevgi
ZAP Architecture		2	YES BY KW	YES	YES	Anastasia, Khushi
TheseWhiteWalls		1	YES By TT	YES	YES	Yusur
Gatti Routh Rhodes		1	YES	YES	YES	Rihab
Turnerbates		2	YES BY KW	YES	YES	Matea, Tasneem
CAKE Industries		1	YES BY KW	YES	YES	Taiwo
David Adjaye Architects	Linda@adjaye.com	1	YES BY CP	YES	YES	Laylaa
MACE	Call mace1	2	YES BY KW	YES	Yes	Ridwan, Joanne
Lewisham Youth Theatre		4	BETHAN	YES	Risk Assessment sent	Sara, Nauma, Osama, Lyes
Vine Architects	Onsite	1	KW	YES	YES	Nic
Haworth Tompkins	Onsite	1	KW DB			Palwasha
Perkinswill	Linzi.Cassels@perkinswil	2	YES TT			Laura + Jordan
Freshorize		4	YES MB AF			Ivanka, Ryan, Ghrunraj, Em
VELOROSE	david@velorose.com	1				Jazmine
Ideas	Christine	2	YES KW	YES		Solveiga, Zainab

5

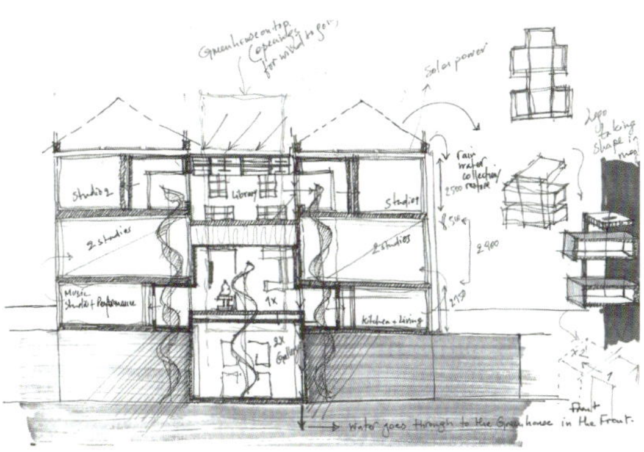

Sectional sketch

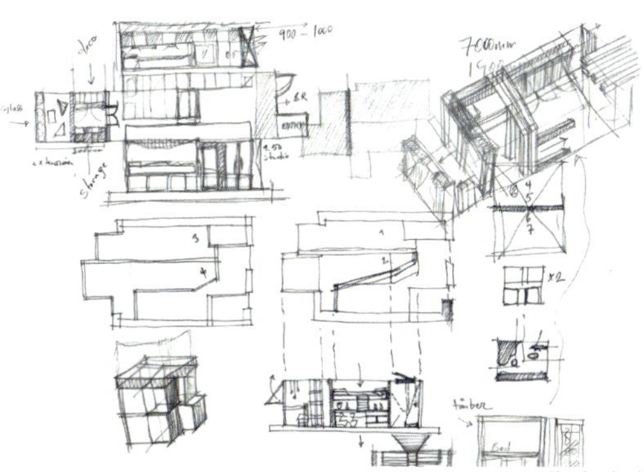
Planning sketch

6

8

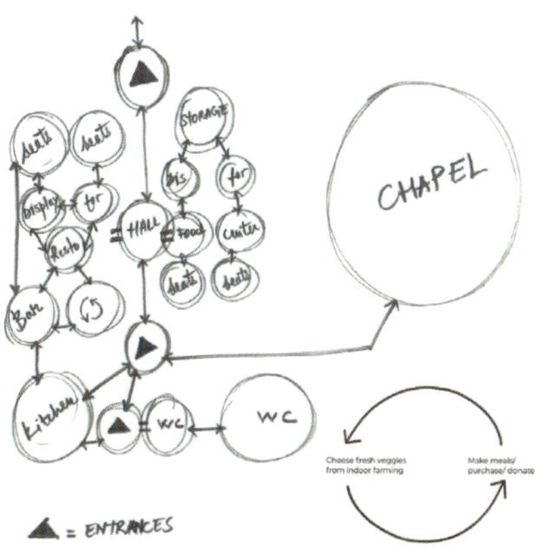

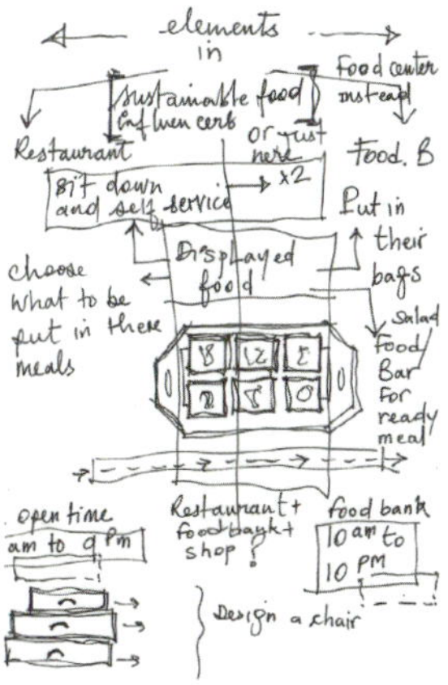

7

9

10

11

12

13

14

15

16

اكليل الجبل

TECHNICAL DRAWINGS AND FINAL DESIGN

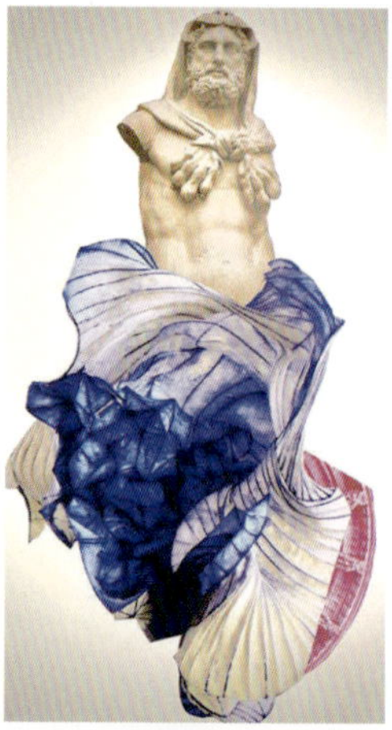

18

19

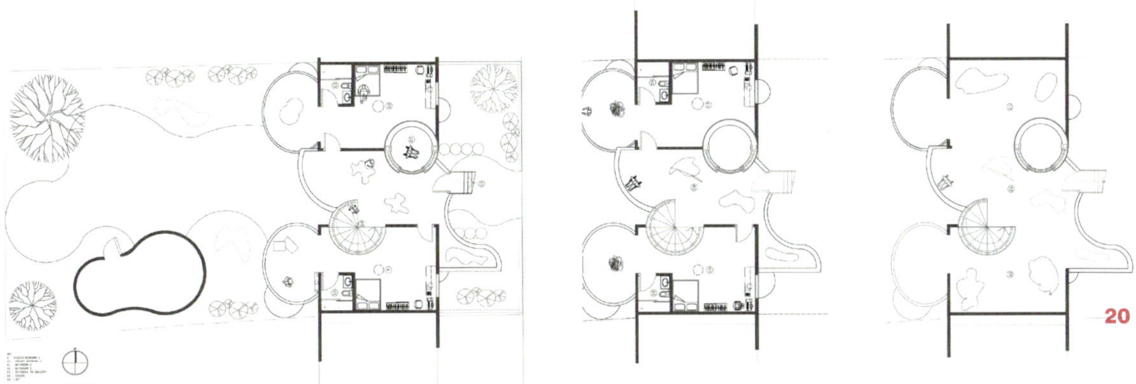

20

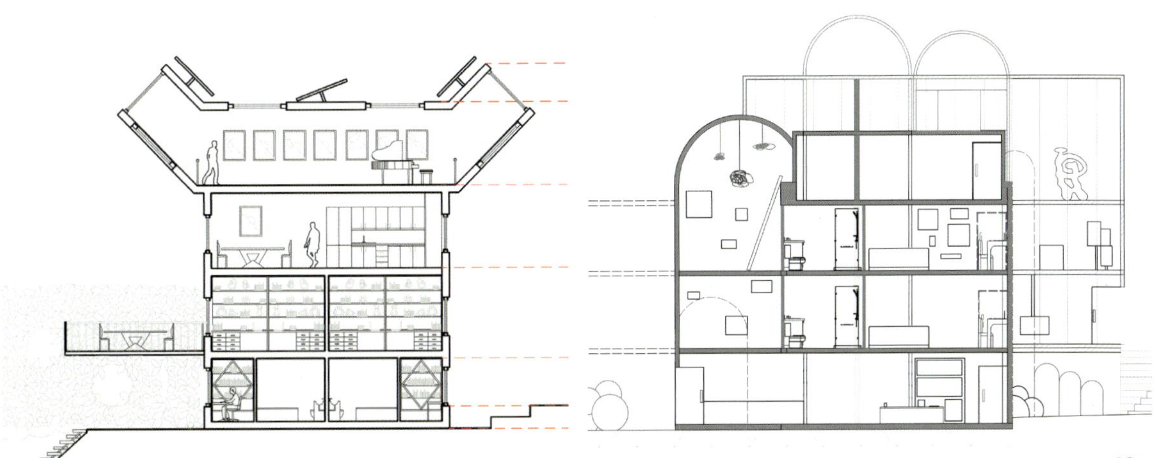

19

DESIGN DEVELOPMENT

22

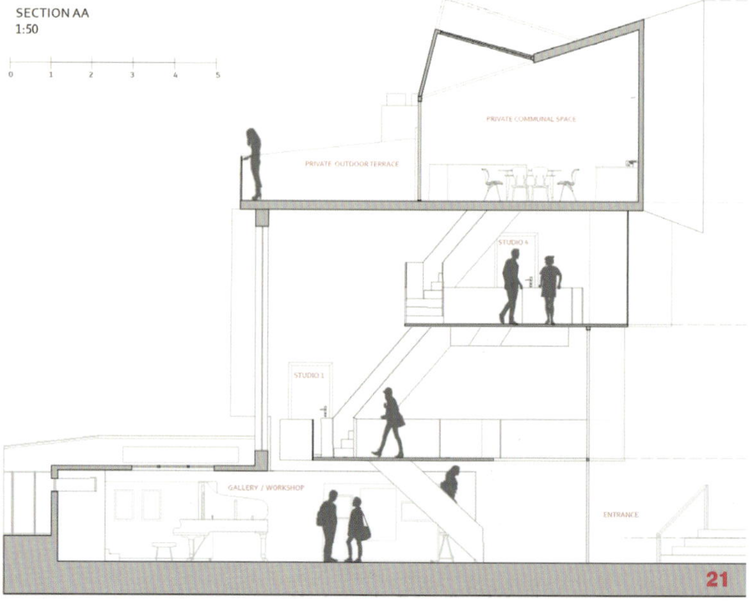

21

2.

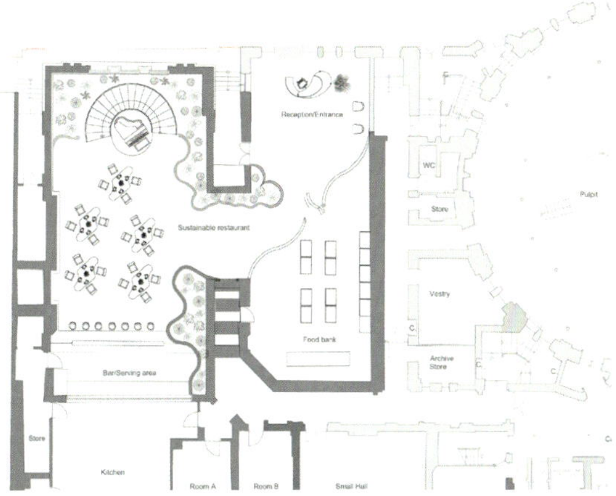

24

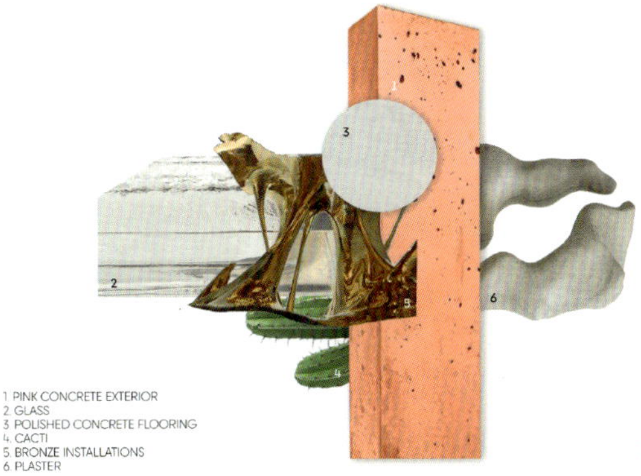

23

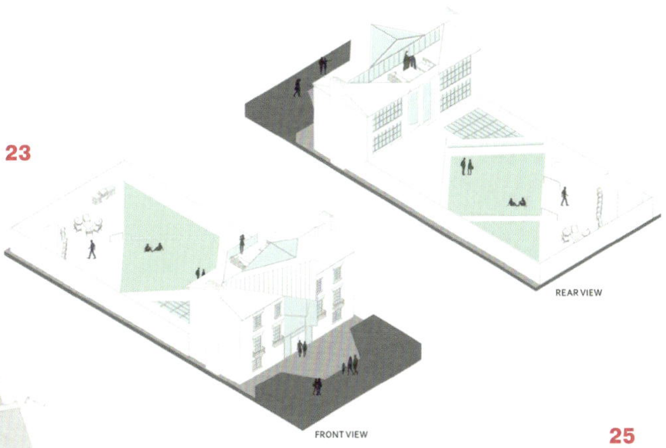

25

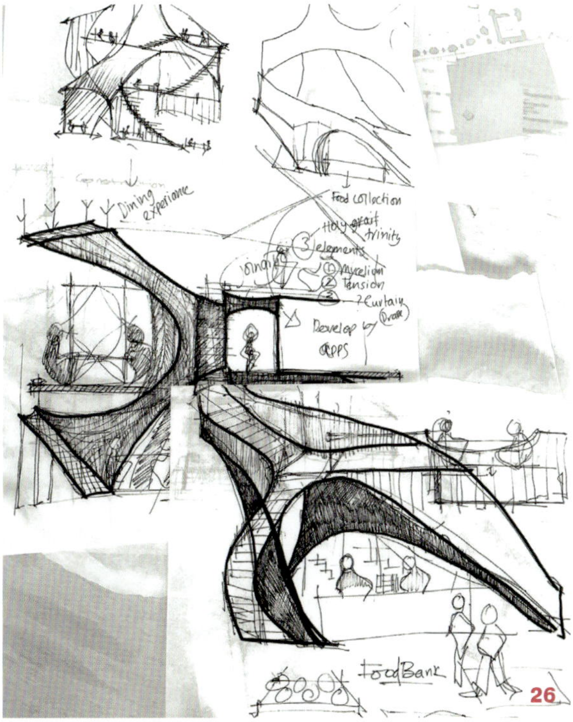

26

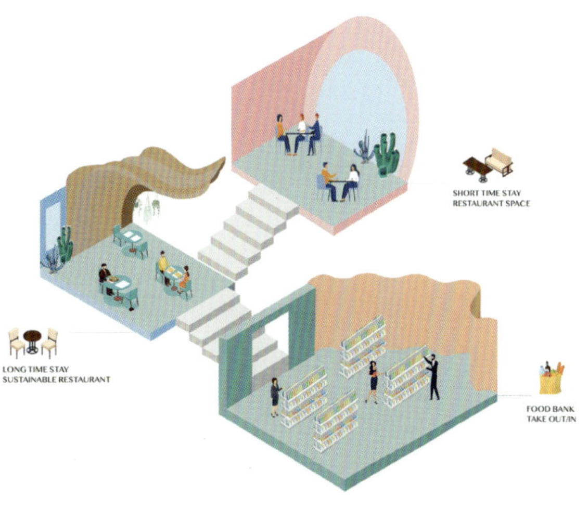

27

SITE ANALYSIS

28

29

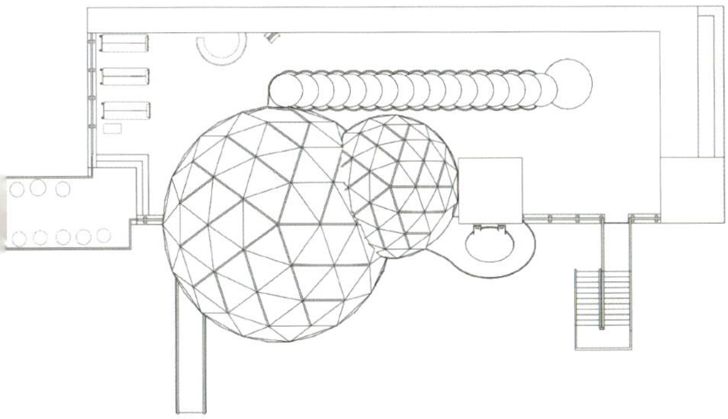

30

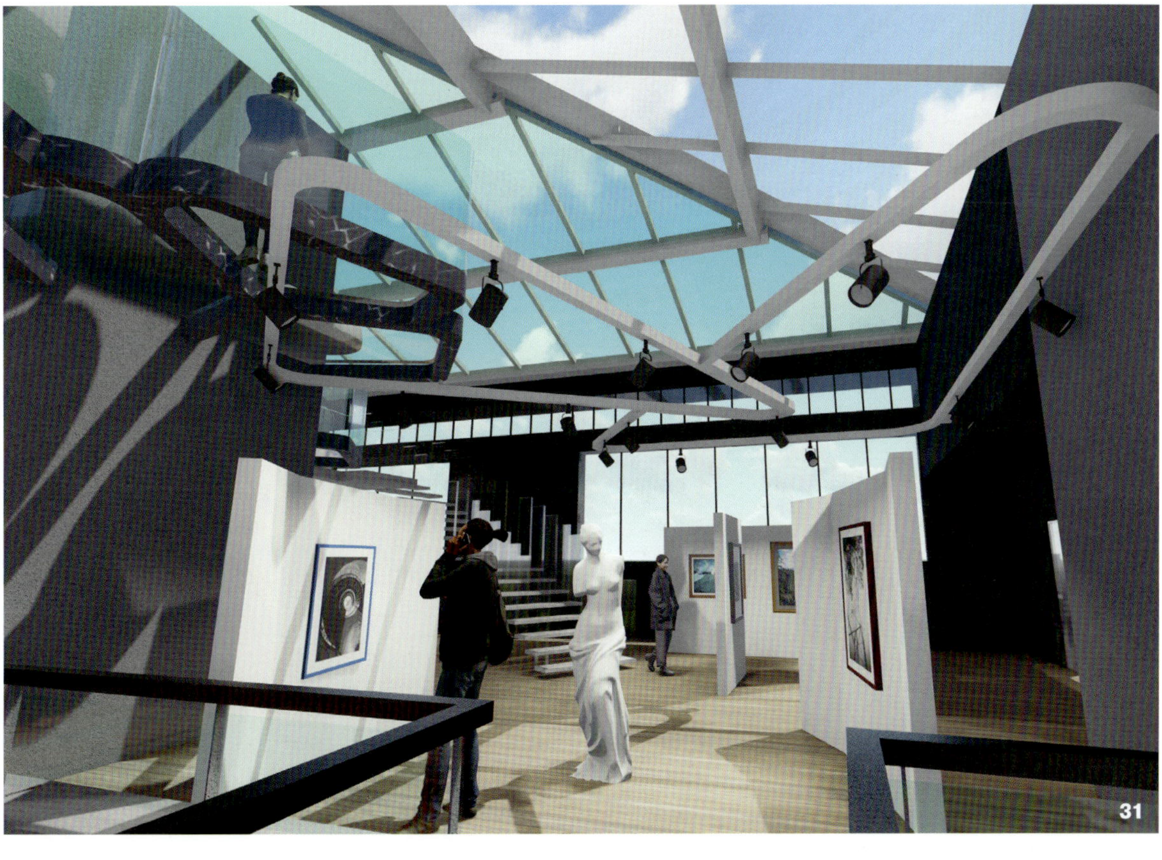

31

32

EXPLODED AXONOMETRIC OF BAR

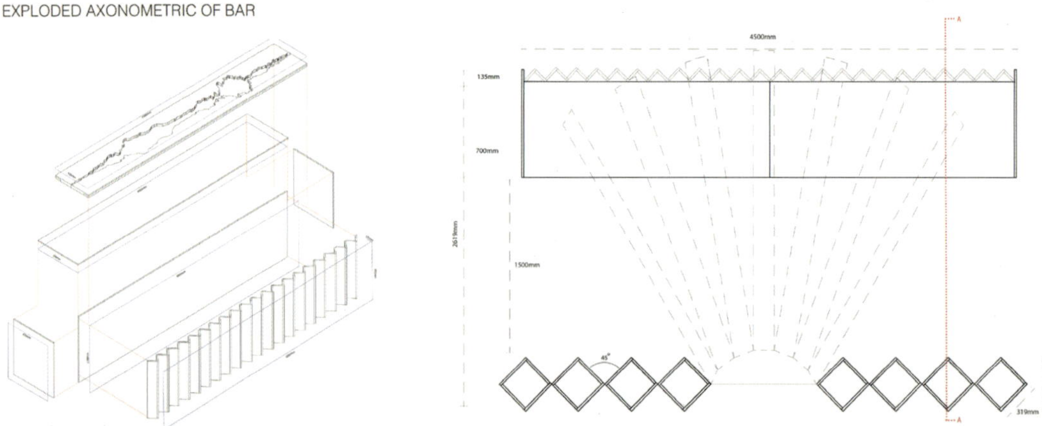

33

34

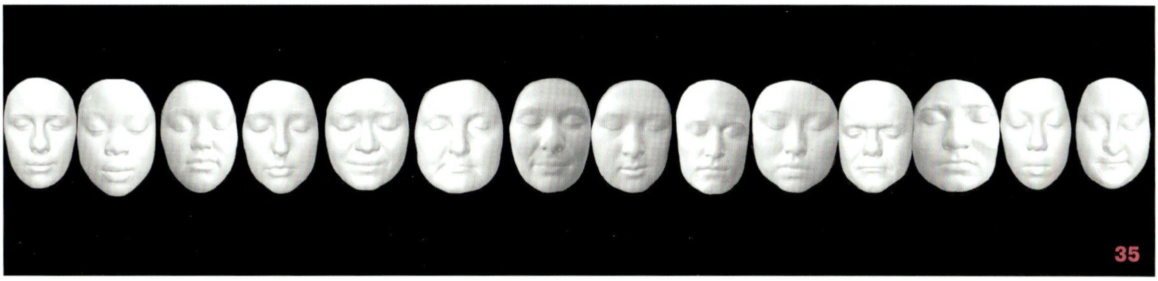

35

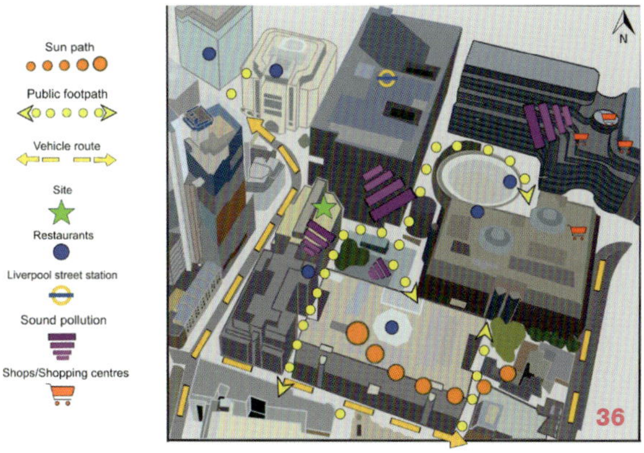
Sun path
Public footpath
Vehicle route
Site
Restaurants
Liverpool street station
Sound pollution
Shops/Shopping centres
N

36

37

ICON
DETAIL
domus

38

39

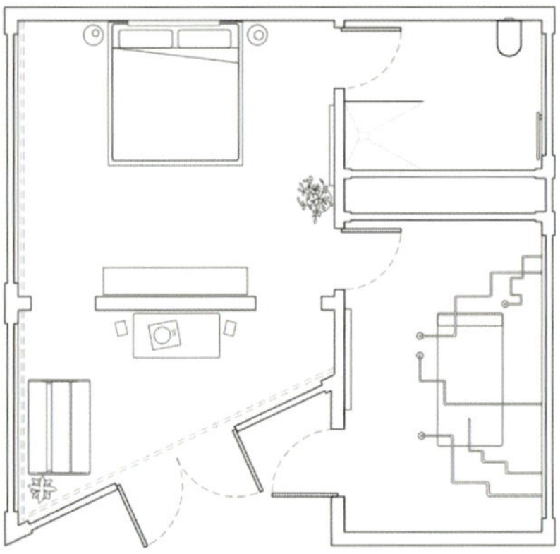

PROPOSED PLAN
DREAM BEDROOM

To make this floor plan I used Adobe Illustrator as it meant I could quickly remove and add parts when I was deciding what furniture I wanted. This was very helpful with the trial and error in choosing furniture, and made the process much more efficient, and also made the final piece neater.

40

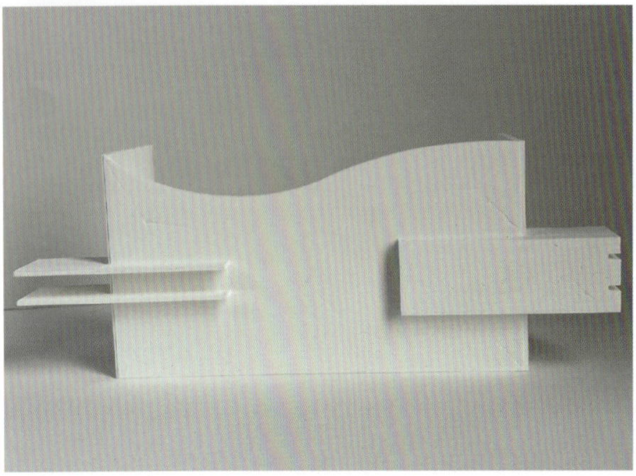

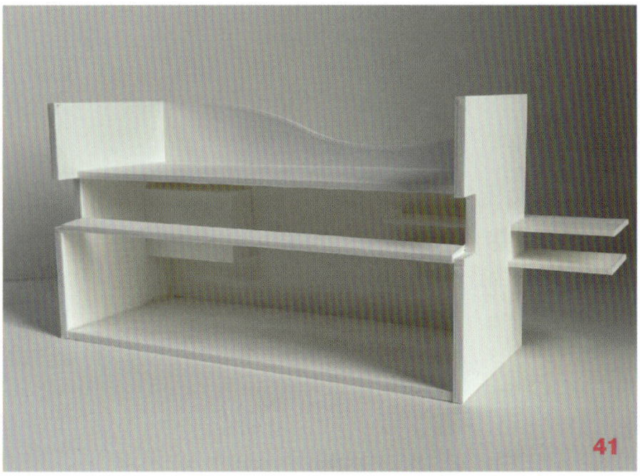

41

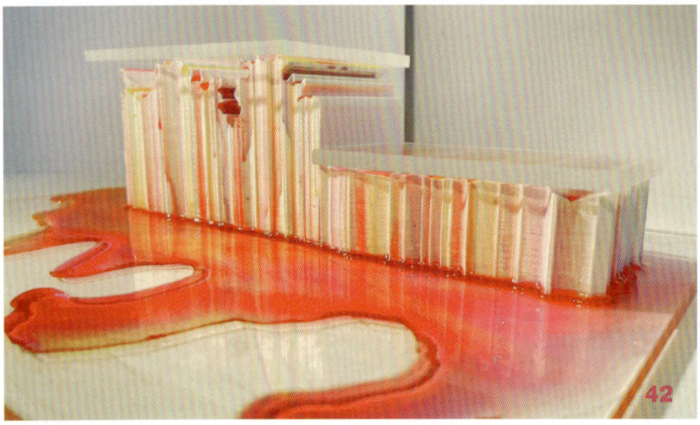

42

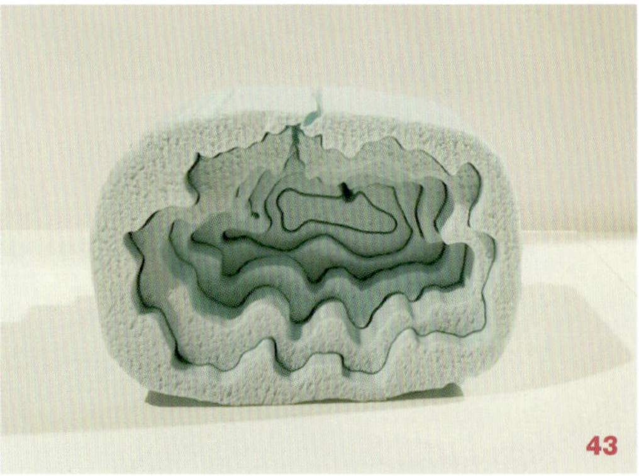

43

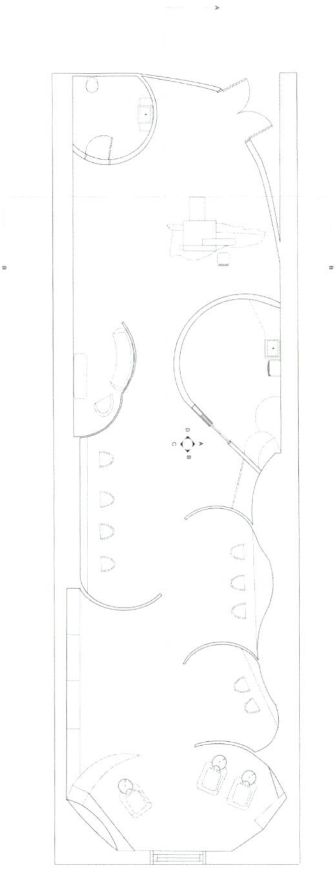

46

44

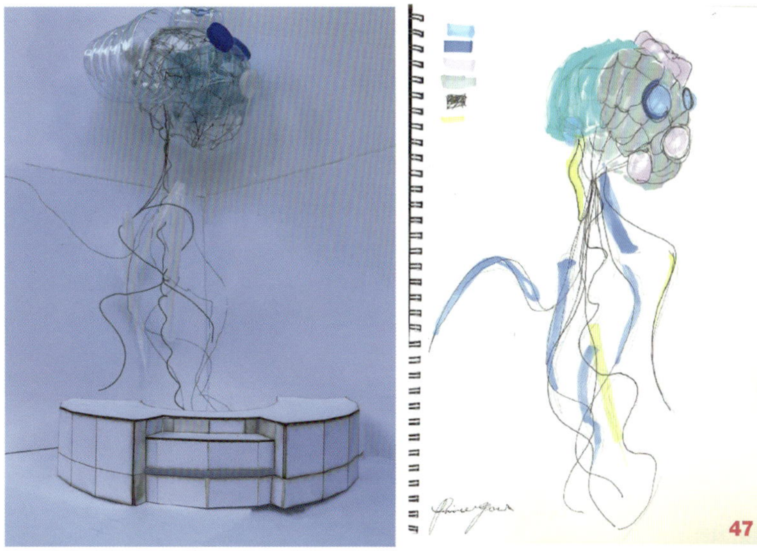

47

45

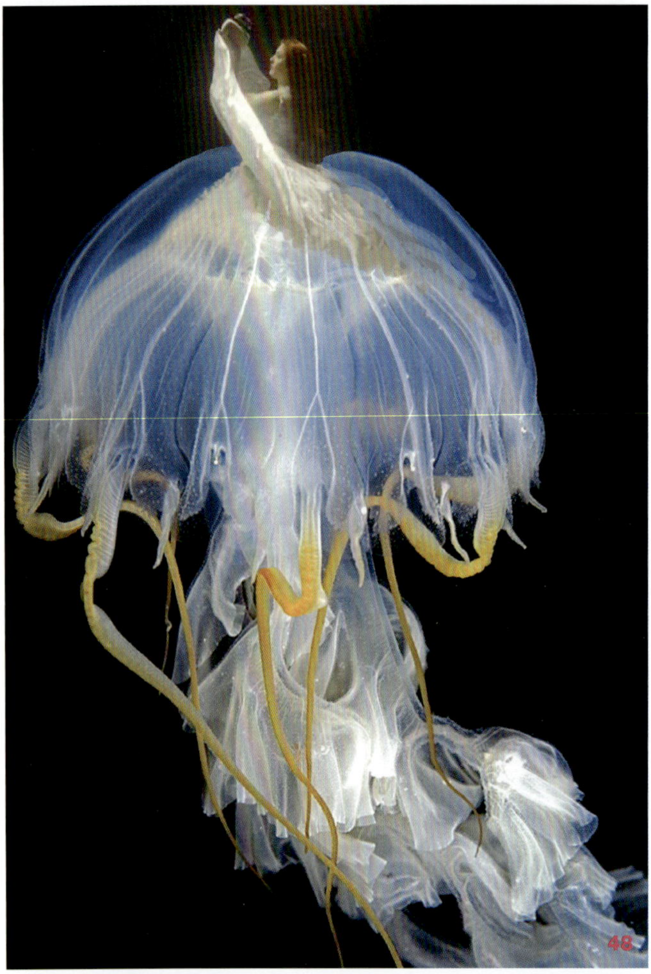

48

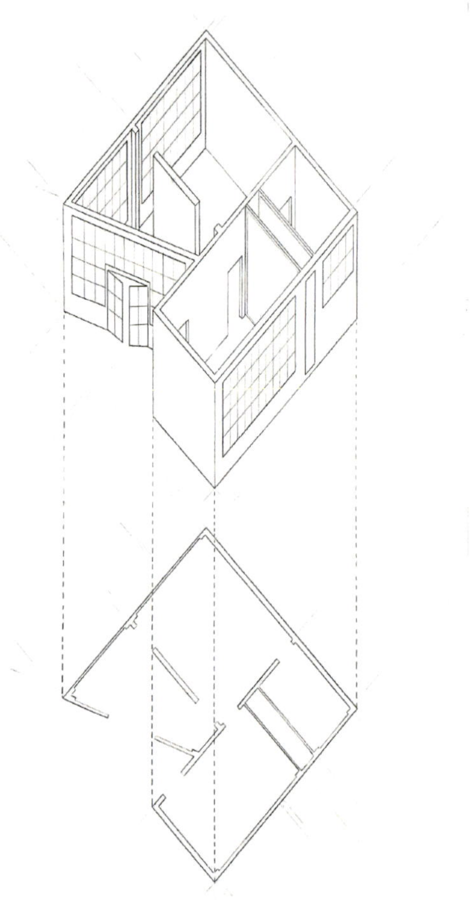

49

50

51

Block Party

Details - Often, when you think about child's play, you can see that buildings blocks are given to kids to help them understand spatial awareness so that they recognise that the circle has to go in the circle hole and the square in the square hole; right?
But I'm deconstructing something logical and making then fit together. Taking the hexagon shape with a circle edge, for example, how can it work in design and functionality?

I am in the process of exploring these types of designs since I think the most stunning ones are those when art meets functionality. I find it meaningful when people can interact with art practically.

52

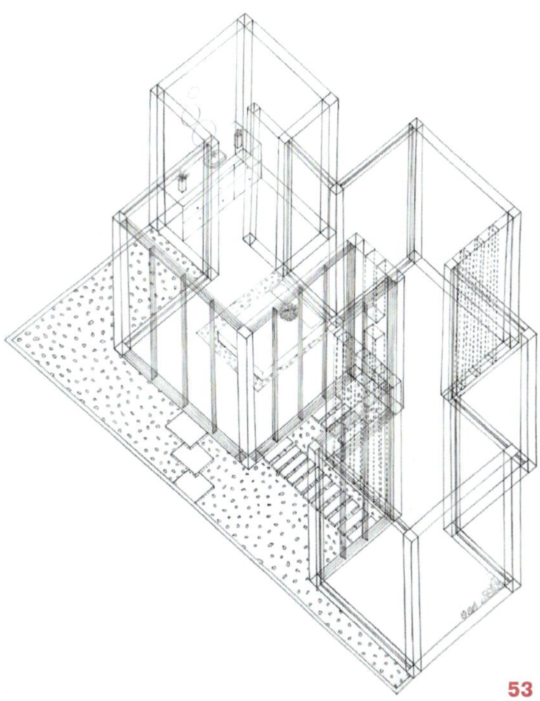

53

Product Design

BSc (Hons)

Andrew Wright, Course Leader
Mathew Brown
Dr Claudia Palma

The Product Design Programme encourages students to analyse and assess social and environmental landscapes to identify opportunities for improvement.

By identifying issues, students undertake primary research to emphasise and identify with their key users, forging a direction for the development of their final designs.

During their journey, students will explore ideas in 2 and 3 Dimensions in parallel to understand and fully represent their design concepts, becoming more refined on their iterative journey of exploration. Encouragement to understand and identify form and function, alongside technical material explorations, helps with the realisation of the final designs, pieces that can be manufactured and realised commercially. The construction of test rigs and jigs on a basic level enables in-depth analysis and evaluation directly with the user, presenting solutions influenced by the client or user's direct input.

By integrating the contextual and professional life elements of the programme to support the design projects, a richer more conclusive outcome is achieved through a body of work that theorises and then directly questions the issues identified central to the user.

BSc (Hons) Product Design Level 6:

Ivanka Ivanova

Final Major Project:

Royal Society of Arts (RSA) Student Design Awards Entry 2021-22:

RSA Brief: Press Play

"How might we support all families, carers and communities to play and learn more creatively at home?"

BSc (Hons) Product Design Level 6:

Ryan Bragg

Final Major Project:

Royal Society of Arts (RSA) Student Design Awards 2021-22:

RSA Brief: Transformation Station

"How might we leverage unrealised spaces in small transport hubs, as catalysts for communities and places to thrive?"

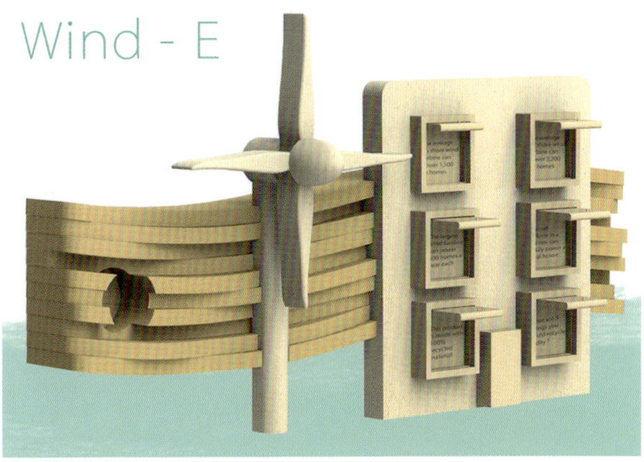

BSc (Hons) Product Design Level 6:

Ghunraj Singh Saran

Final Major Project

A forward thinking insole concept used by care home residents who suffer from Alzheimer's disease. The product would digitally monitor essential personal data which would be shared in real time with nursing staff to help improve patient monitoring and time efficiency

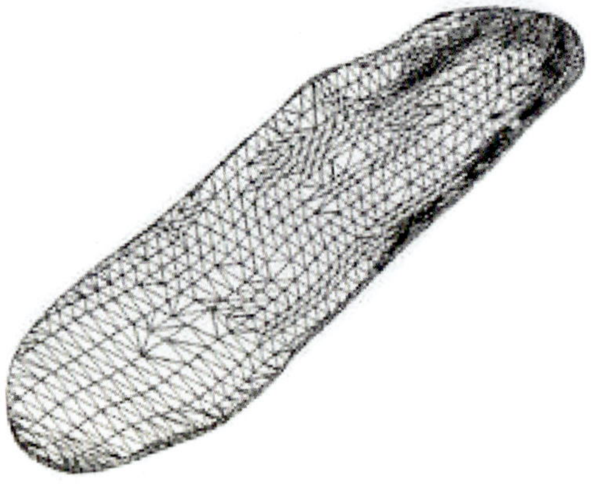

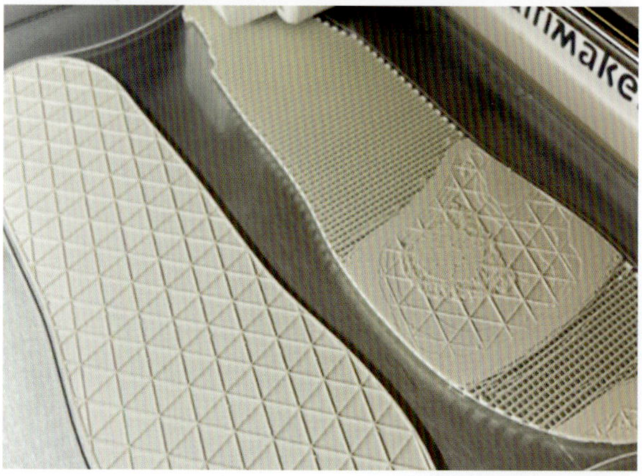

BSc (Hons) Product Design Level 6:

Emily Beth Duckworth

Final Major Project:

Royal Society of Arts (RSA) Student Design Awards Entry 2021-22:

RSA Brief: Without the waste

"How might we use circular economy principles to rethink the storage, delivery and dispensing of tablet medication?"

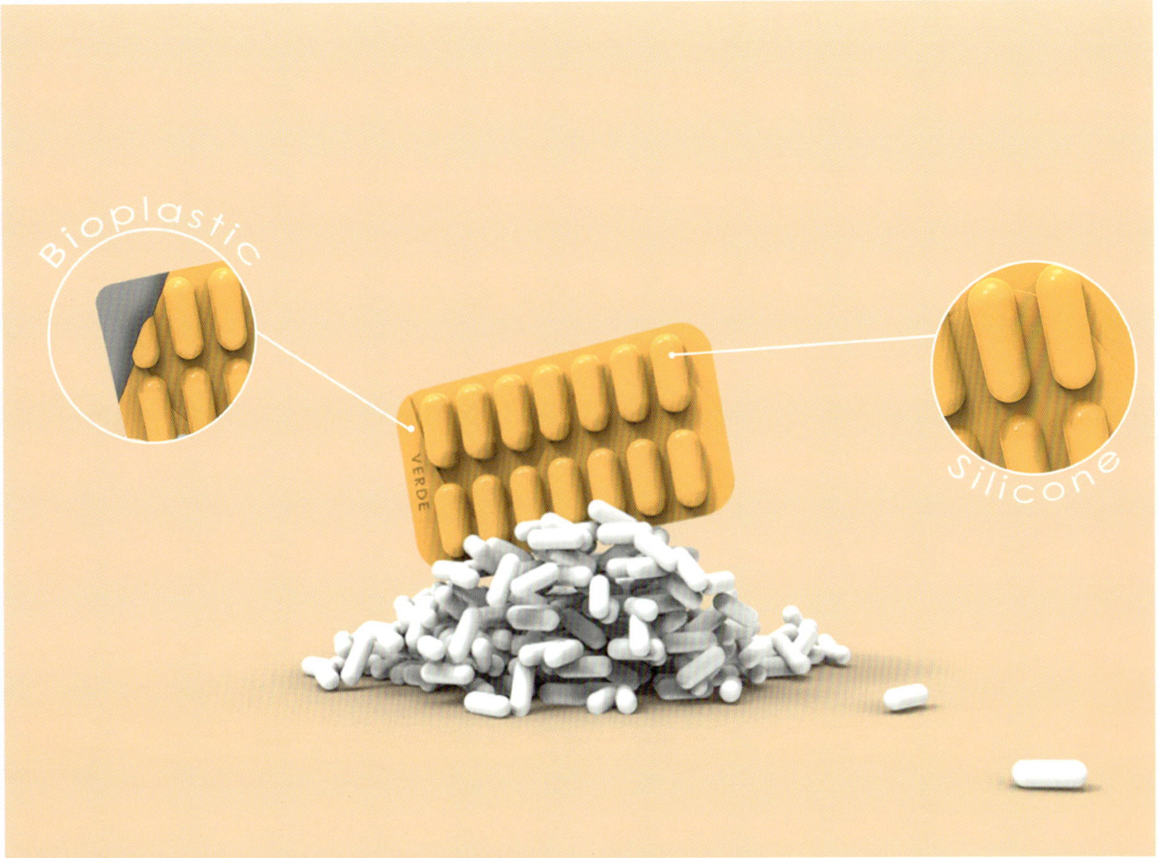

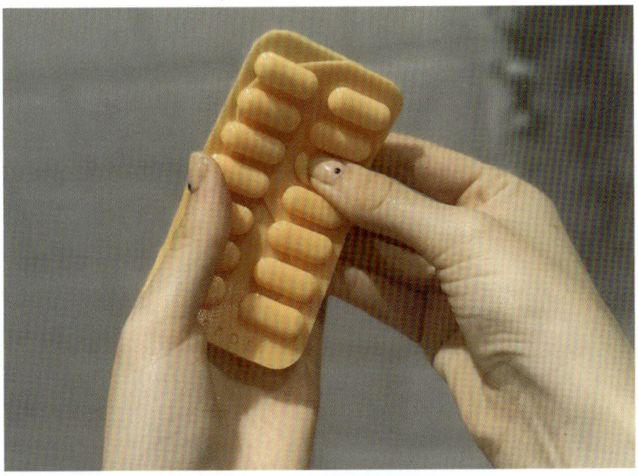

Architecture

MArch Architecture
ARB/RIBA Part 2

Isaie Bloch, Course Leader

Architectural Design Staff:
Unit 2 Christoph Hadrys, Uwe Shmidt-Hess, Tony Fretton
Unit 6 Isaie Bloch, Igor Pantic
Unit 8 Armor Gutierrez, Rosa Rogina

History & Theory teaching staff:
Christoph Hadrys, Anna Minton, Clare Penny, Teresa Serrano, Bridget Snaith, Fulvio Wirz.

Technical & Environmental Studies teaching staff:
Alan Chandler, Armor Gutierrez, Teresa Serrano, Deborah Do-Rosario-Benros.

Professional Studies teaching staff:
Roland Karthaus, Deborah Do-Rosario-Benros.

Technicians & Demonstrators:
Daryl Brown, Luiz Bueno, Garry Doherty, Paul Nichols, Mark Sowden.

External Examiners:
Teoman Ayas, Julian Cross, Raymond Quek, Jessica Reynolds, David Short, Michael Trousdell.

Our school is enriching lives and is addressing the climate emergency. We have developed a strong position in sustainable design and for many years, have developed the shared theme across the course *zero percent carbon one hundred percent people*. The link between environmental and social sustainability has grown our engagement with new and emerging technologies and organisational structures as well as people and communities in need. In this process, we engage students in knowledge transfer, skill-building, research, placemaking, iterative explorations and testing. Our students develop their work through a culture of critical, practical, and creative engagement as designers and thinkers. We ask questions and aim to enable answers, from the things we touch to the world around us and from the individual to society. This approach to sustainability whilst preserving human experience is a core value shared by all staff and students.

Situated in the department of Architecture and Visual Arts (AVA) the close proximity between courses also brings access to a wide variety of technical workshops and labs including the full range of Engineering and Arts workshops, such as photography, the traditional metal, plaster and wood workshops as well as the newer digital fabrication and robotics workshops. Students are encouraged towards a hybrid use of the workshops with project work spanning both traditional and more contemporary digital technologies. As part of our making culture, the hands-on learning by doing is an important aspect of our teaching and learning.

Our professionally accredited part 2 programme at UEL produce directed, environmentally responsible and socially aware graduates that understand architecture as a beautiful, radical tool to make 'place' and engage with the complexities of social and environmental interaction. Through our programmes, our students develop a rigorous and strategic understanding of context encompassing social and environmental, physical and non-physical concerns, enabling them to make engaged and critical architectures. Our teaching is centred on the interface of social and spatial structures, on people and place. At the core of this education are our design units in year 4 & 5, each of which provides students with a particular thematic and methodological approach to design, and as a whole contain a diversity of students and staff that stimulates critical awareness.

The aim of the MArch programme, in Years 4 & 5, is to stimulate students to become critical agents in the social production of space through thorough and in-depth engagement with environmentally sound responses addressing real-life issues and uncertainties. Sustainability is key for us and can only be achieved by aligning human behaviour, use, technology, place and space together. We believe students need more than just a traditional understanding of how to do their job. As such our course does not attempt to replicate office practice, instead it prepares students to push practice forward. We teach how to maximise potential and to generate impact by addressing new methods of project and design development as well as through the use of contemporary technology. We believe that by engaging on a practical level with real-life scenarios you will affect the whole, not just the part. We will stimulate to look at architecture as the opportunist, not the problem-solver only.

Within this process students transform complexity into elegance, animate aesthetics and organise space for social use. Preparation for professional practice and beyond integrates essential technical, philosophical, regulatory and practical knowledge as baseline skills that enable the final thesis at MArch level to critically extend beyond the ARB and RIBA requirements. Decision making and technical innovation, develop from and relate to wider socio-political contexts, grounding the design work and emphasise the importance of the critical task we have in creating better architectures for all generations to come.

Unit 2
Open Space

Christoph Hadrys, Uwe Schmidt-Hess
and Tony Fretton

MArch Unit 2 addresses urban and architectural conditions in locations undergoing critical change and over the years, has worked in North Africa, East London and other places in Europe. Through a combination of research and creative practice, we propose complex buildings, which respond to urban challenges. The Unit explores extremes of interrelated scales, from urban geographies through to building and detail qualities. Our strategies formulate responses to critical contexts, site conditions, architectural sensibilities, as well as structural and material conditions. We aim to create social, spatial and time-based habitats and environments.

This academic year, we focused on architecture between urban developments and green spaces in Kidbrooke, South-East London. Within this location, we explored the guiding theme Open Space.

Around half of London's area is open space, with most of these spaces being in suburban neighbourhoods. But these kind of open spaces tend to be private, gated and fragmented, offering little public and communal life. This in return contributes to further car dependency and isolation. London's housing crisis and the recent pandemic have sparked a move towards suburban locations. This opens urgent questions of sustainability.

Our research area is a microcosm of London's urban, suburban and landscape conditions. During the early 20th century suburbanisation, the area was largely left undeveloped due to a risk of flooding. In the last decade, new developments have started around Kidbrooke station, with high-rise buildings, terraced houses and green spaces. But large parts of the research area remain disintegrated within local neighbourhoods. Here, the research area offers diverse open sites and spaces as well as underutilised sport areas, neglected green spaces, flood-lands and waterways.

As a Unit, we proposed a new urban development framework for the research area that integrates local contexts with a new network of sites, linkages and green spaces. Each student had a choice to work on one of the given sites within the framework. On each site, we combined housing with social amenities to support new landscape strategies and renaturation. The guiding theme Open Space relates to designs that open diverse future possibilities for people and natural habitats alike. We explored ways in which sharing and living together can be part of a synergetic urban life.

> "Nothing exists of itself, but everything is part of a universal harmony. All things interpenetrate and suffer and are transformed into each other. You can only perceive one thing by means of the other..."
> *'A Topography of Feeling' Dimitris Pikionis*

KIDBROOKE, SOUTH-EAST LONDON

Students:
Y5: Shahul Hameed Sadhiq Abdullah Asan Mydeen, Tanvir Ahmed, Sina Fekri, Hussein Ali Kasim, Mariana Andrea Morales Munoz, Alexandra Rogojinaru, Erdjan Ruci, Omer Sabah, Julia Skiba, Karolina Skrzypkowska, Dan Strassburg, Nadira Sultan, Furkan Tarhan, Oliver Tibbenham, Dominika Zielinska

Y4: Luke Day, William Fullick, Thomas Hardy, Ziyad Hasanin, Julian Imossi, Bhakti Panchal, Khushbu Patel

Visiting Crits and Guests:
Kevin Widger, Philip Christou Baruti, Syliva Aehle
Isaie Bloch, Igor Pantic, Armor Gutierrez, Rosa Rogina, Teresa Serrano, Deborah Do-Rosario-Benros

www.march-unit2.blogspot.com

1

1 On the previous page, aerial photo-collage research area in Kidbrooke with student site locations.

2 Landscape strategy for new parkland, wetlands and river-walk, by Thomas Hardy **3** Biodiversity research, education centre and cafe, by Thomas Hardy **4** to **6** Park cafe, by Thomas Hardy

2

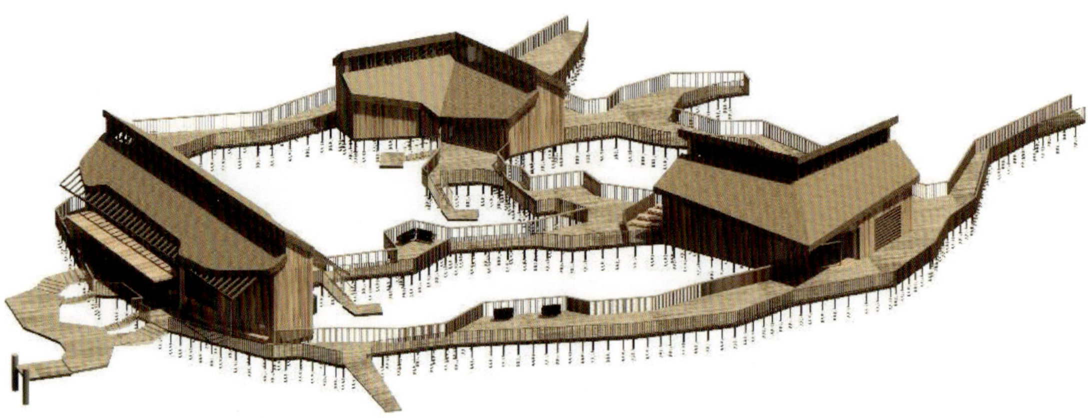

3

4

5

6

7 to **8** Re-naturated parkland and youth centre, plan and section, by Dan Strassburg **9** to **12** Youth centre with workshops for nature crafts and room for story-telling, art, singing and music, by Dan Strassburg

7

8

9

10

11

12

13 New leisure centre and housing with river re-naturation, by Omer Sabah **14** River Quaggy re-naturation and creation of wetlands, topographical landscape transformation, by Tanvir Ahmed **15** to **17** Extension to Kidbrooke centre, station and public spaces with new public amenities, social landscape and housing, by Shahul Hameed Sadhiq Abdullah Asan Mydeen

13

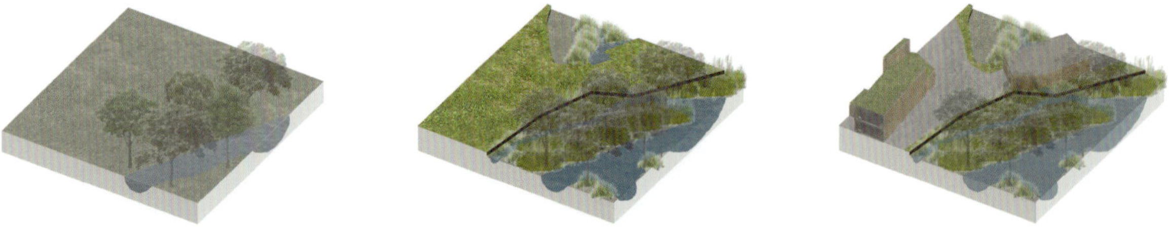

14

15

16

17

18 to **19** Extension to Kidbrooke centre with live-work spaces, multi-generational housing and communal facilities, by Dominika Zielinska **20** to **22** Extension to Kidbrooke centre with new public spaces, co-working facilities and flexible housing, by Karolina Skrzypkowska

18

19

22

23 Axonometric of urban framework design, building group and self-build community with growing houses and shared facilities, by Alexandra Rogojinaru **24** Pattern-book for design guidance, by Alexandra Rogojinaru **25** to **27** Views of the participatory community, by Alexandra Rogojinaru

23

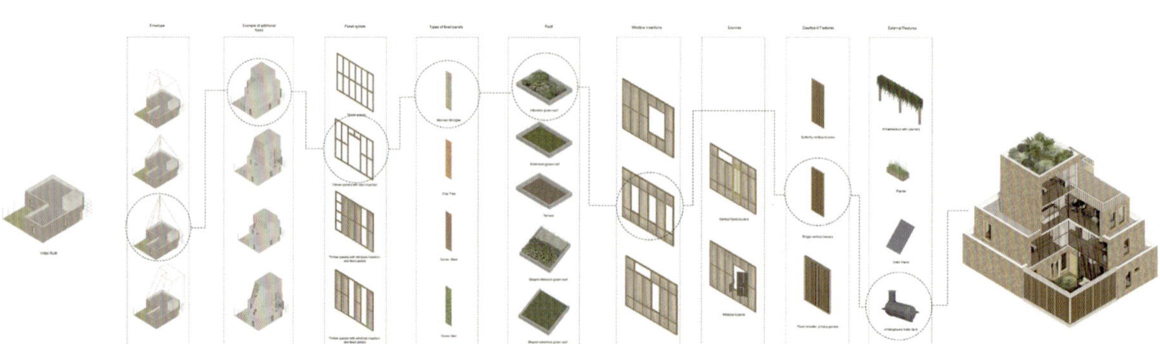

24

25

26

27

28 and **29** Urban framework design for co-housing community, combining living, working, urban agriculture and allotments, view of public/communal street and typical cross section, by Hussein Ali Kasim **30** to **32** Views of co-housing community, by Hussein Ali Kasim

"The neatness of architecture is its seduction; it defines, excludes, limits separates from the 'rest' - but it also consumes. It exploits and exhausts the potentials that can be generated finally only by urbanism, and that only the specific imagination of urbanism can invent and renew."

Rem Koolhaas (SMLXL)

28

29

30

31

32

Unit 6
Sustaining Education or Sustainable Education

Isaie Bloch, Igor Pantic

Across many parts of the world, education costs have become one of the most substantial items families' budget face within their lifetime. Families relate their planning to the cost of education, its duration and location; in the ultimate belief that education brings about change. The growing complexity and sophistication of our civilization presents new challenges both to our educational system and its infrastructure, as well as to its users who often leave university with large financial depths. Our universities cater for the needs of the future; but to keep on doing so they will have to re-envision how to generate sustainable alternative streams of revenue to provide educational acceleration.

In the UK, universities income relies for less then 50% on student tuitions. Governmental funding keeps on plummeting whilst tuition fees are record high, leaving students from the lowest income households to bear the highest levels of depth. The remaining 50% comes from an array of alternative streams of income needed to deliver high level education. Due to this financial stress and the inability of the public sector to aid, little substantial progress has been made in the further development of the educational typology, often resulting in education to occur in un-informed generic structures.

We will aim to prove that architecture can affect the learning process at the deepest level. This ultimate belief will fuel our investigation on educational typologies. Our spatial explorations will account for diversity of human characters, occupancy, hybrid programming and the inherent curiosity human beings possess. Much like the learning process itself we will aim to comprehend, learn, and author the art of construction. More specifically looking into working with materials with close to zero embedded carbon, we will be focussing on engineered timber construction and 3D printed non-fired clay or concrete. Our bottom-up design process will engage with digital design and large-scale digital fabrication in order to apply these learnt principles back into design. Such approach leads to full authorship and gives us total control over the architectural proposition. This opens a great opportunity to contribute to more sustainable futures both politically, environmentally, socially and economically. In order to develop architecture of considered expression we will employ design strategies that synthetize the inner logics of how to deal with material, tectonics and construction processes as to produce comprehensive well crafted architectural propositions.

UEL DOCKLANDS CAMPUS, LONDON

Students:

Y5: Meet Gehi, Surabh Sanjay Jadhav, Ramisa Mahmud, Sribalaji Murugavel, Patrycja Niechaj, Chetan Patel, Mohammed Patel, Rackel Metrona Afat, Rafaa Abubaker Mohamed Elfatih, Harmandeep Kaur Sanghera, Shreyans Sanjay, Foyez Uddin

Y4: Akanksha Barada, Harsh Desai, Vanessa Mawoneke, Wendpagnande Naomi Nakoulma, Nafisa Tailor, Mihriban Ustun, Agis Valsamis

Unit in general:

Unit 6 argues for an architectural ontology based on sharpening the tension between architecture and its parts. Investigating the production of space trough geometrical studies. Increased computational capabilities are able to push our understanding of architecture as a relationship of objects into an unexpected new domain of previously unachievable spatial complexity, materiality, structure and aesthetics as to create informed and well crafted space.

1

During the first workshop of the year students were tasked to work from two pre-selected case studies and in a first instance to duplicate/copy the volumetric model in order to get a thorough understanding of the spatial complexities and opportunities. In doing so students learnt to model in rhino sub-d trough design.

From these initial duplicates students where required to start iterating the masses to personal design developments by including a structural strategy as well as 3D printed parts into the overall mass. These 3D printed parts came in the form of Mega-columns, wall sections, lost formwork, complex joinery, footings.

All teams worked in parallel on several aspects of the proposal simultaniously such as: primary and secondary structure, detailed joinery timber/ timber and timber/clay, preparation of fabrication drawings, documenting all the design iterations, documenting the fabrication process, planar and/or double curved envelope options), relation between unique pieces vs more standardised pieces.

The outcome of the workshop was then eventually built on 1/10 scale using our digital fabrication facilities.

Student work by:

1-2 _MACH Studio group: Harmandeep Sanghera, Chetan Patel, Mihriban Ustun, Agis Panagiotis **3** Mohammed Patel **4** Sribalaji Murugavel **5** Shreyans Sanjay.

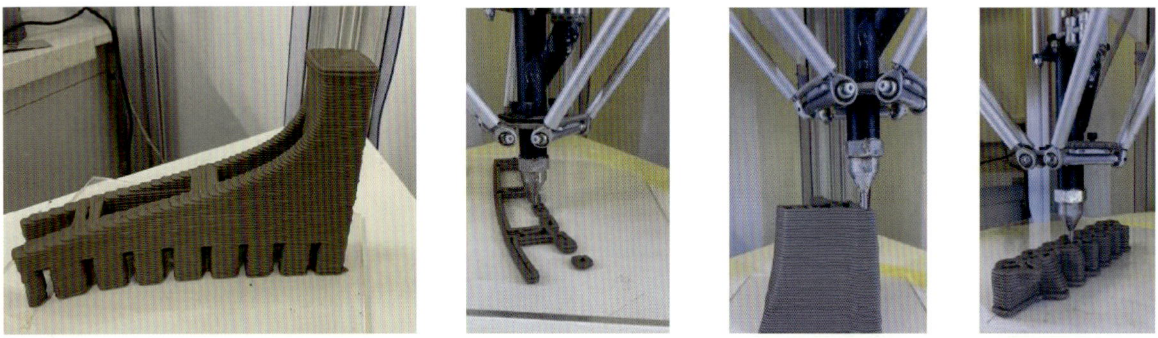

1

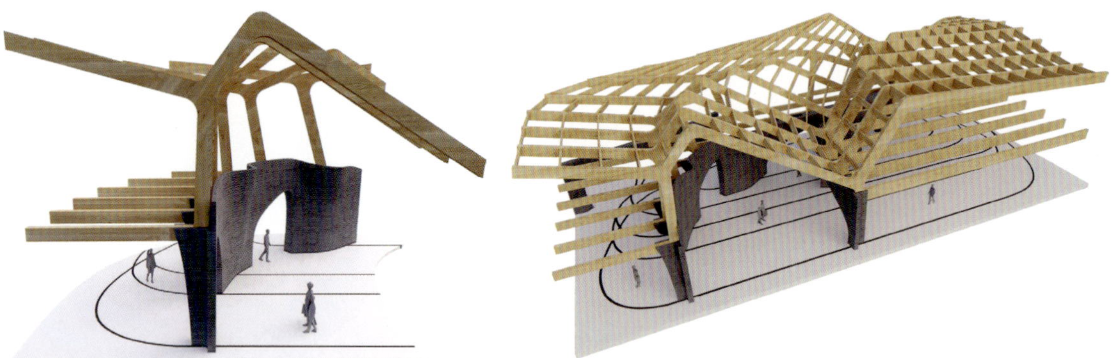

2

3

4

5

Our sites this year are located on UEL's Docklands campus. Students will identify areas on and around our own campus in order to propose novel and more sustainable architectures which suit rapidly changing demands and offer a better integration between study, research and future work whilst providing for its local community. As such it will align with our universities Vision2028 goals which contributes to the UN's Sustainable Development Goals.

Student work by: **6** Mihriban Ustun proposes a half sunken alternative healing centre to aid those with increasing mental health issues. As such, creating an oasis of tranquility and aid. **7** Agis Panagiotis proposes a canoeing club and swimming pool over the existing edge of the docks. Energising the endless edge of the Royal docks.

8 Rackel Metrona Afat proposes to utilize hydrotherapy as a treatment program to treat mental health whilst maintaining ones general physical health. This in collaboration with the existing UEL wellbeing services. **9** Vanessa Mawoneke proposes to replace our existing nursery by a Forest school on top of our existing car park. This model of education can help children and young people to begin to place value, gain awareness and respect for the environment. Thus creating a generation that is more mindful and concious of the effects we have on nature. **10** Rafaa Abubaker Mohamed Elfatih proposes a Human library as an extention to the AVA building, making use of the diversity of educators, students, staff to provide academic, artistic, practical and technical knowledge, as well as life experience struggles and strengths.

6

7

8

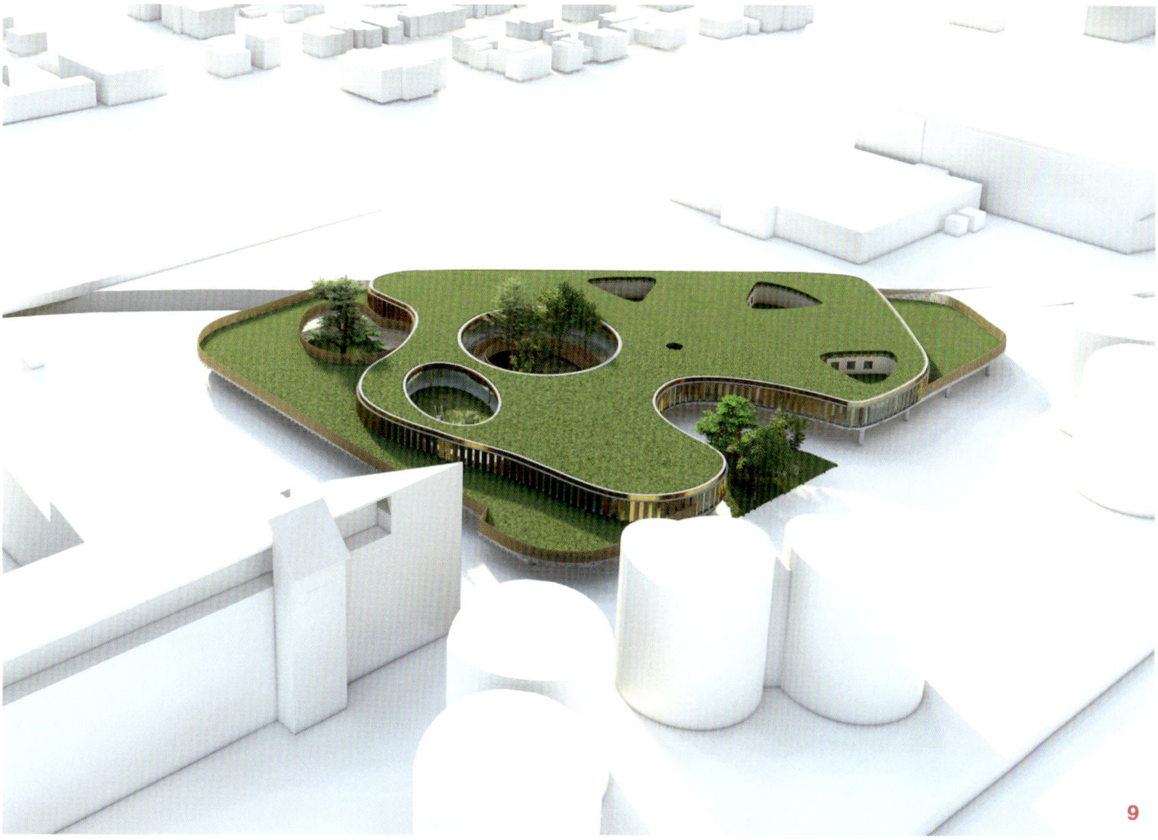

9

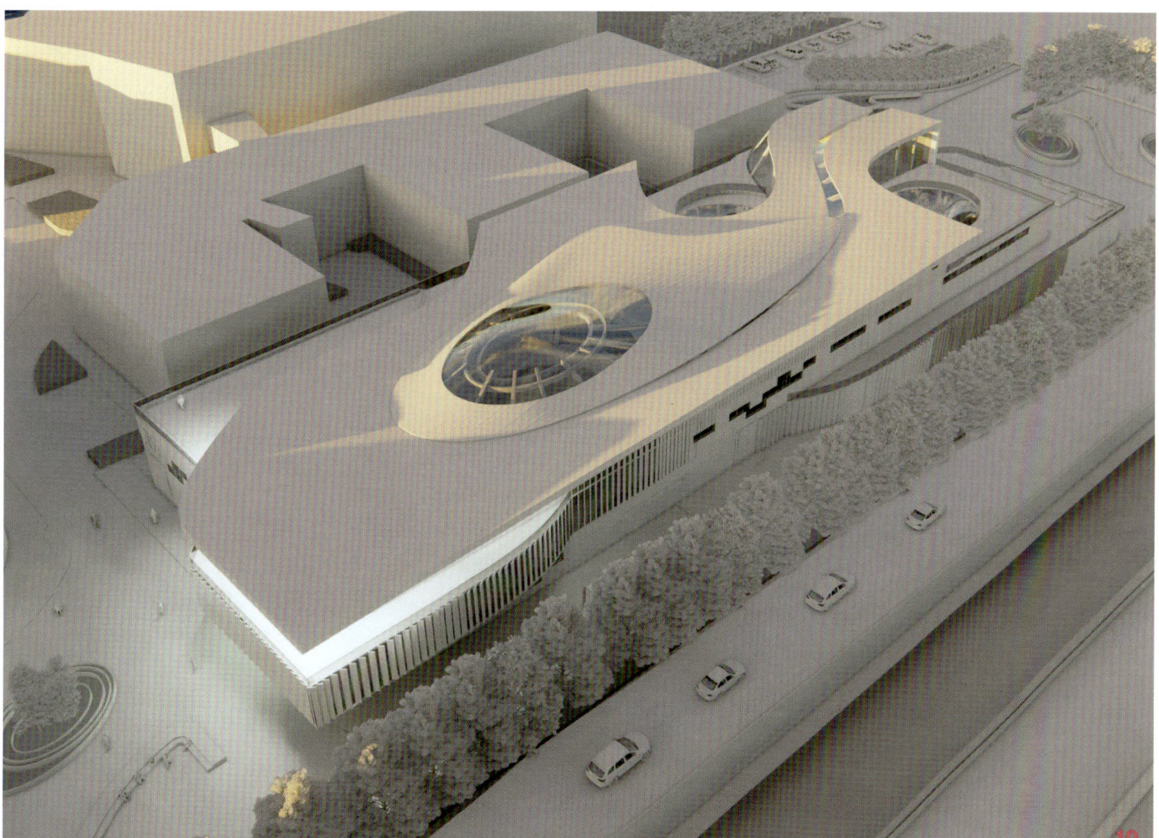

10

A series of a chunk models are developed soon after the start of the second term. These do not only depict constructional material layering as they simultaneously describe chosen envelope strategies which directly influence atmosphere, climatic control and use. These same 3 dimensional chunk models ought to reflect key strategies which are applicable on the whole proposal. In this specifc case, students were looking at the relation between 3D printed concrete or clat parts and planar timber members in order to produce a complex whole.

Student work by:

11 - 12 Harmandeep Kaur Sanghera. Study of infill systems for hollow 3D printed wall sections and chunk model for the new digital making and research spaces in the AVA building.

13 Rafaa Abubaker Mohamed Elfatih. Double layered atrium condition for the human library located in the AVA building.

14 Mohammed Patel. Tripod column supporting mega longitudenal beams which act to supend the first floor structure

15 - 16 Shreyans Sanjay. Elevation and interior rendering of the centre for Education for Sustainable Development. The proposal allows every human being to acquire the knowledge, skills, attitudes and values necessary to shape a sustainable future.Education for Sustainable Development means including key sustainable development issues into teaching and learning; for example, climate change, disaster risk reduction, biodiversity, poverty reduction, and sustainable consumption.

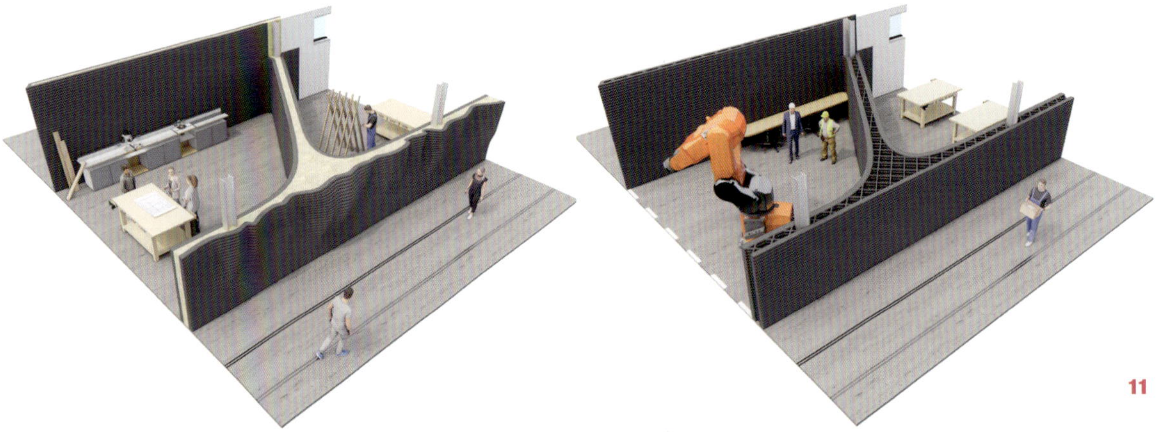

11

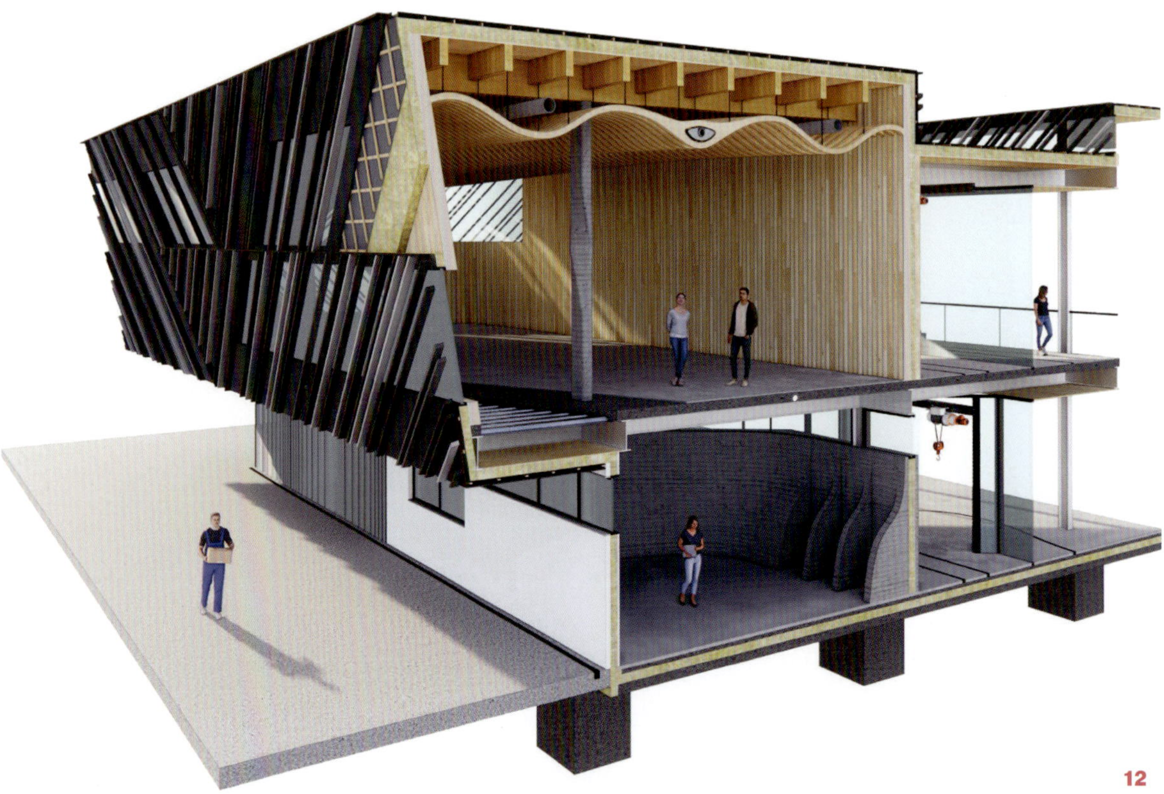

12

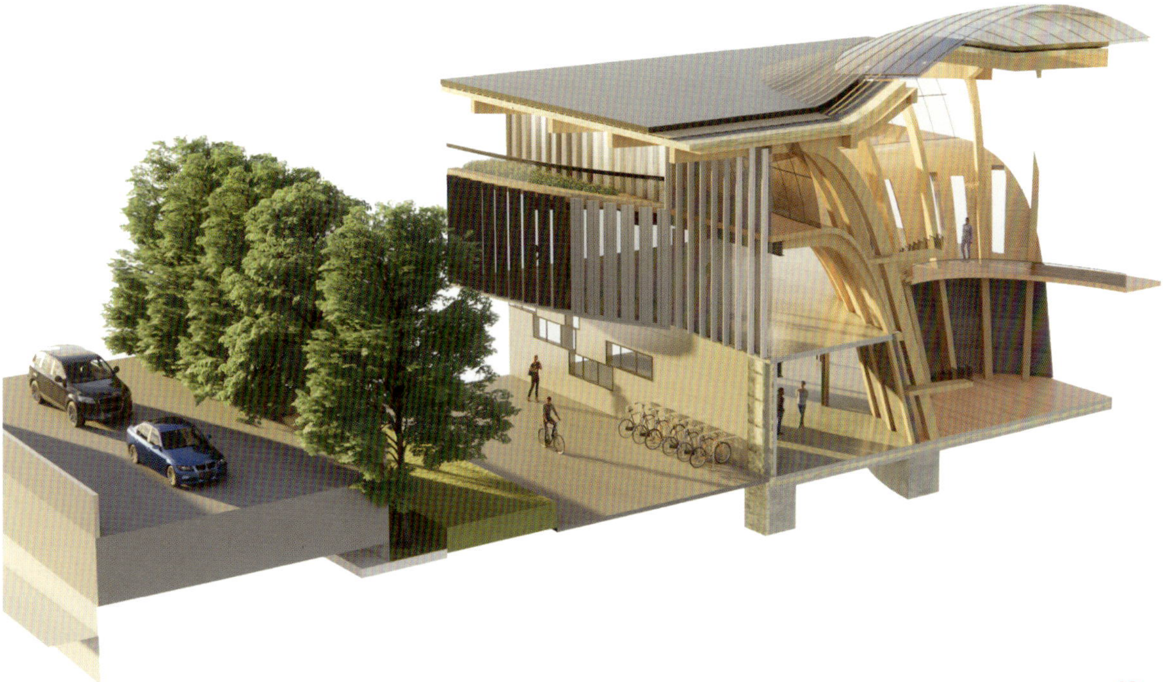

13

14

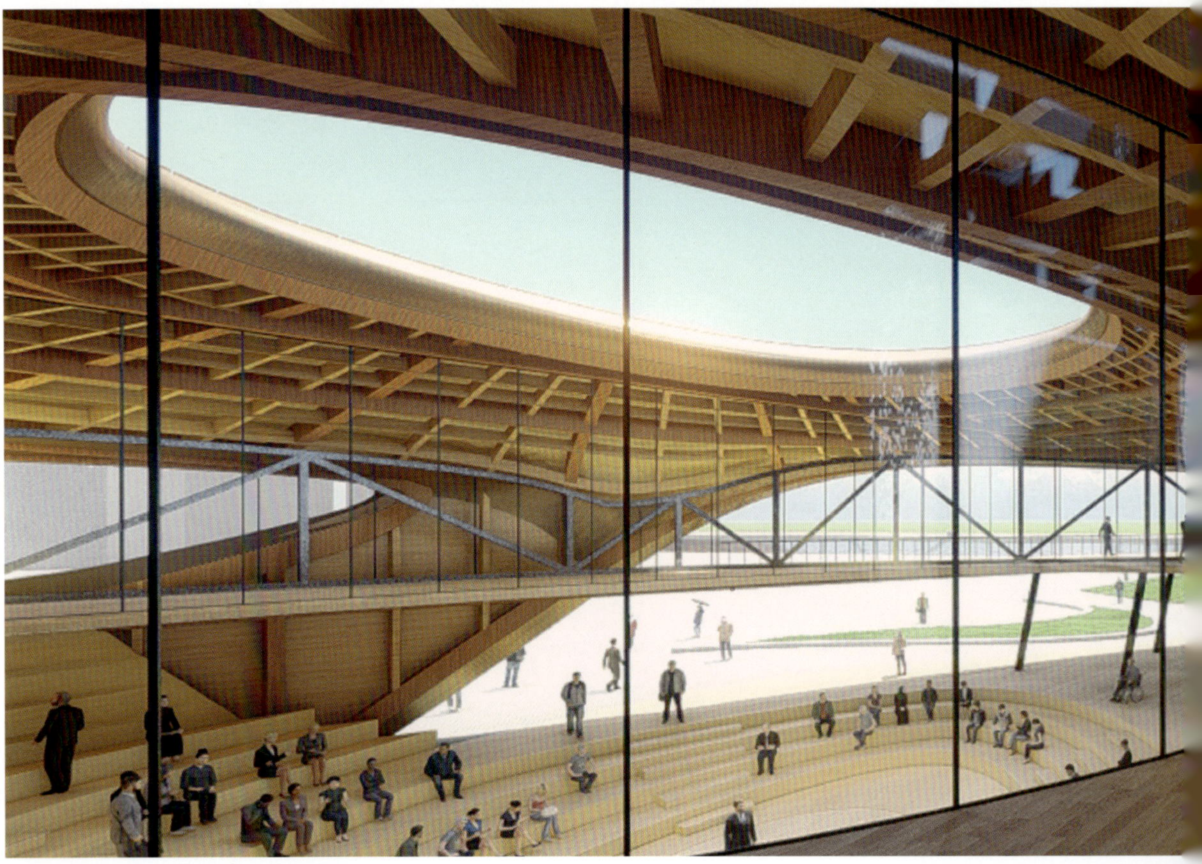

15

16

Unit 8

HWFI: Towards a Sustainable De-industrialization

Armor Gutierrez Rivas and Rosa Rogina

MArch Unit 8 perceives architecture as a social and political practice, and therefore promotes mobilisation of architectural thinking and making as a tool to engage with current matters of concern, both local and global. It explores how can architectural design processes be expanded beyond their conventional role and be utilised as tools for a wider social, cultural and environmental change. The unit looks more closely into territories of spatial and/or social tension and attempts to unpack and address these complex contemporary conditions. By balancing in between identified real-world context, radical imagination and environmental innovation, the students in Unit 8 are encouraged to use the identified tension as a main driver for their design proposal.

This academic year, our design projects look at alternative live-work strategies for creative industries at risk of displacement in Hackney Wick and Fish Island.Once an industrial hub, Hackney Wick remains a home to a whole host of creatives; from innovative green industries working with algae to replace plastic to start ups upcycling food and second-hand clothes. Yet, due to new waves of residential profit-led development, members of this unique ecosystem of independent businesses sharing core values of local empowerment, resource sharing and innovation are being displaced at an alarming rate.

How can Hackney Wick learn from its own intricate past and provide grounds for a new zero-carbon industry model, one that is based on alternative live-work arrangements, adaptive reuse, resource efficiency and circular economy? Can a new zero carbon industry model learn from existing flexible live-work arrangements in the area – and be adaptable, expandable and retractable? Which alternative construction methods and environmental strategies can be used as enhancers to existing meanwhile conditions while minimising local energy consumption?

By using architecture as a form of resistance, Unit 8 will research and document different ways of creative occupation locally. In order to formalise and empower these important but still temporal modes of inhabiting the city, students in unit 8 will be asked to develop a series of new typologies for a more sustainable – both socially and environmentally – live-work set up for the area leading the path for a new De-industrial Revolution.

> "For some years, scaffolding boards and other 'waste' materials from the Olympic Park were used for mezzanine-building, warehouse modifications and much more in Hackney Wick. Almost a decade ago, Tom Fletcher created his Rejuice factory in a Fish Island warehouse, collecting discarded fruit from a wholesale market. Another warehouse-dweller I knew fantasised about closed-circuit hydroponic farms before heading to Kenya to build cooking stove fuelled by their owners' toilet waste. The Wick was not only a playground but a testing ground too."
>
> *Simon Cole, The Wick, 2021*

HACKNEY WICK & FISH ISLAND, LONDON

Students:

Y5: Ozan Nacar, Prabesh Sherchan, Corey Smith, Mahmoud Sayed Abdelmonem Abdellattif, Ana Paula Gomes Kouzak, Safwa Chowdhury, Gayatri Shyam Kashid, Orseer Isreal Gbashah, Rashmi Madagamage Gunathilaka

Y4: Pedro Leite, Jussiley Mendes, Oluchi Obiejesi, Yazmin Abdul Halim, Amaka Edeh, Boon Eng, Mert Erten, Louise Ripper, Slav Savov, Muayad Tuma, Akshay Pravinchandra Koli, Hari Srinivasa Reddiar Thiagarajan, Stephano Binoi Varikkanikkal

Special thanks to visiting Crits and Guests:

Richard Brown (founder of Brown Urbanism), Javier Gonzalez-Adalid (Associate at Foster and Partners), Wilf Meynell (co-founder of Studio Bark), Bamdad Ayati (Material scientist, SRI), Joanne Primiano (Textiles department, UEL)

Isaie Bloch, Christoph Hadrys, Alan Chandler, Teresa Serrano and Deborah Benros

Instagram: @unit8.uel

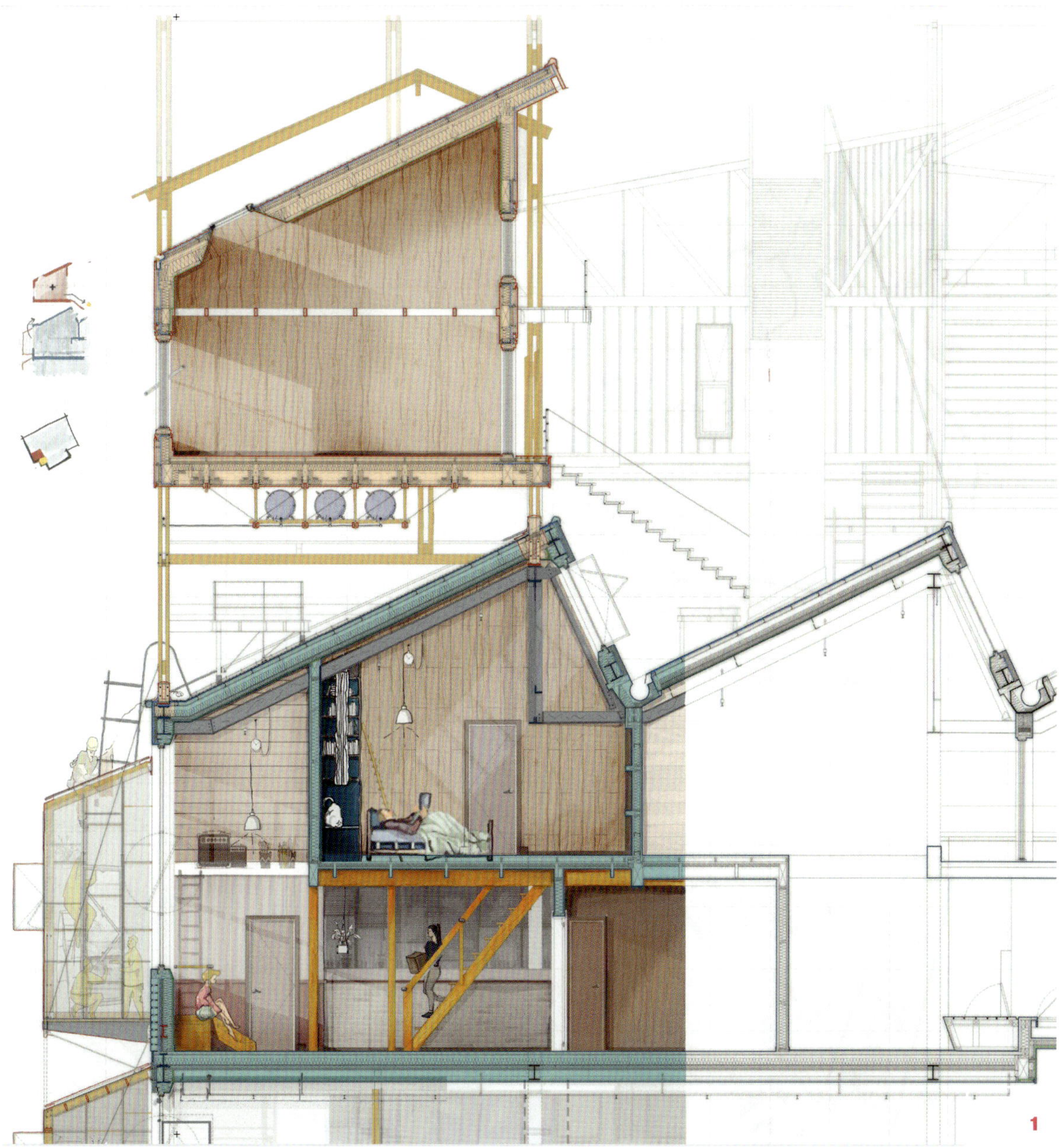

1

1 On the previous page, The Only Way is Up, symbiotes Parasite re-imagining Oslo House, technical section.

The Only Way is Up explores a framework and social platform for the creative community and micro-businesses operating in HWFI to experiment, develop and fabricate different live/work typologies by injecting existing buildings and warehouses with symbiotes and parasites that would enhance, enrich and utilize the existing limited infrastructure of the area.

2 While the project re-imagines Oslo Hose as a testing ground the strategies could extrapolate to other creative venues at risk of displacement elsewhere.

3 Sectional diagrams of intervention stages. **4** Construction axo view exploring symbiotes through environmental enhancers and facade interventions. **5** Cross section indicating interventions to the existing fabric and proposed symbiotes additions.

Project and drawings by Mahmoud Sayed Abdelmonem Abdellattif.

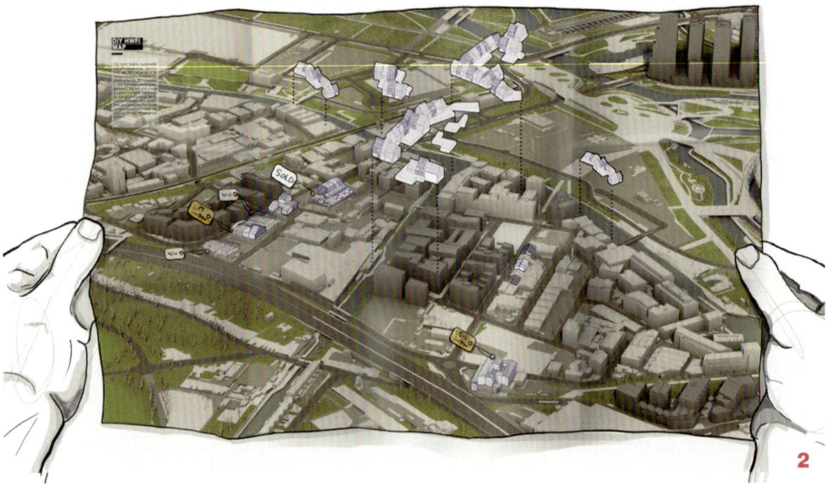

2

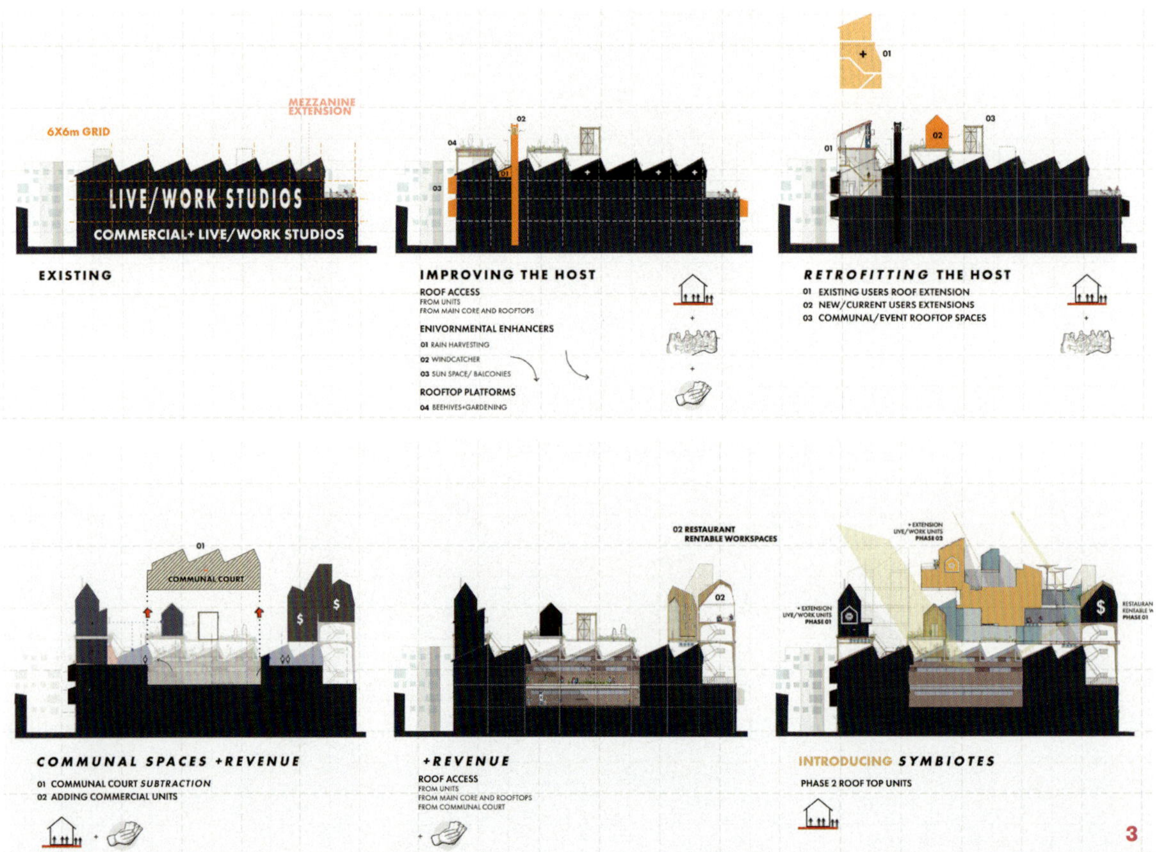

3

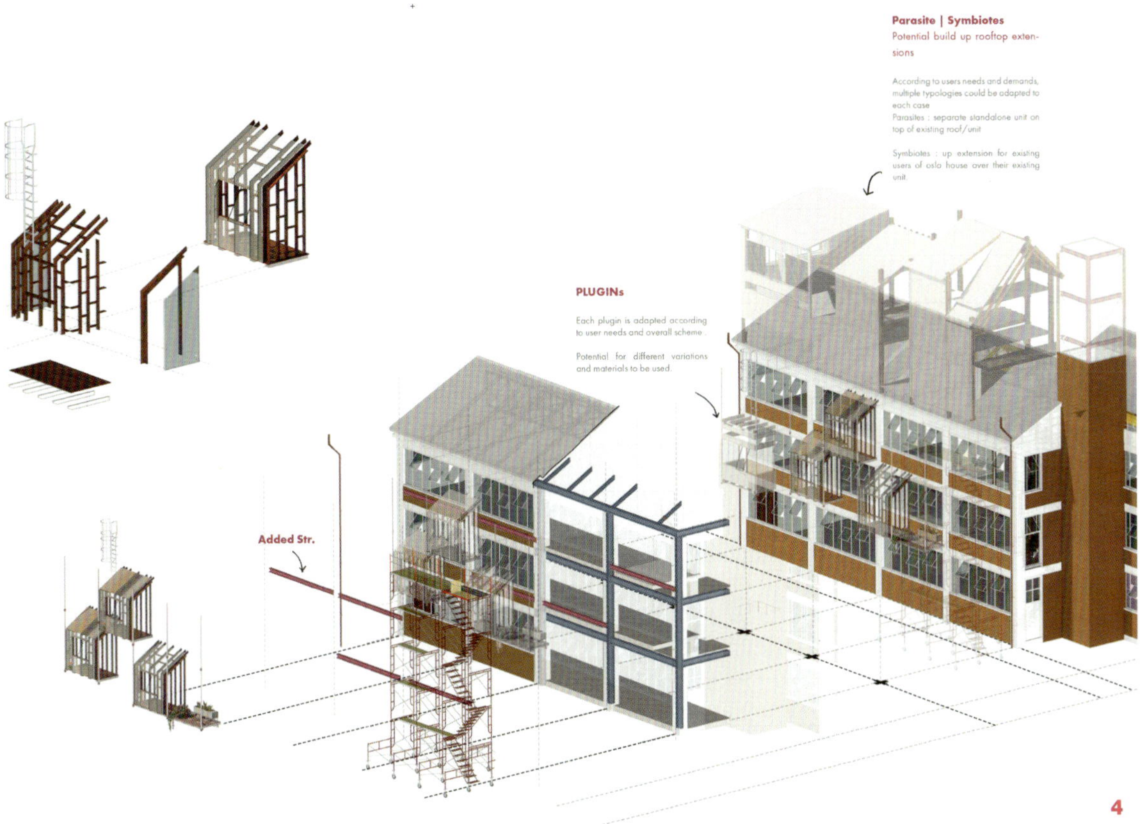
Parasite | Symbiotes
Potential build up rooftop extensions
According to users needs and demands, multiple typologies could be adapted to each case
Parasites : separate standalone unit on top of existing roof/unit
Symbiotes : up extension for existing users of oslo house over their existing unit.
PLUGINs
Each plugin is adapted according to user needs and overall scheme.
Potential for different variations and materials to be used.
Added Str.

4

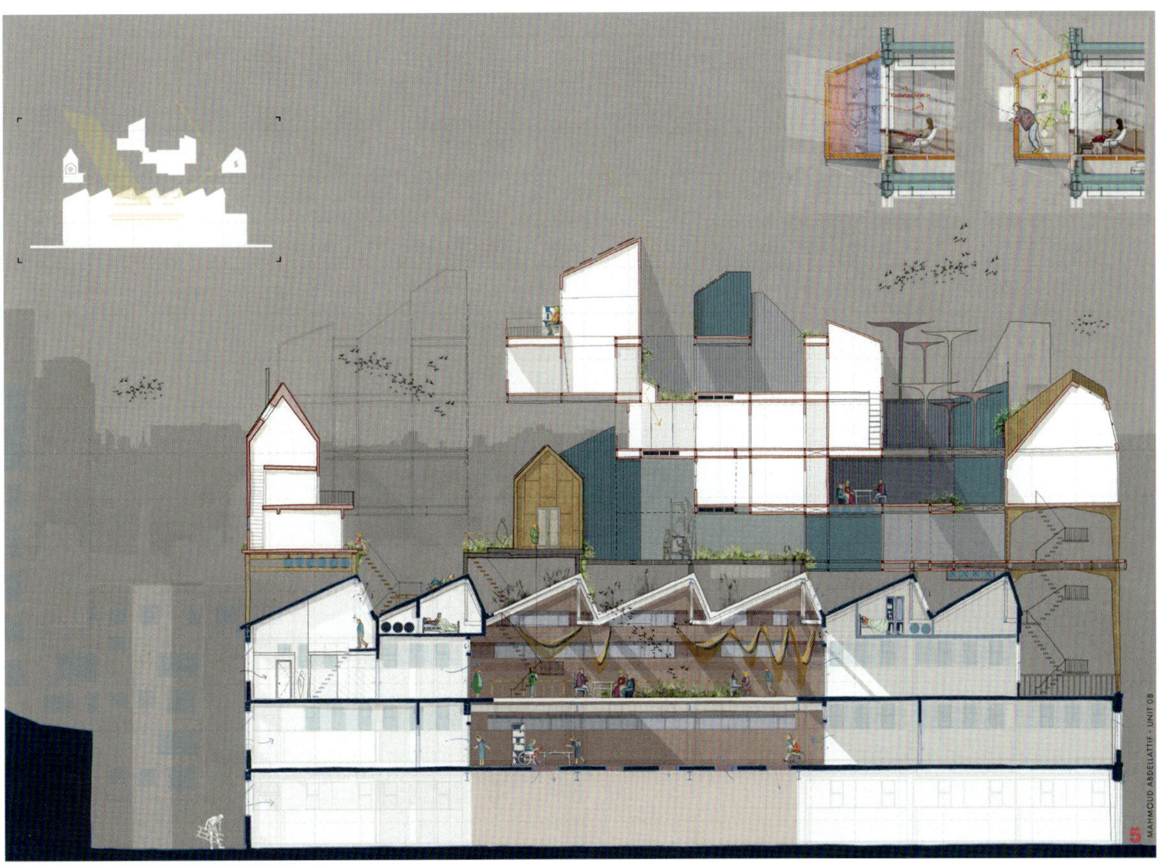
MAHMOUD ABDELLATTIF · UNIT 08
5

Re-create imagines a creative hub in HWFI to exhibit, protect and support local creative industries.

The project aims to bring awareness to the social and cultural values existing in the area, taking advantage of its creative background and exhibiting the work of the existing industries and artists. The proposal accommodates different uses such as an exhibition centre for local productions, workshops that can be used by the existing residents to produce environmental enhancers for their current living conditions, as well as creating a network for the creative community. The project will also accommodate some pilot models of live-work units that can be replicated in other areas.

6 The project uses a community land trust model, where a group of local active residents will own and run the state. Modular and fast construction will serve the community and create the housing pilot models. **7** Welcoming view of the proposal from the Hertford Union Canal. **8** North-west elevation towards Queens Yard. **9** Internal views of the live-work units. **10** The open performance area, workshops and events will fund the capital loan and the residents can be involved as curators for the exhibitions, events and workshops taking place.

Project and drawings by Ana Paula Gomes Kouzak.

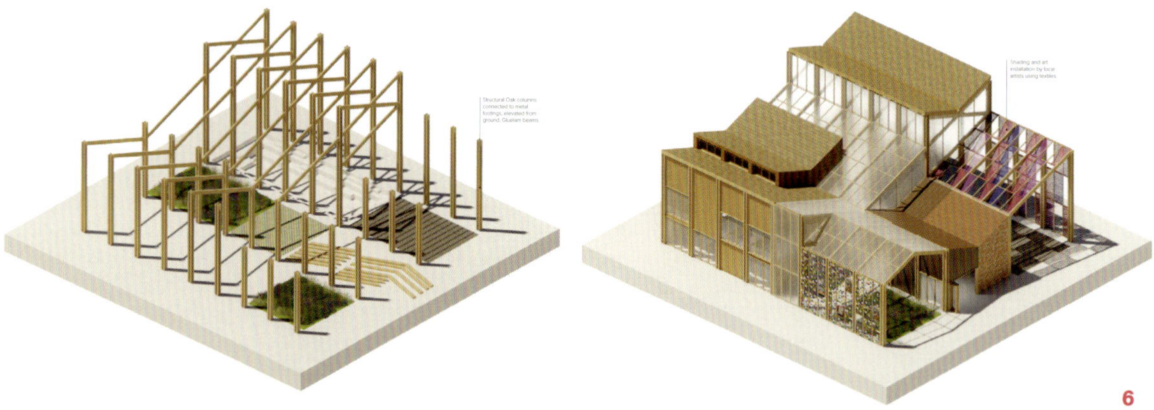

6

7

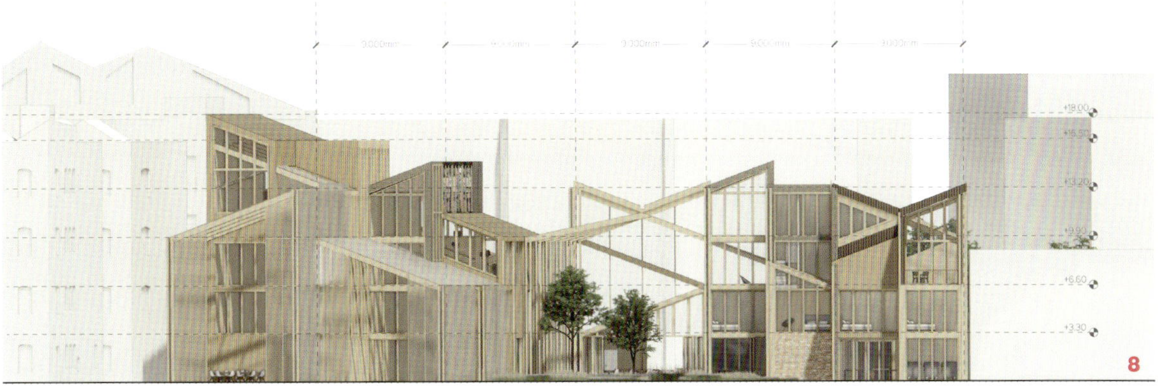
+18.00
+13.20
+9.90
+6.60
+3.30
8

South facing bedroom
Third floor studio
9

10

The Pixel project offers a one-stop destination of exhibition spaces, creative venues and public meeting spaces for the consumption culture and heritage of HWFI and the wider communities, including accommodation for artist in residency and a public display of the work within the double skin façade of the building. An exposé into the exciting creative culture/community of Hackney Wick and Fish Island.

11 Environmental section indicating the relationship with the Green Way and water retention strategy. **12** Axo views indicating structural strategy. **13** Approach view highlighting the use of the double skin facade as an evolving exhibition area.

Project and drawings by Orseer Isreal Gbashah.

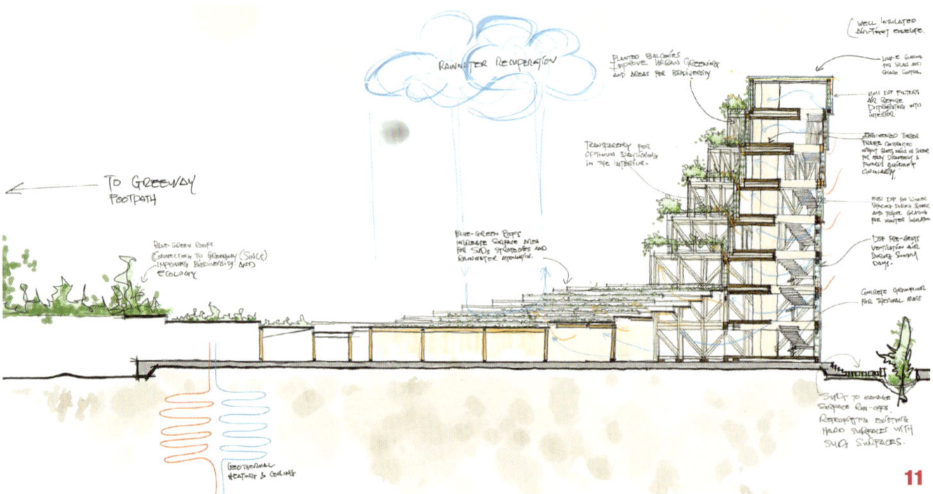

11

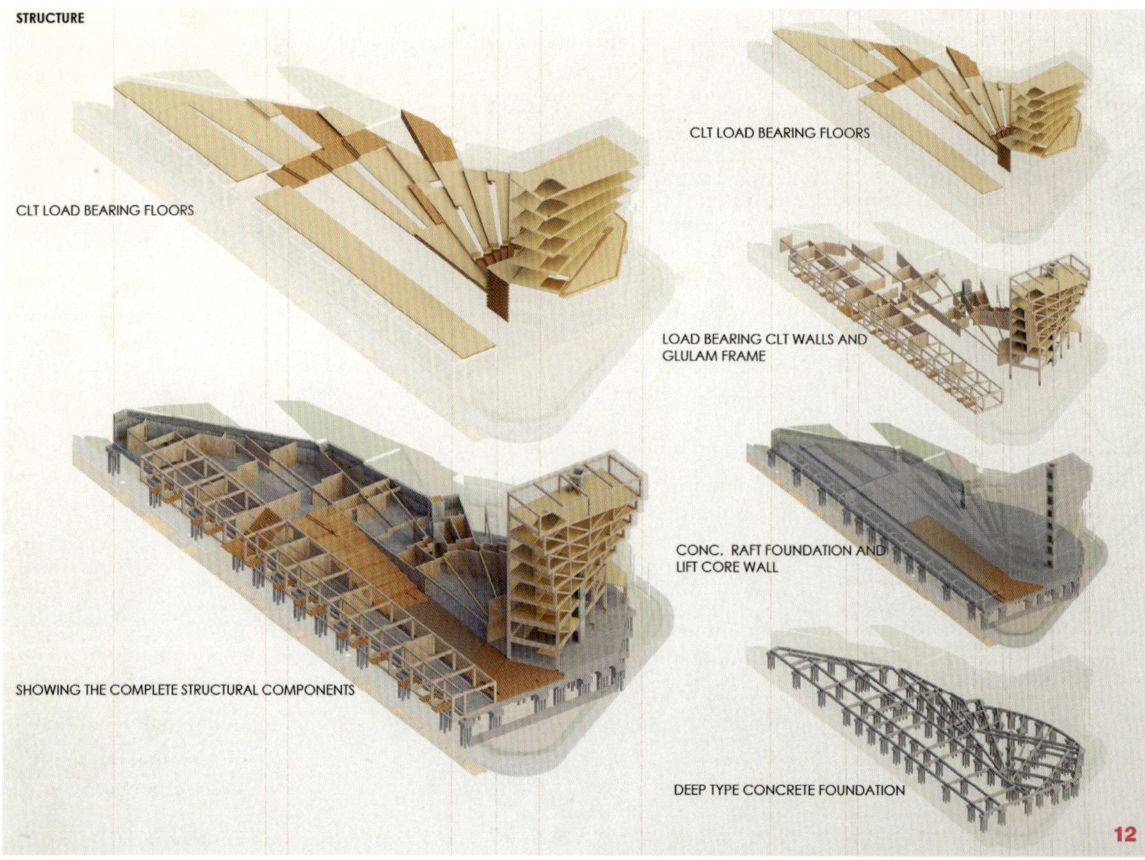

12

13

In The Yards aims to propose a regeneration of existing industries in HWFI, creating a series of interventions to existing warehouses acting as new gateways and areas of creative exchange. The project aims to offer affordable workspaces and community interaction through open workshops for light industry and fabrication, including rehousing local artists at risk of displacement.

14 Material experimentation as cladding using sugarcane by-products from local industries. **15** Axo view of the intervention indicating existing and proposed relationship with existing users. **16** Approach view from the Hertford Union Canal.

17 Main elevation showing the juxtaposition of existing and proposed programs. **18** View of one of the shared workshop spaces. **19** The masterplan intervention is tied together by a colourful exhibition road connection, hosting a bi-annual art event run by local artists to reinforce the importance of the creative community in the area.

Project and drawings by Rashmi Madagamage Gunathilaka

14

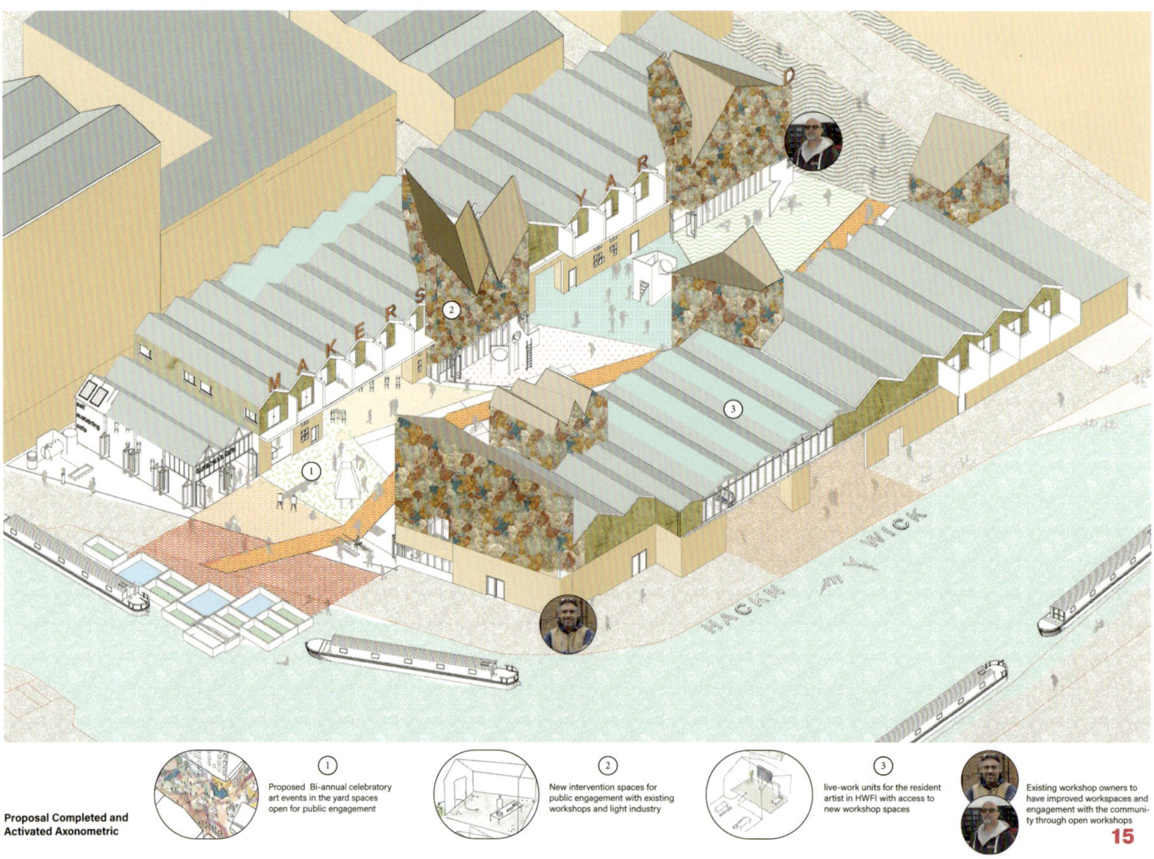

Proposal Completed and Activated Axonometric

15

16

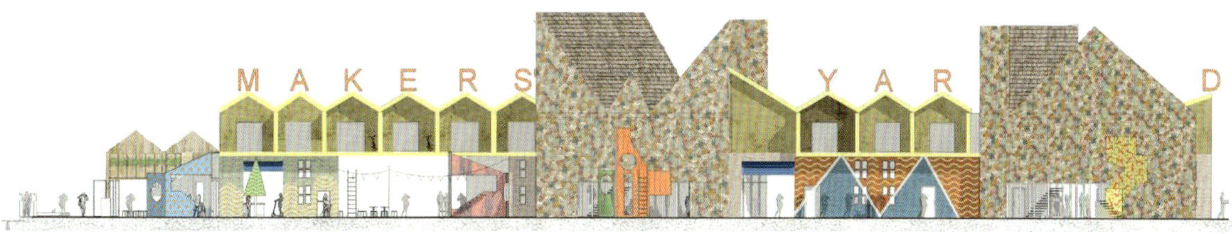

17

18

19

Building Matters

Professional Studies unit-based group project

Roland Karthaus

Building Matters is a group study undertaken by Year 4 MArch students to explore how professional and technical considerations influence the design and construction of buildings. Clients from live construction projects are invited into the school to share their original project aims and objectives and the students research the project planning information. Interrogating this information raises questions that are shaped into structured interviews with the multidisciplinary design teams. The students further interrogate this information to identify key areas within the project that are challenging and complex and seek to understand how these were resolved to meet the brief. They visit the construction sites, to investigate these issues further and experience how knowledge created through the design process results in built form.

The projects are often large and complex and the students are challenged to develop a groupwork method that can tackle the full complexity of the projects, engaging with the technical detail whilst relating it to the client's original aims. At the conclusion, the students present their findings to the clients and frequently bring a fresh perspective, casting new light on the projects.

This year the projects were:

- New mixed use office and older people's 'almshouses' for Southwark Charities
- New older people's almshouses for United St Saviours Trust
- New housing as part of the Gascoigne estate redevelopment for Be First, Barking and Dagenham

The studies explored the potential for housing to support vulnerable people's health and wellbeing and the potential to densify a housing estate whilst increasing community cohesion. Thanks to the clients for providing considerable time and resources to facilitate the study.

Building Matters aims to engage students of architecture with live construction projects, design teams and clients. The process of investigating a complex project as a group reflects the collaborative, team endeavour of designing and constructing a building. Collective knowledge is created, incrementally through a structured process so the final product is fully understood only when it is realised and put into use.

Students:
Luke Day, William Fullick, Thomas Hardy, Ziyad Hasanin, Julian Imossi, Bhakti Panchal, Khushbuben Patel, Akanksha Barada, Harsh Desai, Chidochise Mawoneke, Wendpangnangde Nakoulma, Franko Rrapaj, Nafisa Tailor, Mihriban Ustun, Agis Valsamis, Hidayati Abdul Halim, Stephano Binoi Varikkanikkal, Uzomaka Edeh, Boon Kyiet Eng, Mert Erten, Ashaykumar Koli, Pedro Leite, Jussiley Mendes, Oluchukwu Obiejesi, Louise Ripper, Svetoslav Savov, Harinath Srinivasa Thiagarajan, Muayad Tuma

Visiting Guests
Chris Wilson, Sarah Riley, Martyn Craddock

With thanks to:
United St Saviours, Southwark Charities, Be First, White Architects, Fathom Architects, Witherford Watson Mann

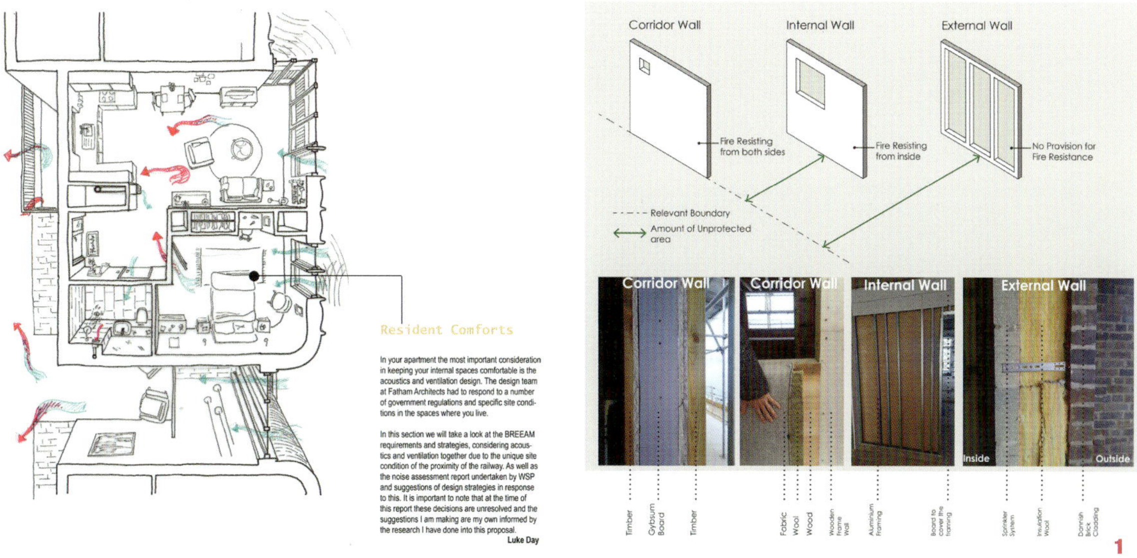

1

2

1 On the previous page: analytical drawings of ventilation and wall construction in relation to fire regulations.

2 Clients from United St Saviour's, Southwark Charities and Be First attending student presentations at UEL.

3 This page: mapping the project process against the RIBA plan of work

4 Site photographs from the Gascoigne Estate, Barking and Dagenham

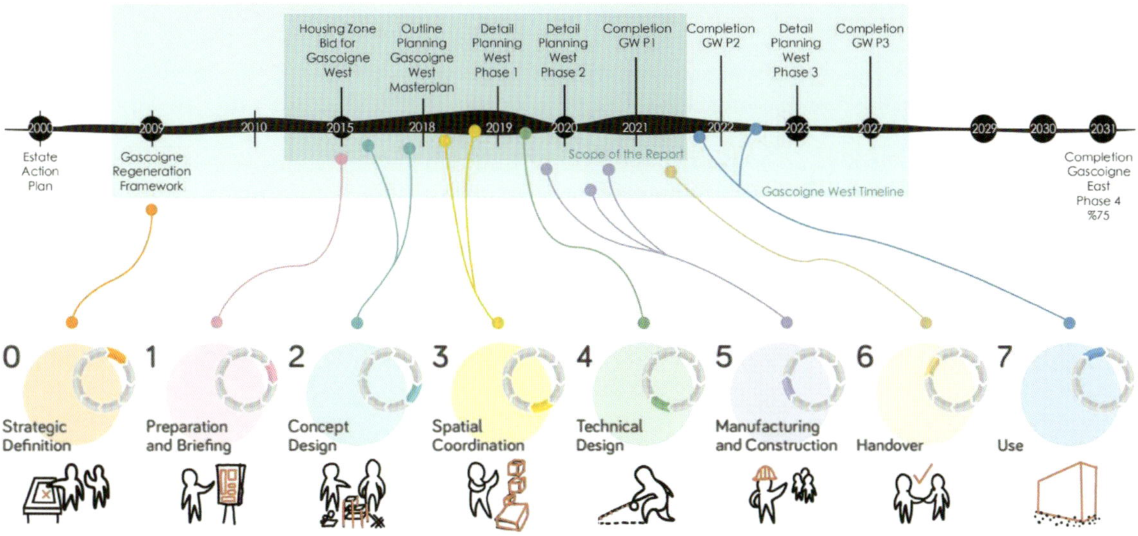
Housing Zone Bid for Gascoigne West
Outline Planning Gascoigne West Masterplan
Detail Planning West Phase 1
Detail Planning West Phase 2
Completion GW P1
Completion GW P2
Detail Planning West Phase 3
Completion GW P3
2000
2009
2010
2015
2018
2019
2020
2021
2022
2023
2027
2029
2030
2031
Estate Action Plan
Gascoigne Regeneration Framework
Scope of the Report
Gascoigne West Timeline
Completion Gascoigne East Phase 4 %75
0 Strategic Definition
1 Preparation and Briefing
2 Concept Design
3 Spatial Coordination
4 Technical Design
5 Manufacturing and Construction
6 Handover
7 Use

3

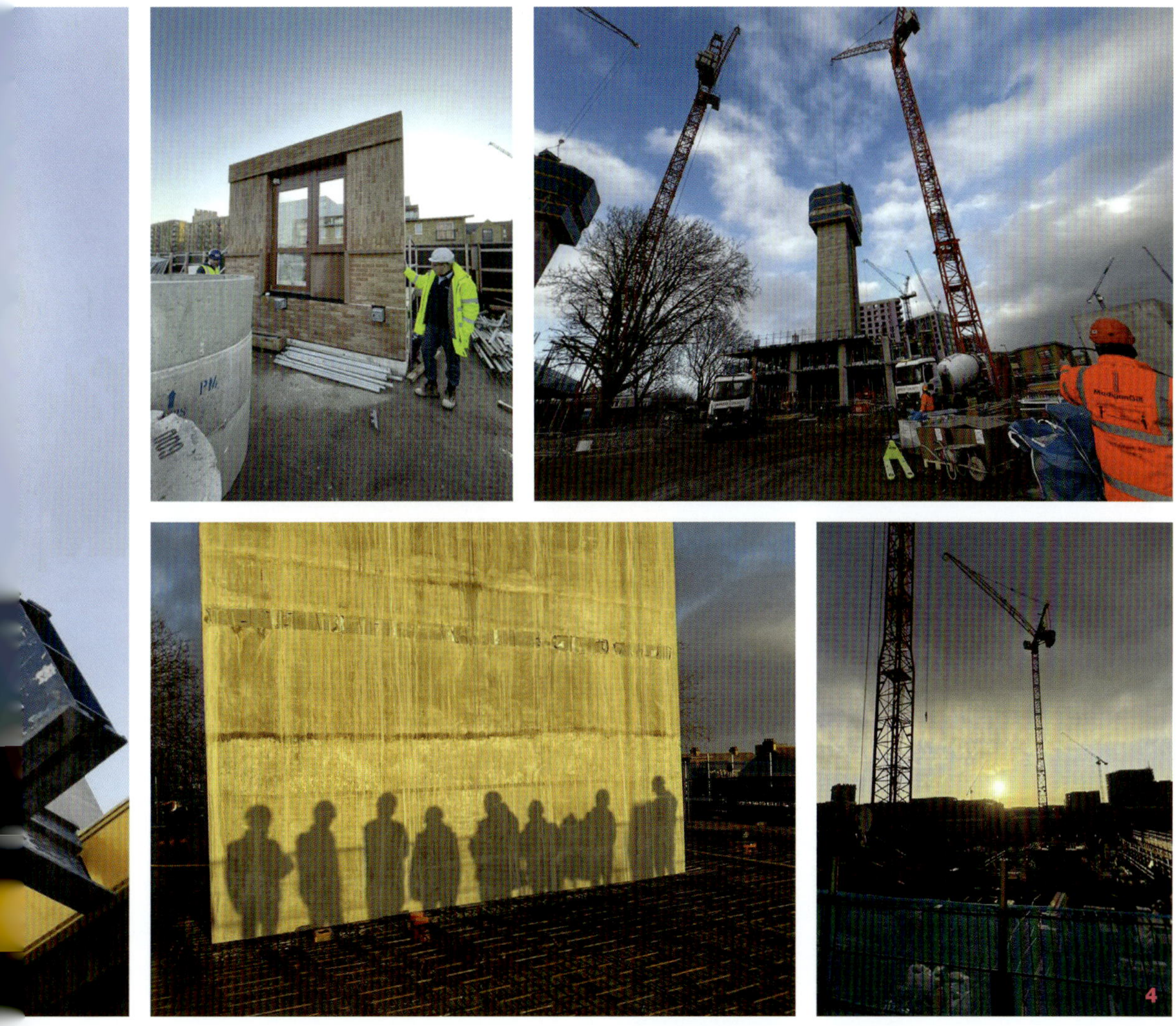

4

MRes Architecture
Reading the neoliberal city

Anna Minton, Debra Shaw

Anna Minton, author of *Big Capital: Who is London for?* (Penguin 2017) and *Ground Control: Fear and happiness in the 21st century city* (Penguin 2009/12), is the Programme Leader on the MRes Architecture. This multi-disciplinary course, sited within the architecture department, welcomes applicants from a wide range of backgrounds. While situated in London's Docklands, the global impact of these processes, which are relevant across the world, provides the context. As this is a small seminar based course, focused on lectures and group discussion, we were able to transfer seamlessly online following lockdown and we continued with blended learning this academic year, meeting online and in person and continuing with our programme of walks through the city.

The course is comprised of four modules: Reading the neoliberal city; Critical Writing and Professional Practice; Ethical Development and the Privatised City. Topics for study include the housing crisis and the privatisation of cities, investigating the financialisation of the urban environment. The modules on Ethical Development and the Digital City investigate potential economic alternatives. The module on Critical Writing focuses on high level writing skills, through written assignments and the study of critical writing about the city, from Situationism to Psychogeography. The modules on Critical Writing and the Digital City are also offered to Diploma students choosing Critical Writing for their Theory component.

Guest lecturers are a key component of the course and include politicians, leading industry figures and activists. This year Lord Moylan, former advisor to Boris Johnson when he was Mayor invited us to the House of Lords where we held a seminar. We also held a workshop with the Leader of Southwark Council, Kieron Williams, James McAsh, Cabinet Member for Sustainability and a student on the course and acclaimed architect Kate MacIntosh.

The MRes provides a pathway to PhD study, with three former MRes students currently doing PhDs with us. Mark Sustr, holder of a UEL PhD studentship is investigating self help housing for homeless communities; Martyn Holmes, also awarded a UEL PhD studentship, is exploring whether community-led housing might provide a solution to the housing crisis and Luke Okende is researching the impact of participatory processes to improve slum conditions in Kinshasa, Democratic Republic of Congo.

We celebrated the end of the academic year with the launch of our 'Best of the MRes' publication, which brought together the best of the students' work since the course began in 2015.

For more information contact:
Anna Minton, Reader in Architecture & Programme Leader (a.minton@uel.ac.uk).

Thanks to Visiting Speakers:
James Murray MP; Daniel Moylan; Leo Pollack; Kate MacIntosh

MRes visit to the House of Lords, hosted by Lord Moylan

Cover of the 'Best of the MRes Reading the Neoliberal City' publication

MA Architecture and Urbanism
Computational Design and Digital Fabrication

Dr Fulvio Wirz

The study paths in Computational Design and Design for Digital Fabrication of the MA in Architecture and Urbanism are developed as a flexible platform to explore the convergence between digital technologies and manufacturing in architectural design.

The programme experiments new possibilities for architectural spaces and cities encouraging students to delineate with their work a clear connection between design processes, technological advances and sustainable strategies.

Students are encouraged to work at all scale using a multidisciplinary approach as the pivotal strategy to achieve creativity and innovation.

This year the programme has been focusing on prefabricated systems applied to residential buildings. The year project had the objective to requalify and adapt a neglected urban space in Canning town transforming it into a cutting edge residential building. The design had to be informed by sustainable strategies and feasibility criteria while taking into account the needs of contemporary society to target an holystic approach to sustainable urban growth.

Students have been encouraged to work in teams to simulate a professional mutidisciplinary environment and promote choices driven by collective intelligence as opposed to isolated thinking.

At the end of the year the teams have entered the prestigious competition " Design Future London" with the objective to tackle the housing crisis in the capital.

This gave them the opportunity to transfer what they learned across the year into practice, achieving outstanding results.

> "Where do new ideas come from? The answer is simple: differences. While there are many theories of creativity, the only tenet they all share is that creativity comes from unlikely juxtapositions. The best way to maximize differences is to mix ages, cultures, and disciplines."
>
> Nicholas Negroponte

Students:
Manali Siddhesh WALKAR, Ubhanayah PATHMANATHAN, Binal PATEL, Hussain Akil SADLIWALA, Mourtada BABOUKARI , Riyad HOSSAIN, Martina COSSU, Venkata Sharat Kumar GOPU, Mohan Ukabhai DUNGRANI, Gunjankumar BAROT, Alina KLIMENTEVA, Brittany Ellen Marie TABER

Special thanks to:
Visiting Critics: Lorenzo Vianello (T&V Architects); Arturo Tedeschi (A>T); Sohith Perera (Kora Architecture, CetraRuddy Architecture), Daniel Widrig (Daniel Widrig Studio)

1

2

Mohan Ukabhai DUNGRANI, Alina KLIMENTEVA, Hussain Akil SADLIWALA, Brittany Ellen Marie TABER : **1&2** Rendered views of " Team Steel" proposal for a Modular Residential Village in Canning Town.

Mohan Ukabhai DUNGRANI, Alina KLIMENTEVA, Hussain Akil SADLIWALA, Brittany Ellen Marie TABER : **3** Top view of the masterplan showing the main circulation, **4** Diagrammes of the urban stategy and zoning, **5** Spatial typologies, **6** Structural assembly showing reused bent steel pipes and 3d printed joints, **7** Abstract combination of modules.

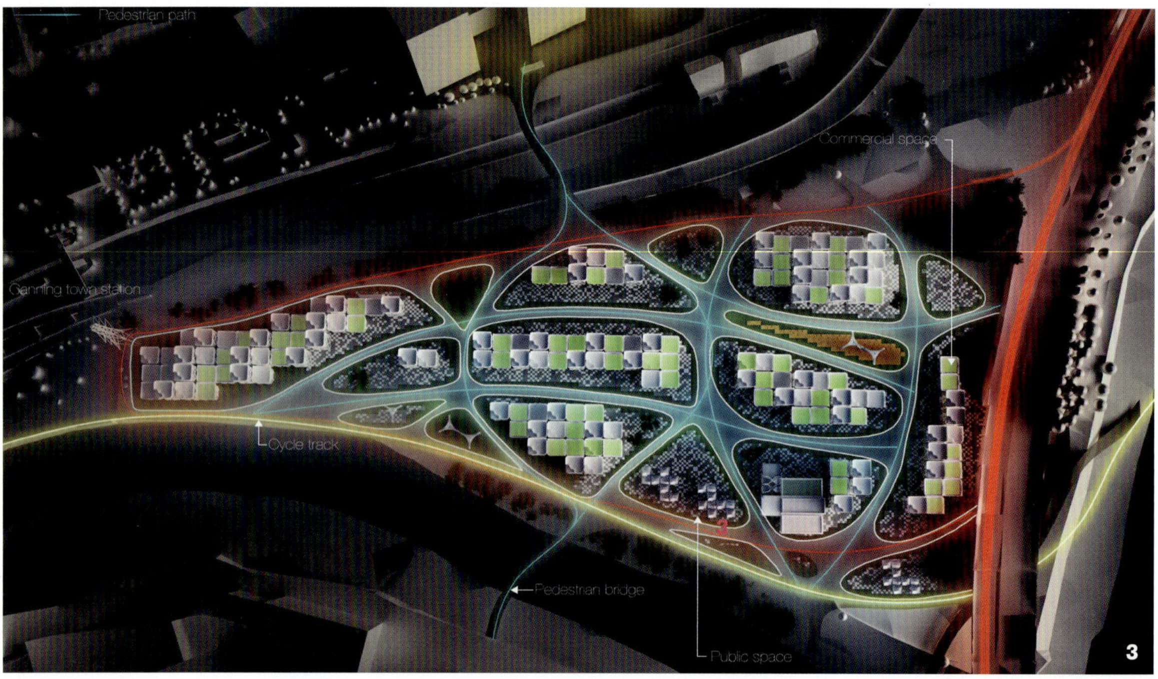

3

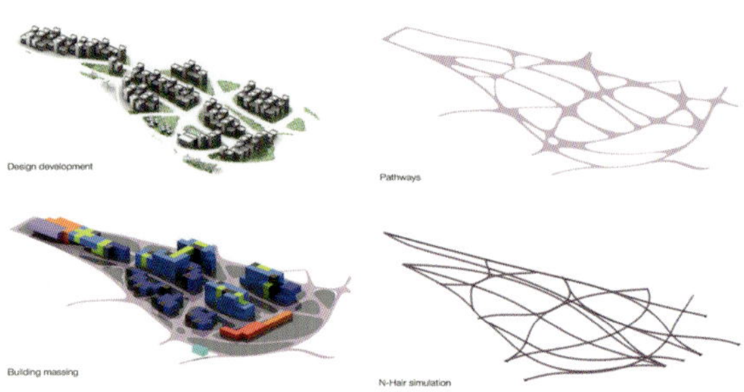

4

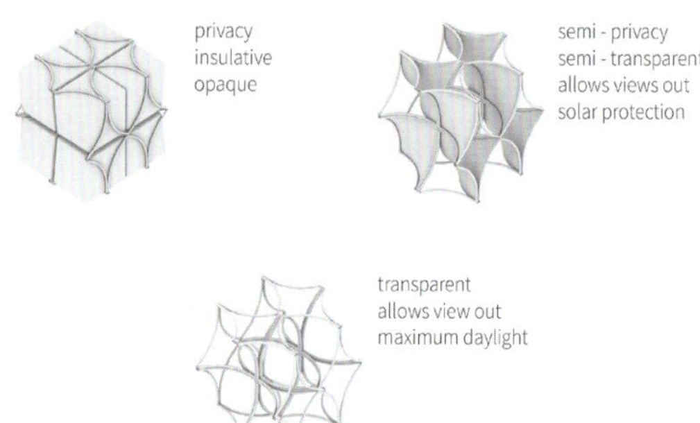

5

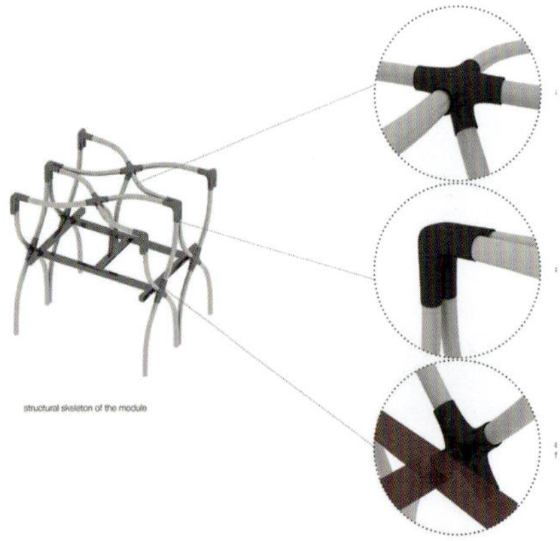

6

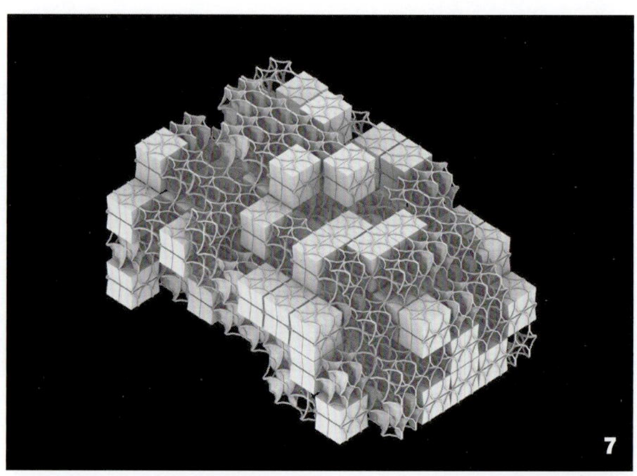

7

Mourtada BABOUKARI , Gunjankumar BAROT, Riyad HOSSAIN, Manali Siddhesh WALKAR : **8** Main perspective view of "Team Timber" proposal for a sustainable village in Canning Town, **9** Axonometric view of the main plans of the building, **10** Early study: physical model exploring form-found vaults, **11** Diagrammes showing the honeycomb aggregation system of various typologies of modular components.

8

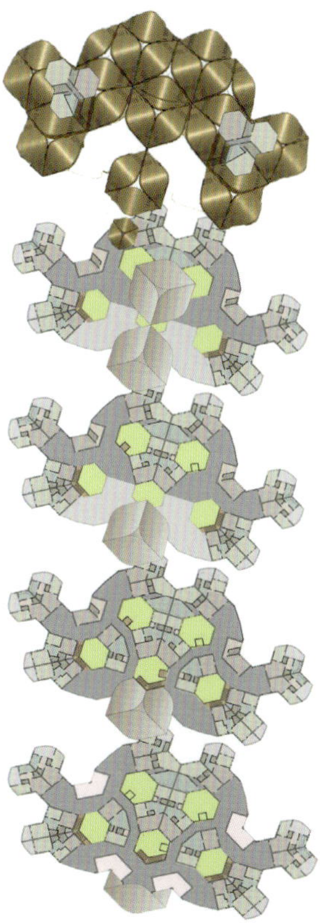

9

10

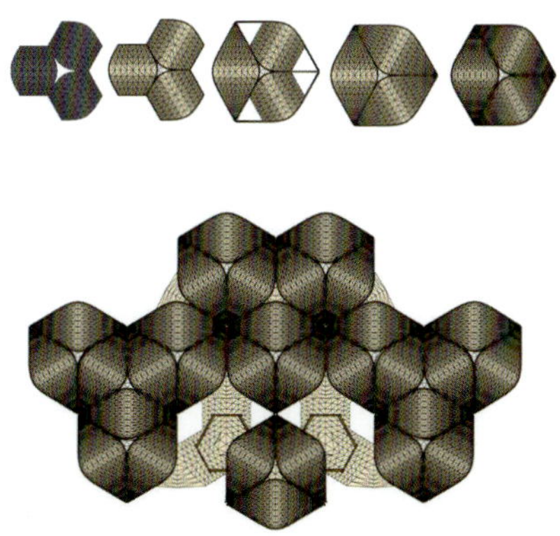

11

Martina COSSU, Binal PATEL, Ubhanayah PATHMANATHAN, Venkata Sharat Kumar GOPU, **8** Visualization of the 3d printed structural reinforcement system **13** Triangulated Modular aggregation of reinforced clay vaults **14** Geometrical studies on triangular vaults **15** Urban studies using computational minimal detour calculation to interconnect the project to Mile End Park.

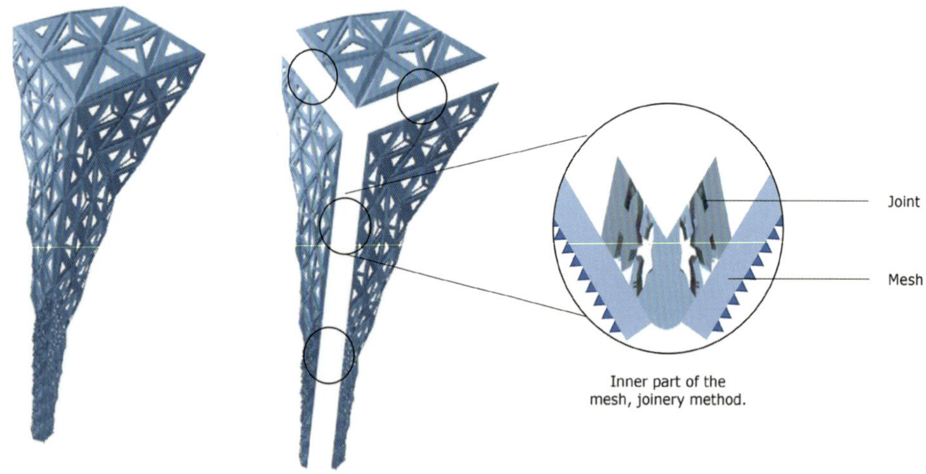

12

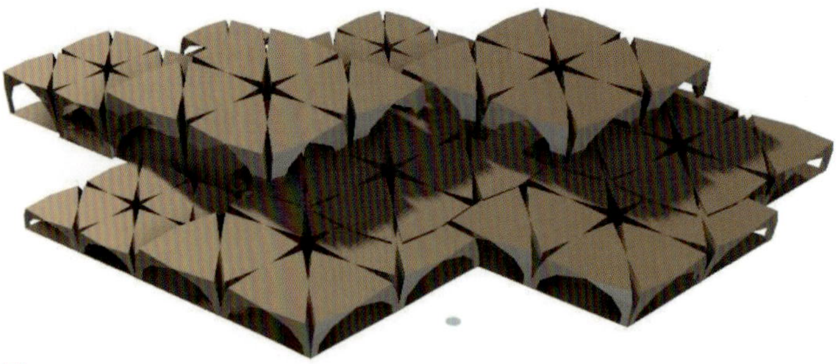

13

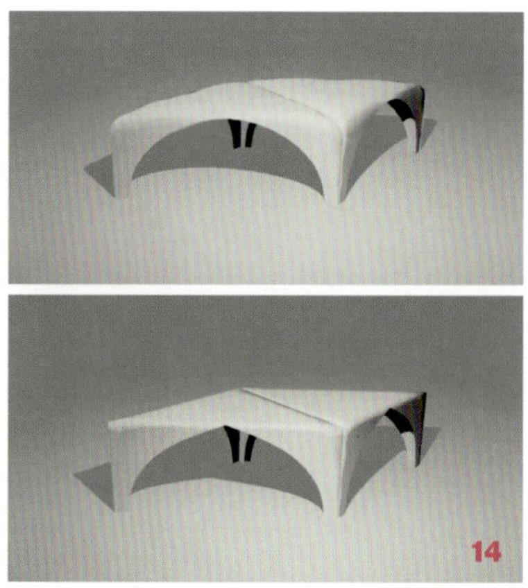

14

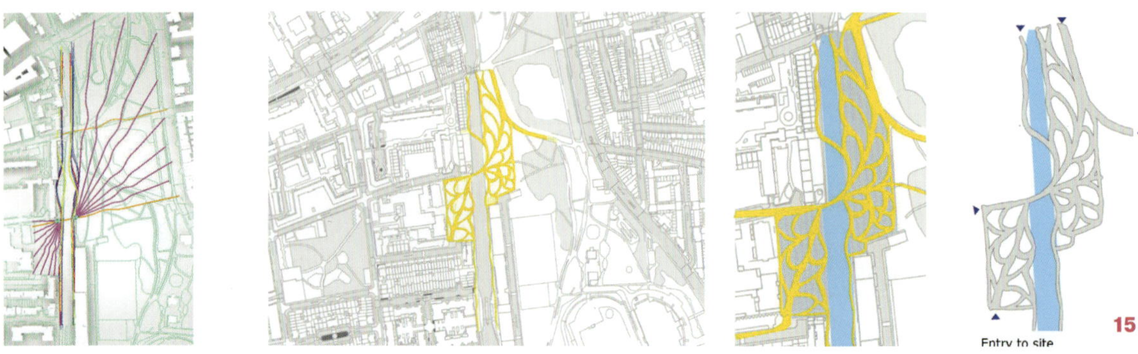

15

Hussain Akil SADLIWALA: **16 & 17** Early studies on vaulted modular systems. Gunjankumar BAROT, Alina KLIMENTEVA, Manali Siddhesh WALKAR : **18** Physical form finding process of minimal surfaces using lycra Alina KLIMENTEVA: **19, 20 & 21** Term 1individual project on plited minimal surfaces.

16

17

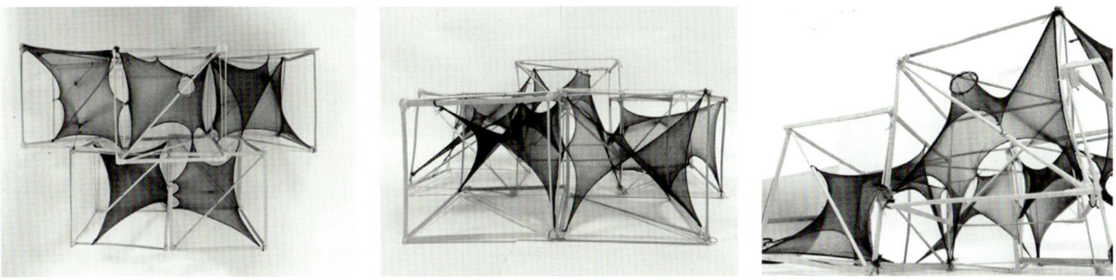

18

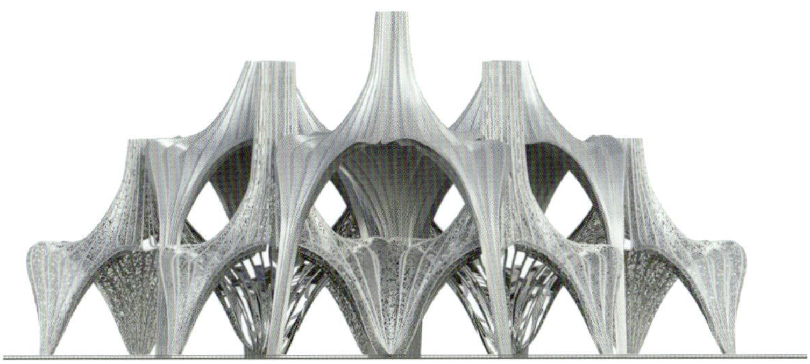

19

20

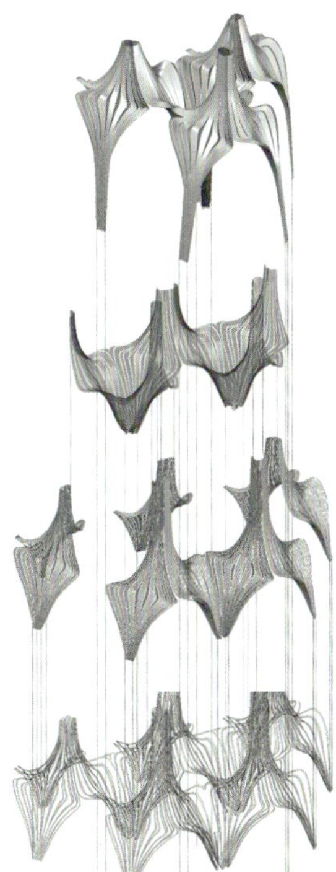

21

Urban Design
Open Studio

Christoph Hadrys

The Urban Design course is part of the MA Architecture and Urbanism Programme. It is the design intensive course for alternative urbanisms at the University of East London. The course is set up to develop both intellectual and practical skills for urban designers and architects. Through interrelated design and theory projects, we search for alternative solutions to complex urban conditions.

The course sets out to explore and develop new forms of urban practice in cities undergoing critical change, where conventional thinking struggles to respond to uncertainties and the necessity for imaginative thinking. It aims to prepare students to work with different geographical settings, urban agendas and economies. We engage directly with communities, sites and contexts, to be able to develop both practical and innovative urban designs, from the scale of regions and cities, all the way through to neighbourhoods and building scales.

This approach is informed by local and international urban practice, but also emphasizes students' individual interests, abilities and intuition, to explore and develop new forms of urbanism. Asking questions, like who is building cities and how to build cities, allows us to open our understanding about finer visible and invisible forces. We research diverse methodologies, like the use of tolerances and time-lines, to enable more dynamic and generative urban processes, allowing a much wider range of people to take part in building cities.

The course provides a platform for the individual student to develop an expertise and an approach to sustainable urban design through the development of urban design strategies and research. As more and more emphasis is put on the importance of sustainable developments by governments and professional bodies, such knowledge and skills will be of increasing usefulness to the students in their professional lives. The programme prepares for work in the public as well as in the private sector.

The masters course has two fully integrated parts: The design intensive studio and the theory component comprising Masters and Professional MArch (ARB/RIBA Part2) students.

The Urban Design course welcomes students as fellow innovators in a programme that is both visionary and hands on in seeking to develop urban futures that are sustainable, distinctive and enjoyable.

Urban Design Studio

The design component aims to prepare students to work with different urban situations and agendas.

In the beginning of each academic year, students engage in a five week induction project, to familiarise themselves with the teaching and learning environment of the course. During that time, we develop design tools and principles, by testing and refining them in various locations.

For the main design project, individual students focus on one site of their choice, for the rest of the academic year. This focus allows very deep explorations of a range of scales and involved urban design issues. Students formulate objectives,

Students:
Brittany Taber, Finlay Jacob Capps, Lajja Ashay Shah

Y4: Stefano Binoi Varikkanikkal, Luke Day, Uzoamaka Edeh, William Fullick, Thomas Hardy, Oluchukwu Okonkwo Obiejesi, Svetoslav Savov, Agis Valsamis

Y5: Ana Paula Gomes Kouzak, Hussein Ali Kasim, Patrycja Adrianna Niechaj, Mohammed Patel, Rafaa Abubaker Mohamed Elfatih, Alexandra Rogojinaru, Omer Sabah, Julia Skiba, Karolina Skrzypkowska, Dan Strassburg, Nadira Sultan, Dominika Zielinska

ma-ud.blogspot.com

briefs, programmes and spatial aspirations of their design work. Throughout the course, we engage in workshops, presentations and tutorials.

Open Studio

This academic year, students select the location and topic of their design, theory and research project themselves. The course offers a rich platform for students' visions for cities.

We formulated strategies that respond to global and site conditions, understanding of scales, architectural sensibilities and local communities, to create social, spatial and time-based habitats and environments.

Urban Theory

The theory component welcomes Masters students and also 4th and 5th year MArch students. The course is 'hands on' and it works in close collaboration with the design component. A lot of urban issues are difficult to explore purely on a visual basis. This has to do with the abstract level of scale and complexity. For example, we can do models of buildings and they will partly tell us spatial and social relationships. In urban design that is different. We can do models of a city, but it is not that easy to understand the underlying forces, that are shaping cities. Concerning issues like migration or globalization, physical models might tell us very little. We have to read, write and talk, to gain a more holistic understanding of urban issues.

Students attend weekly lectures on distinct urban topics, followed by seminars. The fields of studies range from urban history, theory, interpretation and practice to science. Invited guests from different backgrounds enrich the course with diverse talks. We explore complexities of cities through discussions, writings, readings, lectures, drawings, student presentations, movies and excursions.

The theory component is assessed through ongoing course work and an 4000 - 5000 word essay on an urban topic that the students select and research themselves. The studies in urban theory are set up to help articulate a critical context and vision for students' design and thesis work.

Professional Landscape Architecture

Dr B Snaith CMLI, C Penny MA CMLI,
Nick Miller MA CMLI, Dr R Tobe

Our Professional Landscape Architecture programmes span practice and research. Our programmes explore the complex social and environmental issues that inform professional landscape practice every day. Our students are encouraged to consider their place in the world as both humans and landscape professionals and our programmes provide them with the tools to address the social and environmental challenges the world faces.

This year we asked our students to consider the relationship between water and cities in a project called 'Waterlands', focusing on the coastal city of Portsmouth. Portsmouth faces considerable challenges relating to social inequality, access to green space and coastal flooding. These issues are felt across the UK and worldwide, and reflect the range of challenges our profession faces.

This year we returned fully to in-person teaching and were able to work with professionals in person and on site visits. In term one Design Studio students used site survey techniques to develop responses to sense of place, using a wide range of media, including sketching, technical drawing, collaging and model-making. This informed our design project in term one, where our Conversion/PG Dip students worked on a project turning an underused space in Southsea from 'Grey to Green' and Masters students undertook 'Design through Management' in a woodland nature park called the Hilsea Lines. These different approaches to design link closely with our Mental Wealth approach, preparing students for professional life.

In term two Design Studio we undertook area-wide mapping of north Portsmouth, looking at Landscape Character, Green and Blue Infrastructure and Equalities. This mapping informed our term two design project where students developed their own approach to the brief, with some taking a strong ecological and biodiversity focus and others focusing on leisure and recreation. All students had to consider coastal flooding as part of their design.

In theoretical studies, Masters year students explored the challenges of professional practice and urban design theory, selecting topics including Superblocks for Ecosystemic Urbanism and Public Spaces in Dense Metro Cities. Conversion/PG Dip students undertook primary research at Queen Elizabeth Olympic Park and Kings Cross to ascertain how the design of these spaces addresses community needs, and in term two they considered landscape history and theory in the context of contemporary issues such as social inequality, colonisation of landscape and climate change. The student work illustrated here is selected from our MA, MA (Conversion) and PG Dip Professional Landscape Architecture programmes this year.

> "Landscape encapsulates society, politics and our own existence on a planet where we're bound by natural forces. It's how we give form to our land and cities. Ultimately it's how we identify with places."
>
> James Corner, CEO Field Operations

Students:
PG Dip/Conversion: Syed Younus Ali, Nathalie Foster, Lily Garbutt, Khaled Hadi, Jerome Jarrett, Niki Joshi, Susan Reed, Roger Watson, Lucy Williams

MA/Conversion 2: Finlay Capps, Shannon Du Hasky, Lewis Reynolds, Anne-Marie Osei-Sarfoh, Lajja Shah, Joe White

Special thanks to:
PRG: Fenella Griffin (Untitled Practice), Susan Lowenthal (WSP), Tom Lonsdale (Placecraft), Eduardo Carranza (Gustafson Porter Bowman)

Landscape Institute: Sarah McGee, Christina Hirst & Landscape Institute London Branch

With thanks to our visiting professionals:
Madhur Gurjar (London Borough of Lewisham), Charlotte Waters (AECOM), Kirsty Barker (LDA Design), Nicole Yeomans (AECOM), Robyn Grant (Tobermore)

Study Visits: Cain Blythe and Nick May (Ecosulis), Jack Skillen (Team London Bridge), Portsmouth City Council

External Examiner: Saruhan Mosler

1

1 (previous page) Tipner East Masterplan, Lajja Shah **2** Grey to Green Masterplan for Southsea, Roger Watson **3** Section of proposals for Southsea Grey to Green Project, Roger Watson **4** Site Analysis for Tipner East, Lajja Shah **5** 'Waterlands' representation of place through model making, Susan Reed

2

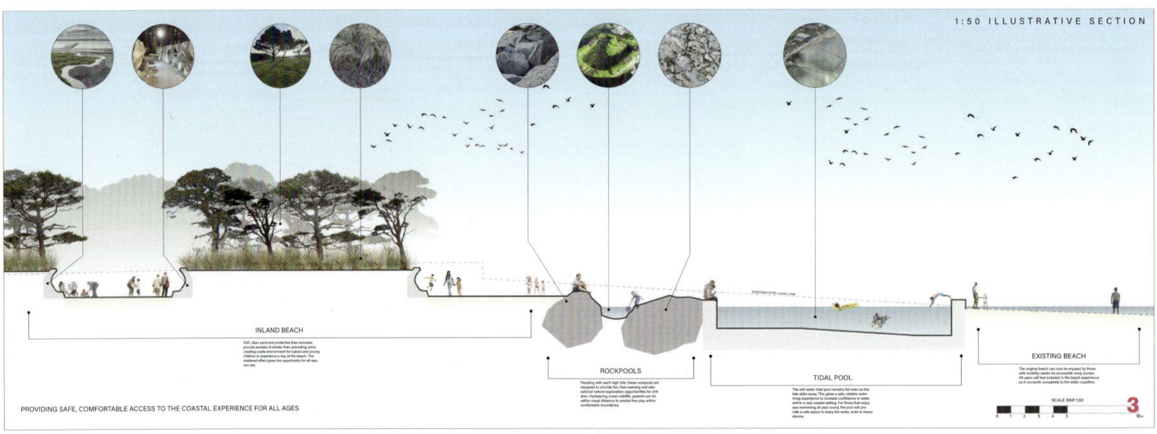

3

Portsmouth Island is densely populated and has minimal open green spaces
Majority open green spaces covered with amenity grassland with low ecological value
Site is covered with loamy soils. The site has high groundwater with adjacent mudflats.
Site is covered with loamy soils. The site has high groundwater with adjacent mudflats.
Sea levels around Portsmouth are due to rise by around 70cm over the next 70 years
PORTSMOUTH HARBOUR
WASTE RECYCLING PLANT
DUMP AND SITE COVERED WITH CONTAMINATED SOIL FROM PREVIOUS INDUSTRIES OF TAR WORKS, TIMBER YARD AND FUEL DEPOT
MUDFLATS
MOUNTBATTEN LEISURE CENTRE
PARK AND RIDE
REMNANTS OF GREY HOUND RACING TRACK
EXISTING WATER BODY
SITE BARRICATION
ALEXANDRA PARK
ALLOTMENTS
STAMSHAW SCHOOL
RESIDENTIAL AREA
N
LEGEND:
IMPORTANT VIEW POINTS TO BE ENHANCED
SITE BOUNDARY
SITE BARRICATION
PREVAILING WIND DIRECTION
EXISTING SEA WALL AND COASTAL WALK
GREEN RIVER PARK
SITE ANALYSIS PLAN
SCALE 1:1250 @A1

4

Create a strong cardboard structure to hold model
Build up clay to create levels
Create textures in clay to represent rocks, sand, shrubs and grass
Mix and pour plaster into mould
Create clay mould for wax
Carefully pour melted wax into mould
Leave to set
Once wax is set, remove clay mould and carefully scrape sides of the model for a clean finish

5

6 Extract from Green and Blue Infrastructure Assessment, Group: Lajja Shah, Anne-Marie Osei-Sarfoh, Lily Garbutt, Roger Watson **7** Extract from Design through Management Plan, Shannon Du Hasky **8** Extract from Design through Management Plan, Finlay Capps **9** 'Selling the Vision' - Hilsea Lido Park, Susan Reed **10** Representing a sense of place, Group: Anne-Marie Osei-Sarfoh, Finlay Capps, Roger Watson, Susan Reed **11** Visualisation of design proposals for Hilsea Lido Park, Khaled Hadi

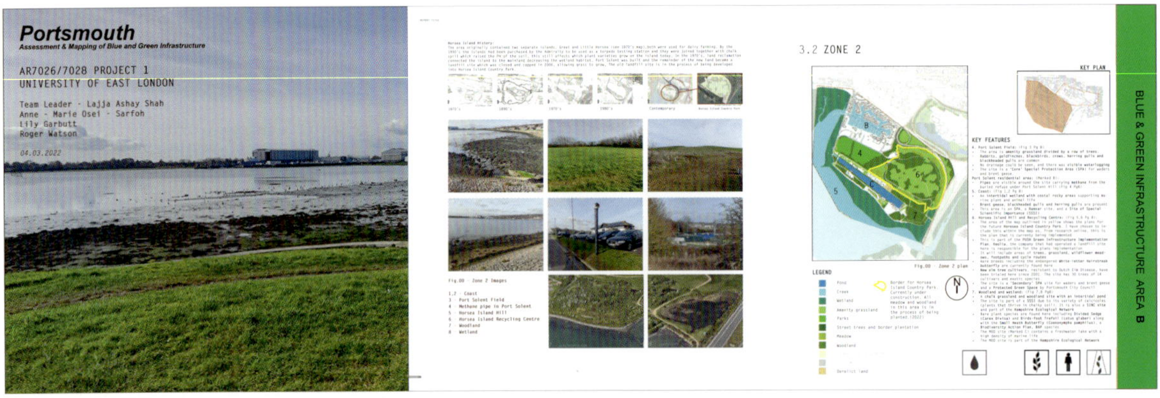

6

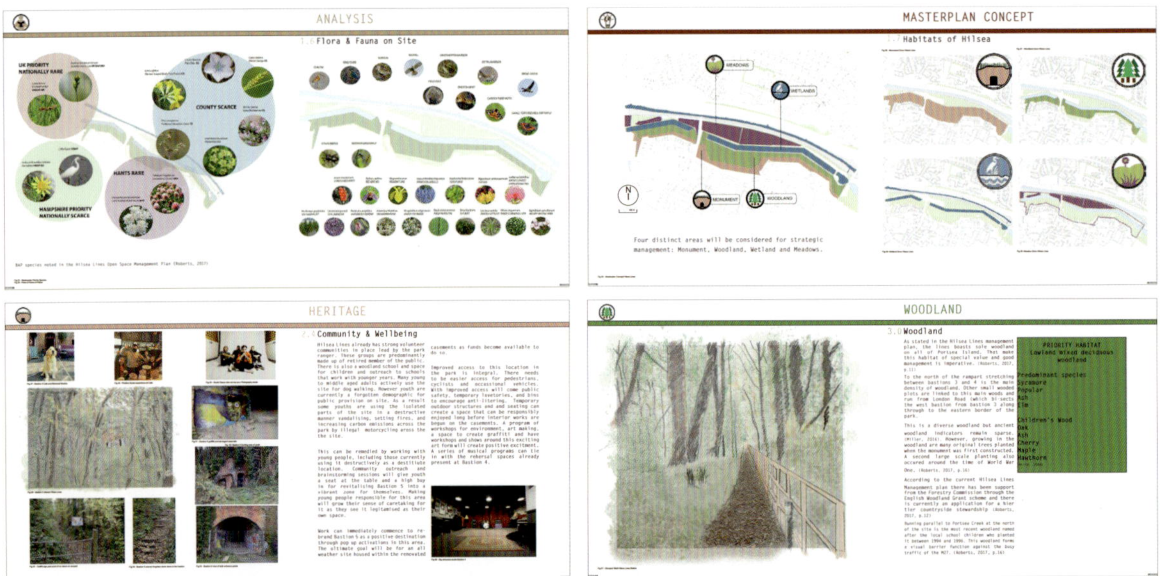

7

8

Hilsea
Lido Park
Nature Trails, Wetland Meadow, Boardwalk, Lido, Wild Swiming, Boating, Aquatic Play & Community Cafe

9

CORVUS CORONE
COLUMBA PALUMBUS
BOMBUS TERRESTRIS
CYANISTES CAERULEUS
CARDUELIS CARDUELIS
CARDUELIS SPINUS
10

11

12 Planting Strategy for Form & Structure and for Environmental Enhancement, Lucy Williams **13** Planting Strategy & Detailed Plan, Lily Garbutt **14** Masterplan and Axonometric Sketch for Hilsea Lido Park, Khaled Hadi

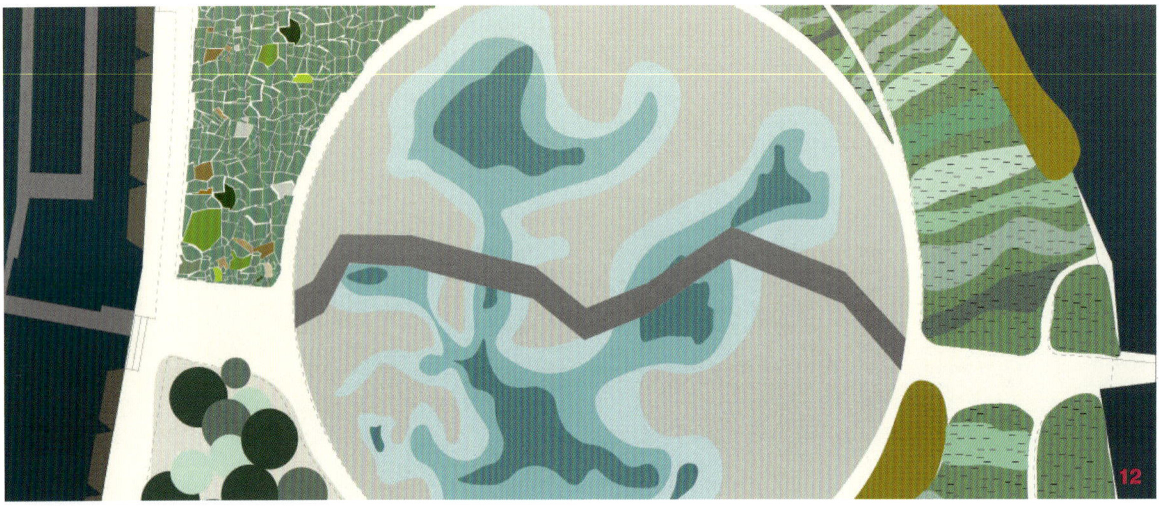

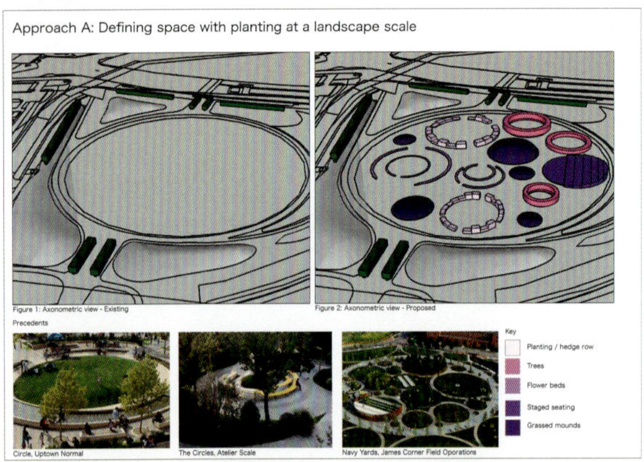

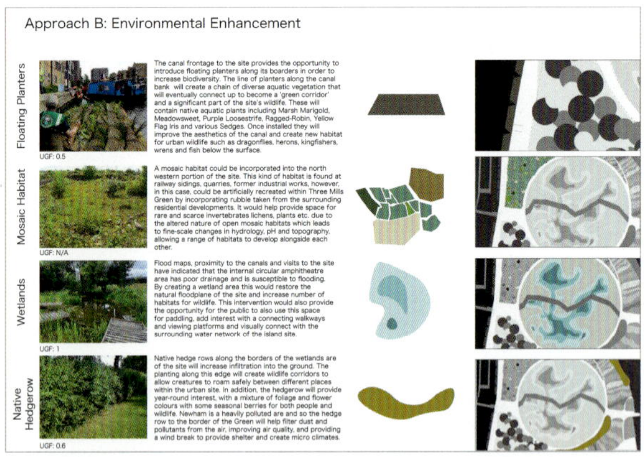

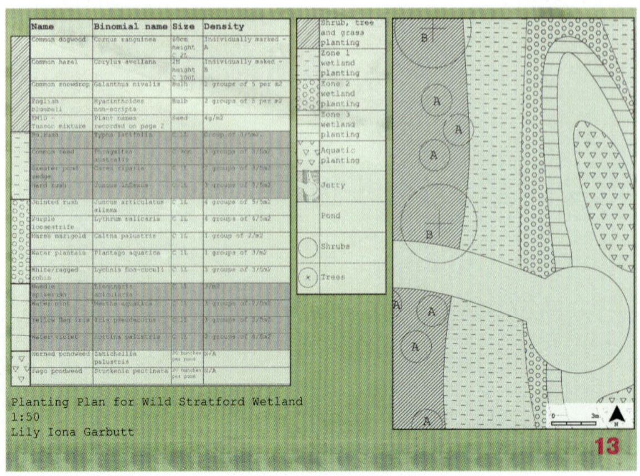

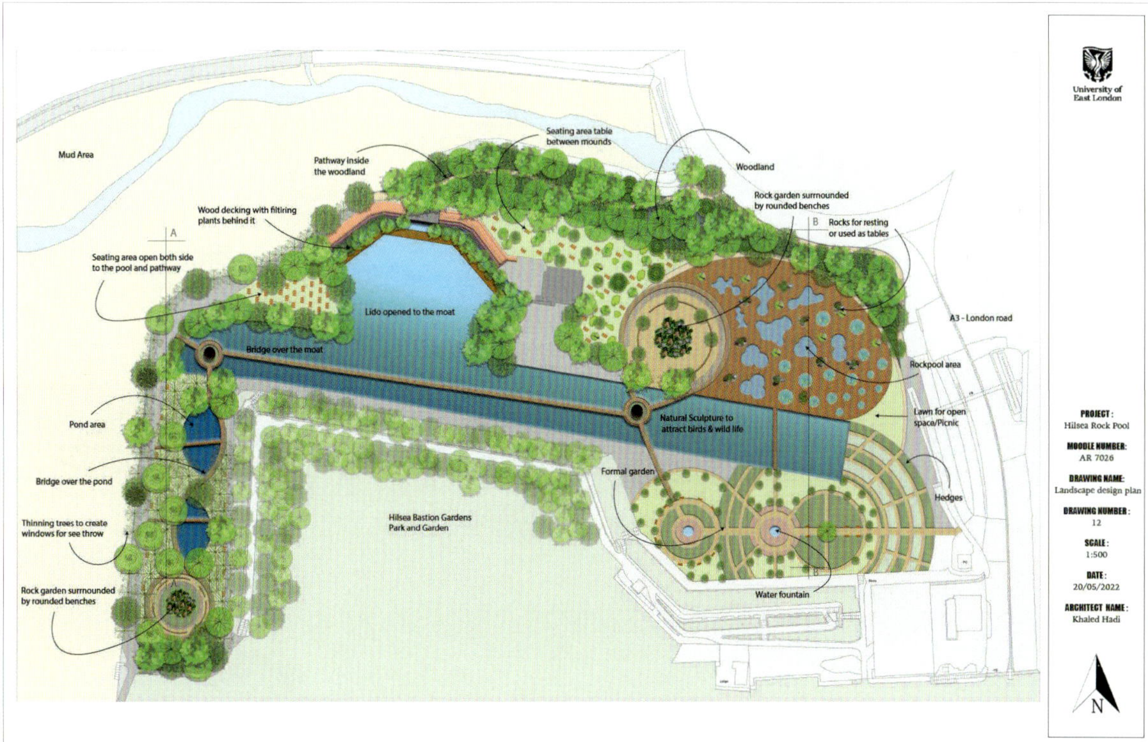
University of East London
Mud Area
Pathway inside the woodland
Seating area table between mounds
Woodland
Wood decking with filtiring plants behind it
Rock garden surrounded by rounded benches
Rocks for resting or used as tables
Seating area open both side to the pool and pathway
Lido opened to the moat
A3 - London road
Bridge over the moat
Rockpool area
Pond area
Natural Sculpture to attract birds & wild life
Lawn for open space/Picnic
Formal garden
Bridge over the pond
Hedges
Thinning trees to create windows for see throw
Hilsea Bastion Gardens Park and Garden
Rock garden surrounded by rounded benches
Water fountain
PROJECT:
Hilsea Rock Pool
MOODLE NUMBER:
AR 7026
DRAWING NAME:
Landscape design plan
DRAWING NUMBER:
12
SCALE:
1:500
DATE:
20/05/2022
ARCHITECT NAME:
Khaled Hadi
N

14

15 Detailed Plan, Site Section and Site model for Hilsea Lido Park, Roger Watson **16** Representation of Form & Structure in Planting Design, Susan Reed **17** Extract from Design through Management Plan, Lajja Shah

15

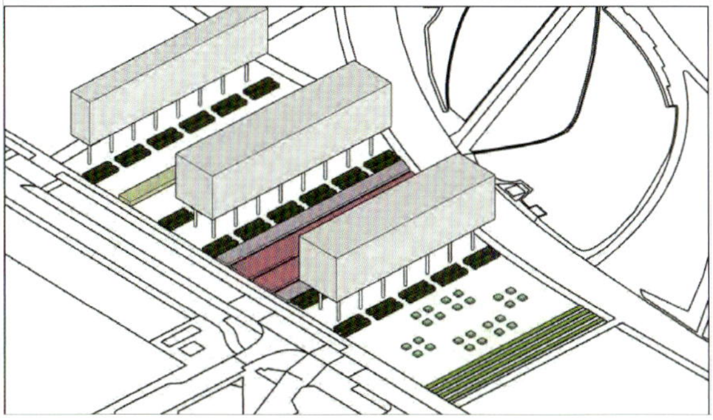

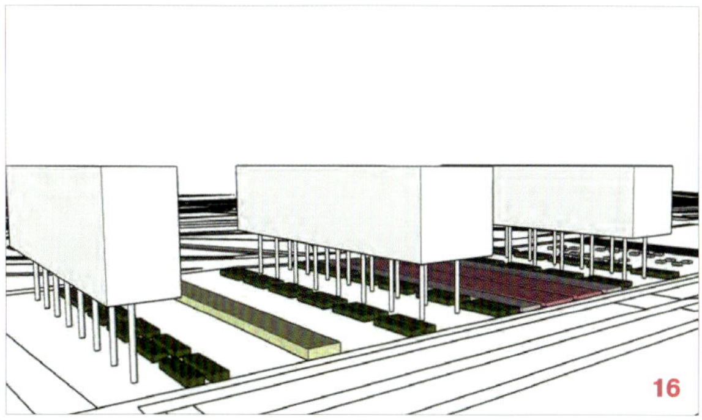

16

HILSEA LINES, PORTSMOUTH
LANDSCAPE MANAGEMENT PLAN
LAJJA SHAH
(2172241)
University of East London
1

Bastion 3
Bastion 4
Bastion 5
Primary walkway loop around moat
Secondary walkway along creek
Walkway on top of Bastions
2.7 Existing Site Features
1. Site access points(A,B,C)
2. Woodland School
3. Woodland
4. Moat
5. Walkway along moat (primary route)
6. Bastions
7. Walkway on top of Bastions
8. Picnic Lawn
9. Meadows
10.Creek
11.Bridge across creek
12.Pond
13. Casemates studio and cafe
14. Parking
15. Moat edge between moat & walkway (with hedgerows in few locations, reed beds in few locations and shrub thickets along most of the stretch)
16. Mudflats
17. Creek edge
University of East London
13

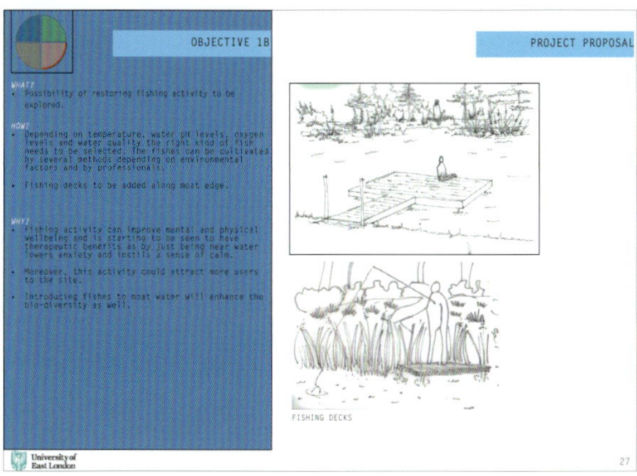
OBJECTIVE 1B
PROJECT PROPOSAL
WHAT?
• Possibility of restoring fishing activity to be explored.
HOW?
• Depending on temperature, water pH levels, oxygen levels and water quality the right kind of fish needs to be selected. The fishes can be cultivated by several methods depending on environmental factors and by professionals.
• Fishing decks to be added along moat edge.
WHY?
• Fishing activity can improve mental and physical wellbeing and is starting to be seen to have therapeutic benefits as by just being near water lowers anxiety and instils a sense of calm.
• Moreover, this activity could attract more users to the site.
• Introducing fishes to moat water will enhance the bio-diversity as well.
FISHING DECKS
University of East London
27

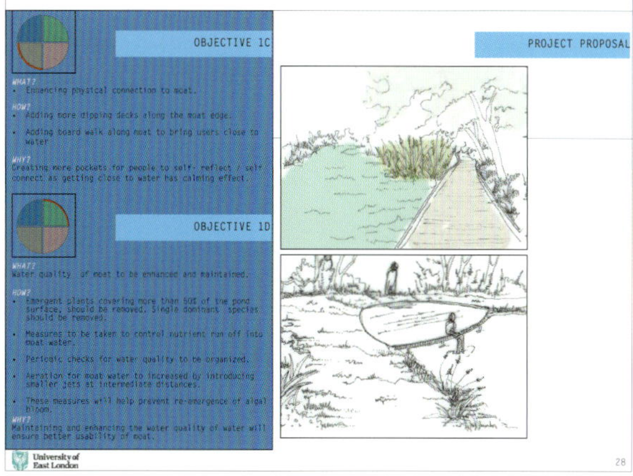
OBJECTIVE 1C
PROJECT PROPOSAL
WHAT?
• Enhancing physical connection to moat.
HOW?
• Adding more dipping decks along the moat edge.
• Adding board walk along moat to bring users close to water
WHY?
Creating more pockets for people to self- reflect / self connect as getting close to water has calming effect.
OBJECTIVE 1D
WHAT?
Water quality of moat to be enhanced and maintained.
HOW?
• Emergent plants covering more than 50% of the pond surface, should be removed. Single dominant species should be removed.
• Measures to be taken to control nutrient run off into moat water.
• Periodic checks for water quality to be organized.
• Aeration for moat water to increased by introducing smaller jets at intermediate distances.
• These measures will help prevent re-emergence of algal bloom.
WHY?
Maintaining and enhancing the water quality of water will ensure better usability of moat.
University of East London
28

17

MA Interior Design

Dr Anastasia Karandinou (Course Leader), Sue Ginsburgh, Miho Nakagawa, Catalina Pollak, Dr Renee Tobe, Kevin Widger.

Design of any scale responds to – and in parallel leads – cultural, political and social change. Our MA course examines the role of design in forming places, connections, communities in a socially and environmentally sustainable way, through speculative and pragmatic design exercises, some of which lead to real-life built projects. Through this MA programme, we challenge the limits of the role of the designer and we explore how design pertains to different aspects of our everyday living. Political and cultural debates are re-articulated and expressed through a hands-on poetic and creative making approach.

Displacement; performative mapping, immersion, montage and active machines

'Thinking involves a wrenching of concepts away from their usual, configurations, outside the systems in which they have a home, and outside the structures of recognition that constrain thought to the already known. Thinking is never easy. Thought-events, like language-bodies, are singularities, which mix with and have effects on other materialities, with political, cultural, cinematic, or architectural events.' Elizabeth Grosz

For Deleuze and Guattari mapping is an open discourse, an open process, 'an experimentation in contact with the real'. Mapping, in this context, as opposed to tracing, reflects on the performative, the immersion in a place. In this type of performative mapping, the distinction between the map-maker's intention and outcome is not valid; intention and outcome are intertwined within the action of its making, which is considered as 'praxis'. 'Praxis' here is meant as 'thinking-in-action', as Gadamer would call it, which does not follow a thinking process but precedes it, encloses it, and, as Snodgrass and Coyne describe it, it breaks down the dichotomies of thought and action, theory and practice. It becomes obvious that in this context there is no clear distinction between mapping/ praxis and designing. The contact with the real, the act of immersion in a place, does not only transform one's understanding of a place, but is transformative for the subject itself. In Zizek's words, 'what is namely an act? The act differs from an active intervention (action) in that it radically transforms its bearer (agent): the act is not simply something I 'accomplish' – after an act, I'm literally 'not the same as before.' In this sense, we could say that the subject 'undergoes the act ('passes through' it) rather than 'accomplishes' it: in it, the subject is annihilated and subsequently reborn (or not), i.e., the act involves a kind of temporary eclipse, aphanisis, of the subject.' Slavoj Zizek

In this Masters course, places are studied in ways drawn from a broad theoretical context, and often discussed in relation to the notion of displacement. Performative acts in a place are acts of immersion and, simultaneously, of displacement. Through such processes a transformative encounter with the place occurs, which – in other words – allows the students to gain a better understanding of the place, while transforming both.

Notes:

Elizabeth Grosz, Architecture from the Outside (Cambridge, Mass.: The MIT Press, 2001). p.61, with reference to Gilles Deleuze, Cinema 2: The Time-Image, trans. Hugh Tomlinson and Robert Galeta (Minneapolis: University of Minnesota Press, 1993).

Deleuze, Gilles, and Felix Guattari. A Thousand Plateaus: Capitalism and Schizophrenia. [1988]. London: Continuum, 2004. p. 13

Snodgrass and Coyne, Interpretation in Architecture: Design as Way of Thinking. p.212

Slavoj Zizek, Enjoy Your Symptom! (New York: Routledge, 2001). p.44, see also: Tony Myers, and Slavoj Zizek (London; New York: Routledge, 2003).

Students
January 2021 start: Shijin Cheruvakkara, Rushil Gaba, Ambika Katta, Shivangi Purohit, Elizabeth Teye, September 2021 start: Jamshid Abdukayumov, Kratika Jain, Jhanvi Patel, Lorraine Ruskin, Nahla Juilany, Rabih Khalil, Josh Mcveigh, Ashna Shakir, Fatemeh Mohanna, Shadi Moradi, Preksha Patel, Jessica Pope-Alkarkhi, January 2022 start: Samreen Naaz, Nandeesha Matha, Aditi Bhole, Merlin John, Victor Omorogbe, Shaymaa Alnaji, Part-time: Martyna Lapinska

www.uel.ac.uk/postgraduate/courses/ma-interior-design
www.instagram.com/uel_mainteriordesign

Special thanks to our guest critics and guest tutors: Amanda Wanner, Rachael Brown, Dina Al-Qusous, Carl Callaghan, Israel Hurtado Cola, Phevos Kallitsis, Belinda Mitchell, Dorian Wiszniewski.

Special thanks also to our collaborators on the Blue Community Space and Cinema project: Russell Dryden; Blue Bermondsey BID Manager, Sanchez Benton Architects, Really Local Group and its founder Preston Benson. Their input, views and conversations were invaluable.

1

The Blue Bermondsey Community space and cinema

In Term 1 the students developed a series of performative processes for encountering and exploring the Blue market square in Bermondsey. They interacted with the local community and developed strategies for designing the new community space currently developed by the Really Local group alongside the new Blue cinema. Poetic processes allowed the students to break away from the division between mapping and designing. They also meant to function as transformative experiences – in contact with the real life of the place. These processes led to design strategies for the community space of the new local cinema.

1, 2 Jamshid Abdukayumov. Drawing-shoes as a medium for mapping movement and interacting with the place and locals.

2

3. Ashna Shakir **4.** Martyna Lapinska **5.** Preksha Patel **6.** Rabih Khalil

Interactive interventions at the site. Performative processes and immersion as a way for engaging with the place and the people. .

3

4

5

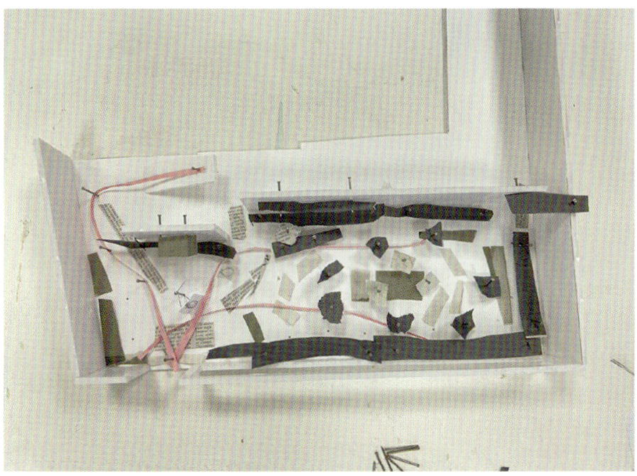

6

7 Josh Mcveigh. Fabric folding and wrapping; performative exploration on site. Fabric as a metaphor for the homely, the comforting, the welcoming.

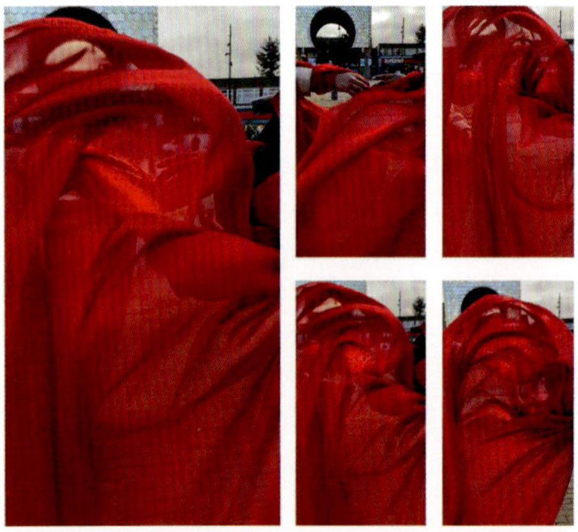

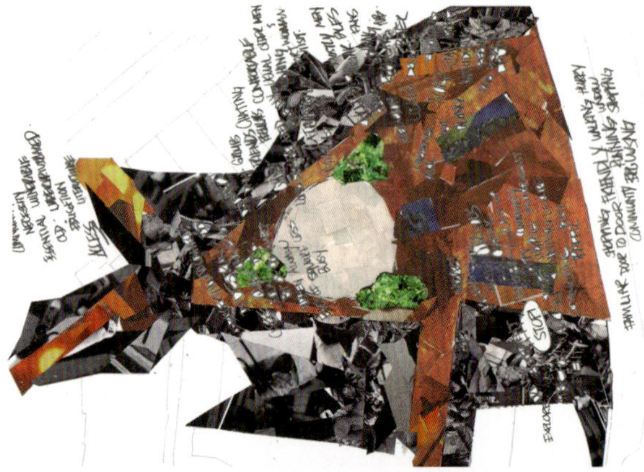

8 Fatemeh Mohanna. Upcycled fabric; shreded fabric used for creating prototypes of blocks and panels, to be used for interior clading and for interior design elements. Plaster, resin, paper, sawdust and other materials tested and used together with the recycled fabric.

Wearable folding table created by the student, and used for serving coffee the locals who were passing by. Through this performative process, the student engaged with the place and the locals.

The experience of both the performative encounter with the site, as well as of the upcycling experiments informed the design strategy for the community space.

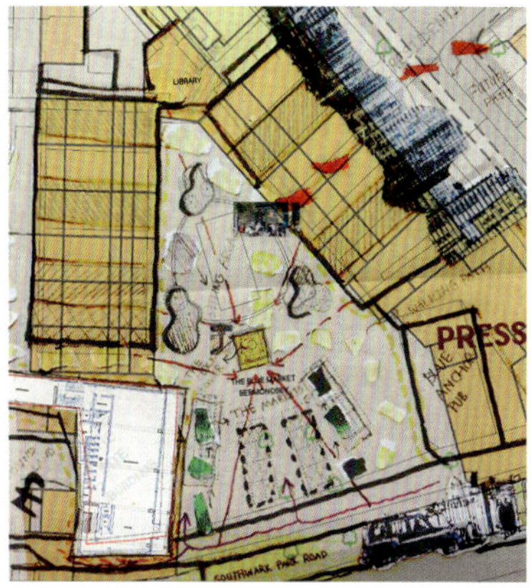

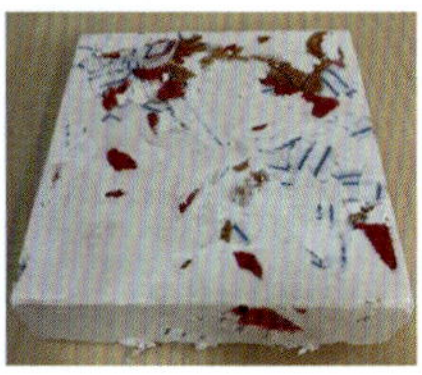

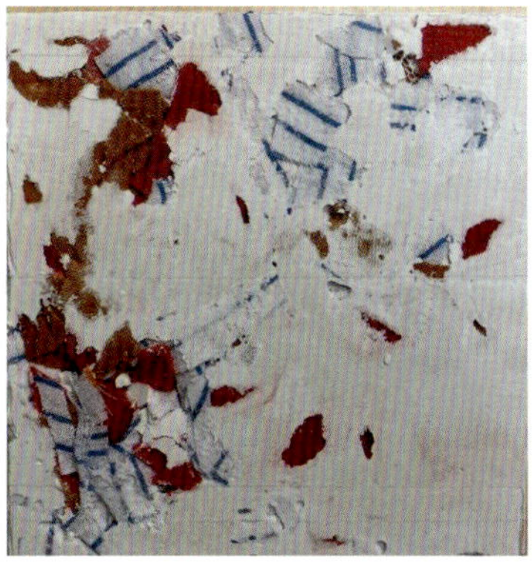

8

The Engine House – Between the Museum and the City

In Term 2 the students developed design proposals for the Engine House; a small Victorian industrial building, situated next to the entrance of the New Museum of London. Each student developed their own brief and vision for this building, addressing this important threshold between a major cultural organisation and the everyday life in the city. The significance and radiance of this location triggered the students to contemplate on what broader change they would like to see happening in London, and on how this small intervention could be employed for testing and manifesting it.

9,10 Merlin John. Recording studio and music space; bringing arts and music in the London city centre again, including emerging musicians.

9

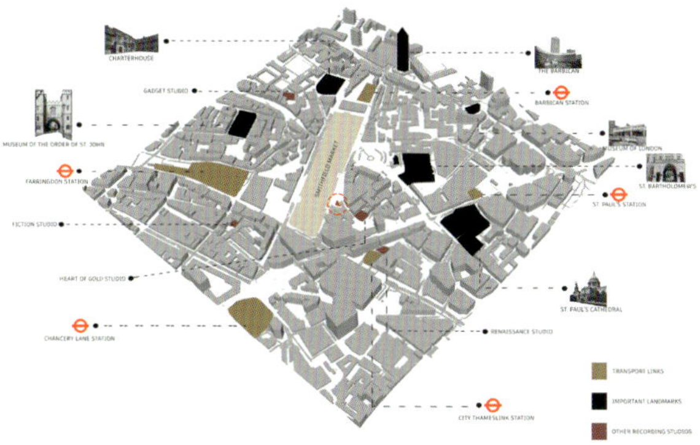
CHARTERHOUSE
THE BARBICAN
GADGET STUDIO
BARBICAN STATION
MUSEUM OF THE ORDER OF ST. JOHN
MUSEUM OF LONDON
FARRINGDON STATION
ST. BARTHOLOMEW'S
SMITHFIELD MARKET
ST. PAUL'S STATION
FICTION STUDIO
HEART OF GOLD STUDIO
ST. PAUL'S CATHEDRAL
CHANCERY LANE STATION
RENAISSANCE STUDIO
TRANSPORT LINKS
IMPORTANT LANDMARKS
CITY THAMESLINK STATION
OTHER RECORDING STUDIOS

10

11, 12 Shaymaa Alnaji. Childrens centre. Pedagogical theories were translated into design strategies and informed the programme and the detailed designing of the space.

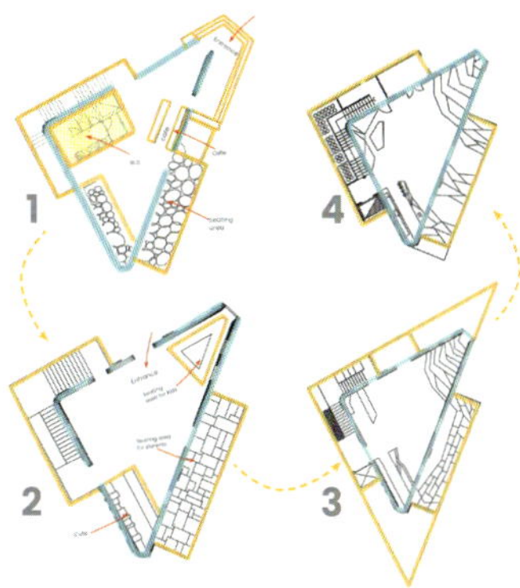

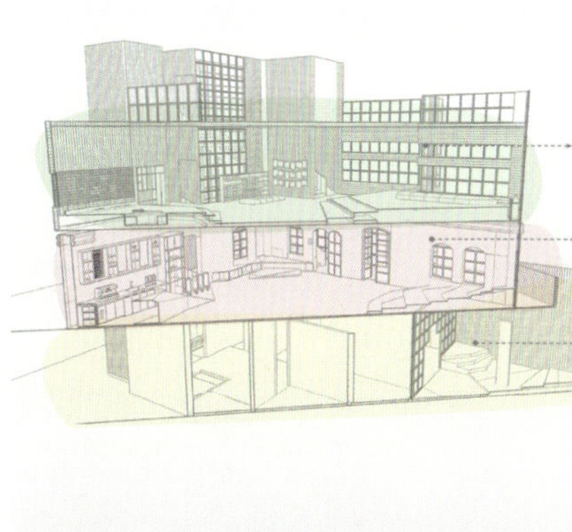

This design of the first floor was inspired by the Montessori approach. The floor restricted area for parents. Only children can use it with some of the staff. The floor is designed to help the children learn and play independently without interfering or direction from adults.

The ground floor is designed as an open cafe for parents and children, and other visitors who want to just grab a coffee go. And the floor has a seating area for children which can be used as a performance area for children, the cafe bar, where children and parents can order drinks and snacks, and there is a reception area where parents can drop their children off on the first floor. Also, the floor has a seating area for single adults and parents. each area was designed to fit the scale of its user.

The basement has WC units which can be used by the people who visit the cafe, and two storage rooms. The basement also has an open outdoor area designed as a playground for children.

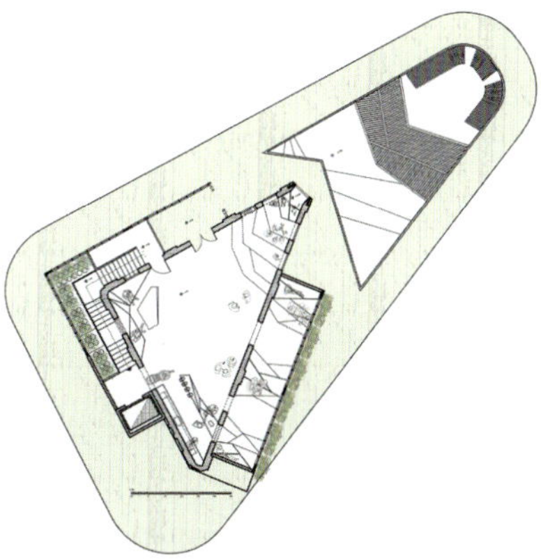

13 Josh Mcveigh. The city as theatre and the theatre as the city. A different space for performing arts; theatre, promenade theatre, bar and open air performances interweave.

14 Jhanvi Patel. Fashion hub.

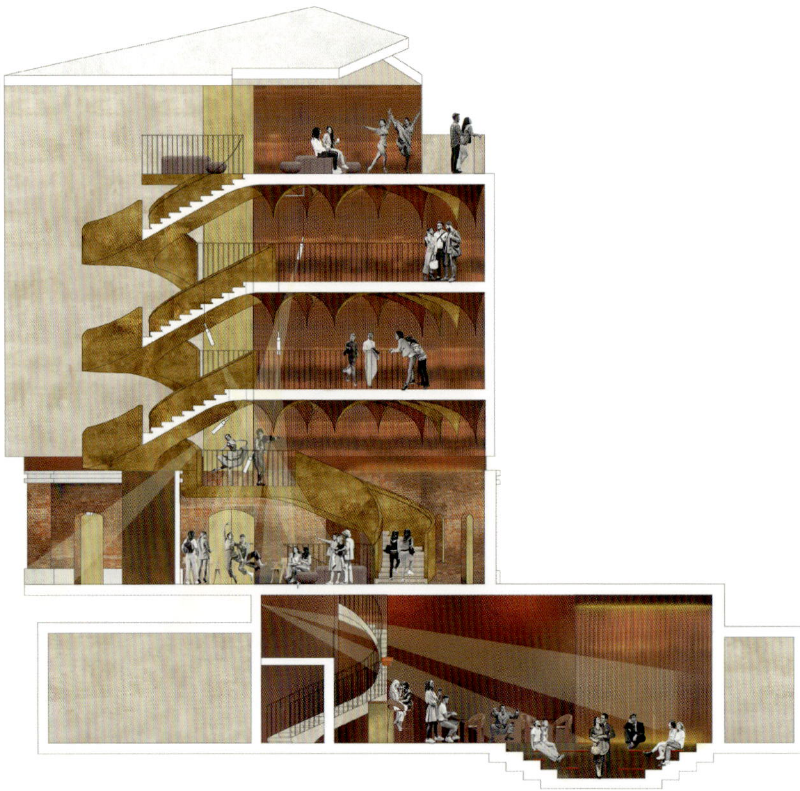

13

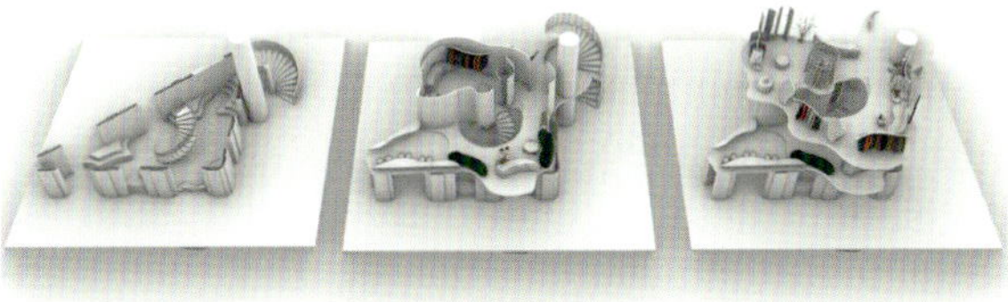

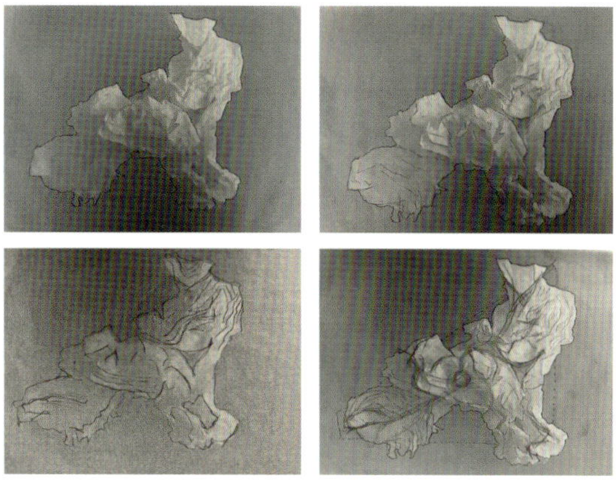

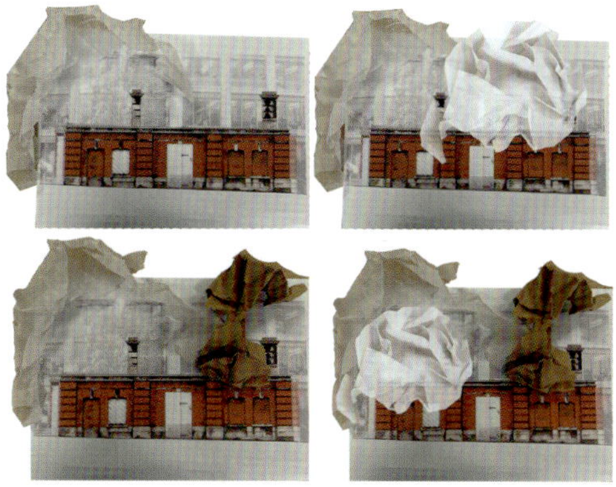

14

15 Jamshid Abdukayumov. Wellbeing and yoga centre. The different levels have different functions, but are also metaphprs of different states of mind.
16 Kratika Jain. Library and book hub with books specialised in the history of London; space for reading, book presentations, cafe.

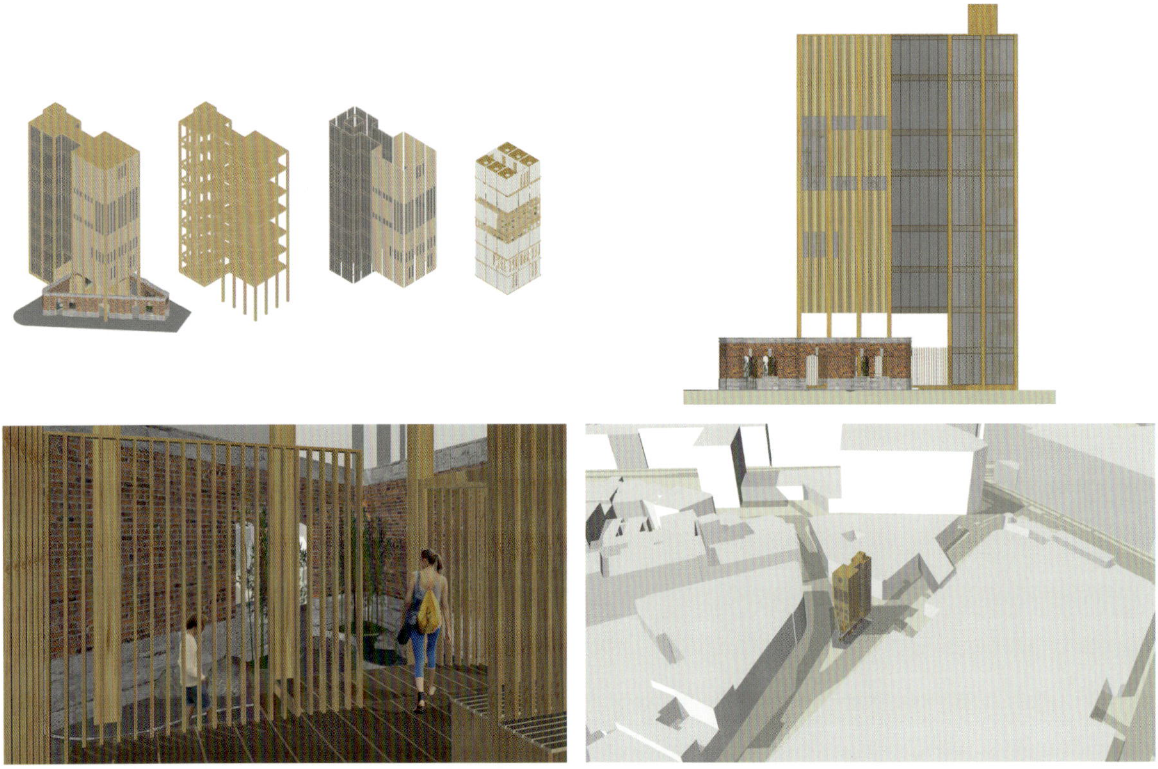

15

16

17 Fatemeh Mohanna. Catwalk in and out of the building and fashion centre. **18** Victor Omorogbe . Photography Gallery. **19** Preksha Patel and Nandeesha Matha. English Cuisine restaurant and cafe.

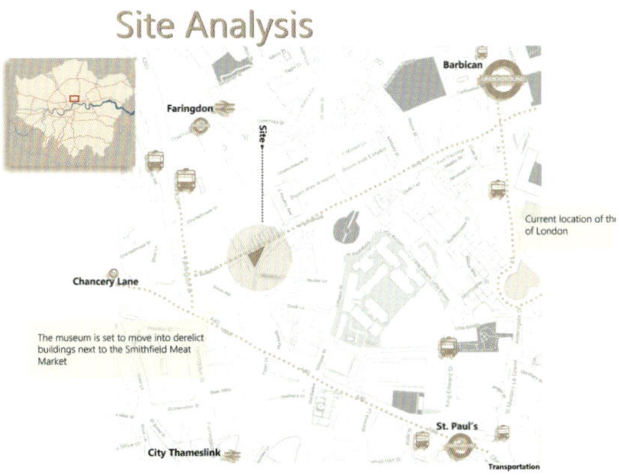

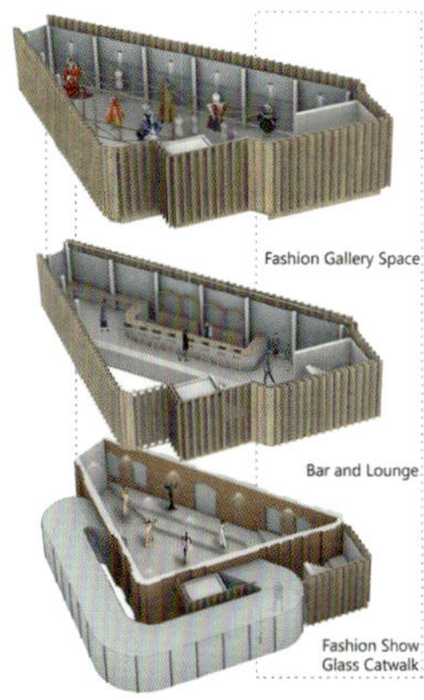

17

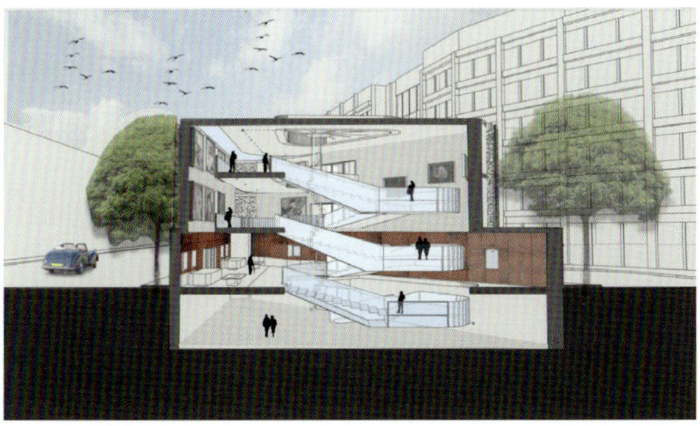

18

19

20 Rabih Khalil. 360-degree compact hotel **21** Jessica Pope-Alkarkhi and Samreen Naaz. Food hub addressing environmental resilience. Timber structure. **22** Shadi Moradi. Arts centre.

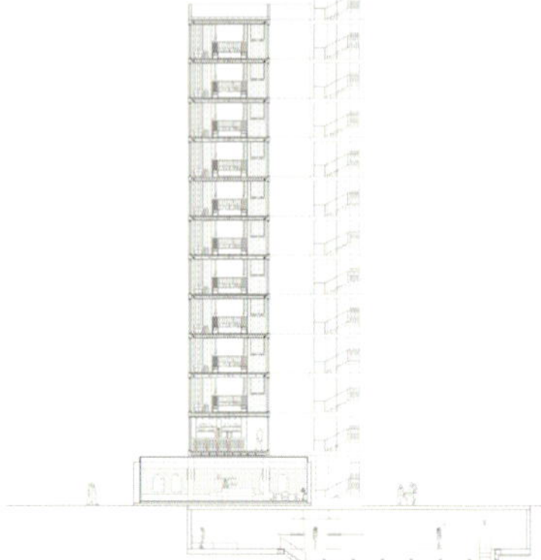

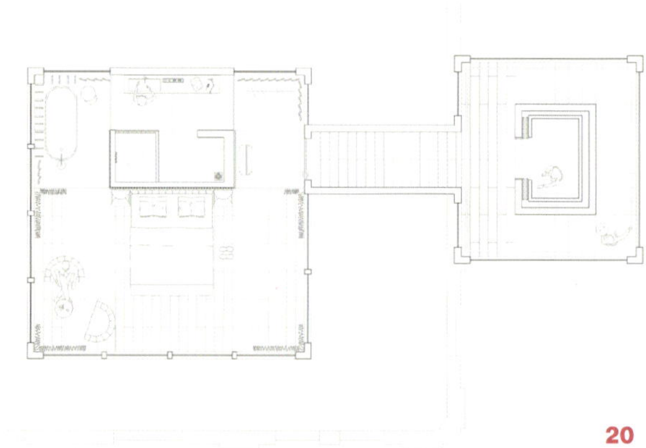

20

21

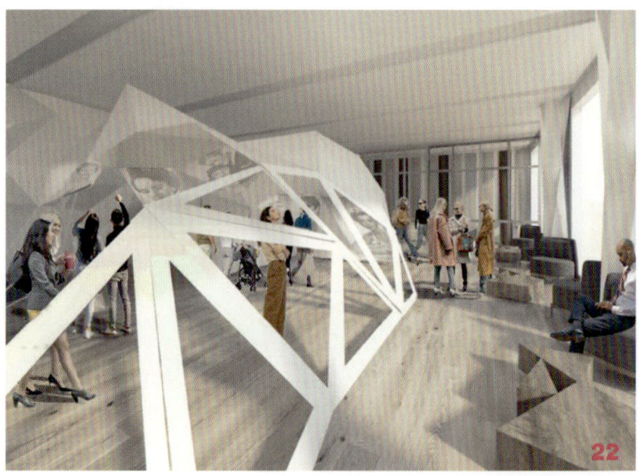

22

23 Martyna Lapinska. Florist centre and cafe; a slow-garden for relaxing in the city centre. **24** Lorraine Ruskin and Ashna Shakir. Jewellery Hub. Recycled Glass facade.

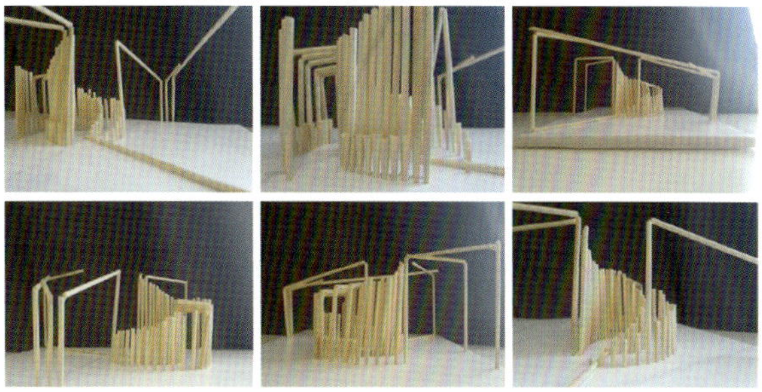

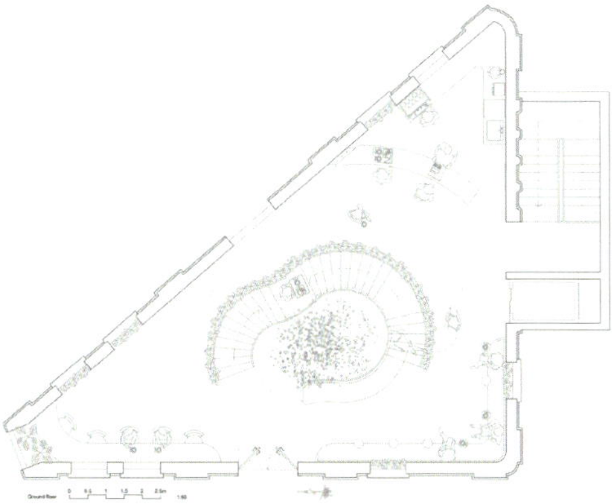

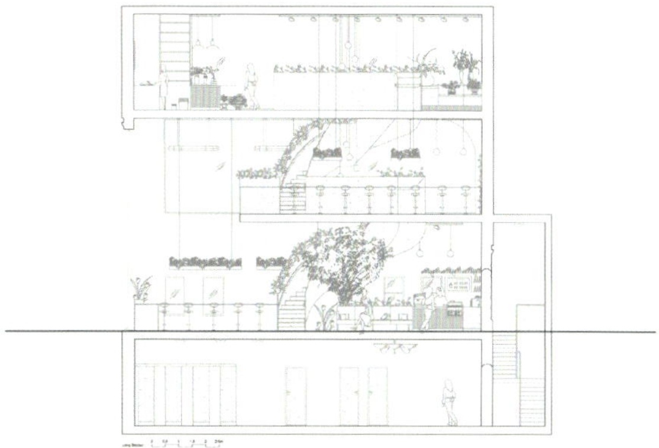

23

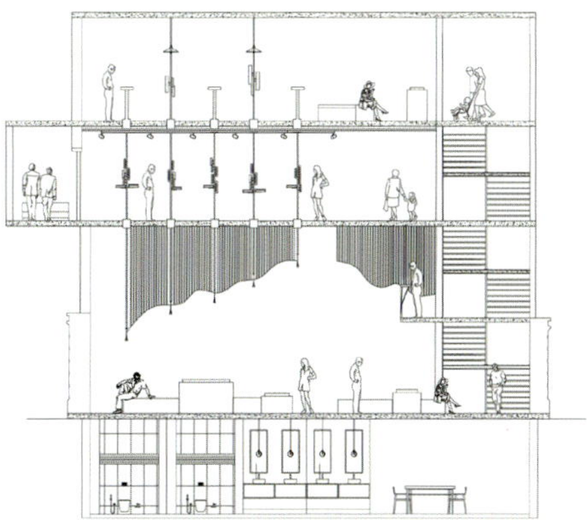

24

PhD by Research

Doctoral research in architecture at UEL is as transdisciplinary as the practice of architecture itself.

High level impact studies that examine smart cities, and intelligent design with contextual analysis mean that we work with both the Sustainable Research Institute (SRI) and colleagues from Humanities. International experts in city design, moving image, sensory perception, retrofit housing, mental health, cultural studies, natural environment, and philosophy guide students through individually develop research projects. The intent of the doctorate is to produce high quality researchers across the different strands of the built environment, that supports students' own concerns as well as funded research investigations.

PhD by Research

An Investigation into the Positive Effects of Interior Design in Care Homes for People Living with Dementia

Investigator: Dina Al Qusous
Supervisors: Anastasia Karandinou, Renée Tobe

This thesis investigates care environments in different cultures, and more specifically different care services in the Western Region and the Middle Eastern/North African Region. Through three selected case studies - each in a different country – the cultural context and differences, traditions around care, prejudices, and assumptions will be examined and discussed. The first case study is The Hogeweyk - Dementia Village in Weesp, the Netherlands which was chosen as the main case studies in care for dementia in this thesis because of its multiple services for the residents. The village was designed in a way to create a community for those with dementia who can walk freely around the space without fear of getting lost or injured due to the detailing of safety that has been taken into consideration when creating the environment.

The second case study, Harmonia Village, located in Dover, United Kingdom was chosen as it was actually inspired by The Hogewyk, Dementia Village. These two care villages located in the Western region are then compared to a care home located in Kuwait, The Farah Specialist Center for the Care and Rehabilitation of the Elderly. The third case study was chosen to show how one of the richest countries in the MENA region establishes care for older people and how traditional and religious values are linked to care services. Awareness of dementia is low to none in this region hence why different services such as home care are much more applicable for dementia users.

Modifying one's environment in order to fit their needs and to adjust it with their lifestyle can help lessen the confusion and distress in their everyday lives. Fortunately, throughout the years, more people are paying attention to designing elderly institutes that are associated for patients with dementia, especially in the UK. Unfortunately, that is not the case for most countries across the world, and especially countries in the Middle East.

Site Analysis: Harmonia Village

The site is located in a convenient location as it's neighboring surroundings include a hospital to it's west which is crucial to be nearby for elderly people especially with underlying health conditions such as dementia. It is also in between other council houses and in a suburban area which allows the residents to be part of a community.

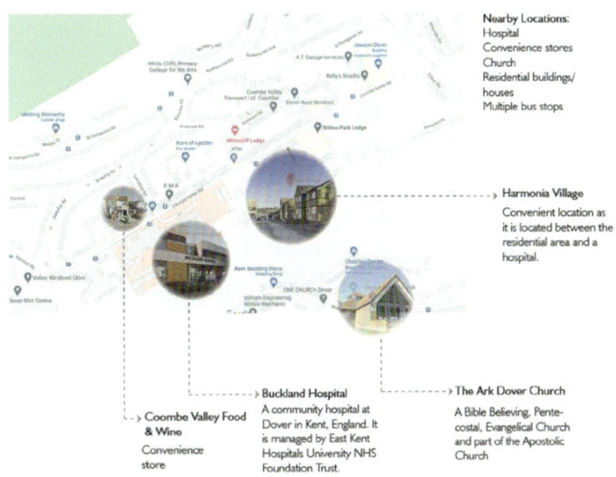

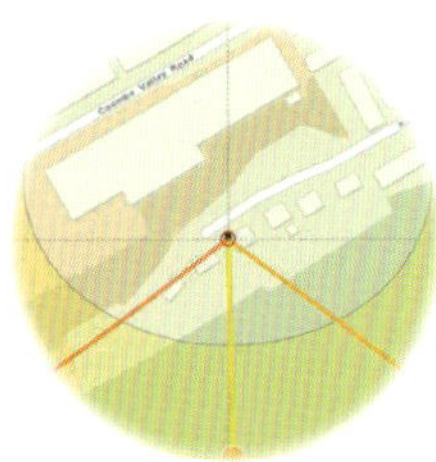

Location: Randolph Road, Dover, Kent, England, CT17 0, GBR
Time: 05.Jan.2021, 11:55 UTC+0
Solar data for the Location Geo data for the Location
Dawn: 07:18:38 **Height:** 35m
Sunrise: 07:57:19 **Latitude:** N 51°7'53.52" 51.13153°
Sun peak level: 12:00:20 **Longitude:** E 1°17'33.6" 1.29267°
Sunset: 16:03:36 **Timezone:** Europe/London GMT
Dusk: 16:42:17
Duration: 8h6m17s
Altitude: 16.36°
Azimut: 178.72°
Shadow length: 3.41 at an object level: 1m

PhD by Research

Can community participation rebalance housing land rights? Case of Kinshasa in the Democratic Republic of Congo

Investigator: Lukangaka Luke Okende
Supervisors: Dr Mihaela Anca Ciupala; Roland F. Karthaus

Like many amongst the African Sub-Saharan cities, Kinshasa the capital city of the Democratic Republic of Congo is confronted to a growing urban deterioration; absence of suitable infrastructures, poor quality of public services facilities and lack of quality housing for largest number of residents. A long period of political instability since the early post-colonial period, prevalent corruption in a context of poor governance and the ambiguous role of traditional chiefdom hierarchies (regarded as the landlords) in the process of urban land acquisitions are identified as keys contextual factors. Nevertheless, an absence of a sustainable urban development strategy, a comprehensive planning model in a city confronted to a fast demographic rate and a decline of socio-economic standard amongst majority of residents over the years, have resulted to an unbalanced dysfunction system which contributed to an urban city development of two independent modes; one side dominated by accumulation of foreign private capital investments while another side by proliferations of informal settlements with a physical manifestation of slums constructions. Contextually, we propose to investigate while looking at a limited intervention adjacent to slums areas in Kingasani and camp Luka with a view to seeing if it can perform well. The essence of this research wishes to test whether community participation can offer an alternative process that can contribute to improving land rights and urban development at the grass-roots level, To fulfil this task we opt for focus groups on minor scale area in Kingasani and camp Luka even that this choice is not fully representative for city of Kinshasa however, it can be extended to big scale with consideration to the particular aspects of each location.

Key words: urban lands acquisitions, chiefdom authority, sustainable housing, community participation, urban poverty, slum constructions, private city space, urban planning.

PhD by Research

Can self-help housing (SHH), empower homeless communities and grow their agency?

Investigator: Mark Sustr
Supervisors: Roland Karthaus, Anna Minton, Renée Tobe

Problems experienced by the homeless cannot always be resolved simply through access to decent housing. Although a stable home is important, it doesn't necessarily address the reasons that originally led to homelessness. Neither does it reconcile the debilitating effect of time spent living on the margins of society, often excluded from social norms. Given this community routinely experience rejection, often moved from public view, or are stigmatised as deviant - the effect is to deny them the sense that they are valued or that their contributions are worthwhile. Such social exclusion is therefore not simply a problem of inequity, but of questionable representation.

Homelessness

Problems experienced by the homeless cannot always be resolved simply through access to decent housing. Although a stable home is important, it doesn't necessarily address the reasons that originally led to homelessness. Neither does it reconcile the debilitating effect of time spent living on the margins of society, often excluded from social norms. Given this community routinely experience rejection, often moved from public view, or are stigmatised as deviant - the effect is to deny them the sense that they are valued or that their contributions are worthwhile. Such social exclusion is therefore not simply a problem of inequity, but of questionable representation.

Increasingly, due to the proliferation of marginal communities and informal settlements, there is a growing global interest in what can be learnt from these communities, in particular the alternative skill sets they possess - born out of a necessity to maximise the potential of the limited resources at their disposal.

PhD by Research

Towards a theory of the Community Led Housing Process

Investigator: Martyn Holmes
Supervisors: Alan Chandler, Anna Minton, Stephen Maddison

Community led housing is an umbrella term, a brand created by a partnership of organizations to deliver that sector and a new space (theoretically) and set of spaces (physically) where CLH realities are being conceived and constructed. This moment in time presents a unique opportunity to study new housing paradigms in formation. A set of paradigms, or world views, that will underpin a new housing sector centred around community participation in the production of the places and spaces we inhabit. A sector that through the involvement of agent and agencies from normative and non-normative housing pathways has the potential to challenge or reproduce the current housing system.

My research examines this conjunctural, intersectional and contested CLH space, where competing histories, values and processes meet, via the lived experience of those who are participating in CLH developments under the current CLH initiative.

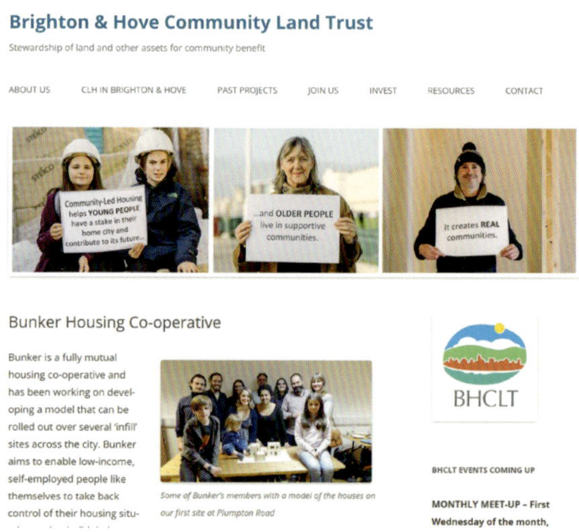

PhD by Research
Roman Concrete

Investigator: Hilal Koztepe
Supervisors: Bamdad Ayati, Alan Chandler

The research aims to assess the alternative construction material to concrete that is sustainable and environmentally friendly because people are concentrating on implementing such strategies that can enhance environmental sustainability. The research will use an explanatory approach and conduct interviews and collect data by presenting questionnaires to the people working in the construction of buildings. In turn, this would assist in finding an effective alternative that has different advantages and benefits compared to the traditional concrete that is the leading cause of environmental pollution.

PhD by Research

Heritage-Led Regeneration Schemes and Heritage Values of Historic Buildings within the UK

Investigator: Umut Gedik Kilic
Supervisors: Alan Chandler, Caroline Watkinson, Maria Segantini

Facing a situation where new regenerative urban development schemes are often led by the priority of financial gain to the detriment and neglect of cultural heritage, sustaining cultural heritage in developing areas and sites of redevelopment is of vital importance for retaining the identity and historic value of a place. The historic value of a place can be understood as both the spatial fabric but also the patterns and scale of uses that it facilitates. Use patterns and ownership frameworks are invariably set aside in large scale developments given the motives and imperatives of the developers who provide a singular set of interests in places that were historically complex networks of human associations. How social fabric is understood as an intrinsic part of historic building fabric requires a very different set of evaluation criteria, the definition of which is the purpose of this research.

AVA